THE WORTH
OF
WOMEN

THE
OTHER VOICE
IN
EARLY MODERN
EUROPE

A Series Edited by
Margaret L. King and
Albert Rabil, Jr.

Moderata Fonte
(Modesta Pozzo)

THE WORTH
OF
WOMEN

ॐ

Wherein Is Clearly Revealed
Their Nobility and
Their Superiority to Men

Edited and Translated
by
Virginia Cox

THE UNIVERSITY OF CHICAGO PRESS
Chicago & London

Virginia Cox is a lecturer in Italian at the University of Cambridge and a fellow of Christ's College. She is the author of *The Renaissance Dialogue: Literary Dialogue in Its Social and Political Contexts, Castiglione to Galileo*.

The University of Chicago Press, Chicago 60637
The University of Chicago Press, Ltd., London
© 1997 by The University of Chicago
All rights reserved. Published 1997
Printed in the United States of America
06 05 04 03 02 01 00 99 98   2 3 4 5

ISBN: 0–226–25681–2 (cloth)
ISBN: 0–226–25682–0 (paper)

This translation was supported by a generous grant from the National Endowment for the Humanities.

Library of Congress Cataloging-in-Publication Data
Fonte, Moderata, 1555–1592.
    [Merito delle donne. English]
    The worth of women : wherein is clearly revealed their nobility and their superiority to men / Moderata Fonte (Modesta Pozzo) ; edited and translated by Virginia Cox.
        p.   cm. — (The other voice in early modern Europe)
    Includes bibliographical references and index.
    ISBN 0-226-25681-2 (cloth : alk. paper). — ISBN 0-226-25682-0 (pbk. : alk. paper)
    1. Women—Early works to 1800. 2. Women—Social conditions—Early works to 1800. 3. Women—History—Renaissance, 1450–1600. I. Cox, Virginia.
II. Title.   III. Series.
HQ1148.F65   1997
305.4—dc21
                                                                        96-52270
                                                                        CIP

♾ The paper used in this publication meets the minimum requirements of the American National Standard for Information Sciences—Permanence of Paper for Printed Library Materials, ANSI Z39.48–1984.

CONTENTS

THE OTHER VOICE IN
EARLY MODERN EUROPE:
INTRODUCTION TO THE SERIES
Margaret L. King and Albert Rabil, Jr.

THE OLD VOICE AND THE OTHER VOICE

In western Europe and the United States women are nearing equality in the professions, in business, and in politics. Most enjoy access to education, reproductive rights, and autonomy in financial affairs. Issues vital to women are on the public agenda: equal pay, child care, domestic abuse, breast cancer research, and curricular revision with an eye to the inclusion of women.

These recent achievements have their origins in things women (and some male supporters) said for the first time about six hundred years ago. Theirs is the "other voice," in contradistinction to the "first voice," the voice of the educated men who created western culture. Coincident with a general reshaping of European culture in the period 1300 to 1700 (called the Renaissance or Early Modern period), questions of female equality and opportunity were raised that still resound and are still unresolved.

The "other voice" emerged against the backdrop of a 3,000-year history of misogyny—the hatred of women—rooted in the civilizations related to western culture: Hebrew, Greek, Roman, and Christian. Misogyny inherited from these traditions pervaded the intellectual, medical, legal, religious and social systems that developed during the European Middle Ages.

The following pages describe the misogynistic tradition inherited by early modern Europeans, and the new tradition which the "other voice" called into being to challenge its assumptions. This review should serve as a framework for the understanding of the texts published in the series "The Other Voice in Early Modern Europe." Introductions specific to each text and author follow this essay in all the volumes of the series.

THE MISOGYNIST TRADITION, 500 BCE–1500 CE

Embedded in the philosophical and medical theories of the ancient Greeks were perceptions of the female as inferior to the male in both mind and body. Similarly, the structure of civil legislation inherited from the ancient Romans was biased against women, and the views on women developed by Christian thinkers out of the Hebrew Bible and the Christian New Testament were negative and disabling. Literary works composed in the vernacular language of ordinary people, and widely recited or read, conveyed these negative assumptions. The social networks within which most women lived—those of the family and the institutions of the Roman Catholic church—were shaped by this misogynist tradition and sharply limited the areas in which women might act in and upon the world.

GREEK PHILOSOPHY AND FEMALE NATURE. Greek biology assumed that women were inferior to men and defined them merely as child-bearers and housekeepers. This view was authoritatively expressed in the works of the philosopher Aristotle.

Aristotle thought in dualities. He considered action superior to inaction, form (the inner design or structure of any object) superior to matter, completion to incompletion, possession to deprivation. In each of these dualities, he associated the male principle with the superior quality and the female with the inferior. "The male principle in nature," he argued, "is associated with active, formative and perfected characteristics, while the female is passive, material and deprived, desiring the male in order to become complete."[1] Men are always identified with virile qualities, such as judgment, courage and stamina; women with their opposites—irrationality, cowardice, and weakness.

Even in the womb, the masculine principle was considered superior. Man's semen, Aristotle believed, created the form of a new human creature, while the female body contributed only matter. (The existence of the ovum, and the other facts of human embryology, were not established until the seventeenth century.) Although the later Greek physician Galen believed that there was a female component in generation, contributed by "female semen," the followers of both Aristotle and Galen saw the male role in human generation as more active and more important.

In the Aristotelian view, the male principle sought always to reproduce itself. The creation of a female was always a mistake, there-

---

1. Aristotle, *Physics*, 1.9 192a20–24 (*The Complete Works of Aristotle*, ed. Jonathan Barnes, rev. Oxford translation, 2 vols. [Princeton, 1984], 1:328).

fore, resulting from an imperfect act of generation. Every female born was considered a "defective" or "mutilated" male (as Aristotle's terminology has variously been translated), a "monstrosity" of nature.[2]

For Greek theorists, the biology of males and females was the key to their psychology. The female was softer and more docile, more apt to be despondent, querulous, and deceitful. Being incomplete, moreover, she craved sexual fulfillment in intercourse with a male. The male was intellectual, active, and in control of his passions.

These psychological polarities derived from the theory that the universe consisted of four elements (earth, fire, air and water), expressed in human bodies as four "humors" (black bile, yellow bile, blood, and phlegm) considered respectively dry, hot, damp, and cold, and corresponding to mental states ("melancholic," "choleric," "sanguine," "phlegmatic"). In this schematization, the male, sharing the principles of earth and fire, was dry and hot; the female, sharing the principles of air and water, was cold and damp.

Female psychology was further affected by her dominant organ, the uterus (womb), *hystera* in Greek. The passions generated by the womb made women lustful, deceitful, talkative, irrational, indeed—when these affects were in excess—"hysterical."

Aristotle's biology also had social and political consequences. If the male principle was superior and the female inferior, then in the household, as in the state, men should rule and women must be subordinate. That hierarchy does not rule out the companionship of husband and wife, whose cooperation was necessary for the welfare of children and the preservation of property. Such mutuality supported male preeminence.

Aristotle's teacher Plato suggested a different possibility: that men and women might possess the same virtues. The setting for this proposal is the imaginary and ideal Republic that Plato sketches in a dialogue of that name. Here, for a privileged elite capable of leading wisely, all distinctions of class and wealth dissolve, as do consequently those of gender. Without households or property, as Plato constructs his ideal society, there is no need for the subordination of women. Women may, therefore, be educated to the same level as men to assume leadership responsibilities. Plato's Republic remained imaginary, however. In real societies, the subordination of women remained the norm and the prescription.

The views of women inherited from the Greek philosophical

2. Aristotle, *Generation of Animals*, 2.3 737a27–28 (Barnes, 1:1144).

tradition became the basis for medieval thought. In the thirteenth century, the supreme scholastic philosopher Thomas Aquinas, among others, still echoed Aristotle's views of human reproduction, of male and female personalities, and of the preeminent male role in the social hierarchy.

ROMAN LAW AND THE FEMALE CONDITION. Roman law, like Greek philosophy, underlay medieval thought and shaped medieval society. The ancient belief that adult, property-owning men should administer households and make decisions affecting the community at large is the very fulcrum of Roman law.

Around 450 BCE, during Rome's republican era, the community's customary law was recorded (legendarily) on Twelve Tables erected in the city's central forum. It was later elaborated by professional jurists whose activity increased in the imperial era, when much new legislation, especially on issues affecting family and inheritance, was passed. This growing, changing body of laws was eventually codified in the *Corpus of Civil Law* under the direction of the Emperor Justinian, generations after the empire ceased to be ruled from Rome. That *Corpus*, read and commented upon by medieval scholars from the eleventh century on, inspired the legal systems of most of the cities and kingdoms of Europe.

Laws regarding dowries, divorce, and inheritance most pertain to women. Since those laws aimed to maintain and preserve property, the women concerned were those from the property-owning minority. Their subordination to male family members points to the even greater subordination of lower-class and slave women about whom the laws speak little.

In the early Republic, the *paterfamilias*, "father of the family," possessed *patria potestas*, "paternal power." The term *pater*, "father," in both these cases does not necessarily mean biological father, but householder. The father was the person who owned the household's property and, indeed, its human members. The *paterfamilias* had absolute power—including the power, rarely exercised, of life or death—over his wife, his children, and his slaves, as much as over his cattle.

Children could be "emancipated," an act that granted legal autonomy and the right to own property. Male children over the age of fourteen could be emancipated by a special grant from the father, or automatically by their father's death. But females never could be emancipated; instead, they passed from the authority of their father to a husband or, if widowed or orphaned while still unmarried, to a guardian or tutor.

Marriage under its traditional form placed the woman under her husband's authority, or *manus*. He could divorce her on grounds of adultery, drinking wine, or stealing from the household, but she could not divorce him. She could possess no property in her own right, nor bequeath any to her children upon her death. When her husband died, the household property passed not to her but to his male heirs. And when her father died, she had no claim to any family inheritance, which was directed to her brothers or more remote male relatives. The effect of these laws was to exclude women from civil society, itself based on property ownership.

In the later Republican and Imperial periods, these rules were significantly modified. Women rarely married according to the traditional form, but according to the form of "free" marriage. That practice allowed a woman to remain under her father's authority, to possess property given her by her father (most frequently the "dowry," recoverable from the husband's household in the event of his death), and to inherit from her father. She could also bequeath property to her own children and divorce her husband, just as he could divorce her.

Despite this greater freedom, women still suffered enormous disability under Roman law. Heirs could belong only to the father's side, never the mother's. Moreover, although she could bequeath her property to her children, she could not establish a line of succession in doing so. A woman was "the beginning and end of her own family," growled the jurist Ulpian. Moreover, women could play no public role. They could not hold public office, represent anyone in a legal case, or even witness a will. Women had only a private existence, and no public personality.

The dowry system, the guardian, women's limited ability to transmit wealth, and total political disability are all features of Roman law adopted, although modified according to local customary laws, by the medieval communities of western Europe.

CHRISTIAN DOCTRINE AND WOMEN'S PLACE. The Hebrew Bible and the Christian New Testament authorized later writers to limit women to the realm of the family and to burden them with the guilt of original sin. The passages most fruitful for this purpose were the creation narratives in Genesis and sentences from the Epistles defining women's role within the Christian family and community.

Each of the first two chapters of Genesis contains a creation narrative. In the first "God created man in his own image, in the image of God he created him; male and female he created them." (NRSV, Genesis 1:27) In the second, God created Eve from Adam's rib (2:21–23). Christian theologians relied principally on Genesis 2 for their understanding of the relation between man and woman, interpreting the creation of Eve from Adam as proof of her subordination to him.

The creation story in Genesis 2 leads to that of the temptations in Genesis 3: of Eve by the wily serpent, and of Adam by Eve. As read by Christian theologians from Tertullian to Thomas Aquinas, the narrative made Eve responsible for the Fall and its consequences. She instigated the act; she deceived her husband; she suffered the greater punishment. Her disobedience made it necessary for Jesus to be incarnated and to die on the cross. From the pulpit, moralists and preachers for centuries conveyed to women the guilt that they bore for original sin.

The Epistles offered advice to early Christians on building communities of the faithful. Among the matters to be regulated was the place of women. Paul offered views favorable to women in Galatians 3:28: "There is neither Jew nor Greek, there is neither slave nor free, there is neither male nor female; for you are all one in Christ Jesus." Paul also referred to women as his co-workers and placed them on a par with himself and his male co-workers (Phil. 4:2–3; Rom. 16:1–3; I Cor. 16:19). Elsewhere Paul limited women's possibilities: "But I want you to understand that the head of every man is Christ, the head of a woman is her husband, and the head of Christ is God." (I Cor. 11:3)

Biblical passages by later writers (though attributed to Paul) enjoined women to forego jewels, expensive clothes, and elaborate coiffures; and they forbade women to "teach or have authority over men," telling them to "learn in silence with all submissiveness" as is proper for one responsible for sin, consoling them however with the thought that they will be saved through childbearing (I Tim. 2:9–15). Other texts among the later epistles defined women as the weaker sex, and emphasized their subordination to their husbands (I Peter 3:7; Col. 3:18; Eph. 5:22–23).

These passages from the New Testament became the arsenal employed by theologians of the early church to transmit negative attitudes toward women to medieval Christian culture—above all, Tertullian ("On the Apparel of Women"), Jerome (*Against Jovinian*), and Augustine (*The Literal Meaning of Genesis*).

THE IMAGE OF WOMEN IN MEDIEVAL LITERATURE. The philosophical, legal and religious traditions born in antiquity formed the basis of the medieval intellectual synthesis wrought by trained thinkers, mostly

clerics, writing in Latin and based largely in universities. The vernacular literary tradition which developed alongside the learned tradition
also spoke about female nature and women's roles. Medieval stories,
poems, and epics were also infused with misogyny. They portrayed
most women as lustful and deceitful, while praising good housekeepers and loyal wives, or replicas of the Virgin Mary, or the female saints
and martyrs. There is an exception in the movement of "courtly love"
that evolved in southern France from the twelfth century. Courtly
love was the erotic love between a nobleman and noblewoman, the
latter usually superior in social rank. It was always adulterous. From the
conventions of courtly love derive modern western notions of romantic love. The phenomenon has had an impact disproportionate to its
size, for it affected only a tiny elite, and very few women. The exaltation of the female lover probably does not reflect a higher evaluation of women, or a step toward their sexual liberation. More likely it
gives expression to the social and sexual tensions besetting the
knightly class at a specific historical juncture.

The literary fashion of courtly love was on the wane by the thirteenth century, when the widely read *Romance of the Rose* was composed
in French by two authors of significantly different dispositions.
Guillaume de Lorris composed the initial 4,000 verses around 1235,
and Jean de Meun added about 17,000 verses—more than four times
the original—around 1265.

The fragment composed by Guillaume de Lorris stands squarely in
the courtly love tradition. Here the poet, in a dream, is admitted into
a walled garden where he finds a magic fountain in which a rosebush
is reflected. He longs to pick one rose but the thorns around it prevent his doing so, even as he is wounded by arrows from the God of
Love, whose commands he agrees to obey. The remainder of this part
of the poem recounts the poet's unsuccessful efforts to pluck the
rose.

The longer part of the *Romance* by Jean de Meun also describes a
dream. But here allegorical characters give long didactic speeches,
providing a social satire on a variety of themes, including those pertaining to women. Love is an anxious and tormented state, the poem
explains, women are greedy and manipulative, marriage is miserable,
beautiful women are lustful, ugly ones cease to please, and a chaste
woman, as rare as a black swan, can scarcely be found.

Shortly after Jean de Meun completed *The Romance of the Rose*,
Mathéolus penned his *Lamentations*, a long Latin diatribe against

marriage translated into French about a century later. The *Lamentations* sum up medieval attitudes toward women and provoked the important response by Christine de Pizan in her *Book of the City of Ladies*.

In 1355, Giovanni Boccaccio wrote *Il Corbaccio*, another antifeminist manifesto, though ironically by an author whose other works pioneered new directions in Renaissance thought. The former husband of his lover appears to Boccaccio, condemning his unmoderated lust and detailing the defects of women. Boccaccio concedes at the end "how much men naturally surpass women in nobility"[3] and is cured of his desires.

WOMEN'S ROLES: THE FAMILY. The negative perception of women expressed in the intellectual tradition are also implicit in the actual roles that women played in European society. Assigned to subordinate positions in the household and the church, they were barred from significant participation in public life.

Medieval European households, like those in antiquity and in nonwestern civilizations, were headed by males. It was the male serf, or peasant, feudal lord, town merchant, or citizen who was polled or taxed or succeeded to an inheritance or had any acknowledged public role, although their wives or widows could stand on a temporary basis as surrogates for them. From about 1100, the position of property-holding males was enhanced further. Inheritance was confined to the male, or agnate, line—with depressing consequences for women.

A wife never fully belonged to her husband's family or a daughter to her father's family. She left her father's house young to marry whomever her parents chose. Her dowry was managed by her husband and normally passed to her children by him at her death.

A married woman's life was occupied nearly constantly with cycles of pregnancy, childbearing, and lactation. Women bore children through all the years of their fertility, and many died in childbirth before the end of that term. They also bore responsibility for raising young children up to six or seven. That responsibility was shared in the propertied classes, since it was common for a wet-nurse to take over the job of breastfeeding, and servants took over other chores.

Women trained their daughters in the household responsibilities appropriate to their status, nearly always in tasks associated with textiles: spinning, weaving, sewing, embroidering. Their sons were sent out of the house as apprentices or students, or their training was

---

3. Giovanni Boccaccio, *The Corbaccio or The Labyrinth of Love*, trans. and ed. Anthony K. Cassell (Binghamton, N.Y.; rev. paper ed., 1993), 71.

assumed by fathers in later childhood and adolescence. On the death of her husband, a woman's children became the responsibility of his family. She generally did not take "his" children with her to a new marriage or back to her father's house, except sometimes in artisan classes.

Women also worked. Rural peasants performed farm chores, merchant wives often practiced their husband's trade, the unmarried daughters of the urban poor worked as servants or prostitutes. All wives produced or embellished textiles and did the housekeeping, while wealthy ones managed servants. These labors were unpaid or poorly paid, but often contributed substantially to family wealth.

WOMEN'S ROLES: THE CHURCH. Membership in a household, whether a father's or a husband's, meant for women a lifelong subordination to others. In western Europe, the Roman Catholic church offered an alternative to the career of wife and mother. A woman could enter a convent parallel in function to the monasteries for men that evolved in the early Christian centuries.

In the convent, a woman pledged herself to a celibate life, lived according to strict community rules, and worshipped daily. Often the convent offered training in Latin, allowing some women to become considerable scholars and authors, as well as scribes, artists, and musicians. For women who chose the conventual life, the benefits could be enormous, but for numerous others placed in convents by paternal choice, the life could be restrictive and burdensome.

The conventual life declined as an alternative for women as the modern age approached. Reformed monastic institutions resisted responsibility for related female orders. The church increasingly restricted female institutional life by insisting on closer male supervision.

Women often sought other options. Some joined the communities of laywomen that sprang up spontaneously in the thirteenth century in the urban zones of western Europe, especially in Flanders and Italy. Some joined the heretical movements that flourished in late medieval Christendom, whose anticlerical and often antifamily positions particularly appealed to women. In these communities, some women were acclaimed as "holy women" or "saints," while others often were condemned as frauds or heretics.

In all, though the options offered to women by the church were sometimes less than satisfactory, sometimes they were richly rewarding. After 1520, the convent remained an option only in Roman Catholic territories. Protestantism engendered an ideal of marriage as a heroic endeavor, and appeared to place husband and wife on a more equal footing. Sermons and treatises, however, still called for female subordination and obedience.

THE OTHER VOICE, 1300–1700

Misogyny was so long-established in European culture when the modern era opened that to dismantle it was a monumental labor. The process began as part of a larger cultural movement that entailed the critical reexamination of ideas inherited from the ancient and medieval past. The humanists launched that critical reexamination.

THE HUMANIST FOUNDATION. Originating in Italy in the fourteenth century, humanism quickly became the dominant intellectual movement in Europe. Spreading in the sixteenth century from Italy to the rest of Europe, it fueled the literary, scientific and philosophical movements of the era, and laid the basis for the eighteenth-century Enlightenment.

Humanists regarded the scholastic philosophy of medieval universities as out of touch with the realities of urban life. They found in the rhetorical discourse of classical Rome a language adapted to civic life and public speech. They learned to read, speak, and write classical Latin, and eventually classical Greek. They founded schools to teach others to do so, establishing the pattern for elementary and secondary education for the next three hundred years.

In the service of complex government bureaucracies, humanists employed their skills to write eloquent letters, deliver public orations, and formulate public policy. They developed new scripts for copying manuscripts and used the new printing press for the dissemination of texts, for which they created methods of critical editing.

Humanism was a movement led by males who accepted the evaluation of women in ancient texts and generally shared the misogynist perceptions of their culture. (Female humanists, as will be seen, did not.) Yet humanism also opened the door to the critique of the misogynist tradition. By calling authors, texts, and ideas into question, it made possible the fundamental rereading of the whole intellectual tradition that was required in order to free women from cultural prejudice and social subordination.

A DIFFERENT CITY. The other voice first appeared when, after so many centuries, the accumulation of misogynist concepts evoked a response from a capable woman female defender: Christine de Pizan.

Introducing her *Book of the City of Ladies* (1405), she described how she was affected by reading Mathéolus's *Lamentations*: "Just the sight of this book ... made me wonder how it happened that so many different men ... are so inclined to express both in speaking and in their treatises and writings so many wicked insults about women and their behavior."[4] These statements impelled her to detest herself "and the entire feminine sex, as though we were monstrosities in nature."[5]

The remainder of the *Book of the City of Ladies* presents a justification of the female sex and a vision of an ideal community of women. A pioneer, she has not only received the misogynist message, but she rejects it. From the fourteenth to seventeenth century, a huge body of literature accumulated that responded to the dominant tradition.

The result was a literary explosion consisting of works by both men and women, in Latin and in vernacular languages: works enumerating the achievements of notable women; works rebutting the main accusations made against women; works arguing for the equal education of men and women; works defining and redefining women's proper role in the family, at court, and in public; and describing women's lives and experiences. Recent monographs and articles have begun to hint at the great range of this phenomenon, involving probably several thousand titles. The protofeminism of these "other voices" constitute a significant fraction of the literary product of the early modern era.

THE CATALOGUES. Around 1365, the same Boccaccio whose *Corbaccio* rehearses the usual charges against female nature, wrote another work, *Concerning Famous Women*. A humanist treatise drawing on classical texts, it praised 106 notable women—one hundred of them from pagan Greek and Roman antiquity, and six from the religious and cultural tradition since antiquity—and helped make all readers aware of a sex normally condemned or forgotten. Boccaccio's outlook, nevertheless, is misogynist, for it singled out for praise those women who possessed the traditional virtues of chastity, silence, and obedience. Women who were active in the public realm, for example, rulers and warriors, were depicted as suffering terrible punishments for entering into the masculine sphere. Women were his subject, but Boccaccio's standard remained male.

---

4. Christine de Pizan, *The Book of the City of Ladies*, trans. Earl Jeffrey Richards; Foreword Marina Warner (New York, 1982), I.1.1., pp. 3–4.

5. Ibid., I.1.1–2, p. 5.

Christine de Pizan's *Book of the City of Ladies* contains a second catalogue, one responding specifically to Boccaccio's. Where Boccaccio portrays female virtue as exceptional, she depicts it as universal. Many women in history were leaders, or remained chaste despite the lascivious approaches of men, or were visionaries and brave martyrs.

The work of Boccaccio inspired a series of catalogues of illustrious women of the biblical, classical, Christian, and local past: works by Alvaro de Luna, Jacopo Filippo Foresti (1497), Brantôme, Pierre Le Moyne, Pietro Paolo de Ribera (who listed 845 figures), and many others. Whatever their embedded prejudices, these catalogues of illustrious women drove home to the public the possibility of female excellence.

THE DEBATE. At the same time, many questions remained: Could a woman be virtuous? Could she perform noteworthy deeds? Was she even, strictly speaking, of the same human species as men? These questions were debated over four centuries, in French, German, Italian, Spanish and English, by authors male and female, among Catholics, Protestants and Jews, in ponderous volumes and breezy pamphlets. The whole literary phenomenon has been called the *querelle des femmes*, the "Woman Question."

The opening volley of this battle occurred in the first years of the fifteenth century, in a literary debate sparked by Christine de Pizan. She exchanged letters critical of Jean de Meun's contribution to the *Romance of the Rose* with two French humanists and royal secretaries, Jean de Montreuil and Gontier Col. When the matter became public, Jean Gerson, one of Europe's leading theologians, supported de Pizan's arguments against de Meun, for the moment silencing the opposition.

The debate resurfaced repeatedly over the next two hundred years. *The Triumph of Women* (1438) by Juan Rodríguez de la Camara (or Juan Rodríguez del Padron) struck a new note by presenting arguments for the superiority of women to men. *The Champion of Women* (1440–42) by Martin Le Franc addresses once again the misogynist claims of *The Romance of the Rose*, and offers counterevidence of female virtue and achievement.

A cameo of the debate on women is included in the *Courtier*, one of the most-read books of the era, published by the Italian Baldassare Castiglione in 1528 and immediately translated into other European vernaculars. The *Courtier* depicts a series of evenings at the court of the Duke of Urbino in which many men and some women of the highest social stratum amuse themselves by discussing a range of literary and social issues. The "woman question" is a pervasive theme throughout, and the third of its four books is devoted entirely to that issue.

In a verbal duel, Gasparo Pallavicino and Giuliano de' Medici present the main claims of the two traditions—the prevailing misogynist one, and the newly emerging alternative one. Gasparo argues the innate inferiority of women and their inclination to vice. Only in bearing children do they profit the world. Giuliano counters that women share the same spiritual and mental capacities as men and may excel in wisdom and action. Men and women are of the same essence: just as no stone can be more perfectly a stone than another, so no human being can be more perfectly human than others, whether male or female. It was an astonishing assertion, boldly made to an audience as large as all Europe.

THE TREATISES. Humanism provided the materials for a positive counterconcept to the misogyny embedded in scholastic philosophy and law, and inherited from the Greek, Roman and Christian pasts. A series of humanist treatises on marriage and family, education and deportment, and on the nature of women helped construct these new perspectives.

The works by Francesco Barbaro and Leon Battista Alberti, respectively *On Marriage* (1415) and *On the Family* (1434–37), far from defending female equality, reasserted women's responsibilities for rearing children and managing the housekeeping while being obedient, chaste, and silent. Nevertheless, they served the cause of reexamining the issue of women's nature by placing domestic issues at the center of scholarly concern and reopening the pertinent classical texts. In addition, Barbaro emphasized the companionate nature of marriage and the importance of a wife's spiritual and mental qualities for the well-being of the family.

These themes reappear in later humanist works on marriage and the education of women by Juan Luis Vives and Erasmus. Both were moderately sympathetic to the condition of women, without reaching beyond the usual masculine prescriptions for female behavior.

An outlook more favorable to women characterizes the nearly unknown work *In Praise of Women* (ca. 1487) by the Italian humanist Bartolommeo Goggio. In addition to providing a catalogue of illustrious women, Goggio argued that male and female are the same in essence, but that women (reworking from quite a new angle the Adam and Eve narrative) are actually superior. In the same vein, the Italian humanist Maria Equicola asserted the spiritual equality of men and women in *On Women* (1501). In 1525, Galeazzo Flavio Capra (or Capella) published his work *On the Excellence and Dignity of Women.* This humanist tradition of treatises defending the worthiness of women culminates in the work of Henricus Cornelius Agrippa *On the Nobility and Preeminence of the Female Sex.* No work by a male humanist more succinctly or explicitly presents the case for female dignity.

THE WITCH BOOKS. While humanists grappled with the issues pertaining to women and family, other learned men turned their attention to what they perceived as a very great problem: witches. Witch-hunting manuals, explorations of the witch phenomenon, and even defenses of witches are not at first glance pertinent to the tradition of the other voice. But they do relate in this way: most accused witches were women. The hostility aroused by supposed witch activity is comparable to the hostility aroused by women. The evil deeds the victims of the hunt were charged with were exaggerations of the vices to which, many believed, all women were prone.

The connection between the witch accusation and the hatred of women is explicit in the notorious witch-hunting manual, *The Hammer of Witches* (1486), by two Dominican inquisitors, Heinrich Krämer and Jacob Sprenger. Here the inconstancy, deceitfulness, and lustfulness traditionally associated with women are depicted in exaggerated form as the core features of witch behavior. These inclined women to make a bargain with the devil—sealed by sexual intercourse—by which they acquired unholy powers. Such bizarre claims, far from being rejected by rational men, were broadcast by intellectuals. The German Ulrich Molitur, the Frenchman Nicolas Rémy, the Italian Stefano Guazzo coolly informed the public of sinister orgies and midnight pacts with the devil. The celebrated French jurist, historian, and political philosopher Jean Bodin argued that, because women were especially prone to diabolism, regular legal procedures could properly be suspended in order to try those accused of this "exceptional crime."

A few experts, such as the physician Johann Weyer, a student of Agrippa's, raised their voices in protest. In 1563, he explained the witch phenomenon thus, without discarding belief in diabolism: the devil deluded foolish old women afflicted by melancholia, causing them to believe that they had magical powers. Weyer's rational skepticism, which had good credibility in the community of the learned, worked to revise the conventional views of women and witchcraft.

WOMEN'S WORKS. To the many categories of works produced on the question of women's worth must be added nearly all works written by women. A woman writing was in herself a statement of women's claim to dignity.

Only a few women wrote anything prior to the dawn of the modern era, for three reasons. First, they rarely received the education that would enable them to write. Second, they were not admitted to the public roles—as administrator, bureaucrat, lawyer or notary, university professor—in which they might gain knowledge of the kinds of things the literate public thought worth writing about. Third, the culture imposed silence upon women, considering speaking out a form of unchastity. Given these conditions, it is remarkable that any women wrote. Those who did before the fourteenth century were almost always nuns or religious women whose isolation made their pronouncements more acceptable.

From the fourteenth century on, the volume of women's writings crescendoed. Women continued to write devotional literature, although not always as cloistered nuns. They also wrote diaries, often intended as keepsakes for their children; books of advice to their sons and daughters; letters to family members and friends; and family memoirs, in a few cases elaborate enough to be considered histories.

A few women wrote works directly concerning the "woman question," and some of these, such as the humanists Isotta Nogarola, Cassandra Fedele, Laura Cereta, and Olimpia Morata, were highly trained. A few were professional writers, living by the income of their pen: the very first among them Christine de Pizan, noteworthy in this context as in so many others. In addition to *The Book of the City of Ladies* and her critiques of *The Romance of the Rose*, she wrote *The Treasure of the City of Ladies* (a guide to social decorum for women), an advice book for her son, much courtly verse, and a full-scale history of the reign of king Charles V of France.

WOMEN PATRONS. Women who did not themselves write but encouraged others to do so boosted the development of an alternative tradition. Highly placed women patrons supported authors, artists, musicians, poets, and learned men. Such patrons, drawn mostly from the Italian elites and the courts of northern Europe, figure disproportionately as the dedicatees of the important works of early feminism.

For a start, it might be noted that the catalogues of Boccaccio and Alvaro de Luna were dedicated to the Florentine noblewoman Andrea Acciaiuoli and to Doña María, first wife of King Juan II of Castile, while the French translation of Boccaccio's work was commissioned by Anne of Brittany, wife of King Charles VIII of France. The humanist treatises of Goggio, Equicola, Vives, and Agrippa were dedicated, respectively, to Eleanora of Aragon, wife of Ercole I d'Este, duke of Ferrara; to Margherita Cantelma of Mantua; to Catherine of Aragon, wife of King Henry VIII of England; and to Margaret, duchess of Austria and regent of the Netherlands. As late as 1696, Mary Astell's *Serious Proposal to the Ladies, for the Advancement of Their True and Greatest Interest* was dedicated to Princess Ann of Denmark.

These authors presumed that their efforts would be welcome to female patrons, or they may have written at the bidding of those patrons. Silent themselves, perhaps even unresponsive, these loftily placed women helped shape the tradition of the other voice.

THE ISSUES. The literary forms and patterns in which the tradition of the other voice presented itself have now been sketched. It remains to highlight the major issues about which this tradition crystallizes. In brief, there are four problems to which our authors return again and again, in plays and catalogues, in verse and in letters, in treatises and dialogues, in every language: the problem of chastity; the problem of power; the problem of speech; and the problem of knowledge. Of these the greatest, preconditioning the others, is the problem of chastity.

THE PROBLEM OF CHASTITY. In traditional European culture, as in those of antiquity and others around the globe, chastity was perceived as woman's quintessential virtue—in contrast to courage, or generosity, or leadership, or rationality, seen as virtues characteristic of men. Opponents of women charged them with insatiable lust. Women themselves and their defenders—without disputing the validity of the standard—responded that women were capable of chastity.

The requirement of chastity kept women at home, silenced them, isolated them, left them in ignorance. It was the source of all other impediments. Why was it so important to the society of men, of whom chastity was not required, and who, more often than not, considered it their right to violate the chastity of any woman they encountered?

Female chastity ensured the continuity of the male-headed household. If a man's wife was not chaste, he could not be sure of the legitimacy of his offspring. If they were not his, and they acquired his property, it was not his household, but some other man's, that had endured. If his daughter was not chaste, she could not be transferred to another man's household as his wife, and he was dishonored.

The whole system of the integrity of the household and the

transmission of property was bound up in female chastity. Such a requirement only pertained to property-owning classes, of course. Poor women could not expect to maintain their chastity, least of all if they were in contact with high-status men to whom all women but those of their own household were prey.

In Catholic Europe, the requirement of chastity was further buttressed by moral and religious imperatives. Original sin was inextricably linked with the sexual act. Virginity was seen as heroic virtue, far more impressive than, say, the avoidance of idleness or greed. Monasticism, the cultural institution that dominated medieval Europe for centuries, was grounded in the renunciation of the flesh. The Catholic reform of the eleventh century imposed a similar standard on all the clergy, and a heightened awareness of sexual requirements on all the laity. Although men were asked to be chaste, female unchastity was much worse: it led to the devil, as Eve had led mankind to sin.

To such requirements, women and their defenders protested their innocence. More, following the example of holy women who had escaped the requirements of family and sought the religious life, some women began to conceive of female communities as alternatives both to family and to the cloister. Christine de Pizan's city of ladies was such a community. Moderata Fonte and Mary Astell envisioned others. The luxurious salons of the French *précieuses* of the seventeenth century, or the comfortable English drawing rooms of the next, may have been born of the same impulse. Here women might not only escape, if briefly, the subordinate position that life in the family entailed, but they might make claims to power, exercise their capacity for speech, and display their knowledge.

THE PROBLEM OF POWER. Women were excluded from power: the whole cultural tradition insisted upon it. Only men were citizens, only men bore arms, only men could be chiefs or lords or kings. There were exceptions which did not disprove the rule, when wives or widows or mothers took the place of men, awaiting their return or the maturation of a male heir. A woman who attempted to rule in her own right was perceived as an anomaly, a monster, at once a deformed woman and an insufficient male, sexually confused and, consequently, unsafe.

The association of such images with women who held or sought power explains some otherwise odd features of early modern culture. Queen Elizabeth I of England, one of the few women to hold full regal authority in European history, played with such male/female

images—positive ones, of course—in representing herself to her subjects. She was a prince, and manly, even though she was female. She
was also (she claimed) virginal, a condition absolutely essential if she
was to avoid the attacks of her opponents. Catherine de' Medici, who
ruled France as widow and regent for her sons, also adopted such
imagery in defining her position. She chose as one symbol the figure
of Artemisia, an androgynous ancient warrior-heroine, who combined a
female persona with masculine powers.

Power in a woman, without such sexual imagery, seems to have
been indigestible by the culture. A rare note was struck by the
Englishman Sir Thomas Elyot in his *Defence of Good Women* (1540), justi-
fying both women's participation in civic life and prowess in arms.
The old tune was sung by the Scots reformer John Knox in his *First
Blast of the Trumpet against the Monstrous Regiment of Women* (1558), for whom
rule by women, defective in nature, was a hideous contradiction in
terms.

The confused sexuality of the imagery of female potency was not
reserved for rulers. Any woman who excelled was likely to be called an
Amazon, recalling the self-mutilated warrior women of antiquity who
repudiated all men, gave up their sons, and raised only their daughters. She was often said to have "exceeded her sex," or to have possessed "masculine virtue"—as the very fact of conspicuous excellence
conferred masculinity, even on the female subject. The catalogues of
notable women often showed those female heroes dressed in armor,
armed to the teeth, like men. Amazonian heroines romp through the
epics of the age—Ariosto's *Orlando Furioso* (1532), Spenser's *Faerie
Queene* (1590–1609). Excellence in a woman was perceived as a claim
for power, and power was reserved for the masculine realm. A woman
who possessed either was masculinized, and lost title to her own
female identity.

THE PROBLEM OF SPEECH. Just as power had a sexual dimension when
it was claimed by women, so did speech. A good woman spoke little.
Excessive speech was an indication of unchastity. By speech, women
seduced men. Eve had lured Adam into sin by her speech. Accused
witches were commonly accused of having spoken abusively, or irra-
tionally, or simply too much. As enlightened a figure as Francesco
Barbaro insisted on silence in a woman, which he linked to her perfect unanimity with her husband's will and her unblemished virtue
(her chastity). Another Italian humanist, Leonardo Bruni, in advising
a noblewoman on her studies, barred her not from speech, but from
public speaking. That was reserved for men.

Related to the problem of speech was that of costume, another, if silent, form of self-expression. Assigned the task of pleasing men as their primary occupation, elite women often tended to elaborate costume, hairdressing, and the use of cosmetics. Clergy and secular moralists alike condemned these practices. The appropriate function of costume and adornment was to announce the status of a woman's husband or father. Any further indulgence in adornment was akin to unchastity.

THE PROBLEM OF KNOWLEDGE. When the Italian noblewoman Isotta Nogarola had begun to attain a reputation as a humanist, she was accused of incest—a telling instance of the association of learning in women with unchastity. That chilling association inclined any woman who was educated to deny that she was, or to make exaggerated claims of heroic chastity.

If educated women were pursued with suspicions of sexual misconduct, women seeking an education faced an even more daunting obstacle: the assumption that women were by nature incapable of learning, that reason was a particularly masculine ability. Just as they proclaimed their chastity, women and their defenders insisted upon their capacity for learning. The major work by a male writer on female education—*On the Education of a Christian Woman,* by Juan Luis Vives (1523)—granted female capacity for intellection, but argued still that a woman's whole education was to be shaped around the requirement of chastity and a future within the household. Female writers of the next generations—Marie de Gournay in France, Anna Maria van Schurman in Holland, Mary Astell in England—began to envision other possibilities.

The pioneers of female education were the Italian women humanists who managed to attain a Latin literacy and knowledge of classical and Christian literature equivalent to that of prominent men. Their works implicitly and explicitly raise questions about women's social roles, defining problems that beset women attempting to break out of the cultural limits that had bound them. Like Christine de Pizan, who achieved an advanced education through her father's tutoring and her own devices, their bold questioning makes clear the importance of training. Only when women were educated to the same standard as male leaders would they be able to raise that other voice and insist on their dignity as human beings morally, intellectually, and legally equal to men.

THE OTHER VOICE. The other voice, a voice of protest, was mostly female, but also male. It spoke in the vernaculars and in Latin, in treatises and dialogues, plays and poetry, letters and diaries and pamphlets. It battered at the wall of misogynist beliefs that encircled women and raised a banner announcing its claims. The female was equal (or even superior) to the male in essential nature—moral, spiritual, intellectual. Women were capable of higher education, of holding positions of power and influence in the public realm, and of speaking and writing persuasively. The last bastion of masculine supremacy, centered on the notions of a woman's primary domestic responsibility and the requirement of female chastity, was not as yet assaulted—although visions of productive female communities as alternatives to the family indicated an awareness of the problem.

During the period 1300 to 1700, the other voice remained only a voice, and one only dimly heard. It did not result—yet—in an alteration of social patterns. Indeed, to this day, they have not entirely been altered. Yet the call for justice issued as long as six centuries ago by those writing in the tradition of the other voice must be recognized as the source and origin of the mature feminist tradition and of the realignment of social institutions accomplished in the modern age.

We would like to thank the volume editors in this series, who responded with many suggestions to an earlier draft of this introduction, making it a collaborative enterprise. Many of their suggestions and criticisms have resulted in revisions of this introduction, though we remain responsible for the final product.

PROJECTED TITLES IN THE SERIES

Cassandra Fedele, *Letters and Orations,* edited and translated by Diana Robin

Veronica Franco, *Selected Poems and Letters,* edited and translated by Margaret Rosenthal and Ann Rosalind Jones

Lucrezia Marinella, *The Nobility and Excellence of Women,* edited and translated by Anne Dunhill

Anna Maria van Schurman, *Whether a Christian Woman Should Be Educated and Other Writings from Her Intellectual Circle,* edited and translated by Joyce Irwin

Arcangela Tarabotti, *Paternal Tyranny,* edited and translated by Letizia Panizza

ACKNOWLEDGMENTS

This edition draws on the fruits of almost a decade's research on Moderata Fonte on my part, and the debts of gratitude I have incurred over that period are many. I should like, in particular, to record my thanks to the staff of the Venetian State Archives for their patience in assisting me with my biographical researches on Fonte, and to Daniela Hacke for her invaluable help in orienting me in these researches; to Michael Clarke, Corinna da Fonseca-Wollheim, John Henderson, Mary Laven, Richard Palmer, David Sedley, and an anonymous reader for University of Chicago Press, for bibliographical advice, comments on the text, and help with obdurate footnotes; to Al Rabil for the support and encouragement he has provided as series editor; to my parents, Greta and Patrick Cox, for their endlessly patient help with proofreading; and above all to Letizia Panizza, for the enormous input of advice, inspiration, and intellectual companionship she has put into this project from the moment of its distant inception.

Virginia Cox

MODERATA FONTE AND
THE WORTH OF WOMEN

INTRODUCTION

Moderata Fonte's *The Worth of Women* (*Il merito delle donne*), written around 1592 and published posthumously in 1600, is among the most original, as well as the most engaging, of all early modern writings by women. This claim to originality does not rest on the novelty of the work's subject matter: women's worth, and men's injustice in failing to recognize it, had been popular subjects of literary debate in Italy and throughout Europe for well over a century before it was written. *The Worth of Women*, however, is very far from simply recapitulating the established commonplaces of this debate; rather, it recharges what had, by this time, deteriorated into a somewhat sterile and formulaic academic exercise by bringing it back into contact with the realities of women's lives. Written in dialogue form, the work purportedly records a conversation among seven Venetian noblewomen of widely varying age and experience, whose discussions, though loosely unified around the theme of men's unjustifiable hostility to women and possible cures for it, range over almost every aspect of their lives, from their wayward husbands' vices to their views on education, from their literary tastes and aspirations to their favorite recipes for fish. Few literary works of the period give us such a vivid insight into the material and imaginative texture of women's lives, and none, perhaps, is as deft in the connections it makes between cultural perceptions of women and the social realities in which they are rooted.

This agile shifting between theory and practice is one of the features of *The Worth of Women* that serve to distinguish it from the majority of other contributions to the Renaissance *querelle des femmes*. Another is its sheer intellectual ambition, best displayed in the second day of the dialogue, with its rapid, witty, and idiosyncratic overview of the wonders of the natural and social worlds. To show women speaking at all, in this period, on such a wide range of scientific and cultural topics was a forceful indictment of the educational barriers that held women back from most areas of study. But the challenge Fonte's dialogue presents to the gender prejudices of her culture does not stop there. The ultimate aim of this section of the dialogue is nothing less than that of critically reshaping contemporary beliefs about nature and the hierarchy of being, in such a way as to secure a place for women consonant with its author's conception of their worth.

LIFE AND EARLY WORKS

The Worth of Women is Moderata Fonte's most substantial work and may be seen as her literary testament. It was completed, according to the memoir by her friend and uncle by marriage, Giovanni Niccolò Doglioni, which is our main source of information on Fonte's life, the evening before her death in childbirth at the age of thirty-seven, in 1592. It is the only prose work of Fonte's that survives. Her earlier published works, mainly written before her marriage to a Venetian lawyer and civil servant, Filippo Zorzi, probably in 1582, are an unfinished chivalric romance, *Il Floridoro* (1581), the libretto of a *cantata* performed for the doge on St. Stephen's Day, 1581, and published early the following year, and verse narratives of the *Passion of Christ* (1582) and the *Resurrection of Christ* (1592). No manuscripts of Fonte's work have been identified, and we cannot know what proportion of her writing this published output represents. Doglioni remarks on her extraordinary speed and fluency of composition and mentions other poems, published anonymously; but he also implies that her literary output was restricted by her domestic duties and by the tyranny of "the misguided belief current in this city that women should excel in nothing but the running of their households."

We may lament, with Doglioni, the constraints that this prejudice placed on Moderata Fonte's development as a writer, but, in many respects, it is less remarkable that this wealthy and respectable young Venetian matron should have encountered obstacles in her writing than that she should have written at all. This is not to say that there was anything extraordinarily novel about a woman writing and having her works published in Italy in this period: there had been celebrated Italian women humanists since the fifteenth century, and from the 1540s, following the striking editorial success of Vittoria Colonna's *Collected Poems* (1538), a steady stream of vernacular women's writing began to appear in print—much of it in Venice, which was at this time one of the publishing capitals of Europe.[1] But, if Venice was a center for the publication of women's writing, it was hardly a center for its production. Elsewhere in Italy, especially in the courts of Central and Northern Italy, upper-class women seem to have had far greater opportunities for social and cultural protagonism than they did in the rigid and conservative aristocratic republic of Venice, where unmarried women of the upper ranks of society were kept in a seclusion no visitor failed to remark on, and even married women appear to have participated only marginally in cultural life. It is striking that in the sixteenth century Venice produced no aristocratic women poets to rank with the Neapolitan Vittoria Colonna, the Emilian Veronica Gambara, or the Tuscan Chiara Matraini. The most considerable Venetian women poets of the century were Gaspara Stampa and Veronica Franco: the former a Paduan and a musical virtuosa, the latter a highly successful courtesan; and thus both released from the rigorous codes of decorum that governed the lives of their Venetian "betters."[2]

As a respectable woman who wrote, then, Moderata Fonte was something of an anomaly in Venice. The anomalousness of her position may perhaps account in part for the anomalousness of her writing, which quite strikingly departs from the conventions of women's writing in the period, especially with regard to genre. The majority of sixteenth-century women's writing, excluding devotional writing, falls into the two categories of the love lyric and the familiar letter. Exceptions, like the *Dialogue on Love* of the Roman courtesan Tullia d'Aragona, or Veronica Franco's brilliant satirical *capitoli*, are far more likely to proceed from writers whose social position made them less shackled than "respectable" women by the dictates of gender decorum.[3] In these circumstances, Moderata Fonte's incursion into two traditionally masculine genres like the chivalric romance (in her early *Floridoro*) and the literary dialogue is worthy of reflection, and it seems legitimate to ask whether her audacity in this respect may owe something to the fact that a woman in her position—so socially segregated that an early admirer of her work could be moved almost to doubt

1. The extent of this vernacular production is indicated in Zancan 1983, 254–64; see also the relevant chapters in Jones and Panizza (forthcoming). On Italian women humanists, see King 1991, 194–204.

2. See Jones 1990, 118–41 and 178–200; and, on Franco, Rosenthal.

3. Both texts are forthcoming in English translation in this series.

her existence[4]—was under less pressure to conform to "feminine" models of writing than women who were more integrated in the literary culture of their cities.

How *did* this improbable literary figure come to write at all, and to write with such commitment and seriousness? Up to this point, I have been stressing the disadvantages of Fonte's comfortable background for the development of her vocation. But there were advantages, as well: most particularly that, like her younger Venetian contemporary, Lucrezia Marinella (1571–1653), in many ways her closest parallel in sociohistorical terms, Moderata Fonte was fortunate enough to have been brought up in a cultivated household and to have male relatives sympathetic to her literary interests. According to Doglioni's *Life*, her poetic talents were recognized and encouraged at an early age by her step-grandfather, Prospero Saraceni, while Doglioni himself, after she moved into his household upon his marriage with Saraceni's daughter, took it on himself to "reveal her previously buried talents to the world" (p. 36). Doglioni's boast is justified: a notary, he was himself a man of literary and intellectual interests, and his sponsorship and contacts were undoubtedly crucial in bringing Moderata Fonte's work to public notice. Fonte's husband, too, Filippo Zorzi, appears to have been sympathetic to her writing, to judge from the prefatory sonnet he contributed to her *Resurrection of Christ* (1592) and from the epitaph he composed for her (p. 40 below), which decidedly emphasizes her erudition and poetic talents over her domestic virtues.

It would be misleading, then, to represent Moderata Fonte as a martyr, silenced by a hostile male literary establishment: she was writing in a culture that allowed a space—if a strictly circumscribed one—for literary expression by women. This should not lead us to underestimate, however, the extraordinary nature of her achievement, nor the remarkable degree of talent, intellectual curiosity, and determination it denotes. There seems little reason to doubt Doglioni's remarks on the impact this "stupendous freak of nature" made on the convent where she spent her early childhood, nor his touching account of the way in which the young Modesta scraped herself an education at second hand by waylaying her elder brother every day on his return from school and persuading him to repeat to her the lessons he

---

4. Sansovino 1587, 201: "Moderata Fonte is a young girl, a respectable *cittadina* of this city, extremely learned in all disciplines, as far as one can gather (for to tell the truth, no one can actually claim to have seen her in person)." An identically worded entry is found in the editions of the same work of 1592 (p. 139) and 1596 (p. 133).

had learned. Nor is there any mistaking the strength of Fonte's ambition or her sense of her literary vocation. Her nom de plume—adopted, Doglioni tells us, to protect her modesty as an unmarried girl[5]—is in fact anything but modest in its implications, jettisoning as it does the timid "Modesta," for "Moderata," with its connotations of self-regulation through reason, and "Pozzo" ("well"), with its connotations of silence and passivity, for "Fonte" (a "fountain" or "spring"). The jaunty self-assertiveness of this pseudonym is not absent, either, from Fonte's first self-portrait, in her youthful romance, *Il Floridoro* (1581), where she places herself at the end of a list of Venetian poets whose sculpted portraits are said to adorn a fountain in the temple of Apollo at Delphi.[6] The portrait she paints of herself there is, again, ostensibly characterized by gestures of modesty: unnamed and clad in a white gown, "befitting her virginal state," the young poet is shown cowering in a corner, not daring to expose her aspirations to the light. This show of self-abasement can, however, hardly dispel the boldness of Fonte's move in literally carving herself a place in a male literary canon. Whether or not, as is tempting, we take up the text's punning hint at a connection between her pen name and the fountain of the god of poetry, it is difficult to ignore the fact that her shrinking self-description occupies a space (two stanzas) which is twice that accorded to any other poet mentioned with the exception of her poetic idol, the august Domenico Venier.[7]

These acts of authorial self-assertion are not the only hints in Fonte's early literary career of the protofeminist sensibility that would find its fullest expression in *The Worth of Women*. The *Floridoro*'s rambling romance plot contains a number of episodes that foreshadow the themes of the later dialogue; most interesting, perhaps, is that concerning the identical twin princesses, Biondaura and Risamante, the former of whom (something of a femme fatale) is the product of a conventionally feminine education, while the latter, kidnaped at birth by an enlightened magus, has been trained up to fight like a man.[8] The moral of the story is driven home in a spirited passage of feminist polemic, which is important as Fonte's first overt public pronouncement on the question of the status of women (see Appendix).

---

5. Goldioni (Doglioni) 1603, 187.

6. Fonte 1995, 161 (canto 10, 37–38).

7. Ibid., 158 (canto 10, 22–23).

8. Ibid., 30 (canto 2, 30–32); see also Valeria Finucci's discussion of the episode in her introduction, 27–34.

Risamante's prowess at arms should not be wondered at, Fonte remarks; rather, it is proof that women have the same innate abilities as men, and, if educated similarly, would prove their equals in the fields of both letters and arms.

As readers familiar with the Renaissance *querelle des femmes* will recognize, this point was by no means a novel one at the time when Fonte was writing, and, as readers of Ariosto will know, there was nothing new in using the figure of a female knight as a starting point for exploring questions of gender.[9] There are elements here, however, that appear to point less to the young author's reading than to her experience. Certainly, it is difficult to read the stanza of the *Floridoro* that speculates about the likely results of giving an identical education to a brother and sister without remembering Doglioni's account of the way in which the young Modesta acquired her own schooling by shadowing that of her brother. It is difficult, as well, to read the story of Biondaura and Risamante—at one point poignantly compared, in their physical likeness, to mirror images of the same woman[10]—without thinking of Fonte's own divided identity, as meek Venetian maiden and audacious aspirant to literary glory. In what was only the second chivalric romance by a woman to be published, the often ambiguous genre cliché of the female knight is charged with a newly personal meaning, as an emblem of a quest for identity beyond the constraints of conventional gender prescriptions.[11] That same quest, translated from the realm of pure fantasy onto the trickier terrain of a finely calibrated quasi-realism, would be pursued with equal imaginative commitment in Fonte's last and most powerful work.

THE WORTH OF WOMEN: STRUCTURE AND ARGUMENTS

It may be helpful, before proceeding with an analysis of *The Worth of Women*, briefly to summarize its argument. As has been noted, the work is structured as a dialogue, and its opening pages are taken up with describing the setting and introducing the speakers: a group of "noble and spirited" Venetian women friends "from the most re-

9. Among the many recent studies on gender in the *Orlando Furioso*, see Shemek 1989, and the relevant chapters in Tomalin 1982 and Benson 1992. Fonte alludes to Ariosto's female knight, Marfisa, as a role model on two occasions in *The Worth of Women*.

10. Fonte 1995, 29 (canto 2, 28).

11. The first chivalric romance published by a woman was Tullia d'Aragona's *Il Meschino* (1560). The element of ambiguity in male chivalric writers' representations of women knights has been stressed recently by critics such as Günsberg 1987 and Finucci 1992.

spected families of the city." We learn first that the dialogue is taking place at the home of one of the women, Leonora, and that it marks the return to the group of another, the newly married Helena, whom the others have not seen since her wedding (p. 46). The situation naturally gives rise to a discussion of marriage and its benefits and trials, which is given further impetus when the women repair to the garden to admire an elaborate allegorical fountain, designed by an aunt of Leonora's as a visual expression of her militant opposition to marriage (pp. 51–55). Understandably, after this, when it is decided to spend the day in conversation, the subject selected for discussion is men and their merits and failings. The dowager of the party, Adriana, is appointed to chair the debate and she divides the other six women into two opposing camps (p. 57). The opponents of men are to be the hostess, Leonora, a young widow determined never to remarry; Cornelia, a married woman with a distinctly jaded attitude to married life; and the scholarly Corinna, who has just announced her intention to renounce marriage altogether and devote herself to the pursuit of literature and learning. On the other side are the young bride Helena, still starry-eyed about her new husband; her contemporary Virginia, an unmarried girl of (as we later learn) quite startling naïveté, and, as a counterweight, Lucretia, an older woman, who, despite her dissatisfaction with her own marriage (p. 71), is prepared to lend her younger companions a not always unambiguous support.

After an initial series of rather inconsequential exchanges, the most theoretically committed section of the dialogue begins when Virginia asks how, if men are as imperfect as her antagonists have been claiming, they have managed to maneuver themselves into such a decided position of superiority over women (p. 59). In two dense and tightly constructed speeches, Corinna counters the thesis that men's political superiority over women is based in nature or God's will, arguing first against the Aristotelian notion that men are naturally framed to command and women to obey, and then against the theological claim—based, she argues, on a misinterpretation of the Creation story—that woman's role is secondary and subservient to man's. The implications of her arguments are drawn out by Leonora: "if women are men's inferiors in status, but not in worth, this is an abuse that has been introduced into the world and that men have then, over time, gradually translated into law and custom; and it has become so entrenched that they claim (and even actually believe) that the status they have gained through their bullying is theirs by right" (p. 61).

After this, the emphasis shifts from the theoretical question of the status of women to the practical one of the ways in which men abuse their undeserved dominion over women. A long litany of complaints is initiated about the ill-treatment meted out to women by their fathers, brothers, sons, and husbands, with husbands' vices being submitted to a particularly coruscating scrutiny (pp. 68–72), based largely on the personal experiences of the speakers. Lovers are next in turn, and the various defects of young, middle-aged, and old suitors are scrutinized in detail, to the distress of the ingénue Virginia, who evidently nurtures romantic fantasies on this score (pp. 73–80). An interesting discussion then ensues on the question of the relative susceptibility of the two sexes to love and, particularly, to lust: an issue of crucial importance in the Renaissance debate on women, in that women's supposed irrationality and consequent incapacity to moderate their sensual appetites was the justification most frequently employed to legitimize the strict constraints imposed on their behavior.

After this digression on love, the conversation meanders back to the question of the "worth of women," at first briefly, in an aside vindicating Eve of blame (or, at least, primary blame) for the Fall (pp. 93–94), then more consistently, from p. 100, where a substantial list is initiated of women's capacities and virtues, as illustrated by heroic figures of the classical past. Here, too, however, the theme of men's cruelty is not forgotten: in fact, after a rather perfunctory rehearsal of the conventional classical exempla of women's achievements in learning, military leadership, and government, Fonte's speakers move on to a fuller and more detailed exemplification of women's devotion to their male relatives, with each example of a heroic mother, daughter, sister, or wife sacrificing herself for her son, father, brother, or husband punctiliously balanced by an example of brutality meted out by a man to a woman. Connections are continually made, moreover, between these glamorous ancient stories, "these few examples of famous and prominent figures," and the less lurid, more persistent misery inflicted every day and "buried and forgotten in the oblivion of time" (p. 107). At the end of the list of exempla, the conversation slides back to these more quotidian abuses, and, in a passage of considerable sociohistorical interest, the speakers discuss the social prejudice that leads fathers to treat a girl's birth as a tragedy, and the injustice of a dowry system that compels women to spend their inheritance buying themselves into the "slavery" of marriage (pp. 112–14).

Dusk falls as the group is discussing the benefits marriage offers to men, and Adriana adjourns the conversation until dawn the following day. The second day's argument, though introduced as a continuation of the first, is in fact very different in character. The day starts with a discussion of love and friendship and their causes, in which women's natural (and dangerous) susceptibility to love is contrasted with men's fatal imperviousness to feeling: a characteristic that renders them not only incapable of romantic love for women, but also—as Corinna claims in a speech that deliberately flies in the face of all classical and Renaissance treatments of the subject—barely even capable of friendship with other men (pp. 123–24). The discussion is then broadened from human affection to the greater cosmic harmony of which it is a part, and the universal forces of concord and discord are invoked (p. 128). This passage marks a shift in the tone and character of the dialogue, introducing, as it does, an ambitious sequence of scientific disquisitions by Corinna, covering the properties and the inhabitants (birds, fish, animals, plants) of, in turn, the air (pp. 129–41), the waters (pp. 147–57), and the earth (pp. 158–88). The conversation then moves from the natural to the social world, covering rhetoric and law, grammar, politics (a subject that triggers an enthusiastic paean to Venetian good government), poetry, music, painting and sculpture, and, finally and perhaps most interesting, heraldry, color symbolism, and dress—"the languages that speak without words" (pp. 230–36). The aims of the second day, as the list of subjects covered indicates, are no less than encyclopedic. Though Fonte is keenly aware of the superficiality of her coverage and makes no pretense at doing more than sketching in the contours of each subject (p. 238), Day 2 of *The Worth of Women* makes a gesture at least toward the ambition that animated many of her contemporaries, of spanning the whole of knowledge within the pages of a single book.[12]

THE WORTH OF WOMEN: THE QUESTION OF UNITY

From the preceding summary, it will be clear that the break between the first and second days of *The Worth of Women* signals a sharp thematic and structural dividing line in the dialogue, between the tightly unified feminist discussions of Day 1 and the encyclopedic meanderings of Day 2. The division is less absolute than might appear from a summary like this, however: beneath its apparent discontinuities—amusingly dramatized throughout the second day in Leonora's

---

12. On the encyclopedic culture of the late sixteenth century, see most recently Findlen 1994.

increasingly irate protests at her companions' digressions—*The Worth of Women* remains faithful to its original concerns. A strong indication that we are intended to perceive continuities between the encyclopedic material of Day 2 and the feminist theme of Day 1 is provided by the semi-serious pretext for the digressions of Day 2, that all this trawling through the resources of the natural and human worlds is directed at identifying some means, natural, magical, or rational, for curing men of their hostility to women. More significant continuities are also hinted at, if less explicitly. After the section on the medicinal properties of herbs, when Leonora objects that all this has very little to do with women, Lucretia corrects her with the observation that "on the contrary, . . . it would be a good thing if there were women who knew about medicine as well as men, so men couldn't boast about their superiority in this field and we didn't have to be dependent on them" (p. 181). A similar feminist impulse is attributed to the whole book in a retrospective comment of Corinna's, when it is put to her that men would find the idea of women discussing natural science and the arts ridiculously incongruous, and she defends their discussions on the grounds that "women have just as much right to speak about these subjects as men have, and if we were educated properly as girls . . . we'd outstrip their performance in any science or art you care to name" (p. 238).

The second day of *The Worth of Women* may be seen, then, among other things, as a symbolic first step toward the task of empowering women by equipping them with the kind of practical and theoretical knowledge of the world from which they had traditionally been excluded by their inadequate education. This is an extraordinarily ambitious enterprise, and an extraordinarily original one: earlier contributors to the *querelle des femmes* had often denounced women's exclusion from education, and proclaimed their potential for mastering traditionally male fields of knowledge, but it is difficult to think of any precedent for this kind of activist response to the problem. This does not, however, constitute the entire protofeminist agenda of Day 2 of *The Worth of Women*. A further aim, it may be suggested, especially in those extensive sections of Day 2 that deal with the wonders of the natural world, is to redeem women from the equivocal and contradictory position they occupied in contemporary accounts of the hierarchy of being and to reassert their dignity as joint rulers of creation alongside men.

Some expansion of this last point may be helpful. It was a commonplace of Renaissance thought that man, created as he was in

God's image and likeness, justly dominated the hierarchy of the natural world, ranging from the animals down to the plants and the lifeless stones. Woman's place on this scale of being, however, was more ambiguous and unstable. Officially, because of her undisputed spiritual equality with men, she was subsumed into the ungendered category "man" and accorded the rank of joint regent over nature. In practice, however, a deep-rooted conviction of women's inferiority to men, fostered both by the Aristotelian scientific tradition that perceived women as "defective males"[13] and by misogynist readings of Genesis of the type that Fonte counters in Day 1 of *The Worth of Women* (pp. 60 and 94), led to a persistent tendency to equate women with subhuman nature and thus to relegate them, explicitly or otherwise, to a point lower than men's on the scale.[14]

That one objective of the scientific disquisitions in Day 2 of *The Worth of Women* may be to challenge this demotion of women from their "rightful place" in the hierarchy of nature is indicated in an important speech of Leonora's at p. 168 of the dialogue, which follows an account of how divine providence has distributed healing properties in plants. Leonora begins by pointing out the anomaly that the cooperative behavior of inanimate plants is more consonant with the Creator's wishes than that of man, who was intended by God to be woman's companion and support, but who in fact behaves more like her enemy, abusing her, depriving her of freedom, and treating her without any respect. This is all the more scandalous, she notes in reply to a point of Lucretia's, in that "all the other creatures recognize us as the rulers of the world, just as much as men, if not more." In insisting on treating women as inferiors, something for which there is no foundation in nature, men are attempting to displace them from their rightful and dignified position in the scheme of things, depriving them of the "reputation, favor, and respect" they should enjoy from "all the creatures of the world."

The passage just quoted is an isolated one, but it does not seem illegitimate to suggest that this concern to reassert women's place in the hierarchy of being is the thread that ties together the various scientific digressions of Day 2 and which binds them to the feminist debate of Day 1. It is by no means fortuitous that in the passage just discussed Leonora refers back to an issue debated in Day 1 of the dialogue (p. 60): the correct interpretation of the Creation myth, which

13. See Maclean 1980.
14. For examples of this tendency, see Thomas 1984, 43.

her culture perceived as a blueprint for both the relation of the sexes and the relation of humanity to the lesser ranks of creation.[15] For Fonte—and this is a profoundly original aspect of her thought—men's abusive postlapsarian appropriation of a position of superiority over women has warped and contaminated not only the relation God had intended to exist between the sexes, but also women's relation with the remainder of creation. In the light of this intuition, Fonte's speakers' descriptive tour of the kingdom of nature in the second day of *The Worth of Women* may perhaps be seen as an attempt to reestablish women's dominion over nature, at least symbolically and verbally; almost, indeed, as a feminist reenactment of Adam's "naming of the animals" in Genesis.[16] On this reading, the thematic gulf that may seem to exist between the first and second books of the dialogue is revealed as more apparent than real. The unity of this apparently disunified text rests ultimately on its radical intuition that rethinking women's status is something that cannot be done without in some sense rethinking the world.

THE WORTH OF WOMEN AND RENAISSANCE LITERARY TRADITION

The Tradition of "Defenses of Women"

As has already been noted, Fonte's *The Worth of Women* forms part of a long-established tradition of writings on women's nature and capacities, dating back ultimately to Boccaccio's *On Famous Women* (c. 1360) and Christine de Pizan's *Book of the City of Ladies* (c. 1405).[17] The issue of women's equality with men became a fashionable debating point in the courts of Northern Italy in the late fifteenth and early sixteenth centuries, and the commonplaces of this debate were shortly afterward given European circulation in works like Castiglione's *Book of the Courtier* (1528), whose third book is largely devoted to the question of the status of women, and Ariosto's *Orlando Furioso* (1532), which wit-

---

15. See ibid., 17–18.

16. A passage from a contemporary treatise defending the thesis of men's superiority is of interest in this context: "And then God [having created Adam], wishing to reveal man's greatness as clearly as possible before he formed woman, brought all the beasts of the earth and all the birds of the air before him, so that he, in his wisdom, could give them all their proper names (a task which was carried out by Adam with all the dignity and majesty one might expect from such a noble creature)." Bramoso 1589, 11–12.

17. On the Renaissance *querelle des femmes*, see, most recently, Jordan 1990; King 1991, 181–87; Benson 1992. On women's contributions to the debate, see Kelly 1984, 65–109.

tily satirizes misogyny in the figure of Rodomonte and champions women's achievements, lamenting their lack of recognition in conventional, male-authored history. Another work of the same period, of comparable influence, was the German humanist Henricus Cornelius Agrippa's *Declamation on the Nobility and Preeminence of the Female Sex* (1529), whose more radical (though often sophistic) arguments for women's superiority to men were widely imitated by writers eager to display their rhetorical skills.[18] Given impetus by these seductive and widely read works, the "defense of women" began to crystallize into a well-defined genre, with an established repertoire of arguments, authorities, and examples. It was an extremely popular one: one recent bibliography, which limits itself to Italian sources, lists around fifty texts in the century from 1524 to 1632, from brief polemical broadsides to vast, heavily documented tomes.[19]

Moderata Fonte was clearly well acquainted with the humanistic tradition of defenses of women, and readers of Castiglione or Agrippa will find much that is familiar here. Many of the key topics discussed in the first book of *The Worth of Women*—the balance of biological and cultural factors in determining gender roles, the role of literature and history in perpetuating misogynist values, the relative dignity and relative guilt of Adam and Eve—were eminently well established in the "defense" tradition, while the long list of classical *exempla* of notable women that occupies a substantial portion of the first book draws heavily on the accumulated findings of two centuries of humanistic research. Despite these fairly substantial debts, however, it would be misleading to portray Fonte's dialogue as in any way a typical product of the genre of defenses of women; indeed, when a comparison is made with a work like Lucrezia Marinella's *On the Nobility and Excellence of Women* (1600), *The Worth of Women*'s relation to the formal tradition of "defenses" is revealed as distinctly semidetached. Marinella's treatise, written in response to a misogynist tract, Giuseppe Passi's *The Defects of Women*, operates consciously within the boundaries of a well-defined polemical context.[20] Sources and authorities are cited and academic conventions of argument respected; even the title, a popular choice with "defenders of women" from Agrippa onward, announces the work's adherence to an established tradition of debate. *The Worth of Women* is quite different in this respect. The

18. Agrippa 1996.
19. Zancan, ed. 1983, 237–46.
20. On Marinella, see Labalme 1980 and 1981; also Chemello 1983.

dialogue does draw extensively on the tradition of "defenses," as has been noted, and Fonte shows an awareness that her work is likely to be read within this polemical context.[21] She makes only the most indirect attempts to engage with contemporary academic debate on the subject, however, and occasionally her speakers' comments even appear to betray a certain skepticism about the utility of the debate as it was conventionally conducted. "Men should be told of these examples," exclaims one speaker, interrupting a list of historical evidence of women's virtues and achievements. "They already know all about them," her interlocutor replies, "They just like to pretend that they don't" (p. 111).

A degree of caution seems advisable, then, when assessing *The Worth of Women*'s relation to the preceding tradition of defenses of women: there are fidelities to, but also departures from, the established conventions of the genre. Perhaps the best way of gauging Fonte's distance from the tradition is to point to the shift in emphasis in her dialogue away from a concern with demonstrating the "nobility and excellence" of women (though this is still a vital part of her argument) to a concern with the concrete consequences for women of men's failure to recognize their worth. As will be clear from my summary of the work, the question of women's equality with men is dispatched in a fairly perfunctory manner at the beginning of Day 1, while most of the remainder of the work is taken up by a litany of complaints about men's cruelty to women, followed by a semi-serious search for a cure. At the end of the work, one of the main speakers, Leonora, expresses her hopes that her arguments may have "converted" some men from their wrongful conviction of their superiority to women. But she makes it clear that her concern is not so much with simply establishing the truth for its own sake as with improving the lot of the "many suffering women" she sees all around her—suffering, precisely, as a result of their menfolk's conviction of their own superiority, which leads them to consider themselves justified in resorting to "any sort of tyranny and cruelty" (pp. 258–59).

Of course, Fonte was not the first "defender of women" to make a connection between misogynist cultural assumptions and concrete social abuses. She is, however, unusual, if not unique, in the insistence and conviction with which she makes these connections.

---

21. See especially the important passage at the end of the First Day, p. 116, where the feminist speakers in the dialogue discuss the possibility of a male backlash against their arguments.

Thus we learn in the dialogue not only of women's exclusion from education (a frequent complaint among humanist "defenders of women") and of the various sufferings visited by husbands on their wives (a common theme among at least the more enlightened writers on marriage), but also of less frequently addressed abuses, from the number of women left without dowries as a result of male relatives' thoughtlessness or greed (p. 63), to men's hypocrisy in censoring women's "provocative" dress rather than acknowledging their own lechery (p. 236), to—most surprising of all, perhaps, especially in the work of a "respectable" married woman—male society's hypocritical condemnation of the rapacity and shamelessness of prostitutes, when many of them have in fact been forced into the trade after being seduced and abandoned by men (pp. 88–89). *The Worth of Women* is hardly a work of unalleviated social realism—much of the time, indeed, it coasts along the borders of fantasy—but the seriousness of its concern with the social expressions of misogyny acts as a ballast even in its flightier moments, and differentiates it quite sharply from most other contributions to the Renaissance debate on women.

This brings us to the delicate question of the seriousness, or otherwise, of the work. Recent critics have rightly stressed the distance that separates the Renaissance and early-modern tradition of defenses of women from the nineteenth- and twentieth-century tradition of political feminism that it appears at times so to resemble. Perhaps the central difference between the two traditions lies, precisely, in the determinedly apolitical character of the former: Renaissance "feminism" tends to limit itself strictly to a theoretical revindication of women's "nobility and excellence," coupled with an occasional proposal for improved educational opportunities for upper-class women. Even those theorists most committed to proving women's capacity to participate in public life on equal terms with men are reluctant to pursue this point to the conclusion that would suggest itself to the modern reader: that society should be restructured to allow women to exercise these talents. Works that can easily strike us, anachronistically, as radical attacks on the patriarchal political order are generally revealed, on closer scrutiny, to be dictated by quite different agendas: writing in defense of women could variously be a way of positioning oneself intellectually (as a humanist rather than a scholastic), or socially (as a courtier and gallant, rather than an unworldly cleric or academic); or a means of courting patronage from women, or displaying one's rhetorical skills. "Sincerity," in the sense of a personal commitment on the author's part to the ideas expressed, should certainly not be assumed in Renaissance defenses of women. We are on safer ground with "courtesy," "ingenuity," or "eloquence": the qualities contemporary readers most frequently praised in such works.

Where does this leave *The Worth of Women*? Certainly, it implies that a degree of wariness is in order, if we are to avoid imposing anachronistic assumptions on the text. When one of Fonte's speakers urges women to "wake up, and claim back our freedom, and the honor and dignity men have usurped from us for so long" (p. 237), it is tempting to interpret this as the heartfelt call to political action it so resembles to modern ears. It is important to be aware, at such moments, that the cultural tradition Fonte is drawing on in *The Worth of Women* was one that had legitimized and, in a sense, neutralized, a set of apparently radical and subversive propositions regarding women's status by relegating them to the twilight zone between seriousness, intellectual gamesmanship, and paradox: the proposition that women were men's natural equals, for example, or that they possessed the same capacities for military leadership and government, or that men's dominance over them was a brutal tyranny with no foundation in nature or providence.

That said, however, the novelty should not be underestimated, within the genre of defenses of women, of the fact that *The Worth of Women* bears on its frontispiece the name of a woman author rather than that of a man. Within any rhetorical performance—which was what such defenses were—the identity and character of the performer is crucially important: a speech by a woman in defense of women demands to be read very differently from a speech by a man. The point made above needs to be considered as well: that the concern Fonte shows for the concrete social consequences of misogynist "tyranny" represents a significant enough departure from the established norms of the tradition of defenses of women to disrupt readers' expectations and perhaps to short-circuit the usual, comfortable response to such works. *The Worth of Women* is certainly far from "sincerity" in the sense of "earnestness," and its tone, like that of other Renaissance defenses of women, is best defined by the contemporary notion of "serious play" (*serio ludere*). What might be suggested, however, is perhaps that in Fonte the proportions of seriousness and playfulness have shifted slightly but crucially from those of the many defenses written by men which had established the rules of the game.

This becomes clear when we consider what is perhaps one of the most delicate interpretive problems raised by the dialogue: what status to attribute to *The Worth of Women*'s many and heated attacks on the institution of marriage, and its enthusiastic recommendations of the pleasures of the single state. There are many indications that we are not intended to take all of these passages entirely seriously (a good example might be Leonora's suggestion that women would be better off spending their dowry on a pig than a husband [p. 114]); and it is acknowledged in the soberer moments of the dialogue that marriage can hold pleasure as well as suffering for a woman, and that in any case, the choice of the kind of independent, moneyed, and carefree single life that the speakers propose as an ideal was an impossible fantasy for the vast majority of women.[22] It would be unwise, however, to dismiss this element in the dialogue as pure "play," pure provocative paradox, especially when it is considered that Moderata Fonte was writing in a period in which, for a series of economic and social reasons, the marriage prospects of upper-class Venetian women were sharply diminishing, and unprecedented numbers were being pressured into taking the veil or kept on as unpaid servants in the family home, deprived of the dowries from which women's economic power and social prestige had traditionally derived.[23] In these circumstances, for a woman writer to criticize the dowry system, however lightheartedly, or to speculate about the possibility of life outside marriage, however fantastically, is something that needs to be read as a political gesture, however oblique. To ignore the humor of *The Worth of Women*, and its playful delight in parading extremist views, would be to miss a great deal of the meaning (as well as the charm), of Fonte's dialogue. But similarly, to fail to detect the undertone of seriousness that is present in even its lightest moments would be to underrate the complexity of this deceptively spontaneous and unmeditated work.

The Tradition of Literary Dialogue

The question of the sincerity—and, more generally, the meaning—of *The Worth of Women* cannot be considered fully without taking due account of the genre in which the work is written. The dialogue was one of the most popular of Renaissance literary genres, in neo-Latin and vernacular literature, and anyone acquainted with the form as used in the period will immediately recognize certain characteristic fea-

22. See especially Lucretia's speech at p. 240.
23. I have examined the social trends referred to here in Cox 1995.

tures in *The Worth of Women*: the setting of the dialogue in a paradisaical *locus amoenus* (pp. 50–51), the ordering of the discussion under
the governance of an elected "ruler" (p. 56), and, more generally, the
tone of semi-seriousness noted above, which tends to wrong-foot
modern readers, accustomed to a greater consistency of tone.

If *The Worth of Women* is formally indebted in many respects to the
tradition of dialogue (and particularly to the more worldly, less academic tradition, running through Bembo's *Asolani* and Castiglione's
Courtier through the works of writers like Agnolo Firenzuola, Stefano
Guazzo, and Scipione Bargagli), in other respects it represents a significant novelty. Fonte's most striking innovation is, without question, her depiction of a group of exclusively women speakers. It is
worth stressing quite what a departure this represents within the
Italian dialogue tradition. Apart from the special case of Lucianically
inspired dialogues between prostitutes, like those of Pietro Aretino,
the number of precedents for all-women dialogues was tiny, and, with
one possible exception, it is very unlikely that Fonte would have been
acquainted with any works in this form when she came to write her
own dialogue.[24] This fact may help to explain the air of liberating
transgressiveness that surrounds the conversation portrayed in *The
Worth of Women*, reinforced by the speakers' frequent remarks on the
delicious novelty of finding themselves "alone," without men.[25] It
may also account for the remarkably fresh and distinctive conversa-
tional idiom Fonte develops in this work. While some individual
speeches (those of the erudite Corinna, in particular) might have
been lifted from other dialogues of the period, it would be difficult
to find a match in such works for the atmosphere of bantering inti-
macy in which the debates of *The Worth of Women* take place, or for the
leisurely, spontaneous, and meandering rhythms of the conversation
portrayed.[26]

Another feature of *The Worth of Women* that lends it a certain dis-
tinctiveness within the dialogue production of the period is its
exceptional "openness" and its deftness in evading any univocal reading. This may seem unremarkable, in that the dialogue form appears
inherently suited to dramatizing conflicts of ideas without attempt-

24. On this possible exception, see p. 20, n. 29, below.

25. See, for example, pp. 47, 53, and 194.

26. It should be noted, however, that *The Worth of Women* may owe something of its air of
spontaneity to the fact that (if we are to believe Doglioni's account of its
composition) its author had no opportunity to revise her work, so that what we are
reading is, effectively, a first draft.

ing to resolve them. In fact, however, this rather sophisticated potential of the form was utilized far less frequently than one might think, especially in the later decades of the sixteenth century in Italy, when a number of factors conspired to favor "closed" (and often overtly didactic) forms of dialogue, in which one or more speakers very obviously act as mouthpieces for the author.[27] It is rare to read a dialogue of this period in which it is quite so difficult as it is in *The Worth of Women* to establish the author's viewpoint, and where the ethos of the speakers is quite so artfully used to nuance and problematize the questions debated.[28] A good example, at a local level, is the discussion of beauty toward the end of Day 2 of the dialogue (pp. 206–9), in which the earnest and bookish young Corinna (whom several critics have identified, perhaps over-hastily, as the author's alter ego) asserts the primacy of moral over physical beauty, and is countered by the much older and markedly down-to-earth Adriana—herself a former beauty and proud of it—who insists first that in practice the headier attractions of physical beauty will always win out over the charms of moral excellence, and, secondly, that attraction is a more mysterious, irrational, and unpredictable process than Corinna is prepared to allow. Few writers of dialogue in this period would have resisted the urge to close this debate on a properly moral and neoplatonizing note, with an unequivocal victory for Corinna. Fonte's resolution, however, is more ambiguous: Adriana may formally concede the point, but her two pungently expressed objections retain a certain resonance in the dialogue, and we come out of the debate with a sense of both the undeniable "correctness" of Corinna's position, and its failure to encompass anything like the full range of human emotional experience.

A similar point might be made in relation to the debate on marriage discussed above. In the closing pages of *The Worth of Women*, this long-running debate appears to be brought to some form of closure, when the young Virginia, who has been half convinced by her companions' arguments against marriage, is persuaded by her mother Adriana to accept it as a necessary evil. At the same time, Leonora, one of the ringleaders of the antimarriage faction, consents to Adriana's pleas that she agree to reconsider her decision never to remarry (pp. 238–40 and 259). Some critics have considered this passage a palinode, inserted to neutralize the subversive charge of Leonora's earlier

---

27. Cox 1992, 65–69.
28. See further on this point Smarr 1995, esp. 22.

diatribes against marriage. This seems an inappropriately heavy-handed reading, however, especially when Fonte's procedure is compared with that of other writers of the period. Where sixteenth-century dialogues intend a palinode, they tend to leave the reader in little doubt of the fact: "wrongheaded" positions, when they are given an airing, tend to be clearly labelled as such and to be followed by an extensive refutation which sets the record straight.[29] The ending of *The Worth of Women*, by contrast, is characteristically ambiguous. Virginia consents to marriage *faute de mieux*, with the warnings of her companions ringing in her ears. Leonora's conciliatory gesture may be read either as a genuine change of heart or a gracious hostess's concession to a persistent guest. As the conversation of *The Worth of Women* meanders to its close, we are left with the sense that it is ending only because nightfall has curtailed it, and not because the last word on its chosen subject has been said. The same might be remarked of the complex and challenging dialogue on gender and identity that Moderata Fonte had been conducting with her readers since her first published work, *Il Floridoro*, and which was destined so tragically soon after she wrote these last pages to be cut short by her premature death.

FORTUNES AND INFLUENCE

The Worth of Women was published in 1600, eight years after its author's death, by the Venetian publisher Domenico Imberti, with a dedicatory letter to the Duchess of Urbino by Fonte's surviving daughter, Cecilia. It seems likely that the work's publication at this time may reflect the new wave of interest in the debate on women excited in the last years of the sixteenth century in the Veneto by the publication of Giuseppe Passi's misogynist treatise *The Defects of Women* (Padua, 1595 and 1599), which occasioned a number of published responses, including, as has been noted, Lucrezia Marinella's *On the Nobility and Excellence of Women* (1600), commissioned by the publisher Giambattista Ciotti. Ciotti's commission suggests that there existed a degree of curiosity among the reading public concerning women's response to the debate on their sex, and this was borne out by the success of his venture: Marinella's treatise received a second edition the following year and a third in 1623.

The Worth of Women does not appear to have enjoyed the publishing

---

29. For an example thematically and chronologically close to *The Worth of Women*, see Cox 1995, 569–75.

success of Marinella's treatise, but it would be misleading to suggest that it sank without trace on publication. From the 1580s, Moderata Fonte's name had been included in the list of important living Venetian writers which featured in the popular guidebook to the city, *On the Notable Features of the City of Venice*, and after her death, the entry on her was expanded (apparently by her biographer Doglioni, who produced a revised edition of this work in 1603) to include in the list of her works "that charming book of hers on the merits of women, in which she defends her sex and shows it to be in no respect inferior to the male."[30] This mention must have brought Fonte's name to the attention of a fairly wide public, in Venice and beyond, and there is evidence of an acquaintance with her writings in the works of several writers of the first half of the seventeenth century, including Luciano Bursati da Crema's *The Victory of Women* (Venice, 1621) and the vast multivolume work by the Florentine Cristoforo Bronzini, *On the Dignity and Nobility of Women* (1624–25).[31] Of particular interest is that Fonte appears to have been read by both her younger contemporary Lucrezia Marinella, and by a Venetian woman writer of the next generation, Arcangela Tarabotti (1604–52), the author of a powerful and compelling denunciation of the widespread practice (of which the author herself had been a victim) of persuading girls without a religious vocation to take the veil in order to save the expense of a dowry.[32] To talk of a direct influence by Fonte on these writers' thought would perhaps be exaggerated, especially in the case of Marinella, who appears to have known only *Il Floridoro* at the time when

30. Goldioni (Doglioni) 1603, 187. The guidebook continued to appear in Doglioni's edition until 1692. See also Stringa 1604, 419r-v.

31. See Bursati 1621, 189 and 192; and esp. Bronzini 1622–24, 30–31; and 1625, 115–18.

32. Editions of Marinella's *Nobility and Excellence of Women* and Tarabotti's *Paternal Tyranny* are forthcoming in this series. For these two writers' references to Fonte, see Marinella 1601, 11, 32, and 34; and Tarabotti 1654, 160 (all referring to the passage of the *Floridoro* translated in the appendix to this edition), and Tarabotti 1994, 95, which quotes the madrigal sung at the end of *The Worth of Women*. There is also some rather more oblique evidence that Fonte's dialogue may have been known to a third Venetian woman writer of the period, the actress and poet Isabella Andreini (1562–1604), in that one of Andreini's published letters, protesting against fathers' unreasonable preference for their male offspring—a theme also touched on by Fonte—contains an admiring reference to the tradition of writings on "the merits of women" (*i meriti delle donne*). That the phrase should be seen as a conscious echo of the Italian title of Fonte's *Worth of Women* is the more likely given that defenders of women conventionally talked of the "dignity," "nobility," or "excellence" of women; Fonte's title, *Il merito delle donne*, is, to my knowledge, without precedent. For the letter in question, see Andreini 1607, 18v–19v.

she wrote her *On the Nobility and Excellence of Women*. It can hardly be doubted, however, that the precedent provided by Fonte's rather dashing embodiment of the role of female defender of women must have been among the factors that encouraged these younger Venetian protofeminists to write, and to write as they did.[33]

After the mid-seventeenth century, until very recently, Fonte's writings appear to have attracted little serious critical scrutiny, although her name continued to be mentioned in biographical compilations and works of literary history, and she features quite prominently in the important anthology of Italian women's poetry edited by her fellow Venetian Luisa Bergalli in 1726.[34] Her modern critical rediscovery began in the 1970s, under the impulse of the feminist movement, and was consolidated in the early 1980s by the publication of important studies of her work (and that of the other Venetian women writers mentioned above) by Patricia Labalme in the United States and Adriana Chemello in Italy. Since that time, a number of other studies have appeared, especially since the publication of a critical edition of *The Worth of Women* (Venice, 1988, edited by Chemello; extracts had earlier been published in Conti Odorisio [1979]). Given its historical interest, its originality, and the quality of its writing, it is difficult to envisage the current fascination with *The Worth of Women* diminishing, and it is to be hoped that as the dialogue is made available through translation to a wider public, the momentum of scholarly and critical work on Moderata Fonte will continue to increase. There certainly remains much important work to be done: Fonte's minor works have as yet attracted little sustained critical attention, and a great deal more research needs to be carried out into the sociohistorical and intellectual context of her writings.

33. It might be noted here that there is some tenuous evidence that Marinella may have learned of Fonte through mutual acquaintances, as well as through her books. One possible connection is Orazio Guarguanti, almost certainly a member of Fonte's social circle, and admitted to the prestigious Venetian College of Physicians in the same year (1589) as Marinella's brother Curzio (*Giornale di medicina* 1763, 388). Another possible mutual acquaintance is Lucio Scarano, mentioned in *The Worth of Women* and the dedicatee of Marinella's *Nobility and Excellence of Women*.

34. See Bergalli 1726, 2: 40–53; also the preface to volume 1, in which Bergalli cites the stanzas from the *Floridoro* reproduced in Appendix 1 below (I am grateful to Corinna da Fonseca-Wollheim for this reference). For further bibliographical references, see Chemello 1988, 106, n. 15.

SUGGESTIONS FOR FURTHER READING

Two very readable introductions to Fonte's work, particularly valuable on the Venetian context, are Labalme (1980) and (1981). Also useful on the position of women in late-sixteenth-century Venice is Rosenthal (1993), which includes a discussion of Fonte. Cox (1995) relates the debate on marriage in *The Worth of Women* to contemporary developments in the social and economic position of upper-class Venetian women. Recent critical discussions of *The Worth of Women* in English include Malpezzi Price (1989 and 1994); Jordan (1990, 253–57) (which is marred by some factual inaccuracies); King (1991, 228–32); Kolsky (1993); and Smarr (1995). The main contributions to scholarship and criticism of Fonte in Italian are Conti Odorisio (1979); Chemello (1983) and (1988); Collina (1989) (which contains valuable new biographical information); and, most recently, Guthmüller (1992). A German edition of the work, edited by Bodo Guthmüller and translated by Daniela Hacke, is currently under preparation.

KEY TO
ABBREVIATIONS

ASV   Archivio di Stato di Venezia

HA   Aristotle, *History of Animals*. In *The Complete Works*, edited by Jonathan Barnes. 2 vols. Princeton, 1986, vol. 1

LP   Diogenes Laertius. *Lives of the Eminent Philosophers*, ed. R. D. Hicks. 2 vols. Loeb Classical Library. Cambridge, MA, 1972

MSD   Valerius Maximus, *Memorable Sayings and Deeds* (*Factorum et dictorum mirabilium libri novem*), edited with an Italian translation by Rino Favanda. Turin, 1971

NH   Pliny, *Natural History* (*Naturalis Historia*), edited with an English translation by H. Rackham and others. 10 vols. Loeb Classical Library. Cambridge, MA, 1938–62

OF   Lodovico Ariosto, *Orlando Furioso*, ed. Cesare Segre. Milan, 1976

RS   Petrarch, *Lyric Poems* (*Rime sparse*), edited with an English translation by Robert M. Durling. Cambridge, MA, 1976

VDH   David Chambers and Brian Pullan, eds. *Venice: A Documentary History, 1450–1630*. Oxford, 1992

A NOTE ON
THE TEXT

No manuscript of *The Worth of Women* has come to light, and the text is known only through the edition published by Domenico Imberti (Venice, 1600), recently re-edited by Adriana Chemello for Eidos (Venice, 1988). It should be noted that in the absence of a manuscript we have no way of knowing how faithful the Imberti edition is to Moderata Fonte's intentions. A comment of her biographer, Giovanni Niccolò Doglioni, suggests that the long poem in *ottava rima* near the end of the work was written separately and may perhaps have been inserted into the text by its editors after Fonte's death, and this may possibly be the case with others of the poems incorporated in the dialogue.

My translation is based on Chemello's edition, where the text and Doglioni's *Life of Moderata Fonte* are concerned. The dedicatory letter is taken from Imberti's edition. I have made one correction to Chemello's transcription (p. 178 [Chemello, 122; Imberti, 105], *uva* for *vua*), and in two cases have modified the text as it stands in both Chemello's and Imberti's editions because the sense appeared to demand it (p. 111 [Chemello, 67; Imberti, 58], where I have substituted *pur troppe* for *pur troppo;* and p. 152 [Chemello, 99; Imberti, 85], where I have amended *Ibernia* to *Iberia*). I have also in a very few cases amended Chemello's punctuation after consulting Imberti's edition. For the two speakers' names whose spelling is modernized in Chemello's edition (Elena and Lucrezia), I have restored the Latinate spelling of Imberti's edition, as it corresponds to English usage.

A NOTE ON
FONTE'S SOURCES

In the notes to the present translation, I have followed the practice of tracing classical references to what seem to me their most plausible classical sources, giving precedence to those works that enjoyed a wide diffusion in Renaissance Italy. It should be noted, however, that a direct acquaintance with the classical texts cited in the notes should not necessarily be assumed on Fonte's part, as the historical anecdotes and classical sententiae she relates are, in the main, among those that had been assimilated into the compendious humanistic "general knowledge" of the period, and that were available by the time she was writing from a very wide range of vernacular sources, including popular reference works such as Mexia (1564), Contarini (1589–97), and Landi (1562) (the last subtitled "a work extremely useful for writers on any subject and from which material may be drawn for speaking on any subject whatsoever"). Given this, speculation about the actual sources of Fonte's erudition must be conducted with extreme caution. On the probably extent of her knowledge of Latin, see below, p. 35, n. 12.

Dedicatory Letter

To My Honored Patroness, Her Most Serene Grace Signora Livia Feltria della Rovere, Duchess of Urbino[1]

When controversies arise, it is usual for both sides in the dispute to seek out the most prestigious protector they can find; indeed, whichever side has secured the support of the more distinguished and eminent person considers itself already to have won half the battle, for it may fairly be assumed in such cases either that one's opponents will be daunted by the learning and authority of one's protector and give up the struggle, or that if they do insist on pursuing the dispute, they will ultimately be vanquished by the power of that person's eloquence. In just the same way, as I unveil the present little work, describing the excellence and the great merits of women and conclusively showing them to be superior to men, aware as I am of quite how little this notion is likely to appeal to men, I thought it well to solicit the defense of a woman capable of putting these detractors, these enemies of female worth, firmly back in their place and reducing them to silence with a single wave of her hand. And, if such a defense is necessary (as I am quite sure it is), what better and wiser woman, what nobler or more exalted protector could I hope to find than Your Most Serene Grace? At the mere sound of your name, all those sophistic ideas and arguments men might use to make out

---

1. Livia Feltria della Rovere, a descendent of the dukes of Urbino, in the Italian Marches, married her distant cousin, the last duke of Urbino, Francesco Maria II (1548 – 1631), in 1599. Cecilia Zorzi's dedication must have been somewhat speculative, as the new Duchess was only fifteen years old and hardly an established patron.

their spurious case will melt away like a thin morning mist in the powerful heat of the sun. And this firm and unshakable resolve of mine is not in any way undermined by the fact that Your Most Serene Grace is joined in marriage to the Most Serene Lord Duke, your husband, who is, after all, a man. For, since the Duke has been graced with all those rare gifts and virtues with which everyone is familiar, he constitutes an exception, to be expressly excluded from any general reflections on his sex; indeed, as a man of the greatest objectivity, I call on him to act as women's defender, alongside Your Grace. And so, with all due reverence, I consecrate and dedicate to Your Most Serene Grace the present work, which was written by my mother Madonna Modesta or Moderata Fonte when I was a child, and brought to the present stage of completion the very day before her death in childbirth, so that she was unable to reread or revise it. And I hope that Your Most Serene Grace will find it an acceptable expression of the depth of my respect for you and the eagerness of my desire to serve you. And I pray you to inscribe me in the number of your most faithful and devoted servants, along with my brother Pietro, who is the only family that remains to me (as the others are now dead, as is our father),[2] and who joins with me in ardently desiring and praying for the continuing happiness of Your Most Serene Grace and the Most Serene Lord Duke, whose revered hands we humbly kiss. From Venice, 10 November 1600.

Your Most Serene Grace's most devoted servant, Cecilia de' Zorzi

ON MADONNA MODERATA FONTE'S
THE WORTH OF WOMEN,
BY HER SON, PIETRO DE' ZORZI

Di quanto avean uomini 'n detti e 'n carte
Le donne tutte indegnamente offeso
Non credea alcun che lor castigo reso
Fosse ch'al merto gisse eguale in parte.

---

2. According to Doglioni's biography, Moderata Fonte had four surviving children at her death: a boy of ten, a girl of eight, a boy of six, and a newborn daughter. Cecilia, who wrote this preface, is evidently the elder girl; Pietro, the author of the two sonnets that follow, the elder boy. The younger boy, Hieronimo or Girolamo, died of fever in 1597; the children's father, Filippo Zorzi, the following year (ASV, Provveditori alla sanità, Necrologie, reg. 827, 77v [15 August] and 196r [26 June]). I have been unable to trace the fate of the younger daughter, who may not long have outlived her mother.

Né credea alcun che donna ingegno ed arte
Avesse e forza a sostener tal peso
O pur a sottentrar l'animo acceso
Ch'a donne il Ciel tal grazia non comparte.
Ecco che sovra d'ogni uman pensiero
Donna è che al sesso suo torna ogni onore
E con la penna e 'l stil l'alza a le stelle.
Potean celar pria gli uomini ogni errore
Loro, ma or noto sie, come di quelle
Ogni virtù da l'Idaspe e l'Ibero.

For all the undeserved abuse, both spoken and written, which men have long showered on women, they never believed they would ever have to suffer any punishment that corresponded even partially to the severity of the offense. And certainly no one believed that a woman could ever have the intelligence, literary skill, and strength of character necessary to take on a task like this, in the absence of true poetic inspiration (for [as they believed] the heavens did not give this gift to women). But here we see, contrary to all expectations, a woman restoring her sex to its rightful honor and, moreover, exalting women to the skies by the power of her pen. Up to now, men could conceal all their misdeeds, but now their flaws, as well as women's true qualities, will be known from one end of the world to the other.[3]

ON THE SAME SUBJECT, BY THE SAME

Chi creduto averia le limpide acque
D'un Fonte a' fiumi esser nemiche e infeste
Sì che scornati le frondose teste [sic]
Sien più di quel che Deianira piacque?
Né a colui forse esser vinto sì spiacque
Come dell'Arno e 'l Po son l'onde meste
Della perduta gloria e ne fan feste
L'onde in mezo di cui Venere nacque.

3. Literally, from the Hydaspes (a tributary of the Indus) to the Ebro, in Spain. The phrase echoes the first line of a sonnet of Petrarch's (*RS*, 210), where it refers to the miraculous uniqueness of the phoenix: an allusion Pietro may well have intended his readers to register.

Se 'l dolce al dolce noce e l'amar giova
Che dir si può? Se non, che man di Dea
L'ordine di natura abbia mutato?
Ma se donna mortal fè questa nova
Stupenda opra, chi negherà che dato
Non gli abbi il Ciel quanto dar gli potea?

Whoever would have thought that the limpid waters of a Spring could have so disturbed and muddied the waters of two great rivers that their great leafy heads were more thoroughly subdued in the encounter than that of Deianeira's admirer?[4] And little as he enjoyed being vanquished, the waters of the Arno and the Po are now perhaps even sadder at their lost glory, while the waves from which Venus was born rejoice at their victory.[5] So we have fresh water working to the detriment of fresh water and the benefit of the salty ocean. What can we say? The only explanation must be that a goddess's hand has changed the normal order of nature. Or, if it really was a mortal woman who was the author of this uncanny and remarkable feat, who can deny that she must have received from the heavens all those gifts the heavens can bestow?

4. The rather tortuous conceit in this sonnet counterposes Moderata Fonte's literary achievements with those of the great traditions of Florence (Dante, Boccaccio, Petrarch) and Ferrara (Ariosto, Tasso), symbolized by the rivers Arno and Po, whose waters are said to have been clouded by the purer waters of her "spring" (a play on the name "Fonte"). Deianeira was the second wife of the Greek hero Herakles, or Hercules; her admirer, Acheloüs, who fought with Hercules, transformed himself into a bull, and, on his defeat, threw himself into the river that now bears his name and drowned. The adjective *scornato* in Italian has the figurative meaning "humiliated," "broken," "subdued," but its literal meaning, "having had one's horns broken," is also relevant here, as prior to Acheloüs's defeat, one of his horns was torn off and thrown into the river by the water nymphs.

5. The "waves from which Venus was born" are those of the Venetian lagoon; such associations of Venice with Venus were not uncommon in the celebratory literature of the period (Rosand 1984, 209–10).

Life of
Moderata Fonte

Life of Signora Modesta Pozzo de' Zorzi, known as Moderata Fonte, composed by
Giovanni Niccolò Doglioni,[1] in the year 1593

In the year 1548, there dwelt here in Venice a certain Messer
Girolamo da Pozzo, who was descended from a respected *cittadino* family.[2] At this time, he was living under the care and protection of his

---

1. Giovanni Niccolò Doglioni (1548–1629), Moderata Fonte's friend and one-time
guardian, was the descendent of a noble family of Belluno, in the Dolomites, but was
born in Venice and lived there most of his life, attaining a certain prominence in the
Venetian civil service (Romanello 1991; Cicogna 1824–61, 2: 23–26). He wrote a number of literary works, including a cosmological treatise, *L'anno* [*The Year*] (1587), a history
of Venice (1598), and a compendium of world history. Doglioni's life of Fonte exists in
a number of manuscripts, suggesting that it was distributed independently after Fonte's
death before being revised for inclusion in the 1600 edition of *The Worth of Women*. My
translation is based on the text in Fonte 1988.

2. The Venetian republic was unusual in recognizing two elite hereditary groups: the
patriciate, the ruling estate of the city and, below them, the *cittadini originari* (lit.
"original citizens"), who were excluded from political office, but otherwise had much
in common with at least the less exalted ranks of the patriciate, in terms of wealth,
education, and lifestyle (*VDH*, 259–60; Zannini 1993). Little is known of Fonte's
father, Girolamo da Pozzo, but some information is afforded by an archival source for
which I am grateful to Daniela Hacke for referring me: the failed application for the
status of *cittadinanza originaria* submitted by Moderata Fonte's brother Leonardo da Pozzo
in 1589, under the new and strict legal regulations governing admission to this estate
introduced twenty years previously (ASV, Avogaria di Comun, Cittadinanze originarie,
Suppliche e scritture inespedite, b. 433, no. 4, 6; also, on the assessment process,
Zannini 1993, 61–83). The testimonials submitted with this document identify
Girolamo's father as a certain Messer Matteo Frances, and suggest that he adopted the
surname Da Pozzo in recognition of a legacy from a member of this long-established
cittadino family, to which he may have been related on his mother's side. The testimo-
nials also confirm that Girolamo and his father were men of means, were born in
Venice, did not engage in any "mechanical trade," and habitually dressed in the wide-

maternal grandmother, having recently lost both parents. And since he was still only a boy, and had a comfortable income from the property he had inherited, he occupied himself by studying the humanities under the learned guidance of Messer *Pre* Ottavio Arnaldo, the parish priest of San Leonardo:[3] a man well versed in the liberal arts and regarded as one of the foremost teachers of the time. This priest had a nephew (his sister's son) called Prospero Saraceni, who had recently married a lady named Madonna Cecilia di Mazzi, with a little daughter named Marietta, the child of her first marriage, which had been to Messer Giacomo dal Moro (all those just named were also from old *cittadino* families). This nephew, although he had a house of his own, in effect lived with his uncle the priest, while working as a lawyer in the courts—a profession at which he excelled.

In this way, Messer Prospero came to know the young Messer Girolamo, who favorably impressed him as a decent and well-mannered young man. So when the time came to marry his stepdaughter, wanting to find the best match possible for her, he thought of Messer Girolamo, and broached the idea to his uncle, who was equally taken with the notion and agreed to act for him and settle the matter. The priest had a word with the young man, who took very little persuading; for, as an orphan, with no one to help him manage his affairs, he realized how useful it would be to him to gain influential friends like the priest and Saraceni. So he agreed almost immediately, and the marriage was arranged. But the priest was a judicious man and realized that this marriage might distract the young man from his studies, which would have been disastrous for him. So after the marriage was concluded, to delay its consummation, he arranged for the young man to be sent away to study in Bologna.[4] And Messer Girolamo remained

---

sleeved robe that signaled patrician or *cittadino* status in Venice. With these qualifications, it may have been the uncertainty regarding the circumstances of Girolamo's change of surname that occasioned the rejection of his son's application, especially given the importance attributed to legitimacy in the male line in the legal definition of *cittadinanza*. In any case, whatever their legal position, it seems indubitable that Fonte's father and brother would still have been considered *cittadini* in the looser sense still current in Venice in this period, embracing all nonpatrician professionals of a certain level of wealth and dignity (Zannini 1993, 93), and certainly she herself appears to have been regarded as of *cittadino* rank (Sansovino 1587, 201).

3. San Leonardo stands just off the Grand Canal, in the *sestiere* of Cannaregio. *Pre* is a Venetian title, a contraction of *prete*, "priest."

4. Bologna University, founded in the eleventh century, was one of the most important centers for the study of law in Europe. For a Venetian to attend a foreign university such as this was, however, in strict terms, illegal in this period and could potentially have caused problems for Girolamo da Pozzo in his legal career (Palmer 1983, 14).

there until he passed his doctorate, which he did in an astonishingly short time and with flying colors, after which he returned to Venice and the enjoyment of his dear wife. On his return, he began to practice as an advocate in civil cases, achieving such remarkable success in such a short time that everyone was amazed.

Girolamo's wife gave him their first child, a son named Leonardo, in 1553. Two years later, on the day of Saints Vitus and Modestus,[5] the girl who is the subject of this biography was born, and at her christening in the parish church of San Samuele,[6] she was given the name Modesta. But before Modesta was a year old, both her parents died, and the poor little orphans were left in a state it is only too easy to imagine. The only good thing that can be said was that their relatives, close and distant, fell over one another to take the orphans into their care—along with their inheritance, which gave them an income of five hundred or more ducats a year.[7] But, since the family could not agree on who should take charge, they eventually decided to choose a steward and pay him a decent salary to manage the estate. The children, meanwhile, were placed in the care of their maternal grandmother and her husband, the above-mentioned Messer Prospero Saraceni, who were diligently seeing to their care and upbringing when suddenly another relative kidnaped the little girl and paid for her to be placed in the convent of Santa Marta.[8]

In the convent, Modesta's lively intelligence proved so engaging that she was showered with love and caresses from all the reverend sisters. The nuns taught her the kind of little recital pieces and other things they usually teach in such places;[9] and her memory

5. This was 15 June, an auspicious date of birth for a patriotic Venetian, as the anniversary of a failed coup attempt in 1310 and the occasion of a great civic procession of thanksgiving (Muir 1981, 217–18).

6. San Samuele stands just off the *campo* of the same name, on the north bank of the Grand Canal, not far from the Accademia bridge.

7. More detailed accounts of Fonte's financial standing are afforded by her tax return of August 1582, a document of 1583 relating to her dowry, and her will of 1585, all cited below. For a discussion, see Rosenthal 1992, 85–86 and 299, n. 73.

8. The convent of Santa Marta (suppressed in 1805) stood in a remote part of the *sestiere* of Dorsoduro, near San Niccolò dei Mendicoli. The custom of sending young girls to convents as boarders was widespread among the moneyed classes of Venice (Grendler 1989, 96–99), and, although no records are available for the period in question, later documents suggest that Santa Marta ran a quite substantial educational establishment (a 1620 pastoral visit, for example, records twenty-three girls in a monastic community of 109 (ACPV, "Archivio segreto," Visite pastorali a monasteri femminili, b. 4: Tiepolo, 1620–27, Santa Marta, 15 August 1620; I am grateful to Mary Laven for this reference).

9. The education received by girls boarding in convents appears to have been limited to

proved so keen and tenacious that no sooner had she read these things once than she could repeat them from memory, to the astonishment of all around. So, whenever some lady came to visit the convent (as is the custom), she would always be taken to see the little girl and hear her perform, as if she were some strange and remarkable freak of nature. And one day it happened that the convent received a visit from Padre Fiamma, the famous preacher, who later became bishop of Chioggia,[10] and, having listened to the child at the urging of the nuns, he was so astonished that he was moved to say that she truly seemed to him like a pure disembodied spirit, "a spirit without a body." At this, little Modesta turned to the cleric, a great whale of a man, and (thinking perhaps, that his words were some kind of insult) retorted as quick as a flash that if she seemed to him a spirit without a body, he seemed to her a body without a spirit. The reverend father was very much struck by the speed of the little girl's riposte and the charming manner in which she proffered it.

Now, when Modesta reached the age of nine, she left the convent and returned to Saraceni's house, where she had as a companion a daughter of the latter, slightly older than herself. And as Saraceni was fond of literature, and especially of poetry, the little girl, to imitate and vie with him, set herself to writing verse herself, as though it was the most natural thing in the world. She succeeded astonishingly well for a child of her age; and Saraceni, recognizing this natural talent on her part, set about stimulating her gift for poetry by constantly suggesting new subjects for her to write about and keeping her supplied with books to read and study, as far as she was able. At the same time (amazing to recount), when her brother came home from school (he was at grammar school by this stage),[11] little Modesta

---

elementary vernacular literacy, needlework, and singing (Grendler 1989, 99). Doglioni's mention of *rappresentazioni* (which I have translated as "recital pieces") is intriguing in this context, as the word usually indicates some kind of sacred or secular dramatic performance, and may indicate the existence of a tradition of convent drama at Santa Marta in which boarding pupils participated (see, for a general discussion of the phenomenon, Weaver 1986).

10. Gabriele Fiamma (1532–85) was one of the most celebrated preachers of his day and a considerable poet (Erspamer 1983, 211–14; Ossola 1976). He was created bishop of Chioggia by Pope Gregory XIII in 1584. Doglioni's remarks about his corpulence are borne out by accounts of his death after "becoming overheated while delivering a speech to the Japanese ambassadors then visiting" (Ossola 1976, 243).

11. The original has *scuola di grammatica:* a secondary school that taught the prestigious Latin curriculum favored by the nobility and the professional classes, rather than one of the vernacular schools that also flourished in this period in Venice (Grendler 1989).

would come up and pester him to show her and explain to her what he
had been taught that day; and she would so fervently impress what he
said on her memory that she retained a great deal more of what he had
learned than he himself did. And she so threw herself into the study
of letters that with the help of the grammar books she read and committed to memory and Saraceni's *arpicordo*, she could soon read any
Latin book very fluently and could even write fairly well in Latin.[12]

As a child, Modesta's dearest object was the diligent care of her
writings, as the following incident shows. Saraceni had some property
in the country, in Villa di Geminiana, near Camposampiero and
Villorba, near Sacile;[13] and, as he was comfortably off and exercised
the legal profession in a rather leisurely way, he tended to spend most
of the summer on his estates. One day, on the way from Geminiana
to Sacile, with the whole family riding along in his open carriage (for
coaches were not in use at the time),[14] as they went over the fast-
flowing river Piave near Lovadina, a little basket containing all the
child's writings fell into the water and was quickly swept out of sight.
Little Modesta was quite devastated and began to weep so bitterly
that her family could not console her, however they tried. And her
sadness remained with her until she had succeeded in rewriting all
her lost works, with the aid of her exceptional memory. In both these
rural retreats—but especially in Sacile, since the beauty of the countryside there made it more suited to such pursuits—Modesta devoted
herself to writing, with extraordinary results. But it was not simply in
writing that she excelled, but in everything she tried. Without any

12. The normal meaning of the word *arpicordo* is "harpsichord." Here, the context would
imply that some kind of language-learning aid is meant, but I have been unable to
establish the precise sense of the term. Where the extent of Fonte's knowledge of
Latin is concerned, it is possible that Doglioni is exaggerating. Certainly, there is no
sure evidence of a knowledge of the language in Fonte's writings: unlike her near-con-
temporary Lucrezia Marinella, she never quotes Latin sources directly, and her main literary points of reference appear to be popular vernacular poets like Petrarch and Ariosto.
Nor do the fairly numerous classical references in *The Worth of Women* necessarily argue a
knowledge of Latin, as not only were most important classical works available in translation by the time Fonte was writing (including the scientific sources on which she
appears to draw in book 2), but much anecdotal material concerning the classical world
was also available in Italian in the popular encyclopedic works that abounded in this
period.

13. Sacile stands on the banks of the river Livenza, just southwest from Pordenone,
about 75 km from Venice. Camposampiero is just northwest of Padua.

14. The widespread use of coaches for transport in Europe began only in the later sixteenth century. The distinction between the two terms Doglioni uses here (*cocchio* and
carrozza) is not entirely clear, but the sense would seem to suggest that he means the
former to indicate an open vehicle, the latter a closed one.

training, she could draw from life any figure placed in front of her, in a way that astounded everyone who saw her. She played the harpsichord and the lute; she sang; her arithmetic was impressive; and her handwriting was so clear, swift, and accurate that few could match her, let alone surpass her. She was also a superb needlewoman, and without any kind of pattern or sketch to guide her, she could embroider any subject or design that was suggested to her, bringing it to life with her needle before the eyes of the amazed lookers-on.

When Modesta had grown up, I married Saraceni's daughter, who had been her companion.[15] And since the girls had grown up like sisters and she could not bear to be parted from my wife, she came to live with us when we were married and stayed on in our house. Up to this point, her talent had been lying buried; but I immediately recognized it and determined, as a lover of excellence, to reveal it to the world. So it was through my agency that her remarkable and unique gifts first began to be known; I encouraged her writing and started arranging for the publication of her works. During her stay in my household, she wrote the *Floridoro* (not just the cantos that appeared in the published edition, but others that have not yet been published).[16] She also wrote the *Passion of Christ* and countless sonnets, canzoni, and madrigals on different subjects, as well as some *rappresentazioni* that were performed before successive Most Serene Doges of Venice, and have also been published, though mainly anonymously.[17]

---

15. The girl's name, not recorded here, was Saracena Saraceni: "Madonna Saracena mia carissima," as Fonte refers to her in her will of 13 July 1585 (ASV, Notarile Testamenti, Atti Sacco, b. 1192 [f. 467]). Saracena's marriage and Fonte's subsequent transfer to Doglioni's house in the parish of San Giuliano (close to St. Mark's Square) must have taken place some time after 1576, as Doglioni lost his first wife and family in the great plague of that year (Cicogna 1824–61, 2: 23). Fonte appears to have lived with Doglioni and Saracena until her marriage in 1583 (ASV, Dieci Savi sopra le decime di Rialto, Condizioni di decima 1581, b. 157bis, no. 751); a further testimonial to their friendship is the fact that the couple named one of their daughters Modesta (ASV, Notarile Testamenti, Atti Bagnolo, b. 86, no. 101: will of Saracena Saraceni fu Prospero, 27 March 1627).

16. The further stanzas referred to here by Doglioni are lost.

17. These *rappresentazioni* (a peculiarly Venetian tradition, though with some similarities with proto-operatic forms developing in Florence in the period) were staged dramatic allegories or mythological pieces performed before the doge in Venice on ceremonial occasions (Solerti 1902). The tradition grew up in the 1570s and was encouraged by Doge Niccolò da Ponte (1578–85), who commissioned annual *rappresentazioni*, performed on St. Stephen's Day (26 December). One identifiable libretto by Fonte survives, *Le feste* (1582), consisting of a debate between a Stoic and an Epicurean philosopher concerning the supreme good, resolved by the Eritrean Sibyl (see Molmenti 1905–8, 2: 352–53). Most of the texts, however, were published anonymously, and it may well be

And so Modesta remained in my house until I decided it was time to arrange a marriage for her; and when, after various other suggestions, someone proposed that distinguished gentleman Messer Filippo de' Zorzi, tax lawyer to the Officio delle Acque,[18] I gave her to him as a wife, after making all the usual inquiries.[19] There are four surviving children of the marriage, two boys and two girls: the eldest is a boy of ten, followed by a girl of eight and a boy of six. Madonna Modesta brought them up with all possible diligence, perfecting the most refined of skills in them; and certainly, few children of their age can be compared with them, for all the three eldest are already competent in Latin and can sing, sight-read, and play the viola, each playing his or her own part, to the amazement of all around. So it seemed as though these children of hers were destined to become the wonder of the world, as a result, especially, of her hard work and patience—until envious Death blocked this happy progress to excellence, when it had barely got under way. For (cruel and bitter fate!) as Madonna Modesta gave birth to another little girl—the fourth surviving child—she was suddenly taken ill and died: a great loss for all

true, as Doglioni states here, that others of those published were hers.

18. Filippo Zorzi, or de' Zorzi (1558–98), was the son of a *cittadino* lawyer, Pietro de' Zorzi, and of Leandra Franco, also from a *cittadino* family. He appears to have had patrician connections through his paternal grandmother Cornelia, the daughter (presumably illegitimate) of the Procurator Filippo Tron (ASV, Avogaria del Comun, Cittadinanze originarie, b. 364, n. 78). The Officio delle Acque, his employer, was the government office responsible for the upkeep of the Venetian lagoon and inland waterways, as well as, less predictably, the mining industry on the Venetian mainland, with which Zorzi seems to have occupied himself in his later career (see Vergani 1989, 302; Cicogna 1824–61, 2: 23).

19. Fonte's marriage to Filippo Zorzi was contracted on 15 February 1583, when she was twenty-seven years old (the date is given in the document relating to Fonte's dowry cited later in this note). The reason for the relative lateness of her marriage, at a time when the average age of upper-class brides was closer to twenty (Davis 1975, 173), may have been that her family was awaiting the outcome of the lawsuit concerning her inheritance that she refers to in canto 3 of the *Floridoro*. Whatever the reason for this delay, one result was that the spouses were much closer in age than was usual in a first marriage in this period: Fonte was, indeed, slightly older than her husband, whereas husbands were usually substantially older than their wives. Perhaps in consequence, their relationship appears to have been an unusually equal one by the standards of the time: a document of October 1583 (ASV, Notarile Atti 7852 [Girolamo Luran], 629v–630v) records that Zorzi, in an exceptional gesture, returned a portion of his wife's dowry to her control during his lifetime, attributing his decision to the "great love and affection" (*grande amore et benevolentia*) he bore her. A further indication of the happiness of the marriage is that Fonte's will of 1585, cited above, not only makes her husband her principal beneficiary, but also makes bequests to his mother, brother, and sisters, while studiedly ignoring her own closest surviving blood relative, her brother Leonardo.

those she left behind, but especially for her children, poor mites, who have now been deprived of the care and schooling she alone could have given them (for their father's time is completely taken up by his work in the law courts), and so will not be able so soon to reach that pitch of excellence that their mother would have guided them to had she lived. (I say "so soon," because each of these children is so naturally gifted that the only ill effect of their mother's death, where their education is concerned, will be to protract the time it will take them to reach the summit of perfection in their studies).

And so, as I said, Madonna Modesta died in the morning of All Souls' Day[20] of the year 1592. Her death left all those who had known her devastated, with a sorrow from which few of us will ever recover. And, after her husband, one of the people most affected by her death was myself; for I had known her ever since she was a child (because I spent a great deal of time at Saraceni's house and, out at Sacile, my family's villa was adjacent to his and our estates bordered on each other's); and then, after that, I had been her guardian and had defended and supported her and arranged her marriage, loving and caring for her as a sister, and sharing in her every happiness and her every sorrow. One remarkable thing is that the very day before she died, she completed the second day of a prose dialogue she had been working on, which she entitled *The Worth of Women*: the very work that is being published alongside this account of her life.

Madonna Modesta was extremely good at running her household: so good, indeed, that her husband scarcely needed to give it a thought and confessed on several occasions that he had no idea what it felt like to have the responsibility of a home and family, for she took everything out of his hands and did it all herself, with extraordinary efficiency and diligence. In conversation, whatever the subject, she always had something sensible to say; and she was so well informed that everyone was always quite astonished to hear her. She had such an amazing memory that I have seen her repeat a sermon word for word when she returned home after church, and after listening a single time to two or three sonnets she would know them by memory as thoroughly as if she had written them herself. She read amazingly fast, retaining so much of what she was reading that she could give a meticulous summary of the whole. She had an amazing gift of foresight and could often use her intelligence to predict

20. 2 November.

exactly what was going to happen, so that it seemed almost as though she were endowed with some divine spirit of prophecy. She wrote poetry so quickly that it seemed almost incredible. I remember one occasion when I was asked by the Illustrious Signor Scipio Costanzo to try to persuade her to write something for the death of his son Signor Tommaso Costanzo, for whom he was attempting to assemble a *mausoleum* of poems.[21] I explained the situation to her one evening and the next morning when she got up she wrote me a canzone, which I took to show to Signor Scipio. When I got to his house, I ran into Signor Giulio Nuti, that rare connoisseur of poetry,[22] who was staying with him at the time, and told him about the poem. The story struck him as completely impossible and he told me that Signor Scipio had wanted people to write new works specifically to commemorate his son's death, rather than adapt existing compositions by changing the odd word. I explained the position; then Signor Scipio arrived and I read the canzone out to him. He listened to the whole thing with tears in his eyes, and Nuti, astounded, asked my pardon for what he had said, exclaiming that he would never have believed anyone could have written a poem like that so well and so quickly. Another time, Madonna Modesta dreamed up a subject for a poem one evening and the next morning woke up and wrote down thirty-six stanzas she had mentally composed on one of love's deceptions, to be published at the end of *The Worth of Women*. The *Floridoro*, too, and all her other things, she wrote in the same manner, for, as a woman, she had to attend to womanly tasks like sewing, and she did not wish to neglect these labors because of the false notion, so widespread in our city today, that women should excel in nothing but the running of the household.

When she had died, in the manner recounted, her husband managed to find a burial place for her in the cloister of the Franciscans near San Rocco.[23] So there she was buried, and a Latin epitaph can be seen carved in the wall, alluding to her life and death, which reads as follows:

21. This anecdote is of interest in that it indicates the extent of Fonte's renown as a poet during her lifetime. Further details of the circumstances of the commission are given in a passage of *The Worth of Women*, where a commemorative sonnet for Costanzo, also presumably by Fonte, is cited.

22. Nuti appears to have been a specialist in commemorative verse in particular: the two independent published works I have been able to trace by him are both in this genre (Cinelli Galvoli 1734–47, 3: 405).

23. Presumably the cloister of the Church of the Frari.

*Here lies Modesta da Pozzo, a most learned woman, who, having felici-
tously given birth to many offspring of the intellect under the name of
Moderata Fonte, both in Tuscan verse, in which she sang of memorable
things, and in prose, while engaged in the labors of natural childbirth,
gave life to a little girl, but at the same time (alas!) death to herself.
Filippo Zorzi, son of Pietro, advocate for the Officio dell'Acque, raised this
stone to his most beloved wife.*

May God, in his infinite goodness, just as in this life he endowed
her with intelligence and virtue beyond the normal lot of mankind,
showing her to be among those souls dearest to him, deign now in
the next life to favor her and admit her among the circle of those
most devoted to him, so that she may enjoy in reality, in contemplat-
ing his omnipotence, what she most faithfully believed here on earth
and most heroically taught in her poetry.

THE WORTH
OF
WOMEN

VERA MODERATÆ FONTIS EFFIGIES,
ÆTATIS SVÆ ANNO XXXIIII.

First Day

*T*he most noble city of Venice, as everyone knows, lies wondrously situated on the farthest shores of the Adriatic Sea; and not only is the city founded on the sea, but the walls that surround her, the fortresses that guard her, and the gates that enclose her are nothing other than that same sea. The sea, divided up and channeled into canals between the houses, forms a convenient thoroughfare, whereby people are ferried from one place to another with the aid of little boats. The sea is the high road of the city and the open countryside around it, through which pass all the goods and traffics that arrive there from various parts; and the same sea is a most diligent tributary and supplier of all that is needed for the nourishment and sustenance of so great a city. Because, as Venice herself does not produce anything (apart from the endless bounty of fishes that the sea proffers up to her daily), it is only through the endless traffic of the ships that constantly arrive there from across the seas with useful provisions that she is kept most abundantly supplied with all that is needed for human life.

And so this city is utterly different from all others and a novel and miraculous example of God's handiwork. And on account of this, and its many other rare and surpassing excellencies, Venice exceeds all other ancient and modern cities in nobility and dignity, so that it may in all justice be called the Metropolis of the universe.[1] The pomp and glory of this nation are beyond calculation; its riches are

1. Venetian writers were lavish in their praises of their homeland, even by Renaissance Italian standards, and many of the features of the city Fonte goes on to praise in this paragraph—its wealth, its beauty, its cosmopolitanism, the devoutness of its people, the prudence of its ruling class—were commonplaces of contemporary panegyric (see Muir 1981, 13–44; Megna 1991, 253–66).

inexhaustible; and the splendor of the buildings, the sumptuousness of the clothes, the remarkable freedom enjoyed by its inhabitants and their friendliness and charm are things that cannot be imagined or described. Venice is both adored and respected, both loved and feared; and it is quite remarkable how everyone loves living there, for it seems as though all newcomers, wherever they may come from, as soon as they have tasted the sweetness of life there, find it impossible to leave. And this means that there are people of every nationality in the city, and, just as the limbs and arteries of our body are all connected to the heart, so all cities and all parts of the world are connected to Venice. Money flows here as nowhere else and ours is a city as free as the sea itself; without needing legislation itself, it legislates for others.[2] And what is most marvelous of all is that although the city harbors such a great diversity of races and customs, nonetheless an incredible peace and justice reign there. This is entirely due to the careful foresight and skill of those who govern the city. Here the finest pick of talents in all the arts and professions gather; here every kind of excellence holds sway, pleasures and delights are enjoyed, vice is extirpated, and virtue flourishes. The courage, good sense, and courtesy of the men are remarkable, as are the beauty, intelligence, and chastity of the women. In short, this most fortunate city is showered by God with all the blessings anyone could desire, owing to the fact that the people are so God-fearing and devout, and so grateful for all God's gifts. And, next to God, it is devoted and obedient in the highest degree to its ruler, the doge, who (just so that nothing should be lacking to such a happy and well-ordered Republic) is unrivaled in his goodness, prudence, and justice.[3]

Well then, in this truly divine city, abode of all celestial graces and perfections, there was once not long ago (and indeed there still is) a group of noble and spirited women, all from the best-known and most respected families of the city, who, despite their great differ-

2. A particular source of pride for Venetians in the later sixteenth century was the status of the "Serenissima" as the last major surviving republic in Italy and the last of the Italian city-states to have retained independence from foreign control. It is this political autonomy that is referred to here in the phrase "without needing legislation itself." The reference to Venice's "legislating for others" is to the city's dwindling but still extensive land and sea empire, extending over much of northeast Italy, and parts of present-day Greece, Croatia, and Albania (*VDH,* 31–35).

3. The doge, the elected leader of the Venetian republic, was currently Pasquale Cicogna.

ences in age and marital status, were so united by breeding and taste that a tender bond of friendship had formed between them. These women would often steal time together for a quiet conversation; and on these occasions, safe from any fear of being spied on by men or constrained by their presence, they would speak freely on whatever subject they pleased—sometimes, their womanly labors; sometimes, their seemly diversions. Sometimes one of them, who was fond of music, taking up her lute or tempering her sweet voice with the notes of a well-tuned harpsichord, would provide a charming entertainment for herself and her companions; or another, whose tastes inclined to poetry, would recite some novel and elegant composition to entertain that judicious and well-informed audience in a fresh and pleasing manner. The women were seven in number.[4] The first was Adriana, an elderly widow; the second, a young daughter of hers, of marriageable age, called Virginia; the third, a young widow called Leonora; the fourth, an older married woman called Lucretia. The fifth woman, Cornelia, was a young married woman; the sixth, Corinna, a young *dimmessa*;[5] and the seventh, Helena, a young bride who had, as it were, temporarily left the group, for she had gone to stay with her new husband in a nearby villa on the mainland, and since the wedding none of the others had had a chance to see her.

4. The number of the speakers in the dialogue is probably not fortuitous: among its many meanings, seven was the number of the liberal arts; of the cardinal and theological virtues, and of the days of Creation; it was also associated with chastity (Kirkham 1978, 314–18; Butler 1970, 34, 39, 69). Seven is also the number of female speakers who gather at the beginning of Boccaccio's *Decameron*, before they are joined by their three male companions (whose company is deemed necessary because women, when alone, are "fickle, argumentative, mistrustful, pusillanimous and fearful" and incapable of interacting in an orderly way without the guiding presence of men [Boccaccio 1987, 37]). The names of the speakers are also allusive. Corinna, Cornelia, Virginia, Lucretia, and Helena were all names of heroines of classical history and myth, famed for their learning (Corinna, a Greek poet; and Cornelia, the mother of the Gracchi, celebrated for her eloquence), chastity (Virginia and Lucretia), and beauty (Helen). The name Adriana had patriotic resonances in Venice, which lies on the Adriatic sea.

5. The phrase *una giovane dimmessa* presents problems of interpretation. The noun *dimmessa* in this period (more usually spelled *dimessa*) most often indicated a member of a female tertiary order started by Padre Antonio Pagani in Vicenza in 1579, which had established a community in Venice by 1587. There is some evidence, however, that the term was used more loosely to indicate any respectable unmarried girl living at home, rather than in a convent (see Cox 1995, 548–50); and this may be the way in which it is being used here, to distinguish Corinna, who does not intend to marry, from Virginia, who is defined as *figliuola da marito*. Another possible sense of the phrase (taking *giovane* as the noun, *dimmessa* as the adjective) would be "a shy young girl," but this seems unlikely, in view of Corinna's forceful character and of the fact that the other women are all defined here in terms of their marital status.

Now this most worthy group of friends, hearing that the young widow Leonora had recently inherited a very lovely house with a very lovely garden, and that she had just moved into it, decided to pay her a visit there at the first opportunity, both for the pleasure of seeing Leonora (a sensible young woman, who, though young, rich, and a widow, was in no hurry to find herself a new husband), and to look over the new house and enjoy for a while the delights of its garden. And so one day they went in a party to pay a visit on this charming young hostess; and after the usual greetings had passed between them, they repaired at her invitation to a light and airy room (for it was the height of summer). There some—the older ones—went out onto a balcony overlooking the Grand Canal, and lingered there for a while enjoying the fresh air and watching the gondolas flying past below. The others, led by Virginia, drew up to a window that overlooked the garden and stood there larking about as young girls do when they are together, affectionately teasing one another and sharing delightful jokes. After a while, a gondola was seen pulling up to the quay; and, as the women looked at it, wondering whose it could be, they suddenly realized that it belonged to Helena. And indeed the young bride had just returned from the country and, hearing that all her friends were assembled at Leonora's, she had come there at once to see them all, and in particular Virginia, who before her marriage had been her closest friend. When the women realized it was Helena arriving, their happiness was complete, for she was a very charming young woman; and she had hardly got up the stairs before they all flocked around her, embracing her and smothering her with kisses in their joy at seeing her again after such a long absence. Then they led her into the drawing room, where they all sat down and feasted their eyes upon her; until finally Virginia spoke up and asked her how she had been all this time and whether she was happy. But before Helena could reply, Leonora, who had a keen wit, cut in with these words:

"My dear Virginia, how can you ask such a thing, when everyone already knows the answer? For popular opinion dictates that no new bride can be anything other than happy."

"Well, let's not say happy," added Lucretia. "Rather, as well as can be expected."

"When I think about it," said Helena, "I'm not sure I can say yet whether I'm happy or not. Certainly I greatly enjoy my husband's company, but there is one thing about him that dismays me a little. He is quite insistent that I should not leave the house, whereas I long for nothing more than to go to all the weddings and banquets to which I am invited—partly because this is my time for diversion,[6] but also because I'm concerned to keep up my own and my husband's reputation by letting the world see that he is treating me well and that I can dress as befits a gentlewoman, as you can see."

"I hope to God," Cornelia interjected, "that you'll never have anything worse to complain of! But you have yet to learn how quickly a wedding cake can go stale."

"Our 'young married,'" said Lucretia, "is still unconvinced of this truth; she can't make up her mind to believe it. And she's quite right, of course, for everything is lovely when it has the charm of novelty."

"What you mean is that everything *seems* lovely when it has the charm of novelty," said Leonora.

"As to that," replied Lucretia, "seeming good in such cases is much the same as being good. For if something I eat, for example, seems good to my palate, even if it isn't, it's as good as if it were."

"Don't make me laugh," rejoined Leonora. "If that's the case, then we shouldn't wonder at the bakerwoman who, after toiling all day over her hot oven, ran outside to strip off her little ones' clothes, in the belief that they too must be suffering from the heat, without considering the fact that it was the depths of winter!"

Cornelia laughed at Leonora's joke and exclaimed, "Praise God that we are free to do just as we please, even tell jokes like that to make each other laugh, with no one here to criticize us or put us down."

"Exactly," said Leonora. "If a man could hear us now, joking together like this, how he would scoff! There'd be no end to it!"

"To tell the truth," said Lucretia, "we are only ever really happy when we are alone with other women; and the best thing that can happen to any woman is to be able to live alone, without the company of men."

"Indeed," said Leonora. "For my part, I derive the greatest happiness from living in peace, without a man. For we all know what a marvelous thing freedom is."

---

6. Venetian society was famed in the sixteenth century for the seclusion in which it kept young women of noble birth (Labalme 1980, 136). This seclusion was stricter before marriage, which marked, among other things, a bride's introduction to the "adult" pleasures of dancing and extravagant dress (Chojnacki [1980], 66–67).

"But surely men can't all be bad?" Helena said.

"Would that they weren't!" replied Cornelia. "And please God that you won't soon be in a position to bear witness to it from your own experience!"

"Who knows?" said Virginia. "What if Helena turns out to be lucky?"

"Well, she just might," said Lucretia. "Don't let's lose all hope."

"However badly you speak of men," Helena rejoined, "I don't believe that you will put Virginia off trying out what it's like to have a husband."

"If it were up to me," said Virginia. "I'd prefer to do without one. But I have to obey the wishes of my family."

"When it comes to that, dear child," said Adriana, "I'd be quite happy to respect your opinion, but your uncles have decided you must marry, because you've inherited such a fortune and it needs to be in safe hands, so I really don't know what else I can do with you. But, anyway, keep your spirits up and don't be afraid. Not all men can be the same, and perhaps—who knows?—you may have better luck than the rest."

"Oh, that really is quite a lifeline you're holding out!" cried Leonora. "That kind of vain hope, which so rarely comes true, has been the ruin of many a poor girl."

"Our boundless hopes often lure us to destruction," said Corinna. "But this vain hope you're talking about doesn't fool *me*. I'd rather die than submit to a man! My life here with you is too precious for that, safe from the fear of any great rough man trying to rule my life."

"O happy Corinna!" cried Lucretia. "What other woman in the world can compare her lot with yours? Not one! Not a widow, for she cannot boast of enjoying her freedom without having suffered first; not a wife, for she is still in the midst of her suffering; not a young girl awaiting betrothal, for she is waiting for nothing but ill (as the proverb says, 'husbands and hard times are never long in arriving'). Happy, thrice-happy Corinna, and all that follow your example! All the more so since God has endowed you with such a soaring intelligence that you delight in the pursuit of excellence, and devote your every lofty thought to the study of letters, human and divine, so that one might say that you have already embarked on a celestial life while still surrounded by the trials and dangers of this world. Though such trials barely touch you; for, by rejecting all contact with those falsest of creatures, men, you have escaped the tribulations of this world and are free to devote yourself to those glorious pursuits that will win you immortality.[7] But perhaps you should devote that sublime intelligence of yours to writing a volume on this subject, as an affectionate warning to all those poor simple girls who don't know the difference between good and evil, to show them where their true interests lie; for in this way you would become doubly glorious, fulfilling your duties to God and to the world."

"It certainly would be a worthwhile thing to do," said Corinna, "and I must thank you for bringing it to my notice; perhaps one day I shall indeed write such a work."

"But in the meantime, surely you must already have written something on the theme: some sonnet, perhaps?" suggested Adriana.

"Well, yes," she replied, "but not, I fear, with much success."

"Oh come!" exclaimed Adriana. "Give us a little something, at least! It would give us all such pleasure."

At this, all the others gathered around Corinna and pleaded with her so earnestly that finally, to appease them, she recited the following sonnet, with a pleasing air of modesty:

> *Libero cor nel mio petto soggiorna,*
> *Non servo alcun, né d'altri son che mia,*
> *Pascomi di modestia, e cortesia,*
> *Virtù m'essalta, e castità m'adorna.*
> *Quest'alma a Dio sol cede, e a lui ritorna,*
> *Benché nel velo uman s'avolga e stia;*
> *E sprezza il mondo e sua perfidia ria,*
> *Che le semplici menti inganna, e scorna.*
> *Bellezza, gioventù, piaceri e pompe,*
> *Nulla stimo, se non ch'a i pensier puri*
> *Son trofeo, per mia voglia, e non per sorte.*
> *Così negli anni verdi, e nei maturi,*
> *Poiché fallacia d'uom non m'interrompe,*
> *Fama e gloria n'attendo in vita, e in morte.*

[handwritten marginal note: — quote from famous epic female knight says it]

The heart that dwells within my breast is free: I serve no one, and belong to no one but myself. Modesty and courtesy are my daily bread; virtue exalts me and chastity adorns

---

7. The desirability or otherwise of marriage for a man was a popular debating point in the Renaissance, and one of the interests of Lucrezia's speech here lies in the way in which it appropriates and adapts one of the favorite arguments of male opponents of marriage, that a woman's company and the care of a household are distractions from contemplation and study (see, for example, Petrarca 1991, 62–64 [2: 18]).

me. My soul yields to God alone, turning back toward its
creator, even while still enveloped in the mortal veil; it
scorns the world and its evil treacheries, that ensnare and
ruin more ingenuous souls. Beauty, youth, pleasures, and
pomp are nothing to me, except as a trophy to my pure
thoughts, offered up of my own free will and not through
chance. And thus in my green years, as in the riper ones
that await me, since men's deceptions cannot obstruct my
path, I may expect fame and glory, in life and death.[8]

The judicious ladies were utterly charmed by the sonnet that the
talented damsel recited for them, on account both of its sentiments,
which all applauded, and of the ease and dignity of its style. So they
all heaped praises on Corinna and begged for a copy of the poem; and
Virginia, who was particularly struck by it, entreated Corinna to sing
it to them, accompanying herself on the harpsichord; which she did,
to universal applause, following it with other songs.

Meanwhile, realizing that the sun had retreated behind some little clouds, they all agreed to go down and enjoy the lovely garden for
a while; and so they set off gaily, taking each other by the hand and
going down the stairs. When they got to the garden, words could not
express how utterly charming and delightful they found it.[9] For there
were rows of little emerald-green espaliered shrubs, in all kinds of
different shapes—some in the form of pyramids, others mushroom-

8. Corinna's sonnet, a manifesto for the single life, contains the first of the dialogue's two references to the figure of the female knight Marfisa, a character in
Lodovico Ariosto's *Orlando Furioso* (1532), and important in this context as a highly unusual (if not unique) instance of a representation in sixteenth-century literature of a
woman committed to independence from men. The second line of the sonnet, in fact,
quotes directly from a famous speech of Marfisa's, in which she rebukes a knight who is
planning to claim her as booty, having defeated her male companions, pointing out
that she is her own woman and that anyone who wants her must win her from herself
(*OF*, 26, 79, 7–8).

9. The description of Leonora's garden that follows is a reworking of a favored topos of
Renaissance literature, that of the *locus amoenus* (literally "pleasant place"): a place of
natural beauty offering shelter from the travails of life, often explicitly or implicitly
associated with the notion of the earthly paradise. The most immediate literary model
for this passage is a description of Caterina Cornaro's garden at Asolo in *Gli Asolani*
(1505), a dialogue on love by the Venetian writer Pietro Bembo (1470–1547), which
itself draws on earlier descriptions of paradisaical gardens in Boccaccio's *Decameron*.
Fonte's description deviates from these models, however, in its greater stress on the
elements of order and artifice. In this, and specifically in details like the topiary and
the shaped lawns, her description accurately reflects contemporary tastes in garden
design (Lazzaro 1990; cf. Bembo 1954, 13–14 [1, 4]).

shaped or melon-shaped, or some other shape—alternating with carefully pruned and beautifully intermingled laurels, chestnuts, box trees, and pomegranates, all cut to precisely the same height, without a leaf out of place. There were the loveliest orange trees and lemon trees[10] to be seen, with such sweet-smelling flowers and fruit that they gladdened the heart with their scent as much as they delighted the eyes. I shall not attempt to list the countless lovely and varied carved urns filled with citrus trees and the daintiest flowers of all kinds, nor the quantities of slender myrtles and the fresh lawns of tiny herbs, cut into triangles, ovals, squares, and other charming conceits. There were jasmine arbors, labyrinths of bright ivy, and little groves of shaped box trees that would have astounded any connoisseur. And the fruit! I shall not attempt to describe it, for there were vast quantities of fruits of all kinds, according to the season; and the useful plants, mingled charmingly with the purely decorative, made up such a lovely sight that the women could not rest from exploring.

And in this way, wandering on from one place to the next, they came upon a lovely fountain which stood in the middle of the garden, constructed with indescribably rare and meticulous workmanship. All around this fountain, at each of its sides, there stood the statue of a very beautiful woman with braided hair, from whose breasts, as from a double fountain, there artfully flowed streams of clear, fresh, sweet water.[11] Each of these statues wore a garland of laurel on her head and carried a slender olive branch in her left hand, with a little scroll

10. The Italian word used here, *cedro*, presents some ambiguity. The term is frequently used in sixteenth-century descriptions of gardens to indicate a type of juniper, *Juniperus phoenicea* (Lazzaro 1990, 25). Another sense of the word, however, is "citrus tree," and, paired as it is here with *aranzi* ("orange trees"), this seems the more probable meaning in this context.

11. The adjectives used here, *chiare, fresche e dolci*, echo the opening line of one of Petrarch's most famous *canzoni* (*RS*, 126). Fountains whose waters flowed from the breasts of female figures were found in a number of Renaissance gardens, the most famous example being the fountain representing Diana of Ephesus at the Villa d'Este in Tivoli; they also feature in the descriptions of ideal gardens in the influential anonymous *Hypnerotomachia Poliphili* (*The Dream of Polyphilius*) (1499). Such figures are normally interpreted as symbolic of the fertility and abundance of nature, but it is relevant to Fonte's use of the image here that the figure of a woman with full breasts also had associations with intellectual and imaginative fertility: such a figure is used to symbolize Poetry in Cesare Ripa's *Iconologia* (1603). It may be the case, then, that the iconography of the fountain is best read as a celebration of the author's own literary creativity, already proclaimed in her chosen pseudonym, Fonte ("Fount," "Spring," "Source"), and further evoked in the wreaths of laurel—the plant of Apollo, god of poetry—worn by the statues. The olive branches carried by the statues are symbols of peace and harmony.

with writing on it wrapped around the branch; while, in her right hand, each carried a different emblem.[12] So that one of them was holding a little snow-white ermine over her shoulder, holding it away from her breast to keep it dry; and the scroll she held in her left hand bore the following verse:

Prima morte, che macchia al corpo mio

Let this body rather perish than suffer any stain.

The next carried in her right hand an image of the phoenix, who lives unique in the world; and in her left hand she bore the message:

Sola vivomi ogn'or, muoio e rinasco

Alone I live for all time; I die and am reborn.   *fame reputation*

The third carried a sun and her motto read:

Solo, porgo a me stesso e ad altri luce.

Alone and unique, I illuminate myself and all around.

The next was holding a lantern, in whose flame a little butterfly could be seen burning to death; and her scroll bore the words:

Vinta da bella vista, io stessa m'ardo

Victim of a vision of beauty, I burn through my own doing.

The fifth had as her device a peach, with a leaf from a peach tree and a verse that read:

Troppo diverso è da la lingua il core.

All too different is the message of the heart from that of the tongue.

But the sixth carried a crocodile and her scroll read:

Io l'uomo uccido e poi lo piango morto

12. The elaboration of emblems—visual riddles encoding moral messages—was immensely fashionable in sixteenth-century Italy and throughout Europe. One important use of emblems, as here, was as personal devices (*imprese*), chosen to express an individual's sense of his or her qualities or aspirations.

I first kill my victims and then, when they are dead, mourn
them.

Besides these verses, the figures had written on their brows a letter each: the first had an A, the second a T, the third an S, the
fourth an H, the fifth an I and the sixth an M.[13] And the statues as
a whole were so precisely carved and so divinely turned that they
seemed rather a natural, living thing than something artificial and a
product of human skill. And as the women gazed on and marveled at
now this thing, now that, in the lovely garden, filled with rapture and
wonder, Adriana said to Leonora, "Come, Leonora, what paradise is
this? You have a real paradise on earth! Who could fail to be charmed
by this place?"

"It seems to me," added Cornelia, "that since this is a paradise in
which food and drink are also on offer, you may be seeing rather a lot
of us here." For in the meantime Leonora's maids had arrived on her
orders with the finest wines and sweetmeats as refreshments for the
group.

"I am only sorry you have not been before," replied Leonora, "and I
hope now you will all wish to return soon."

"I shouldn't make too much of a point of inviting us," said
Lucretia. "For the place is so delightful that we shan't need much
persuading."

"You are all forgetting the best bit in your praises of the garden,"
said Corinna. "You haven't mentioned that among its other charms
there's the very important fact that there are no men here."

"And *you*'ve forgotten an important thing, too," Helena added,
"that the lady of the house is so kind and charming that that alone
would be enough to make us wish to come back often."

"That's true," said Adriana; "Charming, sweet, lovely—no one
could deny it. But it's a pity that you don't think of remarrying,
Leonora, young and lovely as you are."

"Remarrying, eh?" replied Leonora. "I'd rather drown than submit
again to a man! I have just escaped from servitude and suffering and
you're asking me to go back again of my own free will and get tangled
up in all that again? God preserve me!"

13. I have been unable to decipher the meaning of these letters. It is perhaps worth
noting in this context that Fonte's friend and biographer Giovanni Niccolò Doglioni
was the author of a work on codes (1619) (Romanello 1991, 368).

And all the others agreed that she was talking sense and that she was lucky to be in the position she was. And Cornelia, kissing her, said, "Bless you, my sister! You're a wiser woman than I knew."

"Come, that's enough of all that," said Leonora. "Will you not all take some refreshment while the wine is cool?"

And so they went and ate some fruit and larked about for a while, playing *inviti tedeschi*[14] and other silly games, knowing that there was no one there to see them or overhear them (which was what they all enjoyed more than anything). When they had finished eating, Cornelia asked Leonora whether she knew what the figures around the fountain represented and, if so, whether she would be kind enough to explain it to them, together with the significance of their mottoes and devices.

"I shall, with pleasure," Leonora replied. "First, I must remind you that this house, together with this garden, belonged to an aunt of mine: you must have heard about her, though I know none of you can have met her, as she lived in Padua for many years (she has just passed away there, in fact). This aunt, from the time she was a girl, was resolved never to marry and so, on the good income she inherited from my grandfather (and thinking nothing of the expense, for it was her greatest delight) she transformed this garden into the beautiful state in which you see it now; and at the same time she had this fountain built, with these figures, as a statement of the way in which she intended to live her life and of the views she held against the male sex. For the first figure is there to represent Chastity, to which she was devoted; and the meaning of the device and the motto are clear enough in themselves.[15] The next figure represents Solitude and her device is the phoenix, to show that my aunt enjoyed living alone and that she lived on her own terms and, after death, was reborn in the fame she gained by her good works.[16] The third is

14. I have been unable to establish the nature of this game (lit. "German invitations," or, if it is a card-game, "German calls or bids").

15. The ermine as symbol of chastity is a frequent motif in Renaissance literature and art (as in Leonardo's famous portrait of Cecilia Gallerani). In his popular *Dialogue on Emblems* of 1555, Paolo Giovio explains the appropriateness of the symbol by reference to the myth that the ermine prefers to suffer death from starvation or thirst rather than soil its fur by passing through muddy ground (Giovio 1978, 56).

16. The phoenix was a mythical bird, of which classical authors such as Herodotus, Ovid, and Pliny gave varying accounts. It lived to a great age and finally died by throwing itself on a pyre of aromatic herbs, whereupon a new, young phoenix grew from its ashes. The phoenix was popular as a device in the Renaissance among both men and women, mainly to indicate uniqueness, faith in resurrection, or an aspiration to secular

Liberty and her device is the sun, which stands free and alone, giving light to itself and sharing its light with the whole universe, to show that my aunt, living free and alone as she did, won a shining renown through her many fine and respected qualities; and also that she shared the treasures of her mind with every person of refinement with whom she came into contact—something she might not have been able to do under the rule and command of a husband.[17] The fourth figure is Naïveté and her device is the butterfly burning in the flame, signifying that women (poor wretches!), when they are to be married, put too much faith in the false endearments and empty praises of men, who seem so kind and charming that women, believing that they will always live up to the fair image they present at first sight, allow themselves to be caught in their snares and fall into the fire that burns and devours them.[18] The fifth is Falsehood and her device is a peach, which is shaped like a heart and has a leaf shaped like a tongue; and the motto too tells of the deceit and falsity of men, whose words to women all speak of love and good faith, but whose hearts tell a very different story.[19] The sixth is Cruelty; and the device of a crocodile means that men harrow and kill those women who become involved with them and then feign a brutish compassion for their victims."[20]

"immortality" through great achievements, but also, occasionally, as here, a commitment to celibacy, as in the famous cases of Elizabeth I of England, who is portrayed wearing a cameo depicting a phoenix in a famous portrait of the 1570s (in the Tate Gallery, London), and of Ariosto's warrior heroine Marfisa (see Ruscelli 1584, 137–42, for a gloss on this use of the image).

17. The use of the sun to symbolize a virtue and glory that illuminates the entire world is discussed in Ruscelli 1584, 191–93, in the context of the device of the Emperor Philip II; see also Giovio 1978, 103.

18. The image of love as a flame to the lover's butterfly was a frequent motif in the Renaissance literature of love: it is discussed in Pietro Bembo's influential dialogue on love, *Gli Asolani* (1505) and in Paolo Giovio's *Dialogue on Emblems* (1555), where a Pavian noblewoman is described as wearing a dress embroidered with butterflies to warn prospective suitors of their fate (Bembo 1954, 40 [1, 27]; Giovio 1978, 40). For an instance of the use of the image to warn women of the wiles of men, see Matteo Bandello, *Novelle*, 1: 18, where it is observed that women "run toward what will obviously bring about their ruin, just as a butterfly drawn by the beauty of a lamp races toward certain death" (Bandello 1974, 169).

19. A precedent for this emblem is offered by Andrea Alciati's influential and much-translated *Emblemata* (1531), where a peach and a peach leaf are similarly employed to symbolize the heart and the tongue (Alciatus 1985, no. 143). In Alciato, however, the imagery has positive connotations very different from those Fonte gives it here.

20. The crocodile, said to shed tears over the bodies of its victims, was used reasonably frequently as a symbol of hypocrisy in the Renaissance and is identified as such in Erasmus's *Adages*. Paolo Giovio records its use as an emblem by Cardinal Sigismondo

"Excellent," replied Corinna. "We are very grateful to you for having explained these riddles to us and I feel much beholden to the memory of this lady who knew so much about the world and whose opinions are so close to my own. Lord! Why can she not still be here with us today?"

"One thing I can tell you," Leonora added, "is that she brought me up to share in her opinion. In fact, she did not wish me to marry, but my father insisted on it against the wishes of both of us; and now that it has pleased God to liberate me, you may be sure that I am just as she was."

As they were talking away like this, Adriana said to her companions, "Now that we have had this explained to us, what do we wish to do next? For the days are long at the moment and the sun is still very high and, now it's come out again, it's quite impossible to walk in the garden. So I would think it wise for us to retire into the shade of these cypresses and settle down here and amuse ourselves in whichever way took the fancy of each of us, some making music, some playing games, some reading."

"That's a good idea," said Cornelia. "But would it not be better for us to choose some game in which we could participate as a group?"

"Rather than play a game," said Helena, 'it would be more fun if we were to tell each other stories or to have a discussion on some subject that interests us."

And as all the women started disagreeing among themselves, with one suggesting one topic for discussion, another a different one, Corinna stepped in and said, "Come now, let us please elect one amongst us to take command of the others—and let the others obey her, for, in truth, in the private as well as the public sphere, obedience is not merely useful but one of the most necessary virtues. And, that way, we shall harmonize the desires of all."

Corinna's plan met with the other women's approval and by common accord they elected Adriana as their queen,[21] knowing her to be

---

Gonzaga (Giovio 1978, 125).

21. As has often been observed in the case of Boccaccio's *Decameron* and Castiglione's *Book of the Courtier*, the social organization in the miniature societies constituted by the group of speakers in literary dialogues often tends to reflect the political conventions of the broader society to which they belong. Thus Boccaccio's speakers, consistent with Florentine republican tradition, distribute the task of leadership sequentially among all the members of the group, while Castiglione, writing in a hereditary principality, naturally delegates leadership of the group to the unelected duchess. Fonte's speakers, too, fall into this pattern, electing a single "queen" on the model of a Venetian doge, but on the grounds of wisdom, character, and experience (and age, an

a woman of great discernment and someone who, though no longer young (for she was past fifty) was nonetheless very humorous and of an easy and cheerful nature. So they elected Adriana and swore obedience to her for as long as their gathering lasted, and she accepted the charge graciously, saying, "As the oldest of the group, this role you have given me sits well on my shoulders, but, by other criteria, there are others of you who are far more deserving of the honor. However, since this has been your courteous wish, I thank you for it and gratefully accept the governance and command you have assigned to me, and I promise to maintain justice and to govern you in the manner that faithful subjects deserve."

And, after a while, having seated them all around the beautiful fountain on some boxwood seats provided for that purpose, she added, "I had been thinking, since none of us likes to be idle and since evening is still far away, that to pass the time we should tell stories on various themes that I would set for you. But now I have changed my mind and decided, since you have been doing nothing all day but talking about men and complaining about them, that our conversation this afternoon should be on that very same subject. So I hereby give Leonora the task of speaking as much evil of them as she can, and Corinna and Cornelia can join in and take her side. And since I have the impression that Helena is so captivated by the charms of her new husband that she has some leanings toward the male camp, I give her leave to speak in defense of men, if she so wishes, and she may have Virginia and Lucretia as her companions."

When the women heard the Queen's commandment, they were delighted at the idea of talking on this subject; and Leonora said, "Your Highness has given us a most onerous task, which would need stronger shoulders than ours; nonetheless, to obey you, I am ready to plunge into this vast shoreless and bottomless ocean. But I cannot believe that these ladies will be prepared to take on a case in which they know right is not on their side."

"If right is not on our side," replied Helena, "then at least propriety is; and you well know that many disputes are won not so much because of the justice of one side's claims, but because it has decency on its side."

"If that's going to be the whole foundation of your argument, that men have decency on their side," said Cornelia, laughing, "then

important factor in Venice's somewhat gerontocratic political culture), rather than social rank.

you might as well give yourselves up for beaten before you even start. You would as well look for blood in a corpse as for the least shred of decency in a man."

"Oh and that's the least of their faults," said Leonora. "But I am amazed that our respected young bride here, just because she has taken up with one man, should want to defend the whole crew of them and should immediately bring up this matter of their 'decency.' Especially since I'm not sure that her husband has behaved so decently toward her: in fact, I suspect that he has caused her to lose something she had before."

Helena smiled at this and blushed and said, "It cannot be said with any reason that it is indecent for a woman to unite herself physically with her husband, since in that act of generation necessity is the natural mother and license the legitimate daughter. And as you know all things that are licit may also be considered decent. So if the effect—the act of propagation—is not merely decent in itself, but legal and necessary, it can well be said that when a man unites with his wife, he is the agent and cause of a decent act, and hence a decent subject. And for this reason he cannot be said to have taken away any part of the woman's natural decency."

"Where that particular point is concerned," Cornelia replied, "you have made out a very good case. But you are starting to praise men too much, which is against the laws laid down by our Queen; and so I warn you that you will lose the dispute not just because justice and decency are against you, but also because you are disregarding the rules."

"In any case," said Corinna, "Helena has not managed to prove anything except that men do have some merits when they are married—which is to say, when they are united with a wife. Now *that* I don't deny, but without that help from their wives, men are just like unlit lamps: in themselves, they are no good for anything, but, when lit, they can be handy to have around the house. In other words, if a man has some virtues, it is because he has picked them up from the woman he lives with, whether mother, nurse, sister, or wife—for over time, inevitably, some of her good qualities will rub off on him. Indeed, quite apart from the good examples women provide for them, all men's finest and most virtuous achievements derive from their love for women, because, feeling themselves unworthy of their lady's grace, they try by any means they can to make themselves pleasing to her in some way. That men study at all, that they cultivate the virtues, that they groom themselves and become well-bred men of the world—in short, that they finish up equipped with countless pleasing qualities—is all due to women. Just look at the examples of Cimone and many others."[22]

"If it is true what you say," said Virginia at this point, "and if men are as imperfect as you say they are, then why are they our superiors on every count?"

To which Corinna replied, "This pre-eminence is something they have unjustly arrogated to themselves. And when it's said that women must be subject to men, the phrase should be understood in the same sense as when we say that we are subject to natural disasters, diseases, and all the other accidents of this life: it's not a case of being subject in the sense of obeying, but rather of suffering an imposition; not a case of serving them fearfully, but rather of tolerating them in a spirit of Christian charity, since they have been given to us by God as a spiritual trial. But they take the phrase in the contrary sense and set themselves up as tyrants over us, arrogantly usurping that dominion over women that they claim is their right, but which is more properly ours. For don't we see that men's rightful task is to go out to work and wear themselves out trying to accumulate wealth, as though they were our factors or stewards, so that we can remain at home like the lady of the house directing their work and enjoying the profit of their labors? That, if you like, is the reason why men are naturally stronger and more robust than us—they need to be, so they can put up with the hard labor they must endure in our service."[23]

---

22. The argument that women and love were the prime civilizing factors in society was a familiar one in Renaissance defenses of women and is given eloquent expression by Cesare Gonzaga in book 3 of Castiglione's *Book of the Courtier* (Castiglione 1994, 262–64 [3: 51–52]). The reference to Cimone is to Boccaccio's famous development of this theme in the first story of day 5 of the *Decameron*. The story, set in Cyprus (traditionally, of course, a haunt of Venus) concerns a high-born idiot boy, Cimone, who falls in love with a young woman he finds asleep in a forest and, as a result, transforms himself in the space of four years from an apelike figure into "the most charming, well-mannered and accomplished young man the island had ever seen."

23. Corinna's argument here is directed implicitly at the vastly influential tradition of argument stemming from Aristotle's *Politics*, where it is maintained that women are men's natural inferiors, and the pseudo-Aristotelian *Economics*, which maintains that men's and women's differentiated social roles and spheres of activity are rooted in their biological nature (men, strong and active by nature, work outside the house accumulating wealth for the household, which women, weaker and more sedentary by nature, then conserve at home through good household management) (see Aristotle, *Politics*, 1259b1–4 and 1260a1–30; *Economics*, 1343b30–1344a8). Her argumentational technique is the deliberately paradoxical and sophistic one characteristic of at least a substantial portion of the Renaissance tradition of defenses of women: she accepts without demur the premises of her opponents (including the fact, which Fonte challenges elsewhere

"So you're saying that all men's hard labor," said Lucretia, "and all the endless exertions they undergo for us deserve so little gratitude from us that all they merit is the contempt you're expressing! And yet you know full well that men were created before us and that we stand in need of their help: you yourself confess it."

"Men *were* created before women," Corinna replied. "But that doesn't prove their superiority—rather, it proves ours, for they were born out of the lifeless earth in order that we could then be born out of living flesh.[24] And what's so important about this priority in creation, anyway? When we are building, we lay foundations on the ground first, things of no intrinsic merit or beauty, before subsequently raising up sumptuous buildings and ornate palaces. Lowly seeds are nourished in the earth, and then later the ravishing blooms appear; lovely roses blossom forth and scented narcissi. And besides, as everyone knows, the first man, Adam, was created in the Damascene fields, while God chose to create woman within the Earthly Paradise, as a tribute to her greater nobility. In short, we were created as men's helpmates, their companions, their joy, and their crowning glory, but men, though they know full well how much women are worth and how great the benefits we bring them, nonetheless seek to destroy us out of envy for our merits. It's just like the crow, when it produces white nestlings: it is so stricken by envy, knowing how black it is itself, that it kills its own offspring out of pique."[25]

"Not content to charge men with pride, you must label them envious as well," said Helena. "And you full well know that envy reigns only in inferiors, so you are trying to imply that men are inferior. But since it is envy that poisons the tongue of slanderers, if we

---

(p.100) that women are constitutionally more delicate than men), but shows that quite different conclusions may be reached from the same premises.

24. Having dispatched the secular, philosophical arguments for women's inferiority, Corinna moves on to the other pillar of misogynistic thought, the account of the creation and fall of the human race in Genesis. Her points here are not original, but probably derive, directly or more probably indirectly, from Cornelius Agrippa's influential *On the Nobility and Preeminence of the Female Sex* (c. 1529), which contains a discussion of Genesis in which it is argued that Eve's superiority to Adam can be inferred from her name (meaning "life" to Adam's "earth"); the time of her creation (as God's last and, thus, plausibly, best product); the place of her creation (in the "Earthly Paradise" and not outside it, as Adam was); and the material of which she was made (living flesh—Adam's rib—rather than mud) (Rabil 1996, 50).

25. The legend of the crow's rejection of its white offspring derives from the medieval bestiary tradition.

speak ill of men, we shall be taken to be envious of them and, by implication, their inferiors."

"We are not speaking ill of them out of envy," Leonora said, "but out of respect for the truth. For if a man steals (to take an example), he must be called a thief. If men usurp our rights, should we not complain and declare that they have wronged us? For if we are their inferiors in status, but not in worth, this is an abuse that has been introduced into the world and that men have then, over time, gradually translated into law and custom; and it has become so entrenched that they claim (and even actually believe) that the status they have gained through their bullying is theirs by right. And we women, who, among our other good qualities, are eminently mild, peaceable, and benign by nature, are prepared to put up even with an offense of this magnitude for the sake of a peaceful life. And we would suffer it still more willingly if they would just be reasonable and allow things to be equal and there to be some parity; if they did not insist on exerting such absolute control over us and in such an arrogant manner, treating us like slaves who cannot take a step without asking their permission or say a word without their jumping down our throats. Does this seem a matter of such little interest to us that we should be quiet and let things pass in silence?"

"But perhaps they do all this through ignorance," Virginia said, "and not because they wish us any ill."

"Now you really sound like the naïve little creature you are," Cornelia replied. "Ignorance does not excuse a sin and, besides, their ignorance is a willful vice and they are all too aware of the evil they are doing. In fact they accuse *us* of ignorance and senselessness and uselessness. And they are right about one thing: we are indeed senseless to suffer so many cruel deeds from them and not to flee their constant, tacit persecution of us and their hatred of us as we would a raging fire. But we should not think that they behave like this only toward our sex, for even among themselves they deceive one another, rob one another, destroy one another, and try to do each other down. Just think of all the assassinations, usurpations, perjuries, the blasphemy, gaming, gluttony, and other such vicious deeds they commit all the time! Not to mention the murders, assaults, and thefts, and other dissolute acts, all proceeding from men! And if they have so few scruples about committing these kind of excesses, think of what they are like where more minor vices are concerned: just give a thought to their ingratitude, faithlessness, falsity, cruelty, arrogance, lust, and dishonesty!"

"So, if, as I have shown, even amongst themselves they cannot show any mercy but rather despise one other and seek to harm one another, just consider how they will behave toward us. As fathers, as brothers, as sons or husbands or lovers or whatever other relationship they have to us, they all abuse us, humiliate us, and do all they can to harm and annihilate us. For how many fathers are there who never provide for their daughters while they are alive and, when they die, leave everything or the majority to their sons, depriving their daughters of their rightful inheritance, just as though they were the daughters of some neighbor?[26] And then the poor creatures have no choice but to fall into perdition, while their brothers remain rich in material goods and equally rich in shame."

"You have not mentioned all those," said Leonora, "whose cruelty toward their daughters has been such that they have wretchedly deprived them of their honor or their life."

"That is something I can't agree with," said Helena, "and I don't want to hear you trying to make too much capital out of it. For *my* father has shown me every regard and, in a spirit of true paternal love, has seen to it that I was married and married extremely well. But you have no father yourself and that is the reason why you are taking such a desperate line."

"Gently now," replied Cornelia. "Do not interrupt her, please, because one swallow does not make a summer. Besides, what you say does not surprise me. What surprises me is rather that men do not all behave as well as your father did, when we consider that irrational beasts, from whom less charity may be expected, work hard to care for their young, and the pelican in particular is prepared to suck its own blood from its breast to nourish its offspring, motivated purely by paternal love.[27] For every wise and loving father should see to it in good time that his daughters are settled; and if by some accident they should happen to die before they are able to do so, they should at

26. Under Venetian law, daughters were entitled to a share of their father's estate equal to that of their brothers, though daughters' portions took the form of a dowry rather than an independent inheritance (Cowan 1986, 132–42; Ercole 1908, 211–30). This principle, not always scrupulously respected in practice, was in danger of being eroded altogether at the time at which Fonte was writing, as the practice became widespread in patrician families of restricting marriages among their daughters in the interest of conserving family wealth (see Davis 1975, 106–11; Cowan 1986, 148–49; and Cox 1995, esp. 527–29, 544–45, and 558–69).

27. The legend that the pelican fed its young with its own blood derives from the bestiary tradition, and is the rationale for the widespread use of the pelican in art as a figure for Christ.

least ensure that their affairs are in order, so that the poor creatures, seeing themselves disinherited in this way, are not left cursing their fathers' souls after their death.[28] Besides which they are forced, if they want to provide for themselves, to have recourse to those means that (as I have said) are blameworthy and despicable. Then there are others who are lucky enough to be left a dowry by their father, or to receive a share in his estate along with their brothers if he dies intestate, but who then find themselves imprisoned in the home like slaves by their brothers, who deprive them of their rights and seize their portion for themselves, in defiance of all justice, without ever attempting to find them a match. And so the poor things have no choice but to grow old at home under their brothers' rule, waiting on their nephews and nieces; and they spend the rest of their lives buried alive."[29]

But Lucretia, who had been married by her brothers, could not suffer Cornelia to go on any longer and interjected almost angrily, "You are wrong, Cornelia—there are also loving brothers who treat their sisters better than they would their own daughters. And I can testify to that, since my father when he died left me very little and my dear brothers found me a husband using part of their own inheritance. And I believe there are many other such brothers in the world."

"Are you not aware," replied Cornelia, "that God on occasion performs miracles?[30] Besides which many brothers marry off their sisters not out of affection, but just to enhance their standing and improve their own chances of getting a wife, but those who perform this good deed (even for their own interest) are very rare, though it is something all brothers should do, both for the honor of the house and as

28. It is possible that personal experience underlies Fonte's warning to fathers here, as she refers in a passage of her romance *Il Floridoro* (1581) to a lawsuit regarding her inheritance from her father, who had died prematurely when she was an infant (Fonte 1995, 44–46 [canto 3, 3–6]).

29. For further discussion of the fates of such women, see Cox 1995, 546–50. Note that Fonte's speakers do not mention the more frequent alternative method of disposing of unwanted daughters, by encouraging them to become nuns.

30. Fonte's relationship with her own brother Leonardo appears to have been rather chilly, perhaps in consequence of disputes over their inheritance: her will of 1585 makes no mention of her brother, while Leonardo's, drawn up some years after his sister's death, complains that his brother-in-law retains in his possession property that should rightly be his (including, interestingly, the family library: "molte scritture di casa nostra, e in particolare i libri") (ASV, Notarile Testamenti: Crivelli, Girolamo fu Francesco, b. 222, n. 1176; 23 April 1595).

an act of benevolence. Because if there are some men who are prepared to aid other people's daughters and do good to many who have nothing to do with them, how much more is a man obliged to help those who were born of the same womb? Who are of the same flesh and blood as him? But now let us speak a little of sons."

"Oh, now what is there to say about them?" exclaimed Adriana, the Queen.

"What I have to say," replied Cornelia, "is this. How many wretched mothers there are who not only carry their sons for nine months in the womb at the cost of great suffering and give birth to them with great pain and danger, but also feed them, wean them and care for them as children with great love and equally great trouble and, if they have had the misfortune to lose their husbands, toil, sweat, and work their fingers to the bone to bring them up decently, in the hope of reaping that pleasure from them that one has from a job well done—only to find that when these sons have reached the age when they should begin to support their mothers (in their own home or elsewhere, as the mothers desire) they choose instead to reward their many labors and troubles by abandoning them and refusing to help them in their need, completely forgetting that they owe their blood, their early nourishment, their upbringing, entirely to their mothers' care. And, what is worse, if the mothers have money, these sons will squander it all, at the same time making their mothers suffer countless hardships, scorning their loving warnings and treating them with churlish contempt. There are even those who beat their mothers cruelly."

At that point, Adriana, the Queen, spoke almost with tears in her eyes:

"Ah, but Cornelia, if you had had the son it pleased the Lord to give me and then to take from me, I am not sure whether you would speak in the same way. For he was an angel of goodness—nothing at all like his father, who was a cruel husband to me. But when I lost my husband, and my son soon afterward, I was forced to marry again to have children and I had this one (pointing at Virginia). But though I hoped for something better from this second marriage, it turned out exactly the opposite, for if my first husband was bad, this one was worse and I cared little for the deaths of either of them compared with that of my poor son."

"This son of yours," Cornelia replied, "may have indeed been an angel of goodness, as you say, or else, by great good fortune, he simply happened to take after you more than his father. Or it could be that he was going to turn out worse than other men, for you do not know whether he would have changed character with the years—it's something you can't know, if we are to believe that line,

La vita il fine, e 'l dì loda la sera.

The quality of a life is revealed by its end; of a day, by the evening.[31]

And it is all the more plausible that he should have been destined to change for the worse, if the Lord God took him from you early, so you did not have to witness this wretched spectacle. For I can tell you quite surely that having a wicked son is the worst misfortune a woman can suffer in this life: for if, as the proverb goes, the worst of husbands is still better than the best of sons, what can we say about a bad son? And the reason is this: that just as wounds hurt us more the more deeply they penetrate our flesh, so the son who goes to the bad, being flesh and blood with the mother, will afflict and torment her more than her father or husband could, because the bond goes deeper. And, since, in addition, love flows downward rather than upward, a mother in her tenderness will always suffer her son's evils, however wicked he may prove, as she cannot abandon or disown her own flesh. That isn't the case where her husband is concerned: if she is unable to live with him because of the extent of his wickedness, after suffering long and hard, she can at least finally leave him, if circumstances permit. It's something one sees every day, in fact: many sensible women, unable to put up with them any more, leave their wicked husbands to avoid a living hell.[32] The same is true of fathers, because, besides the fact that as I have said, love flows downward rather than upward, it is also easier and less painful for daughters to leave their unloving fathers, who do not care for them as they should. But sons may be far more wicked and cause them far more grief and yet women will put up with their offenses, however grave, so great is the power of maternal love. And children in return are much indebted to their mothers and should by rights treat them as well as they would their own selves."

Then Corinna said, "The other day I was sent a stanza on this subject written from the point of view of a young woman whose father, husband, and son were all in grave danger of death and she

31. The line quoted is from one of Petrarch's most famous *canzoni* (*RS*, 23, 31).
32. On the incidence of marital breakdown in Venice in this period, see Ferraro 1995.

had the power to save just one of them, whichever she wished.[33] But she, not knowing whose life to spare, since all three were extremely dear to her, asked advice on how to resolve so great a problem, in these lines that I shall now recite:

> *Lassa, che in mezzo a le nimiche squadre*
> *Veggio il mio sposo, il genitor, e 'l figlio,*
> *E l'un d'essi o 'l marito, o 'l figlio, o 'l padre,*
> *Posso ad eletta mia trar di periglio.*
> *Deh, sarò miglior sposa? o figlia? o madre?*
> *Chi porge a l'alto mio dubbio consiglio?*
> *Qual am'io più, che più prezzar debb'io,*
> *O 'l natal, o le nozze, o 'l parto mio?*

Wretched me! In the midst of the enemy throng I see my husband, my father, and my son, and one of these three— spouse, child, father—I may choose to release from danger. Alas! shall I choose to be a better wife? or daughter? or mother? Who can offer an answer to this cruelest of dilemmas? Whom do I love most, whose life should I most value—he who gave me life, he who joined himself to me in marriage, or he to whom I gave birth?

The women were all extremely attentive as Corinna recited this stanza, listening to it with great pleasure and satisfaction; and when it was over, after they had all praised it highly, some of them said that the woman should save her husband from the incipient danger, since he was one flesh with her, while others considered that she should save her father's life, since she had herself received life from him. But Corinna said, "Just listen first, please, to the view of someone who replied with this other, very beautiful stanza and then say what you think."

And she went on:

> *Salva da le crudel nimiche squadre,*
> *Se sei pietosa madre, il caro figlio,*
> *Che dando vita al sposo, o al vecchio padre,*
> *La stessa vita tua poni in periglio.*
> *E'naturale amor quel de la madre,*

---

33. The rather tortuous dilemma envisaged in this stanza is perhaps inspired by a historical (or quasi-historical) anecdote mentioned later in the text (see p. 106 below).

Verso il padre è pietà, l'altro è consiglio;
Quanto pietà e consiglio avanza Amore,
Tanto il parto, le nozze, e 'l genitore.

If you are a loving mother, you must rescue your dear son
from the cruel enemy ranks, for, if you choose to give life
to your husband or your aged father, you are endangering
your own life. A mother's love is instinctive, natural love,
while a woman's love for her father contains an element of
duty, that for her husband, an element of principle. And,
by as much as love outweighs duty and principle, so the
bond of maternity outweighs those of marriage or filial
obligation.[34]

It would have been impossible to express how well satisfied the
women were by this elegant response; if the first stanza had pleased
them, they praised the second a thousand times more. The Queen
and the others all insisted that Corinna must have composed both of
them, since it was her habit to share her new creations with them
under the pretense that they were written by someone else, and she
was finally compelled to pledge her word that the reply was by someone else, a person of great refinement whose skill far outstripped the
powers of her poor wit and of whose worth and wisdom she would be
grateful to possess a thousandth part.

"Well, in any case," said the Queen, "the subject of the poem
and the problem it poses are very relevant to our discussion, but what I
like most is the opinion expressed by this highly judicious man, as
well as the happy wit he shows in his writing. And since Cornelia, as
well, has argued so convincingly that our love for our children is
greater than any other love, my own final judgment would be to confirm the sentence given: that the woman in question should save her
son rather than her father or husband from the danger described."

After this she gestured to Cornelia that she should continue
with the discussion; and Cornelia, remembering that the next topic
to discuss was husbands, announced the topic with considerable relish:

"Well, having spoken about fathers, brothers, and sons, it is high
time we talked a little about the evils of husbands."

---

34. The second stanza is something of a showpiece, using as it does, for the first six
lines, the same rhymes (and, indeed, rhyme words) as the first. For the conventions
governing such *risposte* ("reply poems"), see Ruscelli 1563, 148–53.

Almost the entire company was in full agreement with this plan, except for Helena and Virginia.

"It seems to me," said Helena, "that you will not find very much to say on the subject."

"Oh, but what are you saying?" replied Leonora. "It's all too obvious that where marriage is concerned you haven't got past the opening words of the speech. You are just like someone drawing close to a fire on a winter evening: at first, you begin to warm up and the feeling is quite delicious, but then as you draw closer and stay longer, you start baking in the heat, or get covered with soot or blinded by the smoke."

"Let Cornelia speak," Corinna added. "She may speak ill of marriage, but it will be the truth."

"You have about as much experience of marriage as I do," said Virginia. "What do you know about it? Anyone who did not know you and listened to you talking in that way would think you had had a hundred husbands."

But at that point Cornelia, interrupting their argument, continued, "Women who are married—or martyred, more accurately—have endless sources of misery. First there are those husbands who keep their wives on so tight a leash that they almost object to the air itself coming near them; so that the poor things, thinking that by marrying they are winning for themselves a certain womanly freedom to enjoy some respectable pastimes, find themselves more constricted than ever before, kept like animals within four walls and subjected to a hateful guardian rather than an affectionate husband. And it cannot be doubted that husbands such as these, through this kind of contemptuous treatment, cause the downfall of countless women who would be better behaved if their husbands were more kind and loving."

"You might add that there are some men," said Leonora, "who convince themselves that being so jealous and making life so unpleasant for their wives is the best way to keep them in line. Little do they know, poor fools, that their wives, seeing how little they are respected and how little faith their husbands have in them, finish up behaving as badly as they can! Whereas when a wife can see that her husband trusts her and is not going to interfere with her freedom, then she takes the yoke on her shoulders of her own free will and becomes jealous of herself. Because, quite apart from the respect she gains through her behavior, when a wife is treated so well by her husband, it would never occur to her to repay him so badly for his kindness, however many opportunities came her way; she would prefer to abstain and suffer and conquer temptations. And truly there is no better guardian of a woman's honor than her own will and resolve. So I would never advise a man to take it on himself to police his wife's behavior in a cruel, overbearing way, because he will finish up making a misery of both of their lives and very often he will finish up getting what he deserves."

"I have a fear that my own husband may turn out to be one of these jealous and brooding types," said Helena, "for he is already showing signs of it. And I am very sorry for it, for I would never be one of those who would wish to risk my soul, my honor, and my life to avenge myself on him."

"Just pray to God," Cornelia retorted, "that he turns out to have no worse vice than this! Think of all those men who have wives as young and beautiful as angels and who, even so, neglect them and make fools of themselves over some shameless woman (for inevitably you do find a few such amid the masses of virtuous women), who may even be getting on in years and have very little going for her. Such men inflict endless sufferings on their wives, even stripping them of their most treasured things to give them to prostitutes;[35] besides which, they very often make mistresses of their servants and fill the house with bastards and expect their wives to keep quiet and bring them up for them; so that the poor wives see themselves turned from the mistresses of a household into the prioresses of an orphanage."

"That's just what my first husband was like, my dear," the Queen interrupted. "I was young and regarded as one of the beauties of this city, but he showed no interest in me at all, and after two years he fell in love with a prostitute, who was quite old and none too salubrious a proposition—fell in love so violently that it was as though the sun shone out of her face—and my beauty and my caresses were of no avail and my patience no use in the face of his obsession. He seemed to hate his own home, our home; and all the time he should have

---

35. I have translated *meretrice* here as "prostitute," though the word was also used more loosely in this period to indicate any woman living in an "irregular" relationship (Martin 1989, 235). The word *cortigiana* ("courtesan"), used below by Adriana, is more specific, designating the kind of high-class prostitute whose clientele derived mainly from the social elite of the city. The problem discussed here must have been a real one for many Venetian noblewomen of the period: Venice was famed for the number and sophistica-tion of its courtesans, and some, at least, do appear to have made considerable fortunes from their liaisons with Venetian patricians (see Barzaghi 1980, Casagrande 1968, Santore 1988, and Rosenthal 1992).

been spending with me, he frittered away at the home of that corrupt courtesan of his."

"Perhaps she had cast some kind of spell on him, so that he couldn't help himself,"[36] Lucretia suggested.

"That won't wash," Cornelia replied. "Believe me, all that talk about magic spells is just words: men do what they do because they want to. And if you want proof, you will find men who are just as obsessed, or even more obsessed, with gambling as they are with women. So you can see what the problem is: men have vicious tendencies, to which they give too free a rein, and that's the explanation for all the crazy things they do."

"It's quite true what you say," replied the Queen. "For it was just my luck as a wife that after a first husband who was so intent on running after other men's women that he didn't have any time for his own wife, I then took a second who was so taken up with gambling that I can't tell you what a wretched life he led me, until it finally pleased the Good Lord one fine day to take him off my hands."

"You've never said a truer word," Cornelia continued." They get so wrapped up in that cursed game of theirs that they stay out all day and all night with their gambling companions and leave their poor wives at home, so that instead of enjoying their nights in bed with their dear husbands, they have to spend their time sitting by the fire, counting the hours passing, like the watchmen on guard at the Arsenal, and waiting until dawn for their reprobate husbands finally to come home. And when they do come home, if by some unlucky chance they have lost, it's the wives who have to suffer for it, because the scoundrels take out all their anger on them, poor wretches. That's quite apart from the fact that they use up and squander all their wives' resources with this kind of perverse and vicious habit.

"Then there are those husbands who spend all their time shouting at their wives and who, if they don't find everything done just as they like it, abuse the poor creatures or even beat them over the most trivial matters, and who are always picking fault with the way in which the household is run, as though their wives were completely useless. And the poor women who are married to men like this gradually come to realize that they haven't, as they'd thought, left their childhood

36. Belief in the efficacy of spells and love potions was widespread in this period in Venice, as the records of Inquisition trials for witchcraft testify; and there is much evidence that courtesans were perceived as particularly given to the practice of love magic (Martin 1989, 103–10 and 235).

home to go and run their own household (which is the office of a wife, just as it is the husband's task to bring in the money and deal with the world outside); instead, it's as though they'd been sent to a strict schoolmaster. In fact, the poor things are so cowed and angered by the fury and nagging of their overbearing husbands that rather than loving them and longing to spend time with them, they find them irksome and want them to spend as much time as possible out of the house and out of their sight. You can tell from that quite how much pleasure the poor things get out of their husbands' bullying, to which they are condemned for life! And you can find endless examples of husbands who are irascible and intolerable in this way, though there may be different reasons why they are like that: some are bad by nature, while others undergo some kind of humiliation outside the home and then come home and try to give vent to their frustration by taking it out on their hapless wives."

"While we're on the subject," Lucretia said, "I can think of one example, at least, of a woman whose husband is so foul-tempered that she has no peace except when he leaves the house."

"That woman isn't you, by any chance, is she?" Corinna asked with a smile.

"Would that she were not!" replied Lucretia.

"Well, if it's not one thing, it's another," said Leonora. "My husband was one of those men who are so mean they're afraid to eat because it costs money."

"Oh yes!" Cornelia continued. "Misers are often regarded as good men, yet they too put their wives through agonies—they keep them short of money for food and clothing and, if their wives complain, they start putting the word around that the wives are ruining them and wasting their substance and have no idea how to run a household; so that the poor things find that without having taken a vow of poverty they have become nuns in all but habit, with respect to all the basic necessities they are lacking. Then there's another group of bad men who are regarded as good because they lack the kind of obvious vices we've been talking about up to now, but who do have the vices of ignorance and ill judgment. Those are the men who throw away their money without realizing what they are doing and finish up mismanaging things to such an extent that they are left without a penny to call their own. And if their wives, who may well be shrewder than they are, try to warn them tactfully about the consequences, they refuse to listen and ignore their wise and loyal advice, so that they often reduce themselves to poverty and their wives have to pay the price for their faults. And one of my dearest friends, whom you all know, has had the ill luck to marry someone like that."

"I might just have an inkling whom you mean," said Corinna.

"I shan't attempt to disguise it," Cornelia continued. "I am that unfortunate woman. For I can see clearly that things are going to rack and ruin through his mismanagement and I keep reminding him in the kindest possible way to be careful about things and not to throw away his money, but he always takes it badly and doesn't want to listen. So, to sum up, we women are tortured and racked in such a countless number of different ways by these murderous sadists, these covert enemies, that it would be impossible to tell the thousandth part of what they do to us."

"You've told us quite enough," Lucretia said. "After all, when it comes down to it, women are the cause of all evils that befall men. That's what men like to claim, anyway, as they scornfully dismiss our every attempt to advise them and set them straight, accusing us of stubbornness and capriciousness and all those other vices they like to attribute to us. And yet I'd be prepared to stake that if men were good, no woman would be bad; for, if there are bad women around, it is their husbands who have made them so, by not knowing how to handle them. Anyway, whatever faults a woman has in her are not really her own, but are inherited from her father; and a wise and good husband (if there were such a thing) would deal with it by helping his wife along and correcting that little flaw in her disposition through kind words and even kinder actions. For, if you can tame irrational beasts by being kind to them and giving them what they need, how much easier should it be to convert an artless young girl who has inherited some stubbornness of character from her father?"

"That's quite true," said the Queen. "When we want to keep and tame a puppy, we give it bread; with a little bird, we feed it millet— whereas, if we hit it, it would get angry and fly off."

"That's why I'm telling you that the fault is all the husband's," said Lucretia. "He can't have much judgment or wisdom if he can't communicate some of it to his wife. And if both husband and wife are bad, why place all the blame on her, without giving him his share? It's really both of them that should be blamed, or neither, or just the husband, for the reasons we've been discussing."

"Let's leave this complaining about husbands to one side for a moment," said Corinna, "and talk about the worse type of man there is: the false and deceitful lover."

"Now there you're really talking about a task that's not for light-weights,"[37] said the Queen. "Not because of the loftiness of the subject matter, of course: I'm talking about its sheer difficulty. In fact, I can't imagine you'll be able to cover the tiniest part of what there is to say on the subject, let alone to find a safe route across this mighty ocean, unbounded on all sides. Still, plunge in happily, for on the way out, you can always ask Love to lend you his wings.[38] If not, you will need the waxed wings of Daedalus to make your escape, before those countless lovers against whom you are preparing to speak all turn their wrath against you."[39]

"Or rather," Lucretia said, "she will need Leombruno's magic cloak so that she can escape hidden and invisible."

"I have nothing to say against true lovers (if any such exist)," replied Cornelia. "My targets are those who pass as lovers but who are actually quite the opposite."

"Oh, come now, Cornelia dearest,' said Virginia. "Are you now going to try to claim that lovers are as flawed as you have shown all other conditions of men to be? I could never believe, if I saw before me a well-mannered young man, behaving respectfully, sensibly, and politely, not staring at me, not complaining, not asking for anything, but just showing with his burning sighs and other subtle signs that he loves me and will serve me faithfully and that, in short, he is mine and mine alone—I could never believe, as I say, that such a man would ever deceive me. On the contrary, it would seem to me as though I could see his heart lying open before me and I should be overcome by his displays of love and humility and would not be able to help loving him in return."

"You have just painted the outward semblance of a lover, as though his inner self must necessarily conform to this appearance," replied Cornelia. "You poor thing, it's very clear that you've had no

37. The phrase used in the original (*da coturni e non da socchi*: lit. "for the tragedian, rather than the comedian," referring to the characteristic footwear of actors in the two genres in classical antiquity) echoes a line of Petrarch's *Triumph of Love* (4, 88).

38. The God of Love, Eros or Cupid, was conventionally represented as a winged boy. This sentence is obscure in the original and the sense has been reconstructed conjecturally.

39. Daedalus, in Greek mythology, created a pair of wax wings for his son Icarus. The latter, however, on his test flight, forgetting his father's advice flew too close to the sun, whereupon his wings melted and he plummeted to his death. I have not been able to identify the source of the allusion to "Leombruno's cloak," immediately following in the text.

experience in these things—and please God you may remain so innocent! Not that I'm speaking from experience myself, but surely you
too must have read or heard all those endless cautionary tales, which
have enabled a woman like me to learn all too well, at others' expense,
what this love business is all about? Believe me, lovers such as you
described scarcely exist (ones that truly love, I mean, rather than just
look the part). And it's these ingratiating striplings of yours who are
to be avoided most of all, for, being young and thus more fiery in
their passions than older men, they are also (however much they try
to hide it) more impetuous and unstable in their affections. They are
also foolish, even though they think they know better than anyone
else; besides which they are proud, insolent, and utterly shameless, so
that even though they hardly know what the word 'love' means, they
expect to be loved, obeyed, granted favors, and, in short, given everything they demand. And these young men go about everything so
indiscreetly and openly that everyone knows about it. As soon as they
are the least bit in love, they lose all patience; once they realize that
they are loved, they lose all discretion; if they are given some favor,
they want the whole world to know about it; if they deceive a woman,
they boast about it, do her down in public and glory in their cunning;
and, if they manage to possess a woman, they immediately lose interest in her. Their love is no more than a flash in the pan; their loyalty, a laugh in the tavern; their devotion, a day out hunting the hare;
their fine appearance, a peacock's tail. The only good thing about
these young boys, from a woman's point of view, is that being so
fickle and changeable, as I have said, they cannot—they would not
know how to—hide their falseness and treachery for long. They are
like bronze with a layer of gilding: it takes very little for that thin
layer to start peeling off and showing it was just a false coat, so any
woman with half a brain becomes aware very quickly what they're up to
and doesn't allow herself to be trapped so easily in their snares; she
either casts them aside or uses these frivolous creatures as a pastime,
to amuse herself—like a fan made of light plumes, whose only use is
for cooling you down in the summer."

"Oh, you really have it in for these poor little lads," Helena said
at this point. "You're following the advice of that poet who advises us
to:

> *Coglier i frutti non acerbi, e duri,*
> *Ma che non sian però troppo maturi.*

Pick fruits when they are no longer hard and unripe, but
not ones that are overripe, either.[40]

What do you have to say about more mature lovers? Can't we trust
older men, at least, when they appear to love faithfully?"

"We can trust them even less than those I've been talking
about," Cornelia replied. "For their experience has taught them not
to love more truly, but rather to deceive more effectively. Dearest sister, the greatest threat to our innocence comes precisely from these
more experienced lovers, fiendish creatures that they are! And you
mustn't be taken in for a moment when you see them pining away in
front of your eyes, consumed by their love for you, looking up at you
with their piteous eyes and speaking honeyed words. Just think of
them as an unreliable clock that tells you it's ten o'clock when it's in
fact barely two. These men never really take a woman into their
ungrateful hearts. When they meet a woman they pretend to be her
slave and to love her desperately, but at the same time they are laying
down traps for every woman they see, trying out each one in turn,
deceiving them all, saying the same words to each and laying down
the same nets—they aren't fussy about who it is, as long as they have
some woman in their power. These men, if nature has endowed them
with some talent or charm or beauty or prowess, are so proud and vain
that they behave as though (and genuinely believe that) women
should be grateful to them for courting them; and if they realize that
these qualities of theirs have made a woman fall in love with them,
they immediately demand a full satisfaction of all their desires, and if
they encounter any difficulty or resistance they immediately get
offended and pretend they want to claim back that heart which in
reality they never gave away. They complain that they are not loved,
because they haven't seen any of the proofs they were demanding—
and, believe me, these men who are obsessed with having this 'proof'
are a perfidious breed and of the nature of the Jews:[41] they don't

40. The quotation is from Ariosto's *Orlando Furioso* (*OF*, 10, 9), where, following a tale of
monstrously callous infidelity on the part of a young man, the middle-aged poet slyly
advises his women readers that they are safer with men of his age.

41. Antisemitism was obviously too widespread a phenomenon in this period to need
particular comment, but Cornelia's remark may perhaps be seen as reflecting a hardening
of attitudes toward Jews in Venice at the time Fonte was writing, partly as a result of
the intolerant climate fostered by the Counter-Reformation, which resulted in increasingly stringent restrictions being placed on Venetian Jews' business activities and
freedom of movement (see Pullan 1971, 538–78).

really love the woman, as they claim, but rather nurture a mortal hatred against her. And this is very clear, because when, as sometimes happens, these men attain what they desire, once they have won their victory by deceiving some poor girl, they immediately despise her and abandon her; and to free themselves of any obligation to love her, they try to justify themselves by pretending to believe that she did not grant them the favors they asked because she was carried away by an overwhelming love for them, but just out of caprice or shamelessness. And then the poor girl, who has been led into doing wrong by the strength of her feelings, thinking that this will make her seducer love her all the more, realizes at once that she has picked up a snake along with the flowers she has been gathering and that all that her labors have gained her is the loss of her faithless lover. So sensible women will regard this kind of lover as being like the panther, the cruelest of all animals, which, when it is hungry, pretends to be dead, so that other animals do not fear to come near it; and the poor incautious little things, attracted by the beauty of its spotted coat and lulled into a false sense of security by its cunning, are emboldened to come up and play around it; until finally it leaps on them and dispatches them ferociously and devours them, feeding ravenously on their flesh.[42] The only advantage mature lovers have over younger men is that being older and wanting to be thought wiser and better than they in fact are, they conduct things rather more discreetly than the others and handle things rather more shrewdly."

"My dear Cornelia," said Virginia. "What you're saying is sowing confusion throughout the whole kingdom of love. What of all the famous stories of lovers in the past? All the faith of those in the present day? You're turning everything on its head. Haven't you read about all those countless men who have died for the great love they have borne for women?"

'Do you really believe,' Cornelia replied, 'that everything historians tell us about men—or about women—is actually true? You ought to consider the fact that these histories have been written by men, who never tell the truth except by accident. And if you consider, in

---

42. I have been unable to find a source for Fonte's description of the panther's hunting habits that corresponds in every detail with the account given here (for example, ancient and medieval sources that mention panthers' mysterious powers of attraction tend to attribute this to the animals' scent rather than the visual enticements of their coat). See, however, McCulloch 1960, 148–50; and Pliny (*NH*, 8, 23, 62–63). Regarding the panther's spotted coat, it should be noted that Pliny and many medieval sources use the term "panther" to describe a species of leopard.

addition, the envy and ill will they bear us women, it is hardly surprising that they rarely have a good word to say for us, and concentrate instead on praising their own sex in general and particular members of it, as a way of praising themselves.[43] But, even accepting that there have been many men who have gone wretchedly to their deaths while flaunting their love for a woman, do you believe that the real reason for their downfall is the overwhelming passion they feel for the woman? Not on your life! The cause of death is their overwhelming rage at not having been able to achieve their end and not having enjoyed the victory they so longed for: the triumph of deceiving and ruining these women whom they purported to love. As evidence of this, you'll find that very few men, if any, have died for love *after* achieving the supreme end of love. The only exceptions are those men who are caught in the act and wretchedly put to death, as often happens—but their deaths are brought about not by their love for the woman but by their eagerness to satisfy their disordered desires. In fact, if they really loved the woman, they would take care not to put themselves and her in such a dangerous situation, so as not to be the ruin of her."

"Well, that's enough about these middle-aged lovers," said Virginia. "Are you saying that we should love old men, then, since we can't have youths, still less men in their prime?"

"That's not my point at all," replied Cornelia. "Because, as they say, 'a bird in a child's hand and a girl in an old man's both spell danger.' Old men are just as crafty as middle-aged men—worse, in fact; and, besides, they are deficient in many ways, because their years of happiness are long over and all their charm and beauty have faded: they've used up all the best of their flour and there's nothing left in them except what they call chaff or bran. Besides which, they are

---

43. The point made here by Cornelia about male historians' lack of objectivity was a staple argument of Renaissance defenders of women, first employed by Christine de Pizan in her *City of Ladies* (c. 1405). The theme received what is perhaps its most sustained development in the period in a work with which Fonte may possibly have been familiar: Luigi Dardano's *Fine and Learned Defense of Women* (Venice, 1554), the bulk of which consists of a critical "trial" of celebrated and reviled male and female figures from history, conducted by a male and a female advocate. The most prominent discussions of the issue, however, are those found in Ariosto's *Orlando Furioso*, in the proem to canto 37, which deals with the problem of gender bias in history at some length, and in the proem to canto 20, which treats the same question in a more offhand manner. There may be an ironic allusion to this latter passage in Fonte's phrase *invidia o mal voler* ("envy or ill will"): compare *OF*, 20, 2, 8, where men's failure to record women's achievements is more generously attributed to their *invidia o non saper* ("envy or ignorance").

extremely jealous and suspicious by nature, lazy and averse to the dangers, the ordeals, and the long vigils lovers have to suffer; and they are also fussy and mean. Though when I talk about their being mean, it's not because I think lovers, whether old or young, should seek to buy their way into a lady's good graces, or that any woman should wish this or seek this of her lover, because that would be to behave like a whore. The reason I mention meanness is that when a man is mean with money (which is the last thing in the world we should care about), that's a sign that he must be just as mean, or more so, with his heart and his word. Because a man who loves truly and so gives up his heart and his soul and his whole self will not make a fuss about giving up his money and what he owns, since it isn't a part of him. So when a man is mean with what is no part of himself, how do you think he will behave when he himself and his heart and his faith are concerned? And that, after all, is the most precious jewel, the greatest treasure a lover can give to his lady and that she can give him in return; and that's the reason why true love is said to make people liberal and magnanimous, noble and brave. And, since old men are for the most part just the opposite of this, because of their age and all the ailments that go with it, let us leave them to one side. For they are more fitted to find their pleasure in drinking good wine than in chasing pretty girls; and better qualified to give advice than to act themselves."

"Now which men are you defining as old?" asked Virginia. "Up to what age do men deserve to be loved (if they themselves love truly, that is)?"

"A man of forty-five or even fifty may deserve to be loved as long as he is decent and steadfast in character," replied Cornelia. "But I'll leave it to you to try to find such a man. For, young and old alike, not one of them truly loves from the heart."

"But tell me, pray," Virginia went on. "Those men who have labored so hard and spent so much time writing works in our praise (and there are many, many such men)—do you refuse to believe that they, at least, love our sex in general and the particular women who are the objects of their affection?"[44]

44. In addition to the many works of the period devoted to arguing the case for women's equality with (or even superiority to) men, Virginia is probably thinking of the massive output of Neoplatonizing love poetry in the period, which, following the conventions established by Dante, Petrarch, and more recent writers like the Venetian Pietro Bembo (1470–1547), portrayed women as beings of such supernatural perfection that a man could ascend through a meditation on their beauty and virtue to a contem -

"I'd say that they are no different from other men," Cornelia said. "None of these writers has been driven to write by the intensity of his love: in fact, the majority of them, believe me, have taken on the task of praising us more out of self-interest and concern for their own honor than out of any genuine concern for ours. Because knowing that they have few merits of their own to win them fame and glory, they have used the achievements of our sex instead, clothing their fame in our virtues and perfections—just like those men who want to attend some ceremony even though they are not in favor with the Prince and have nothing decent to wear, and who take advantage of the invitation and the wardrobe of a friend and tag along with him to watch the festivities. There are many, as well, who praise us in the belief that we are like that crow who let himself be tricked by the hungry fox, who saw the crow carrying off a great piece of cheese and started praising it extravagantly and, at the same time, begging it to sing a little, because it had heard so much about the crow's lovely voice; when the crow finally opened its beak to give the fox a song, it dropped the cheese and the fox snatched it up and ran off with it [45] In the same way, men think that if they praise a woman enough, she'll be so carried away by vanity and self-love as to allow herself to be tricked into releasing her grip on her own will, so that they can get their hands on it, along with her honor, her soul, and her life. And, anyway, what do you say about all those many men who have written attacks on our sex? Because for every one man who praises us, speaking the truth, there are a thousand who attack us quite without motivation. So you should let none of these vain discourses persuade you that any man loves as he should, perfectly and sincerely."

"So we should love no one, since, as you insist, no man loves truly," said Virginia. "Is that what you're saying?"

"I don't mean to imply that there are no exceptions," replied Cornelia, "just as I acknowledged in the case of fathers, brothers, sons, and husbands. But what I do say is that those who love truly are

---

plation of the divine. Though this lyric tradition was undoubtedly important in offering a counterpoise to contemporary misogynistic views of women as base and animalistic, most modern critics would share the skepticism Cornelia expresses in her reply (below) concerning the degree to which Petrarchism's exaltation of women may be attributed to feminist motives.

45. The story of the fox and the crow (like that of the lamb and the wolf, mentioned below) derives from the collection of moral fables attributed to the shadowy figure of Aesop (sixth century BC), which enjoyed immense popularity throughout the Middle Ages and Renaissance, and was still, in this period, used in some Venetian schools as an elementary Latin text (Grendler 1989, 175).

so rare that they are lost among the vast hordes of false lovers; and it is extremely difficult to identify them and pick them out. It's just like those tokens you use playing the lottery:[46] among all those thousands of blank cards you find maybe eight or ten winning cards, which only come up by an amazing stroke of luck; and whether you win or lose depends on luck, not on judgment."

"But surely," said Helena, "there must be some distinguishing feature or particular trait that would let us identify these few good men who you admit do exist among the whole mass of them? Some sign that would teach us how to avoid the deceits and treachery of those countless lying predators who are stalking us to take away our freedom? And that would allow us to reward those few deserving lovers by returning their love?"

"Well, yes, my dear," said Cornelia. "But, as I've said, it's extremely difficult, because both true lovers and false

Dimostran tutti una medesima fede

All outwardly display the same faith.[47]

But if you were by some chance to find one who showed all the devotion and had all the good qualities Virginia was talking about, but who persisted in his love over time, without ever demanding anything from you that compromised your honor or your soul, so that if you loved him in return you could be sure that there was no other woman in the world he was courting, and that all his energies were concentrated on pursuing your love and pleasing you in every way he could, then such a man would be a true lover and you could believe that he loved you from the depths of his heart. Another sign by which you can tell a man who is truly in love is that if he happens to catch sight of the person he loves or hears her name unexpectedly, his heart turns over, his expression changes, his voice and whole body start trembling; he grows pale, sighs deeply, and speaks with a broken and troubled voice. The man who loves from the depths of his heart desires nothing, hopes for nothing, and demands nothing except to

46. Public numbers lotteries like that referred to here were known in Italy from the early sixteenth century, and were organized on occasion by the Venetian government (Endrei and Zolnay 1986, 41–42).

47. The line (slightly misquoted) is taken from the first stanza of canto 19 of Ariosto's *Orlando Furioso*, which deals with adversity as the test of true friendship.

be loved in return; he keeps within the bounds of decency; stands in awe of the woman he loves; loves her in her presence; praises her in her absence; interests himself not only in her but in everything that concerns her, as though it were his own business. And if a man who has all these qualities deceives you by pretending to love you, though in fact you find out the opposite is true, then you can just laugh it off, for such a love cannot harm you much and he has little to gain by it."

"Well," said the Queen, "if all those who professed to be lovers were men of this kind and loved truly, then love would be the sweetest of things. For if men contented themselves with little and women were prepared to give them that little, the sweetest and most blissful harmony and peace would reign between them, and you wouldn't keep hearing all these complaints from men who want what they can't have, or from women who have given away what they can never take back."

"And what exactly do you mean by this 'little' with which lovers should be content?" asked Lucretia.

"That the woman does not object to being loved, sincerely and within the bounds of decency," replied the Queen.

"One writer has observed on this subject," added Cornelia, "that a refined love will extend only as far as a sigh, meaning that it is permissible for the woman to sigh at the anguish she sees her lover going through for her sake, and that her lover must be satisfied with her sighs."

"As the poet said," added Corinna:

Certo il fin de' miei pianti,
Che non altronde il cor doglioso chiama,
Vien da' begli occhi al fin dolce tremanti
Ultima speme de' cortesi amanti.

And certainly the end of my weeping (for my sorrowing heart aspires to nothing else) will come from those lovely eyes, when at last they will turn on me, gentle and trembling—the utmost ambition of the courtly lover.[48]

"Well, either way," the Queen went on, "a love as restrained as

---

48. The lines are from Petrarch's canzone "Gentil mia donna, i' veggio" (*RS*, 72), one of his most confident assertions of the ennobling power of a sublimated love.

this would be, if not quite the father of virtue, then at least a school of manners, a source of happiness, and a breeding-ground for all the graces."

"It may be seen from experience," added Cornelia, "that those few men who have loved truly have acted virtuously as well and have never been a cause of scandal to anyone. True love makes the proud humble, the ignorant learned, the timorous brave, the irascible gentle; it makes the foolish clever, and madmen wise. In brief, it can change men's nature, make the bad good and the good better. That's why love is often compared to fire: just as gold is refined in the fire, so man reaches a state of perfect refinement in the flame of true love. But, then, those who have none of the qualities we have just listed strive to appear what they are not, and, as I have said, they often succeed very well (much to our harm and peril), in concealing their falsity and ill intentions beneath an appearance of decency. So even if a man does seem, over a long period, to display that loyalty and true love that we have talked about, I should advise any woman who is sensible, well-respected, and virtuous to proceed cautiously, if she values her virtue and her reputation. Thus when some man sets himself to courting her, however sincere his courtship appears to be, she should never take him seriously in any way, and should neither allow herself to believe him, lest she find herself loving him in return, nor accept his messages or his favors, lest she find herself in his debt. In fact, right from the start, she should energetically defend and protect herself against these temptations (it should not be difficult for her), and she should behave this way with everyone who tries to lure her, rejecting each man's advances equally and refusing to listen to anyone, whether seriously or even in jest (in case she falls into the trap of those who feign sleep and finish up falling asleep in earnest). But above all things, even if she does feel some leaning toward a lover, she should on no account let this be understood: she should hide her feelings as much as possible and not give the man the least encouragement, in case he becomes arrogant and importunate, and dares to try and tempt her to something more serious. Because it can often happen that over time the pestering and the constant pleading of someone one loves and trusts are enough to move a heart, especially the heart of a tender, trusting, and impassioned woman—for, as the proverb says, even the hardest stones are worn away by drops of water."

"That would be fine," Leonora replied to this, "if it were something within our power to do. But we women are so trusting, so kind and sensitive by nature that we are quick to trust; and then, since we are also compassionate and warmhearted, we cannot help loving in return (though in a sincere and virtuous manner). For we assume that men are like us, both in truthfulness and in purity of motives; and this tendency to judge men by ourselves is the cause of our downfall."

"Tell me, my dear, sweet Corinna," said Helena. "Why is it that women, as Leonora says, are kinder and more innocent and trusting than men?"

"In my view," Corinna replied, "the explanation for this lies in women's natural disposition and complexion, which is, as all learned men agree, cold and phlegmatic.[49] This makes us calmer than men, weaker and more apprehensive by nature; more credulous and easily swayed, so that when some lovely prospect opens up before us, some enticing vista, we immediately drink in the image as though it were true, when it fact it is false. But despite all that, where our natural disposition is at fault, we should bring our intellect into play and use the torch of reason to light our way to recognizing these lovers' masks and protecting ourselves against them. In fact, we should pay about as much attention to them and give them about as much credence as the sensible little lamb gave to the wolf when it was imitating its mother's voice and begging it to open the gate."[50]

"That makes good sense to me," said Helena. "For women's nature is such that ferocity cannot dominate in it, since choler and blood make up a relatively minor part of our constitution. And that makes us kinder and gentler than men and less prone to carry out our desires,

49. The passage that follows rests on the theory, central to medieval and Renaissance thinking on medicine and psychology, that a person's psychosomatic makeup ("complexion") was determined by the combination in his or her body of the four essential bodily fluids or "humors" (blood, phlegm, yellow bile or choler, and black bile or melancholia), which in turn were combinations of the four essential properties ("qualities" or "contraries"), hot and cold, moist and dry. A dominance of blood (hot and moist) in the complexion made a person extrovert and "sanguine" (the word derives from the Latin for "blood"); while choler (hot and dry) made one quick-tempered ("choleric"); phlegm (cold and moist), dull and placid ("phlegmatic"); and melancholia (cold and dry), melancholic. The notion that women were by nature less hot than men (and thus, by implication, duller, more sedentary, and more timid) derives from Aristotle, whose views on sexual difference dominated medical thought on the subject throughout the Renaissance (see especially *HA*, 608a19–608b15, where the psychological implications of the distinction are most clearly brought out). This argument was frequently used to provide support for the thesis of women's inferiority to men (see Maclean 1980). However, by the early sixteenth century, defenders of women had elaborated a set of strategies for responding to it, similar in some respects to those found here (see for example Castiglione 1994, 221–28 [3: 12–18]).

50. The reference is to a fable of Aesop.

while men, by contrast, being of a hot and dry complexion, dominated by choler—all flame and fire—are more likely to go astray and can scarcely contain their tempestuous appetites. And that is the reason for the fierceness, waywardness, and fury of their anger, and the urgency and excessiveness of their burning, intemperate desires, carnal and otherwise. Desire in men is so powerful that their senses overpower their reason; and since that is the way in which men function (following their senses, without the controlling influence of reason), then you can hardly wonder if most of them have little time for virtuous deeds and give themselves up entirely to the pleasures and promptings of vice. For when the human spirit is joined to a body so constituted, the effects that follow can hardly be other than those that the nature and properties of the cause dictate. Isn't that the case?"

"Indeed," replied Corinna. "But by saying that, you are not refuting the claim that women are superior to men. On the contrary, you are rather lending further weight to it, because, in addition to what has already been said, you are now adding the fact that women's physical nature is superior to men's and that women act according to reason rather than appetite and thus refrain from evil and devote themselves to good. The same is not true of men, even though they certainly could be good and emend their nature if they wished to, considering the perfection of their intellect, resulting from the greater liveliness of spirit they are said to possess. But they do not care to use their intellect, nor to make the effort to contain their sensuality, and thus they go from bad to worse. So men are vicious both by nature and by will—and they try their best to corrupt us as well."

"So women's goodness derives from their nature rather than their will," said Helena. "Which means that since we are less naturally inclined to evil than men, if we abstain from it we hardly deserve much credit for it, while if we do succumb, our sin is a grave one— for, if the urgings of our nature are not strong, it implies a conscious decision to sin. Men, on the other hand, are almost forced into sin by their nature, as we have been saying; and when they succeed, through sheer moral strength, in controlling their urges, then their virtue must be recognized as outstanding and they deserve great credit for it."

"Aha!" said Corinna. "Even now, you are still having to admit that women are superior in nature to men; indeed, your whole argument rests on that assumption. And a consequence of that is that women are more perfect then men and of greater dignity. But you are wrong when you assert that for this reason men are more praiseworthy than us when they refrain from evil, because their urge to sin is greater and more powerful than ours. That is something I cannot concede, for it's easy to find any number of examples of women who have suffered the torments of sensuality more violently than many men. It may be that the inclination toward sensuality is stronger in men than in women, because their nature is more capacious and their will more imperious. But that does not mean that women are not just as fiercely assaulted as men by these natural forces and powers of the soul, or that women are not drawn toward sensual pleasures by as strong an urge of the will as their nature will allow. It's just as though there were two glasses, one large and one small: when both are filled with water, the large obviously contains a greater volume of water, but that does not change the fact that both glasses are full, brimming, and fully occupied with that volume of water which their maker designed them to hold. And thus we must conclude that women have fewer mental and physical resources for resisting temptation, but are still, within the limitations of their nature, as subject to the temptations of the senses as men—perhaps even more so, because of their yielding and unsuspecting nature, which lends them to be all the more easily carried away and overcome by natural passions. Yet women struggle to be good and resist their evil inclinations with a stout heart. And women do not simply face the obstacle of their own inclinations; they also need to summon enough strength to pit themselves against men's corrupting influences. A double strength, then; and a kind of strength, you might say, that comes all the less easily to women because of their natural gentleness and kindness, which make them inclined, in all other areas of life, to put others' good and others' pleasures before their own. In this case, though, because they know that virtue must come above their own life and others', they accept the need to repress their desires and deny all pleasure both to themselves and the men they believe love them. But they do so at the cost of great violence to their hearts, and they deserve an infinite amount of credit for their victories."

"But even if I were to allow, for the sake of argument, that we women were less naturally inclined to error than men, then it must be taken into account that we are also less well equipped than they are to restrain ourselves; for if we want to claim that men are naturally more inclined to sensual desires, then they are also possessed of greater strength and judgment, so they can guard against those

desires and rein them back. So when we women carry off our double
victory, over our own desires and those of others (for that is, for the
most part, what happens), then the honor we win for ourselves should
be all the greater, just as a captain placed in charge of a well-manned
fortress does not attain any particular glory when he defends it, for
even when the attackers are many, he has many more in defense. The
real praise goes, instead, to those who defend themselves with few
supporters and succeed in defeating and beating off their enemies. It
scarcely matters if those enemies—some of whom may lie within their
own walls—are also few in number, for where there are few defenses,
there is a real danger that the fierceness or length of the siege will
bring the city to its knees. So we must conclude that women are more
virtuous than men both by nature and through the exercise of their
will."

"You are quite wrong, Corinna," Lucretia said. "In fact, would to
God women were as steadfast as you make out, for then men would
behave in a more reasonable way. What really happens is that men
learn from experience that we are all too easy and yielding, and it is
this that encourages them to try their luck with us. So they set
themselves to tempting and pleading with such dedication that in
the end they carry off the victory over some woman or other—something that would not happen if women behaved with true womanly
dignity[51] and rejected them firmly right from the start, as they
deserve. Because when a woman really sets her mind to it, she can
dismiss any lover, however importunate and shameless he may be, with
a single gesture."

"It is rather you who are in the wrong when you try to attack
women in this way, Lucretia," Corinna retorted, "as though it were
women who provided the opportunity for enterprising men to start laying traps for them. On the contrary, it is men who are the origin and
source of all the evil, for women are like the flint in a tinderbox,
which, though it encloses a potential flame within itself, does not
issue that flame except when it is persistently struck by the steel.
And, if men through their actions are the efficient cause and the
prime movers in awakening women's senses (and we see the proof of
this every day, watching the way they solicit women and molest
them), then why should women bear the blame for something they do
under duress? For a sin that arises from accidental causes and not from

51. The original (*se le donne fessero da donne*) puns on the etymology of the Italian word for
"woman," *donna* (*domina*: "lady of the household," "woman of power and standing").

their own nature or from a clear act of will on their part? For something men have goaded them into? Women can hardly be expected under these circumstances to be colder than water or harder than iron; and even water and iron change their form when heated.

"And besides all this, to reply to what you say about women being able to lift this burden from their shoulders if they only wanted to, I tell you that all women do try, and it sometimes works for them and sometimes doesn't, either just through bad luck or because they happen to be dealing with particularly bad men. For there are some men who will never desist from their enterprise, fueled as they are by vain hopes arising from their overwhelming arrogance and their conviction of being so desirable that women should be chasing after them rather than the contrary and practically hurling themselves out of windows to please them. And with this conviction firmly in their mind, these men simply cannot believe that sooner or later the women they are courting will not soften in their behavior toward them (they are convinced, of course, that their *hearts* have already softened, and that they are acting coldly toward them only to keep up appearances and preserve their reputation for virtue). So we women encounter just the same problem as farmers do when they sow the same crop in different fields: each may pull his weight and try as hard as he can to ensure a good harvest, but they do not all get the same results, as they ought when they are using the same seed; instead, one gets a splendid crop, while the other's withers and comes to nothing. In just the same way, women's virtuous reproaches and dissimulations and rejections, when planted in the hearts of more reasonable men, produce the harvest of remorse and goodness on their part and make them forget their follies, but with men like those just mentioned, the same methods are no use at all; on the contrary, instead of producing a good crop, they often just serve to turn the wheat fields into a bed of nettles. For if their feigned love never got a real foothold in their hearts, once they are disabused of their foolish illusions they become possessed of a hatred for us that is genuine and heartfelt; and through pique, they try to convince people by words that they enjoyed those favors they were denied in deed. How many women suffer this fate!"

"Those cursed scandalmongers!" exclaimed the Queen. "Don't I just know about them! I have come across endless examples. How many poor women are slandered, alas! who are quite innocent."

"Well, let them talk away," said Corinna. "And let us concentrate on behaving well, because the truth always comes out in the end."

"Oh, come now!" Helena spoke up at this point. "Surely you're not trying to deny that women too have their part in sin, despite what you've been saying about men being the instigators and causes of all evil and it always being men who put us up to it? For the most part, that's nonsense. To take their part for a moment (for, after all, we are alone here and they can't hear us), what about all those shameless and corrupt women who dishonor our sex publicly, soliciting men openly and selling off their honor to the first bidder? Such women destroy men, stripping them of all their money and often bringing them to the point of death. And men certainly aren't going to let us forget they exist—especially since many of them are upright and virtuous, like Scipio, Xenocrates, Alexander, and the others we read about in history."[52]

"Well that last point is true as far as it goes," replied Cornelia. "But you aren't going to find men like that often: they are like patterns of virtue that God sends into the world for others to imitate (though few manage to get anywhere near the mark), and that's the reason why historians pick them out for special mention, as something remarkable, outlandish, and memorable, like those amazing comets that appear once in the course of many years. By contrast, there have been endless good and virtuous women. But where shameless women are concerned—and I am not trying to deny that such women exist (would that they didn't!)—I repeat what I said earlier, that the source and the true cause of this terrible evil lies in the men who trapped, tempted, solicited, and lured on these women while they still had their honor, leading the most naïve and easygoing of them to fall head-over-heels to their ruin. But for all that, these women, wretched as they are, preserve a little more dignity than the men they consort with, because at least they aren't the ones paying the men; whereas men fall into their traps like animals and pay for *them*, however corrupt, vile, and wretched they are. Which is something that certainly wouldn't happen if they kept their heads and

52. The episodes referred to here are among the most famous classical exempla of male chastity: Alexander the Great's continence in refraining to take advantage of the wife and daughters of Darius, King of Persia, after his defeat of the latter in 331 BC; the similar restraint shown by the Roman general Scipio Africanus on his successful campaign in Spain in 210 BC; and the exemplary self-control displayed by the Greek philosopher Xenocrates (fourth century BC), who preserved his chastity through a night with a famous courtesan, Phrine, despite her energetic attempts to seduce him. All three exempla are wittily debunked in Castiglione's *Book of the Courtier* by Cesare Gonzaga, who points out that Scipio and Alexander had sound tactical reasons for their self-restraint, while Xenocrates' continence should be attributed to his decrepitude and drinking habits, rather than his virtue (Castiglione 1994, 253–54 [3: 44–45]).

showed some of that modesty and virtue we find in women. Just tell me: have you ever come across the case of a young girl, a virgin, so bold and shameless as to tempt a man into vice? It cannot be doubted that when a virgin loses her honor, it can be blamed entirely on a man who has shamelessly flattered and solicited her in all the ways he can find: eventually, as I say, he takes advantage of her naïveté and gradually strips her of all her natural feminine dignity and power until she is finally reduced to prostitution, either because he has abandoned her, as often happens, or because some other hardship forces her into it. And once the wretched creatures are reduced to this state, knowing as they do that men, with their tricks and relentless pestering, have been responsible for their downfall, they decide to get something back for the great harm they have suffered and resolve never to love a man again, since they have been so deceived by them, but rather to give them a taste of their own medicine and, just as men once preyed on their honor, they prey on men's purses; they pretend to love them and if, by some chance, a man falls in love with one of them (for it does happen sometimes that men get more involved with these women than with decent women, because these women have become like men and share their propensity to vice)—if that happens, I can tell you, he's had it, because they will drain him to the last penny, just as he deserves.[53]

"And besides all this, those poor women have only one sin (and that one caused by men, as I have said), whereas most men have endless vices. So why should so much blame be heaped on our sex? I'm not denying that it is a most shocking and shameful thing, but it is unfair that all women should be blamed for the transgressions of a few, or that their vice should reflect on women in general. Though even those few do not deserve to get all the blame while men stand by smugly congratulating themselves, because I have not come across any divine law that absolves men of this sin and punishes women alone. And even in human law, when the courts find themselves with a great number of culprits on their hands after some major crime, they generally try to establish who the ringleader was; and once they find him, they very often absolve his accomplices and punish only the

53. The degree of sympathy for prostitutes evinced here is unexpected in the context of a work by a "respectable" woman. It should be noted, however, that this was a period that saw several important new religiously inspired initiatives in Venice directed at rescuing "fallen women" and sheltering young girls perceived to be in danger of being drawn into the trade (Pullan 1971, 276–394, esp. 386, 393, on Venetian noblewomen's participation in these initiatives).

principal mover in the crime. So you can see that both human and divine laws demand that wicked men should receive the same oppro-brium and punishment as wicked women—indeed more, since they are the cause and the instigators of women's errors, as I have pointed out. And besides all this, those few women who fall into sin in this way (I am not talking about prostitutes any more) are led into it, as I have said, by their good nature and compassion."

"Oh come now, Cornelia dearest," said Lucretia. "You're not try-ing to tell us that vice is goodness? That really is a load of nonsense you're trying to make us swallow."

"But when you hear men talking," said Cornelia, "all they ever do is speak ill of women. 'Did you know what such-and-such a women is up to with such-and-such a man?' 'And that other one! What a whore! What a slut! I'd never have believed it: she seemed like such a saint!' 'Oh, these women all make out that they're so prudish because they haven't got the opportunity. If they had, they'd all be at it; there'd be no stopping them.' And they can keep up these curses and insults all day without once looking down at themselves and seeing that they may need to take some of the blame. And I don't quite know how they've managed to make this law in their favor, or who exactly it was who gave them a greater license to sin than is allowed to us;[54] and if the fault is common to both sexes (as they can hardly deny), why should the blame not be as well? What makes them think they can boast of the same thing that in women brings only shame?"

"Oh, let them get on with it!" said Corinna. "They think they have shamed and lowered us by introducing this convention into the world, but in fact it works to our advantage and their disadvantage, because it teaches us to avoid their company, which, in any case, is beneath us."

"Who knows?" said Leonora. "Perhaps it was women themselves—some wise and courageous women of ancient times—who first intro-duced this distinction between the ways in which men and women are treated. For when a man has amorous concourse with a woman, the result is the greatest shame for her and a certain amount of credit and praise for him; so that the woman always tries to disguise it as much as

54. The wording here recalls a passage in Castiglione's *Book of the Courtier* in which a male speaker acknowledges that the sexual double standard in society is due to the fact that "we [men] have by our own authority claimed a license to consider trivial or even praise-worthy in men those same offenses which are in women regarded as punishable by a shameful death or, at the least, perpetual infamy" (Castiglione 1994, 247 [3: 38]; trans-lation modernized).

possible, while the man cannot wait to tell the whole world about it, as though his glory and happiness depended on it. Surely this is a way of declaring clearly the dignity and nobility of women and the corresponding indignity of men. Because, since this great gulf in perfection exists between the sexes, it *is* a very shameful thing when we, who are so far superior to them, stoop so far as to have anything to do with these inferior creatures—especially outside the necessity of marriage, which, since it is imposed on us, we can hardly avoid. But even in marriage, this intercourse with men abases us. For the ancient Romans held virgins in great esteem and treasured them and honored them as something sacred—as have all peoples, in fact; and the same thing applies in our own day, right across the world. The vestal Tuccia, who had never had intercourse with a man, was able to carry water in a sieve.[55] Claudia, too, another vestal, was able to pull to the shore with her girdle the ship that so many thousand men had been unable to shift. For a woman, when she is segregated from male contact, has something divine about her and can achieve miracles, as long as she retains her natural virginity. That certainly isn't the case with men, because it is only when a man has taken a wife that he is considered a real man and that he reaches the peak of happiness, honor, and greatness. The Romans in their day did not confer any important responsibilities on any man who did not have a wife; they did not allow him to take up a public office or to perform any serious duties relating to the Republic. Homer used to say that men without wives were scarcely alive.[56] And if you want further proof of women's superior dignity and authority, just think about the fact that if a man is married to a wise, modest, and virtuous woman, even if he is the most ignorant, shameless, and corrupt creature who has ever lived, he

55. The Vestal Virgins, in ancient Rome, were priestesses of the temple of Vesta, goddess of the hearth fire. They were sworn to chastity and any who transgressed were punished by being buried alive. The two mentioned here by name were both accused of unchastity, but cleared their names by performing miracles: Tuccia miraculously carried water in a sieve without its leaking, while Claudia, with her girdle, dragged free a ship that had run aground at the mouth of the Tiber. Both figures were frequently represented in art and literature as exemplars of chastity, and both gained a quasi-sacred status in the Middle Ages, when they were perceived as prototypes of the Virgin Mary.

56. I have not been able to identify the source of this supposed view of Homer's. Where the point about Rome is concerned, Fonte may have been thinking of the Augustan legislation that sought to encourage marriage and procreation by making celibacy socially and economically disadvantageous for men between the ages of twenty-five and sixty. This legislation did not, however, extend so far as to exclude unmarried candidates from office: it simply introduced mechanisms for favoring the election of married men, especially those with large families (Treggiari 1991, 66–75, 83–84).

will never, for all his wickedness, be able to tarnish his wife's reputation in the least. But if, through some mischance, a woman is lured by some persistent and unscrupulous admirer into losing her honor, then her husband is instantly and utterly shamed and dishonored by her act, however good, wise, and respectable he may be himself—as if he depended on her, rather than she on him. And, indeed, just as a pain in the head causes the whole body to languish, so when women (who are superior by nature and thus legitimately the head and superior of their husbands) suffer some affront, so their husbands, as appendages and dependents, are also subject to the same misfortune and come to share in the ills of their wives as well as in their good fortune."

"It's quite true," said Cornelia, "that if we were not by nature so kind, compassionate, and meek, then these facts alone would be enough to make us avoid men's company altogether, since it can bring us only harm, shame, and downright ruin. We should be more circumspect, and preserve our dignity and our natural feminine authority, without mixing so much with these creatures, who are not only unworthy of us, but also speak ill of us into the bargain, when it is they who are responsible for all our ills."

"Listening to all these dire things you're saying," said Virginia, "I'm being to get frightened and to go off the idea of men. Who knows? I may even start to have second thoughts about marriage."

"Steady now, daughter," said the Queen. "These ladies would not wish to deny that there are a few good men among all these scoundrels."

"No, indeed," said Cornelia. "For, apart from anything, men may inherit some of the innocence and goodness of their mothers. It is said that in generation the father contributes more to the son than the mother does;[57] and that is the reason why sons turn out to resemble their fathers more (in other words, to be as bad as their fathers). So it can be said that the least bad men are those who have taken most from their mothers."

"Oh, but when all's said and done," said Lucretia, "with all these arguments of yours, you surely can't deny that women have been and still are the cause of countless evils in the world. That's the reason

57. The reasons for this are discussed at length in Aristotle's *Generation of Animals*, 4, 3 (767a36–768b14), though Fonte is very far from sharing the misogynistic premises of Aristotle's arguments (on which see Maclean 1980, 36–37).

they are known as 'women,' in fact: the word *donna* derives from *danno* ['harm'].["]58

"That's not true!" replied Corinna. "Women are called *donne* to signify that they are a *dono celeste*, a gift or donation sent from heaven to bring goodness and beauty to the world. Why *danno*, for heaven's sake?"

"You're asking me why?" Lucretia retorted. "Don't we read that the fall of Troy and the ten years of continual war that led up to it were caused by a woman?59 What do you have to say to that?"

"I say," Corinna replied, "that even though the woman of whom you are speaking admittedly did go astray, overpowered by love and by the flattery and entreaties of the man who solicited her (and who, indeed, sought her out precisely for that purpose, at a time when she wasn't giving him a thought), her example serves rather as further evidence of the dignity of her sex. First, because it was the man who went to seek her out, not she him: which, besides demonstrating her superiority, also excuses her in great part and reveals her as innocent, and a victim of his wiles. And also, because both her lover and her husband were prepared to countenance such ruin, such expense, so much death and destruction, over so long a period, the one in order to keep her, the other to win her back; both, in fact, whether it was love that moved them or honor, felt the loss of this one woman as something grave enough to justify all this. Whereas it has never happened that a woman has stolen a man, or carried him off, or done anything of this kind for the sake of a man. Nor, for that matter, have men ever shown themselves to hold one of their own sex in such high regard, or undertaken any such enterprise for the sake of another man."

At this point, Helena broke in, "So who was the cause of the Fall, if not Eve, the first woman?"

"On the contrary, the blame lies with Adam," replied Corinna.

---

58. Arguments from etymology (often extremely fanciful ones) were a much-favored technique among both defenders of women and their misogynist opponents. For a pertinent example, see Bramoso 1589, 35, where *danno* is defended as the etymology of the word *donna* over both *dono*, proposed below in the text by Corinna, and the correct *domina* (see Daenens 1987, esp. 22–23).

59. The reference is, of course, to Helen, the wife of the Greek leader Menelaos, whose abduction by her Trojan admirer, Paris, was the stimulus for the Greek invasion of Troy. Similar vindications of Helen may be found in earlier defenses of women: see, for example, Maggio 1545, 25v–26r; also, for a later example, Marinella 1601, 117–18.

"For it was with a good end in mind—that of acquiring the knowledge of good and evil—that Eve allowed herself to be carried away and eat the forbidden fruit. But Adam was not moved by this desire for knowledge, but simply by greed: he ate it because he heard Eve say it tasted good, which was a worse motive and caused more displeasure.[60] And that is the reason why God did not chase them from Paradise as soon as Eve sinned, but rather after Adam had disobeyed him—in other words, he didn't respond to Eve's action, but Adam's prompted him to give both the punishment they deserved, which was and is common to all humankind. And, besides, how about the woman chosen above all others to redeem that sin? God never created any man (a man who was simply a man, that is) who could match that woman who was entirely a woman. Just you try finding me a man in all the annals and chronicles of ancient times, however wise and virtuous, whose merits stretch to the thousandth part of the rare excellencies and divine qualities of our Lady, the Queen of Heaven. I don't think you're going to have much luck there!"

"I must say I don't really know how to reply to that," said Lucretia.

"Do you really believe," Leonora said, "that men do not recognize our worth? In fact, they are quite aware of it, and, even though envy makes them reluctant to confess this in words, they cannot help revealing in their behavior a part of what they feel in their hearts. For anyone can see that when a man meets a woman in the street, or when he has some cause to talk to a woman, some hidden compulsion immediately urges him to pay homage to her and bow, humbling himself as her inferior. And similarly at church, or at banquets, women are always given the best places; and men behave with deference and respect toward women even of a much lower social status.[61] And

60. This defense of Eve appears to have originated in a work by Bernardo Spina of the 1540s: see Ruscelli 1552, 18v, where he congratulates Spina for being the first defender of women to attempt to defend Eve, rather than simply concede her guilt and attempt to counterbalance the slur by the example of the Virgin Mary. For an influential example of this latter, more conventional, strategy of defense, also drawn on by Corinna later in this same speech, see Castiglione 1994, 228 (3: 19).

61. The ingenious argument that the deference shown to women by men may be seen as a kind of involuntary acknowledgment of women's natural superiority is also found in Veronica Franco and Lucrezia Marinella (Marinella 1601, 24; Franco 1995, 149–50 [24, 103–11]). A possible source is the first of the Roman examples in *MSD*, 5, 2, 1 ("On Gratitude"), where it is recounted that in recognition of the part played by Coriolanus's mother in saving Rome from the ambitions of her son, the Roman Senate decreed that men should cede precedence to women in the streets and that women

where love is concerned, what can I say? Which woman, however low-born, is below men's notice? Which do they shrink from approaching? Is a man of the highest birth ashamed to consort with a peasant girl or a plebeian—with his own servant, even? It is because he senses that these women's natural superiority compensates for the low status Fortune has conferred on them. It's very different in the case of women: except in some completely exceptional freak cases, you never find a noblewoman falling in love with a man of low estate, and, moreover, it's rare even to find a woman loving someone (apart from her husband) of the same social status. And that's why everyone is so amazed when they hear of some transgression on the part of a woman: it's felt to be a strange and exceptional piece of news (I'm obviously excepting courtesans here), while in the case of men, no one takes any notice, because sin for them is such a matter of course and an everyday occurrence that is doesn't seem remarkable any more. In fact, men's corruption has reached such a point that when there is a man who is rather better than the others and does not share their bad habits, it is seen as a sign of unmanliness on his part and he is regarded as a fool. Indeed, many men would behave better if it were not for the pressure of custom, but, as things stand, they feel it would be shameful not to be as bad as or worse than their fellows."

"Well, that's the way it is," said Cornelia. "The good and the wise cannot live as they would any more; they have to behave badly in spite of themselves. It's like that story of the seven philosophers whose great wisdom allowed them to foresee an epidemic of madness that was about to fall on their city, and who agreed among themselves, without saying a word to anyone, to take certain preventive measures to ensure that they alone would remain sane.[62] Their idea was that once all the others had gone mad, it would be easy for them as wise men to take control of the madmen, and that their wisdom would allow them to become the lords of the city and seize everything for themselves. The plan was a bold one, their hopes infinite; they impatiently waited their moment. When the time arrived and everyone in the city suffered the mishap of losing their wits, out jumped these characters, who were sane and who recognized that their moment had come, and they strolled wisely into the midst of

---

should be allowed to wear purple robes and gold adornments, otherwise reserved for those in positions of power (another detail noted by both Franco and Marinella).

62. I have not been able to identify the source of this story.

their fellow citizens, who were all dancing and cavorting around and generally behaving like madmen, and signaled to them to calm down. But as soon as the madmen saw these people who weren't cavorting around like them, but instead soberly trying to command them—these people who weren't behaving in what they saw as a sane way—they concluded that they must be mad and turned on them with such fury, using their fists or sticks or stones or whatever came to hand, that the poor wise men found it wisest to leave their wisdom on one side and to dance and cavort around with all the others and behave like madmen, even though they weren't. And that's just the way that men behave: since most of them are chasing around madly after all kinds of ridiculous things, the few good men get jeered at. So, through bad example as much as anything else, they go from bad to worse, without there being anyone to reprimand them, because they are all tarred with the same brush."

"And who, precisely, would you expect to reprimand them when they do something wrong?" Cornelia said. "We women, perhaps, who are too meek to open our mouths in their presence? Or they themselves, who, as you say, are all up to their necks in it as well?"

"I remember reading," said Helena, "that in antiquity they used to punish women's transgressions extremely severely by law, while men went unpunished."[63]

"Well, the reason is obvious," replied Corinna. "Men may be wicked but they aren't stupid, and since it was they who were making the laws and enforcing them, they were hardly going to rule that they should be punished and women go free. And anyway, they made that law knowing that they would only rarely have to enforce it, since so few women went astray, whereas if they had wanted to punish men in the same manner, they would have had to kill them all, or most of them."

"Oh, come now," said Lucretia. "Surely we've said everything there is to say about these poor men?"

"Oh, anyone who wanted to could easily carry on," said Cornelia.

63. Fonte is perhaps thinking here of the legislation passed by Augustus which brought adultery under Roman criminal law for the first time. Although the Augustan laws did stipulate punishments for the male lovers of married women, as well as the women themselves, they were certainly anything but symmetrical: while men were entitled (and sometimes obliged) to punish or repudiate adulterous wives and daughters, no corresponding entitlement or obligation existed for women (Treggiari 1991, 277–98; Gardner 1986, 127–29).

"In fact, you'd never get to the end of it: the volumes would pile up, you'd wear out all known languages, and need to live as long as Methuselah or Nestor. All we've done is to point to a tiny fraction of men's baseness and iniquity, but even so it's enough to make you wonder how women can bear to so much as look at them, let alone love them."

"That's exactly what I was trying to say just now," said Lucretia.

"So you're all quite convinced by this fantasy of yours that, as men aren't capable of loving sincerely, they don't deserve to be loved in return?" said Virginia.

"We are indeed," said Cornelia. "But there's more to it than that. I've said before and I'll say again that even if a woman does find a man who is genuinely in love with her, unless he is her husband or in a position to marry her she should refuse to love him and should stay out of his way so as not to fall into those dangers and errors women fall into so often because of their innocence and goodness. That's what I've always said and I'm reaffirming it now."

"And what dangers are these?" said Virginia.

"I haven't told you yet," Corinna stepped in. "The dangers are these. A woman in love is in danger, whether she conquers her desire or is conquered by it. If she stands firm so as not to fall into error, what greater emotional turmoil can be imagined than the battle taking place within her and the anguish of knowing that she will never be able to fulfill her desire? Death would be a thousand times more welcome to her than continuing to live in such torment. But, then, if she lets herself be vanquished by her desire, won over by the flattery and pleading of her lover, you can very well imagine the dangers she is laying herself open to: her reputation is at stake, her life, and, gravest of all, her immortal soul. So, for all these reasons, women should avoid the love of men—though, as Cornelia has said, many find it hard, because they are so kind and good they cannot spurn men, however bad men are."

"Well, as far as that's concerned," said Virginia, 'you're quite right that we shouldn't fall in love with men if we can possibly help it, to avoid the two dangers you mentioned, even if we could find men who were virtuous and loved us sincerely. I'm not trying to contradict you on that. I just think there's more to say on the subject. One thing I don't want to let pass, in particular, is this idea that men in general are bad and that they don't love us genuinely, from the bottom of their hearts. Come now! Surely if they didn't love us, they wouldn't spend so much time and energy in courting various women from dawn to dusk, as we're always seeing?"

"Oh don't make me laugh," said Corinna. "You're such a baby! This courtship of yours is just a pastime for young men with nothing better to do. Haven't we talked enough about the kind of courtship that men go in for? Hasn't Cornelia already told you it's nothing but a hare hunt? Don't you remember the words of the Ferrarese poet?

> *Come segue la lepre il cacciatore*
> *Al monte, al bosco, a la campagna, al lito,*
> *Né stima poi che già presa la vede,*
> *E sol dietro a chi fugge affretta il piede.*

> Just as the hunter tracks the hare, through mountains,
> woods, fields, and shores, and then, when he catches her,
> loses all interest in her and is only interested in pursuing
> those that flee from him . . .[64]

And he goes on to compare young lovers to these hunters, and so on."

"Aha!" said Leonora. "I think our poor Virginia herself must have one of these young striplings chasing her—someone who, apart from her beauty, has heard she has a considerable dowry awaiting her and has set himself to tempting her innocence with the kind of flattery and feigned love we've been talking about. And because she's just a little girl still, she has fallen for the idea that this man is dying of love for her, and that's why she's claiming men really do love women."

"That's not true!" said Virginia, blushing a little. "That's not at all the reason why I said it. It's just that that's how things seem to me—or, at any rate, how things should be."

"But, as Cornelia said," replied Corinna, "it's not because they love us that they go in for all these displays of love and undying devotion; rather, it's because they desire us. So that in this case love is the offspring, desire the parent; or, in other words, love is the effect and desire the cause. And since taking away the cause means taking away the effect, that means that men love us for just as long as they

---

64. The lines are from Ariosto's *Orlando Furioso*, from a passage already alluded to earlier in the dialogue (see n. 40 above), in which the poet warns his women readers about the faithlessness of young men.

desire us and once desire, which is the cause of their vain love, has died in them (either because they have got what they wanted or because they have realized that they are not going to be able to get it), the love that is the effect of that cause dies at exactly the same time. But when *we* love, love is the cause and the father (as it were), desire the effect and the child. And just as the father can exist without a child and the cause without an effect, but not the child without the father or the effect without the cause, so in a man you can find desire without love but not love without desire, while in a woman you find love without desire but never desire without love."

"But perhaps," said Virginia, "the reason why men don't love us is that we don't deserve to be loved. I know you and Cornelia will claim that's not true, but you're not going to convince me unless you tell me your arguments and prove them with examples."

"Do you really think that's the reason?" replied Corinna. "We've already proved that on all counts—ability, dignity, goodness, and a thousand other things—we are their superiors and they our inferiors. So I don't see any reason why they shouldn't love us, except for the fact that, as I said before, men are by nature so cold and ungrateful that they cannot even be swayed by the influences of the heavens. Though another factor, as we were saying earlier, is their great envy of our merits: they are fully aware of our worth and they know themselves to be full of flaws that are absent in women. For where men have flaws, women have virtues; and, if you need proof, it's quite obvious that in women you find prudence and gentleness where men have anger, temperance where men have greed, humility in place of pride, continence in place of self-indulgence, peace in place of discord, love in place of hatred. In fact, to sum up, any given virtue of the soul and mind can be found to a greater degree in women than in men."

"What poor wretches men are," Cornelia exclaimed, "not to respect us as they should! We look after their households for them, their goods, their children, their lives—they're hopeless without us and incapable of getting anything right. Take away that small matter of their earning money and what use are they at all? What would they be like without women to look after them? (And with such devotion!) I suppose they'd rely on servants to run their households—and steal their money and reduce them to misery, as so often happens."

"It is we women," said Leonora, "who lighten men's burden of worries. When we take charge of household affairs (and we do so not in order to dominate our husbands, as many men claim, but simply in order to give them a quieter life), we take over a part of their work, overseeing the whole household. And it's certainly true that a man can never really find true domestic contentment and harmony without the fond companionship of a woman, whether she be a wife or a mother or a sister; without someone to look after him and take care of all his needs, and to share all the good times and the bad times with him. So it cannot be said with any truth that women are a source of harm in the world: on the contrary, they bring great benefits to the world with their wisdom, their virtue, and their goodness.

"And besides all that (and besides their physical beauty and grace) women have other merits that should give them a claim on men's love. There's our fortitude, for one thing—fortitude of mind *and* body, for if women do not bear arms, that isn't because of any deficiency on their part; rather, the fault lies with the way they were brought up. Because it's quite clear that those who have been trained in military discipline have turned out to excel in valor and skill, aided by that peculiarly feminine talent of quick thinking, which has often led them to outshine men in the field.[65] And, as proof, just think of Camilla, of Penthesilea, the inventor of battle-axes, of Hippolyta, Orithya, and all those other warlike women whose memory not even the history written by men has been able to suppress.[66] And where

65. This defense of women's capacity to excel at warfare, if given the proper training, takes on a particular significance when one considers how central a place arguments derived from women's supposed physical inferiority to men had within the Aristotelian tradition of misogynist thought. Fonte's arguments here are not original: defenders of women from the fifteenth century onward had used classical allusions to physically developed women, from the Amazons to the athletic female "guardians" of the fifth book of Plato's *Republic*, as evidence that contemporary women's physical weakness was the result of their upbringing rather than any innate deficiency. Over the same period, female warriors like Ariosto's Bradamante and Marfisa became popular figures in chivalric romance (see Tomalin 1982); and Fonte herself, in her romance, *Floridoro*, includes a female warrior, Risamante, whose prowess at arms is presented explicitly as evidence of women's suppressed potential.

66. Here Leonora initiates the second part of the "feminist" camp's response to Virginia's challenge to prove women's merits by "reason and example." The listing of examples from classical history and mythology was an essential element in most Renaissance defenses of women and, by the time Fonte was writing, two centuries of research on women's history had unearthed an impressive range of recondite anecdotal evidence. Camilla, a native Italian warrior princess, features in Virgil's mythological account of the founding of Rome in the *Aeneid*. The other figures named were from the legendary race of warrior women in Greek myth, the Amazons. Orithya was joint ruler of the Amazons at the time of their defeat by Hercules. Hippolyta, the sister of the other queen, Antiope, was taken to Athens by Theseus as a spoil of battle, provok-

letters are concerned—well, that's obvious: it was a woman, Carmenta, who first invented the alphabet, and poems are called *carmina* after her. And what shall I say of Sappho, who was counted among the sages of Athens? Or Corinna of Thebes, who outshone Pindar in eloquence? Or all those famous Roman women: Hortensia, Sulpicia, who dedicated the Temple to Chastity, Lucan's wife Bella, Pliny's Calpurnia, Laelia, Proba, Pythagoras's sister, Aristippus's daughter; or the Sibyls, to go further back; or all the others, who are innumerable?[67] And if women should be loved for their courage and for famous deeds, think of Judith's remarkable deed,[68] or Tomiris's revenge against

---

ing a retaliatory attack by the Amazons. Penthesilea was the successor to Orithya and Antiope, and was killed by Achilles while assisting Priam in the defense of Troy.

67. Fonte's rather perfunctory list of learned women of antiquity reproduces, with some errors and omissions, lists found in earlier defenders of women like Galeazzo Flavio Capra (1525) (see Capra 1988, 90–93). Carmenta, or Nicostrate, is a legendary figure of the prehistory of Rome: the mother (or, in other sources, the wife) of Evander, the exiled king of Arcadia, founder of a city that later became part of Rome. She was credited, among other things, with the invention of the Latin alphabet. Sappho is the famous Greek love poet (sixth century BC); Corinna, another, slightly earlier, Greek poet, of whom a few fragments remain. Hortensia was the daughter of the Roman orator Quintus Hortensius Hortalus (114–50 BC). During the period of the second Triumvirate, in a famous speech, she successfully pleaded the case of Roman women against a proposed measure of punitive taxation, earning Quintilian's later tribute that her father's eloquence seemed to breathe again in her words (Hallett 1984, 58–59). Sulpicia was a Roman poet of the Augustan age, some of whose love poetry is included in book 3 of Tibullus's work. Fonte appears to have confused her with an earlier figure of the same name, however: the Sulpicia mentioned in Pliny (*NH*, 7, 35, 120) and Valerius Maximus (*MSD*, 8, 15, 12) as having been elected to the honor of dedicating a temple to Venus Verticordia, in recognition of her chastity. Polla (not Bella) Argentaria was the wife of the poet Lucan. A poet herself, she helped her husband in his revision of the first three books of his *Pharsalia*, and was praised by Statius in his *Sylvae* as a model wife. Calpurnia was the wife of the younger Pliny, who praises her in his letters for her love of reading (especially her husband's works). Laelia, the daughter of the orator Gaius Laelius (consul, 140 BC), was praised for her eloquence by Cicero and Quintilian (Hallett 1984, 338). Little is known of the early Christian (fourth-century) poet [Falconia] Proba except that she wrote a poem made up of verses from Virgil, adapted to convey a Christian meaning, which won lavish praises from Boccaccio in his *On Famous Women* and was published well into the sixteenth century. Of the last-named figures (Greek, of course, rather than Roman, as Fonte states), Pythagoras's sister Themistoclea, supposedly a priestess at Delphi, is unfortunately an apocryphal figure, the result of a linguistic misunderstanding (Caujolle-Zaslawsky 1989, 350). Aristippus's daughter, Arete, was, by contrast, a historical figure, who studied philosophy under her father and ran his school after his death. The Sibyls, in Greek legend, were priestesses who dwelt in shrines and were consulted for their enigmatic prophecies. One, the Eritrean Sibyl, makes an appearance at the end of Fonte's *Le Feste*, published in 1582.

68. Judith is the only biblical heroine included in Fonte's list of famous women. The story of her deception and beheading of the enemy general Holofernes (told in the

Cyrus,[69] or Cleopatra's undaunted soul,[70] or the greatness of Semiramis,[71] of whom the poet says:

> *Ch'una treccia raccolta, e l'altra sparsa*
> *Corse alla Babilonica rovina.*

> With one tress bound and the other loose,
> She raced to the destruction of Babylon.

Or think of the wars and the prowess of Zenobia,[72] or that great
episode of the women of Aquileia, during the war against Maximinus,
when, faced by dire necessity, they cut off their hair and gave it to
their men to make bowstrings with which to defend themselves. And
the women of Carthage and Rome did the same thing on other occasions.[73] And then there are the women of Sparta, who, when their
men went to war, used to lace on their shields with the words, 'with

---

Apocryphal books of the Old Testament) was an immensely popular subject for
Renaissance writers and artists.

69. Tomiris or Tamiris was a legendary warrior queen of the Massagete, who fought
against Cyrus, King of Persia, to avenge his murder of her son. After defeating him in
battle, as the legend goes, she plunged Cyrus's severed head into a bucket of blood "to
slake his thirst."

70. Cleopatra (69–30 BC) is the famous last queen of Egypt, the ally and lover of Mark
Antony. In speaking of her "undaunted soul," Fonte may have in mind the celebrated
episode of her suicide after Antony's defeat by Octavian.

71. Semiramis was a perhaps legendary warrior queen of Assyria, of the thirteenth century BC: a successful military leader, best remembered, however, for her sexual excesses.
The lines quoted here, from Petrarch's *Triumph of Fame* (lines 104–5), recall a famous
anecdote associated with her: that being informed about an invasion while halfway
through having her hair dressed, she raced off to war with half her hair up and the rest
flowing over her shoulders (Boccaccio cites the episode in his *On Famous Women* as
striking evidence of how miraculously Semiramis succeeded in transcending the natural
vanity of her sex).

72. Zenobia, the last individual figure mentioned here, was another warrior queen, this
time a historical figure: she was Queen of Palmyra from 266 to 273 AD and fought
against the Romans. Chaste and learned as well as warriorlike, and eventually defeated
and reduced to genteel retirement in Rome, she proved a more congenial figure to
Renaissance defenders of women than the bloodthirsty Tomiris or the lustful
Semiramis, appearing, for example, as a speaker in Sir Thomas Elyot's *Defense of Good
Women* (1540).

73. The story of the sacrifice of the women of Aquileia (328 AD) derives from the
Roman historian Julius Capitolinus, as does the account of the similar sacrifice of the
women of Rome during the Gaulish siege of 390 BC. The source for the parallel
Carthaginian episode is Lucius Annaeus Florus (I, 31). From this point in the list of
examples of women's courage, as in her listing of learned women, Fonte appears to be
following a source deriving from Capra (see Capra 1988, 83–84).

them or in them,' meaning that they must return either victoriously alive or gloriously dead; and in this way, they inspired them to prefer victory or death to cowardly flight.[74] And then there are the Roman women whose great love of their country and desire to free it from the Gauls led them freely to give up all their riches and ornaments and give them to the nation—an action which prompted the Senate to give them the right to ride in chariots. It was the men of Rome who started a war by carrying off the Sabine women and it was the women who then restored the peace. And the part played by Coriolanus's mother, in persuading her son to give up his ill will toward his country, is no less famous.[75] The past—and the present[76]—hold countless other examples of magnanimity and patriotism among women: far too many to list them all now.

"But if another good reason to love people is because of the love they show us, then what can we say about the love women have displayed toward their male relatives? What about that story of Cimon's daughter who, when her imprisoned father was dying of starvation, kept him alive for a long time by surreptitiously feeding him on her visits with her own milk?[77] And what shall we say of Erigone who,

74. The proverbial austerity and patriotism of Spartan women, mentioned below in the text, is recorded in Plutarch's *Sayings of Spartan Women*, from which the exhortation cited by Fonte derives (Plutarch 1927–69, 3: 465 [241, 16]); see also *MSD*, 2, 7, Foreign Examples, 2).

75. Of these last Roman examples, the episode of the women of Rome giving up their jewelry to help defend the state against the Gauls (in 390 BC) is told by Diodorus Siculus (14, 116, 9). The story of the abduction of the Sabine women by the men of Rome forms part of the legendary prehistory of the city recounted by Livy in the first book of his history: see especially I, 13, 1–4, where the story is told of their courageous intervention to make peace in the battle between their enraged menfolk and their Roman abductors. The story (also legendary) of Gnaeus Marcius Coriolanus being persuaded out of his plan to attack Rome by his mother Veturia (or Volumnia) is recounted by Livy and Valerius Maximus (Hallett 1984, 41).

76. A striking feature of Fonte's listing of celebrated women, and one that differentiates it from many other such lists in Renaissance defenses of women, is its near-exclusive classical bias: no recent or contemporary examples are cited, and only one medieval one, which Fonte may well have remembered as classical, in any case. It should be noted, however, that the seventeenth-century defender of women Cristoforo Bronzini claimed in a work of 1625 (it is unclear on what evidence) that Fonte had intended to include in the work "some Trophies of past and present women," presumably left unfinished at her death (Bronzini 1625, 117).

77. This story, which became a popular subject in art, as an allegory of charity, is told by Valerius Maximus in his chapter on filial devotion (*MSD*, 5, 4, Foreign Examples, 1). The name of the father given there, however, is Mycon, rather than Cimon (the daughter's name is Pero). The confusion of names, found in many Renaissance—and some modern—sources is probably due to the fact that the name Cimon occurs in the

after searching long for her father, was finally alerted to the truth by her faithful dog, who dragged her over with its teeth to where his dead body lay? She was driven to despair by her grief and hanged herself on the tree under which his body was buried.[78] And what do you say to the daughters of Oedipus, King of Thebes—what patience they showed, what filial piety, in looking after their blind father in his misery, without ever leaving him, come what might?[79] And the filial devotion of Mestra is remarkable, as well: Mestra who let herself be sold many times by the famished Erysichthon and then, fleeing from the men who had bought her, returned spontaneously to her father so he could buy food for himself.[80] But think, by contrast, how cruel it was of a father to barter his daughter for his own needs."

"Oh, come on," said Helena. "He was forced into it by necessity: it wasn't any lack of affection on his part. And when his life was at stake, it wasn't such a terrible thing for him to take advantage of her filial piety and obligation in order to save his life."

"Well, many fathers wouldn't have done the same for their daughters, if *they* were dying," Cornelia retorted. "Many fathers who could have given their daughters a new life by marrying them to the men they loved have preferred to see them die of love."

"Don't make me laugh," said Lucretia. "I'd much rather be dying of love than of hunger, like Erysichthon!"

"So should I!" said Helena.

"Let's drop the subject," Cornelia continued. "Death is death, all

---

following anecdote (De Ceueleneer 1919, 182n).

78. Erigone, in Greek myth, was the daughter of Icarius, the first mortal to receive the gift of wine from Dionysius: an unenviable honor, since he was later murdered by some shepherds, whom he had unintentionally intoxicated and who suspected him of poisoning them. After her pitiful suicide, described here, Erigone was transformed into the constellation Virgo.

79. The daughters of Oedipus, the ill-fated king of Thebes, were Antigone and Ismene. After her father's self-blinding, Antigone accompanied him on his wanderings until his death at Colonus.

80. The bizarre myth alluded to here is told at length by Ovid (*Metamorphoses* 8, 738–878), who is hardly more sympathetic to the male protagonist of the story than Leonora is here. Erysichthon shows disrespect to the goddess Ceres and, in punishment, is afflicted by a ravening and insatiable hunger. Having sold all his goods to buy food, he sells his daughter Mestra as a slave, but she appeals to Neptune (who has previously seduced her) and he, taking pity on her, endows her with the gift of metamorphosis, which allows her to escape her new master. On her return to her father, he sells her again and again, under different human and animal forms, until finally, driven mad with hunger, he devours himself.

the same. But what about those fathers who have killed their daughters without mercy just because they were in love?"

"Are you saying that a father should put up with that kind of shame, in his own home?" asked Lucretia.

"No, I'm not saying that," replied Cornelia. "But the father should see to it, in some discreet way, that the lovers do not have the opportunity to meet (which is the prudent way to manage things, without causing scandal and setting everyone gossiping about one's private business). He should do everything in his power to dissuade his daughter from the affair, sending her away, threatening her—trying everything, in fact, short of the horrendous last resort of killing her. Because, apart from the inhumanity of such a course, it doesn't even remove her stain; on the contrary, it almost certainly results in the damnation of her soul, which is the gravest thing of all."

"The pagans didn't have too many scruples on that count," said Corinna. "Because when Pontius found that his daughter had been led astray by her tutor, he killed her without a second thought.[81] And Blandemo, Zeuxis's son, did the same. And I don't know whether Verginius deserved praise or blame for the fact that his first thought was not to kill the decemvir Claudius or himself but to slaughter his innocent daughter with his own hands."[82]

"So you're suggesting," said Lucretia, "that men in such cases should let reason be their guide, rather than passion."

"Yes," said Corinna. "And that they should follow the laws of nature: that is, treat others in the manner they would like others to treat them."

"You had such a lot to say in praise of women's devotion to their families," said Lucretia. "But what about the way in which Tullia

81. The figure in question is Pontius Aufidianus, a Roman knight. Valerius Maximus in his chapter on chastity (*MSD*, 6, 1, 3), praises him for his strength of character and resolve. I have not been able to identify the other figure mentioned here. It should be noted that Roman law in the Imperial age condoned the killing of an adulterous daughter by her father, with the proviso that he must have discovered her in the act and killed her lover at the same time (Treggiari 1991, 282–83).

82. Verginius is a semilegendary figure, a humble citizen of Rome (fifth century BC) who is said to have killed his daughter Verginia rather than have her succumb to the lust of the decemvir Appius Claudius Crassus Inrigillensis (see Hallett 1984, 119–20). Her death, like that of Lucretia, acquired political connotations for Roman historians, since both prompted uprisings against the political tyranny their seducers represented. Fonte's inclusion of Verginius in this list of cruel fathers is interesting, since most Renaissance sources, taking their cue from Livy and Valerius Maximus, tend to represent his action sympathetically, as necessary and honorable.

behaved toward her father, watching her father's dead body being trampled by horses and saying to those who reproached her that there was nothing so sweet as revenge on one's enemies?"[83]

"That's certainly true," replied Corinna. "But she was a freak of nature, a complete anomaly; and, anyway, as far as we know, she didn't actually have her father killed, even if after his death she was led by her anger into such a shocking act. But that one example is nothing in the face of the devotion women in general show toward their fathers, brothers, sons, husbands, and other relatives. Didn't Erigone, Orestes's sister, die from a broken heart after his death?[84] And how about Cassandra, Hector's sister?[85] And think what Intaphrenes's wife did to save her brother from Darius's hands! Darius had seized her husband, her children, and her brother, and she had persuaded him through her tears and entreaties to release one of the prisoners, whichever she wanted—and she left her husband and children, saving only her brother, saying that she could get another husband and other children, but never another brother, since her parents were already dead.[86] And there are countless others I could mention, if there were time.

"But, looking at the other side, how can we begin to describe the cruelty brothers have shown toward their sisters? I'm not talking about

83. Tullia was the daughter of Servius Tullius, one of the legendary kings of early Rome, and wife of his successor, Tarquin the Proud. After her father was ousted (in a conspiracy to which she was party) and assassinated in the street, Tullia had her charioteer run over his dead body. Her story is told by Livy in the first book of his *History*, and Valerius Maximus gives her pride of place in his chapter on wrongful words and wicked deeds (*MSD*, 9, 11).

84. Erigone was the daughter of Aegisthus and Clytemnestra and thus half sister to Orestes. Legends conflict concerning their relationship: some classical sources have her thirsting for revenge after her parents' murder and committing suicide through frustration when Orestes was acquitted; others have Orestes harboring murderous designs against her, which are foiled by Artemis's intervention; still others present the siblings as marrying and producing a son, Penthilus (Grimal 1986, 150). It seems probable that Fonte's variant of the story results from a contamination between the first and the third of these versions, whether due to her or some intermediate source.

85. Cassandra was the daughter of King Priam of Troy and sister to the Trojan hero Hector. In speaking of her sisterly devotion, Leonora may be thinking of the episode in book 24 of the *Iliad*, in which Cassandra, watching from the rooftops of Troy, is the first to see Priam returning from the Greek camp with Hector's corpse.

86. The anecdote derives from the third books of Herodotus's history. Intaphrenes was a Persian nobleman of the fifth century BC, who, along with Darius and five others, conspired to regain the Persian throne from the usurper Smerdis. After Darius had assumed the throne, he threw his former companion into prison under suspicion of treachery, but was sufficiently moved by the grief of Intaphrenes' wife to grant her the dubious privilege described here.

their appropriating their sisters' worldly goods (that, for them, amounts to a positive act of courtesy); I'm talking about the many brothers who have gone so far as wretchedly killing their sisters. What do you say to Ptolemy, who killed his sister Eurydice (who was also his wife) in order to take a harlot as his lover?[87] Or Cambyses, who also killed a sister he had taken as his wife, just because she was weeping over the death of another brother whom he had had killed?[88] Not to mention the pitiful case of the sister of the Horatii, who was mourning the death of her husband, one of the Curiatii killed by her brothers, when these same brothers, in their anger, cruelly murdered their sister as well.[89] And what a cruel trick it was that Ptolemy Ceraunus played on his sister Arsinoë! He pretended to marry her, swore undying fidelity to her—and then killed her children and seized the kingdom from her.[90] I'm just listing these few examples of famous and prominent individuals, because historians do not record the countless examples of humbler folk, but you can imagine that cases like these happen every day and remain buried in the oblivion of time.

"And then, what shall we say of the love mothers show for their sons? Rutilia was happy to leave behind the comforts of her homeland to follow her son when he was banished, saying that she would prefer to suffer a long exile than to be without him.[91] And the strength of Tomiris's love for her son is shown by the great revenge she later took

87. This may be Ptolemy I of Egypt (d. 283 BC), who repudiated (but did not kill) his wife Eurydice for a young widow (hardly a "harlot"), Berenice, who then became his queen (Macurdy 1932, 102–3).

88. Cambyses, king of Egypt and son of Cyrus the Great, was notorious for his tyranny and excesses. The source for this anecdote is Herodotus, 3, 32.

89. In Roman legend, Horatia was killed by her sole surviving brother (not brothers, as Fonte states here) after she had publicly mourned for her fiancé, one of the three enemy champions whom her brothers had killed in a six-man combat intended to settle the dispute between Rome and Alba (Livy, 1, 24–26). Roman historians tend to present the sororicide in a positive light, stressing Horatia's father's public vindication of his son (Hallett 1984, 114–15).

90. The figure referred to here is Arsinoë II Philadelphos (c. 316–270 AD), who became queen of Egypt by her third marriage, to her brother, Ptolemy II. The Ptolemy Ceraunus of the text was her second husband and a half brother. The story of Ceraunus's treachery and Arsinoë's children's death is recounted with great pathos by Justin in his epitome of Pompeius Trogus, 24, 1–3 (though it should perhaps be noted, as a counterbalance, that Arsinoë was not a stranger to this kind of treachery herself, having been implicated in the death of her first husband's son [see Burstein 1982]).

91. Rutilia was the mother of Gaius Aurelius Cotta, who was exiled in 91 BC but returned with Sulla in 82 and was consul in 75. Seneca praises her courage and maternal devotion in his consolatory letter to his mother Helvia (16, 7).

on Cyrus. Agrippina's love for Nero, as well, can hardly be denied, for, when she heard from the oracle that her son would be emperor, but would kill his mother, she said, 'Let him kill me, then, as long as he becomes emperor'—and he fulfilled the prophecy.[92] And Nero was not alone in this cruelty, for we also read of Antipater that he killed his mother and others of his family.[93] Aristobulus, son of Hyrcanus, killed his mother;[94] and Alcmaeon,[95] and Orestes."[96]

"Oh, come on!" Lucretia interjected. "Orestes acted quite rightly—she was a shameless woman."

"I'm not saying he was in the wrong," said Corinna, "but I can assure you that men are swayed more by their natural irascibility and cruelty than by any real zeal for honor, because if the latter were their real motive, then they would first make sure not to do anything

92. Nero's mother was Agrippina the Younger (15–59 AD), daughter of Germanicus and wife of (among others) Claudius. In murdering her, Nero was rather following in her footsteps, since she herself had murdered at least one husband. The anecdote recounted here derives from Tacitus.

93. Antipater (d. 294 BC) was the son of Cassander, king of Macedonia and Thessalonica, sister of Alexander the Great. After the deaths, in close succession, of his father and elder brother, he fought for the succession with another brother, Alexander, killing his mother in the course of this feud on the suspicion that she favored his brother.

94. The story of Aristobulus I, King of Judea (d. 103 BC), resembles that of Antipater in the previous example, in that both killed their mothers in the course of a struggle for the throne. Aristobulus achieved power after his father's death by imprisoning all his brothers except one, whom he later killed; when his mother challenged his authority, he imprisoned her too and left her to starve to death in a dungeon. The source is Josephus in his *Jewish Antiquities*, 13, 302, though it is likely that Fonte drew her knowledge of this, and perhaps others of her more obscure historical anecdotes from her friend and biographer, Giovanni Niccolò Doglioni, who is likely, at the time of her composition of *The Worth of Women*, to have been engaged on research for his *Compendio historico universale*, published in Venice in 1594 (see, for example, on Aristobolus, Doglioni 1594, 91–92).

95. With this example, Corinna moves on to less sure moral ground (as earlier, with the example of Agrippina). Alcmaeon was the elder son of the soothsayer Amphiaraus, who was driven to the war against Thebes against his will by his scheming wife, Eriphyle, who had allowed herself to be bribed by the gift of Harmonia's divinely crafted necklace. Eriphyle was later corrupted again into inducing her son to lead a second expedition against Thebes, but on his return, he slew her, honoring a request of his dead father.

96. The story of Orestes' murder of his mother Clytemnestra and her lover Aegisthus in revenge for their murder of his father, Agamemnon, the victor of Troy, is one of the most famous of Greek myths. As Lucretia is quick to point out in the text, the example is a rather equivocal one; in fact, after being hounded by the Furies, Orestes was ultimately acquitted of his crime in Athens.

dishonorable themselves and then worry about punishing others. And if you want proof, what had those other poor mothers been guilty of? Yet their sons were still not ashamed to kill them, just as other men are guilty of other excesses; but men rely on their sheer shamelessness to disguise their faults, whereas women's faults are magnified by the shame they feel.

"But all that we have been talking about is nothing to the heart-wrenching love that wives feel for their husbands. Think of Evadne, who after Capaneus's death threw herself into the flames and ended her life on the funeral pyre where her husband's dead body was burning.[97] And who was it who saved the life of Admetus, King of Thessalia, who was stricken by a grave infirmity and heard from the oracle that he could recover only if another died in his place? Did his brothers step forward to save him? His friends, perhaps? His servants? No one did, except his dear and faithful wife Alcestis.[98] And what shall I say of Hypsicratea, who followed Mithridates into the fierce wars posing as his serving man?[99] And Pantheus's wife did the same, as did Cleombrotus's and Lentulus's.[100] Panthea, on the death of her husband, whom she had urged to go to the wars, felt that she had been the cause of his death and, in her great misery and wretchedness, put an end to her own life.[101] Artemisia, when her husband

97. Capaneus was one of the seven legendary Greek kings whose assault on the city of Thebes is described in Statius's *Thebaid*; he died during the attack, struck down by a thunderbolt after defying Jupiter. Evadne's suicide after her husband's death is recounted at *Thebaid*, 12, 800–802.

98. The story of the self-sacrifice of Alcestis, daughter of Pelias, king of Iolcus, is recounted most famously by Euripides in the tragedy of that name.

99. The devotion of Hypsicratea, the wife (or, in other sources, a concubine) of Mithridates VI, King of Pontus (120–63 BC), is described in admiring tones by Valerius Maximus in his chapter on conjugal love (*MSD*, 4, 6, Foreign Examples, 2).

100. The wife of Pantheus, a general of Cleomenes III, King of Sparta (third century BC), was executed by her husband's political enemies after his death (Plutarch, *Life of Cleomenes*, 38). Plutarch praises her courage and tells, in a pathetic aside, how, as a young bride, she had been forbidden by her parents to accompany her husband to Egypt, but had procured herself a horse and some money and run away to join him. The story of Cleombrotus's wife, Chilonis, derives from the same source (*Life of Cleomenes*, 17–18): the daughter of an earlier king of Sparta, Leonidas, she successfully pleaded for her husband's life when he had been condemned for usurping her father's kingdom and insisted on accompanying him into exile, despite her father's pleas that she stay. The third figure mentioned here, Sulpicia (first century BC), disobeyed her mother's orders and disguised herself as a man to follow her exiled husband Lentulus Cruscellion into exile in Sicily. Her story is included by Valerius Maximus among his examples of faithful wives (*MSD*, 6, 7, 3).

101. The story of Panthea, the beautiful and loyal wife of Cyrus's general Abradatas, is

died, took his ashes and wept so copiously that his remains were mixed with the water of her tears; and she sipped the mixture until she had drunk all his ashes and at the same moment her life failed.[102] Oenone, whom Paris had abandoned for Helen, on seeing her husband dead, shortly afterward died of grief.[103] And what of Porcia, Brutus's wife, who, after her husband's death, was deprived of any instruments with which she might injure herself, yet still managed to kill herself by swallowing burning coals?[104] And Julia, Pompey's wife, on seeing his clothes drenched in blood and fearing for his life, was so affected that she miscarried and died immediately afterward.[105] I shall not repeat the stories of Laodomia, Polyxena, and others, who did not wish to survive their husbands' deaths;[106] as well as those of the countless wives who were their husbands' companions in their

---

told in Xenophon's *Cyropaedia*. The account of her suicide (an event so moving that three eunuchs in her entourage were impelled to follow suit) can be found at book 7, 3, 15.

102. Artemisia was the Queen of Caria in Asia Minor (d. 350 BC), famed for her devotion to the memory of her dead husband, Mausulus, to whom she erected a celebrated monumental tomb, the Mausoleum. Fonte's mention of her suicide is perplexing, but it may be a result of her misremembering the detail relayed by Valerius Maximus (*MSD*, 4, 6, Foreign Example, 1), that Artemisia drank her husband's ashes in order to convert herself into a "living tomb."

103. Oenone, in Greek mythology, was a river nymph and Paris's lover before he fell in love with Helen. Wounded at Troy, Paris called on Oenone, who was famed for her knowledge of herbal medicine, for help. Having initially rejected his plea, she relented and went in search of him, only to find him dead, whereupon she killed herself by throwing herself on his funeral pyre.

104. Porcia was the daughter of Cato the Younger and the wife of Marcus Junius Brutus, Julius Caesar's assassin. Her "virile" and uncompromising courage was testified, besides this story of her suicide (queried by Plutarch), by the famous anecdote of her wounding herself to demonstrate to her husband during the conspiracy against Caesar that she was worthy of being let into his confidence (see Hallett 1984, 57–58).

105. Julia was the daughter of Julius Caesar and Cornelia, daughter of the consul Cinna. She was married to Pompey in 59 BC and died in childbirth five years later. The story of her miscarriage and death in horror at the false report that her husband was dead is included by Valerius Maximus among his examples of conjugal devotion (*MSD*, 4, 6), along with that of Porcia's suicide.

106. Laodomia was the young bride of Protesilaus, the first Greek hero to be killed at Troy. One version of her story has her beg the gods to allow her to restore her husband to her for three hours, at the end of which, losing him again to Hades, she killed herself. Polyxena was the daughter of Priam, King of Troy, loved by Achilles and sacrificed on his funeral pyre after his death. The version of her story referred to here, in which she reciprocates Achilles' love and throws herself willingly into the flames, is an obscure one (though it is recorded in some Renaissance editions of Philostratus's *Imagines*); far more commonly, Polyxena's sacrifice is represented as an involuntary act, forced on her by Achilles' Greek comrades after his ghost has requested it in a dream.

travails and exiles, and who remained utterly loyal and devoted to them even at their death, because I know full well that you are as well acquainted with them as I am. And then, finally, there's the example of those Indian women who, after their husband's death (since their custom was for a single husband to have several wives), would fight among themselves to establish which of them had been the favorite, and the winner would happily burn herself to death alongside her husband."[107]

"You haven't mentioned those women in Sparta," said Cornelia, "who, when their husbands were in prison, obtained permission from the enemy to visit their men and then removed their feminine clothes and dressed their men in them, remaining in the prison themselves to be killed as a punishment while they sent their men out of danger."[108]

"And then there were those other women," added Lucretia, "whose city was captured and who obtained permission from the enemy to leave in safety with all the possessions they could carry with them. And, leaving everything else behind them, they carried away their husbands or fathers or children or brothers, leaving their homeland with all their possessions in prey to the enemy.[109] There are countless other examples of our love for our husbands, but it would be superfluous to tell you them all."

"It's men who should be told them," said Leonora.

"Oh, they know them well enough," added Corinna. "They just pretend not to. And then, on the other side, think of how many husbands have treated their wives badly (and still do). It's such a common, everyday occurrence that it's unnecessary to recite examples of it: they're almost all the same. And lovers—well, I scarcely need to tell you about them, for there have been only too many women who have suffered as a result of their love for some man and who have eventually been tricked by him, betrayed and abandoned. But enough

107. The custom in India of wives immolating themselves on their husbands' funeral pyres is reported by Valerius Maximus in his chapter on foreign customs (MSD, 2, 6, 14).

108. The story is told by Plutarch in his collection of exempla of female virtue and by Valerius Maximus, in his chapter on conjugal love (MSD, 4, 6, Foreign Example, 3).

109. This is the only instance in Fonte's list of a postclassical exemplum, though the vagueness of her reference suggests that she may not have remembered its provenance. The city in question is Weinsberg, near Heilbronn in Germany, besieged by Conrad III shortly after his election as king in 1138. The story was frequently included in lists of exempla of women's courage, though Fonte could also have heard it from Doglioni, who includes it in his Compendio historico universale of 1594 (Doglioni 1594, 289–90).

of this—if women deserve to be loved for their chastity, then the case is quite clear, and there's no need for me to say any more than what has already been said about women's constancy. So I shan't go into the thousand examples of chaste women of antiquity, Christian and pagan; nor shall I recall the episodes of Lucretia, Polyxena, Dido, Zenobia, and the German girls,[110] nor all the others historians mention. And if kindness and tenderness are enough to merit love, it is well known that women are incapable of hating anyone, however greatly they have offended them, and that a single good word is enough to make them forget all the abuses they have suffered.

"So I'm not sure, my dear Virginia, what remaining cause men can possibly have for not loving us, for we have every claim on their love. And if I wanted to prove this more clearly, I would need the pen of an angel rather than a mere mortal, for the merits of women are infinite, and the blessings they bring to the other creatures of the world. For the world would be in a sorry state if it were not for women: it would be stripped of all happiness and beauty, and there would be no respite from the miseries of life. And since women are a source of such honor and consolation, the Lord ensures that they are born in greater numbers than men; and for the same reason, when a daughter is born, there should be the most profound rejoicing across the whole family. But, on the contrary, when a father is told that his child is a girl, he is put out and dismayed, and gets angry with his wife.[111] In fact, there are endless husbands who make their wives' lives a misery over this, as though the wives alone were responsible and they had noth-

---

110. Lucretia, one of the most lastingly famous of Roman heroines, killed herself from shame after being raped by Sextus Tarquinius, thus indirectly prompting the revolt that led to the establishment of the Republic in Rome (Hallett 1984, 112–14). The story of Dido, Queen of Carthage, is best known, of course, in its Virgilian version, in which the widowed queen betrays the memory of her dead husband, Sichaeus, carried away by her passion for Aeneas, and kills herself from grief and shame when the latter abandons her. An alternative (and older) version of the story, however, which enjoyed considerable currency in antiquity and the Renaissance, has Dido as a faithful widow, who kills herself to escape a remarriage that is being forced on her. Zenobia was so devoted to chastity, according to Boccaccio, that she not only remained faithful to her husband's memory after his death, but, even in marriage, consented to sex only for the end of procreation. Valerius Maximus, in his chapter exemplifying chastity (*MSD*, 6, 1, Foreign Example, 3) recounts how the wives of the Germans conquered by Marius (consul in 107, 104–1, and 86 BC) pleaded with the victor to be allowed to join the temple of the Vestals in Rome and killed themselves when refused this request.

111. Disappointment at the birth of a daughter is, of course, by no means an experience limited to Venice in this period, but there is reason to think that it may have been particularly acute at a time of dramatic inflation in dowries (see Davis 1975, 106–11; Cowan 1986, 148–49).

ing to do with it; and they want nothing to do with their daughters. What malice there is in all this! Men should be delighted at the birth of a daughter, who will grow up meek and quiet and, in many cases, look after them and their households with devotion and love, but instead they long for the birth of males, who, when they grow up, will squander their money and swagger around looking for trouble, in constant danger of getting killed or killing others and being sent into exile—sons who will gamble or marry some unsuitable woman, or who are so eager to be the head of the household and to be free to squander its resources at will that they long for their father's death and cannot wait to see him out from under their feet. These, in the main, are the delights, joys, and pleasures that result from male offspring, as we can see every day from experience. It's completely different with daughters, who give no trouble at all: all their fathers have to do is provide a dowry for them to buy themselves a husband, so they have every reason to be grateful to their daughters, even though in practice the opposite occurs."

"These days," said Leonora. "[. . .]:[112] that's why they say the world belongs to the brash."

"That's not true," said Helena. "Dowries are paid to husbands because when a man marries, he is shouldering a great burden; and men who are not rich could not maintain a household without the subsidy of a dowry."

"You've got it all wrong," Corinna retorted. "On the contrary, the woman when she marries has to take on the expense of children and other worries, she's more in need of acquiring money than giving it away. Because if she were alone, without a husband, she could live like a queen on her dowry (more or less so, of course, according to her social position). But when she takes a husband, especially if he's poor, as is often the case, what exactly does she gain from it, except that instead of being her own mistress and the mistress of her own money, she becomes a slave, and loses her liberty and, along with her liberty, her control over her own property, surrendering all she has to the man who has bought her, and putting everything in his hands— so that he can run through the lot in a week?[113] Look what a good

112. The text is obscure here (*chi diè* [= *diede*] *da far comandar*) and may be corrupt. The sense may be "it's a seller's market" [for husbands].

113. Corinna's speech interestingly reflects the frustration some women must have felt at a system that made married women the nominal owners of often very large sums of money, without giving them any effective control over this wealth, at least for the duration of their marriage. A woman's dowry, in Venetian law, corresponded to her share

deal marriage is for women! They lose their property, lose themselves, and get nothing in return, except children to trouble them and the rule of a man, who orders them about at his will."

"It would be much better for most of them," said Leonora, "if, instead of taking a husband, they just bought a nice pig for themselves every Carnival, which would fatten them up and keep them in grease rather than keeping them in grief."

"That's enough of that!" said Corinna. "Even if it were just the case that dowries didn't have to be given to men and that men gave dowries to women instead, then marriage would be a little more tolerable. Though they would still be getting the best out of the bargain, because for a very small outlay they would be getting a great return: the treasure of the sweet companionship and true love of a dear wife. And that should be a sufficient dowry for them, since they have so much more than we do, anyway."

"But surely it would not be much of an honor for us to receive a dowry from them," Cornelia said. "Women have too much sense of their dignity ever to deign to be bought by men. And besides, we are like jewels so precious as to be beyond price."

"There's not much that I know," Lucretia said. "But one thing I have always heard people say is: 'If you want to make a man wise, give him a wife.' Which is as much as to say, saddle him with a weight, a burden, a trial, that will take up all his time and interfere with all his pleasures and turn everything sour for him. When a man takes a wife, he can wave farewell to the good times."

"You've got it completely wrong, Lucretia," said Corinna. "Don't try to twist things around. Do you know why people say: 'If you want to give a man wisdom, give him a wife'? It's not at all for the reason you said. On the contrary, it means that when a man takes as his companion a wise, sensible, virtuous, sweet, and loving woman, he must, whether he like it or not, turn his previously wayward and perverse passions onto a better path and return to the fold of reason. He will feel compelled to, as I say, both because of the new love he will

---

of her father's inheritance and was something to which she had a legal entitlement (Cowan 1986, 133; Chojnacki 1975, 575). On her marriage, the dowry was paid to her husband, who retained control of it for his lifetime, though he had the right to use only the interest, not the capital, which, on his death, reverted to his widow (Chojnacki, 1988). It is interesting to note in this context that Fonte's own husband appears—most unusually—to have waived his right to control of her dowry during her lifetime (see above, p. 37, n. 19).

naturally feel for his bride and because of the good example of decent and sensible behavior his wife will place before his eyes."

"Imagine a carriage drawn by two horses," said Leonora, "one noble, handsome, well-trained, and docile to the bit, going steadily down the right path; the other moody, restless, fiery, capricious, and given to going astray, always in danger of finishing up in a ditch somewhere with a broken neck, if it were not for the influence of the good horse beside it, pulling it back onto the straight and narrow.[114] And that's the ill service wives perform for their husbands in marriage: they drag them off the path of evil and onto the path of good."

"How blind they are! How misled!" added Cornelia. "Women are sent to them by the heavens as an oracle, a consolation, and a glory (quite an undeserved one); and they act like that cockerel who found a jewel in the dirt and ignored it because he didn't know what to do with it and instead rooted around after some disgusting piece of filth, recognizing his natural diet.[115] If men have no respect for the most excellent creature in the world, then what will they respect? No other created thing is the equal of woman—not even man, as men themselves must needs confess."

"And what's more," said Corinna, "women's worth is so great that they are prized even in hell. For it is said that Pythagoras, when he descended to hell, found many souls suffering great torments there who turned out to be those of men who had refused to marry when they were alive.[116] When Menedemus was asked whether it was the act of a wise man to marry, he replied: 'Do I seem like a wise man to you?'; and, when the other replied: 'What are you saying? The wisest of them all!' he replied: 'Well, *I* am married.'[117] And Diogenes said that any man who dared to harm so much as one hair on the head of his wife deserved to be put to death in the cruelest possible man-

---

114. The imagery here probably derives from the famous allegory of the soul in Plato's *Phaedrus*, 246b and 253c–254e (Plato 1961, 493 and 499–500).

115. The fable of the cock and the jewel is from the beginning of the collection by Aesop, where it serves as a warning to readers incapable of recognizing the value of what is to come.

116. Many strange legends surrounded the life of the sixth-century (BC) Greek philosopher Pythagoras. Fonte may be thinking here of a passage in Diogenes Laertius (*LP*, 8, 21), in which the story is reported that Pythagoras visited Hades and saw, among other damned souls, those of men who had been unfaithful to their wives.

117. Menedemus of Eretria was a Greek philosopher (c. 339–265 BC), known for his pithy and caustic style. This riposte is recorded by Diogenes Laertius (*LP*, 2, 129).

ner.[118] And the elder Cato considered good, loyal husbands to be as deserving of praise as the most eminent senators, while those who beat their wives he judged to be as wicked and impious as men who desecrated temples or other sacred things."[119]

"You're right," said the Queen. "Men are completely wrong when they claim such superiority over us and refuse to recognize our great worth, when ultimately a man without a woman is like a fly without a head. And while we're on the subject, I remember going to the houses of various male relatives and friends of mine, who were unmarried. You'd think you were going into a workhouse: they were so filthy and messy, with everything lying around all over the place, looking less like a gentleman's residence than a rag-and-bone man's shop."

"Just think," said Corinna, "if men could have heard what we've been saying about them, how many much worse things they'd say about us in return. Because men will never put up with being outdone in malice (though it hardly counts as malice on our part to speak the truth)."

"They'd probably write some contemptuous book about women as a reply," said Lucretia.

"Oh, they wouldn't be doing anything they haven't already done a thousand times," said Corinna. "I can tell you, men haven't been sitting around waiting for us to attack them."

"Yes, we can hardly aspire to come up with anything as old and tired as those arguments they keep churning out against us, without a shred of truth in them," said Leonora.

"Oh, as to that," said Corinna, "let them go ahead and keep conjuring up these groundless chimeras and fantasies, which aren't worth the paper they're written on and which I'm certainly not going to bother reading. But that kind of pigheadedness just brings shame on them, not honor, and it's not something to be taken seriously, especially since what's behind it all is obviously just the great envy they feel for women (which is also, as I was saying earlier, the explanation for why they can't bring themselves to love us sincerely)."

"Oh come now!" said Lucretia. "If men are as bad as you've been

118. Diogenes (fourth century BC), was a Greek philosopher and founder of the Cynic sect. I have been unable to trace the source of the comment quoted here by Fonte, which contrasts oddly with the caustic and often misogynist tone of most of his recorded remarks.

119. Like Diogenes, the Roman statesman Marcus Porcius Cato (234–149 BC) was not famed for his positive attitude to women. The remark quoted here is, however, reported by Plutarch in his *Life of Cato the Elder*, 20, 2.

insisting today, then why are we still inclined to love them? What is it that leads us to yield up our hearts to them and offer ourselves to them as willing slaves for life?"

Corinna was on the point of replying to this when the Queen stepped in, and said, "I can tell that you two are launching off on a debate that isn't going to be settled in a hurry. But since I can see that the sun is now leaving us to go and give light to the other hemisphere, I feel we should call it a day and not sit around here in the open air keeping company with the glowworms. And so, as your Queen, I order you to postpone your debate until tomorrow, when Corinna must undertake to answer Lucretia's question and to cover all the ground we have not been able to cover today."

As the Queen spoke, she got to her feet and made as if to stir up and rouse the others, who had been so absorbed in the conversation as to be hardly aware that evening was upon them. There was some discussion about where they should meet the following day, but Leonora said, "What are you saying? We have started our conversation here, and it is here that we must finish it. Indeed, so that we can get off to an early start, I invite you, beg you, and *order* you (if I may) to come around for breakfast tomorrow morning. That way, we'll have more time for talking, and you'll have more time to make the most of my garden, as well, which you've barely had a chance to enjoy today."

And she insisted so much that the others, overcome by her courtesy, all promised to return the following day. And then, after a brief wander in the shade and cool of the trees, they all took leave of one another and set off from Leonora's house, with the intention, as agreed, of returning the following morning to complete their interrupted debate.

Second Day

The fresh, rosy dawn had already made her appearance at the windows of the East and the rest of the sky was white and blue, bathed in the purest of light: a sign to mortals of a clear and radiant day to come. So Adriana and her daughter, and the other women in their own houses, having risen and dressed in happy anticipation, and performed their usual devotions, all climbed into their gondolas and headed for Leonora's house, which they all reached at almost the same time. For intent as they were on making the most of the garden which they had barely glimpsed the previous day, they had decided that this was the best time of the day to see it. So, when Leonora had greeted them with her usual affectionate courtesy, the Queen said to her:

"So, Leonora, you must be impressed at how well we have kept yesterday's promise. We promised to come and have breakfast with you, but in fact we've arrived almost in time to join you in bed: if we'd come a few minutes earlier, I'm sure we'd have found you still asleep."

"If you had come earlier," said Leonora, "you would have interrupted a strange dream I was having this morning—just around dawn, in fact. I dreamed (perhaps because of our conversation yesterday evening) that I was fighting hand to hand with some of those dreadful men of yours, and that I was wreaking havoc on them and giving no quarter, hacking them to pieces and massacring so many that they were all put to flight. There was so much noise that I woke up, terrified, to find that it was already day—and then I realized that all this racket had been caused by a battle between my little cat and a troop of valiant mice, of which she had made mincemeat, so that my room, when I woke, was full of blood and corpses. So that explained my dream."

The other women laughed at this ridiculous story, and Virginia said, "It would have been better if we had stayed with you yesterday, and then you wouldn't have had to go through all that bother. Because I'm sure, if we had, you'd have had so little chance to sleep that you wouldn't have had the chance to perform all these amazing feats in your dream and show such prowess and valor against those poor men; and nor would your cat have had cause for her real battle with the mice."

"It's certainly true that if we'd stayed here last night, there'd have been no need to carry on today," said Cornelia. "We'd have carried on chattering away about what we were talking about yesterday, and we wouldn't have slept a wink, so we'd have finished today's conversation already overnight."

"Wouldn't we just!" said Leonora.

"Well, do you know why we've come over to invade you so early?" said the Queen. "We want to take advantage of the cool of the morning to wander around your garden for a while."

"Quite right," said Leonora. "You've chosen just the moment to enjoy it, because the sun is still not too strong. Let's go! We can pick some figs and plums, and the grapes are starting to ripen as well."

So she led them into the garden and left them to wander around and enjoy themselves there for as long as they wanted, while she devoted herself to organizing breakfast. And when she had everything set out and was sure that nothing was lacking, she summoned the noble company and they all merrily sat down at the table. After they had eaten their fill, laughing and joking, they went back into the lovely garden. They settled themselves, by order of the Queen, in the same place as the day before, though much earlier in the day, and Corinna started speaking.

"The question you put to me yesterday, Lucretia, was a very important one. But don't go thinking that I've spent the night preparing my response. I shouldn't want to lose sleep over such a trivial thing, especially since the question is so easily resolved; in fact, if we'd had enough time for it yesterday and the Queen had permitted it, I'd have settled the issue for you yesterday evening. Your question was why it should be that, even though men are a thoroughly bad lot, as we proved in so many different ways, many women—decent, sensible women—still love them very deeply. My reply is that there are three different causes at work here. We need to make a distinction first between the different manners in which women may love men. A first case is when their love is sensual in nature and they are enticed by that love into committing illicit acts. The root cause in cases like this is women's naïveté and their wish to satisfy the desires of the men they love: a weakness which is the only real defect of our sex (though it is not one that afflicts every woman—and in any case you can't really complain about it, as only God is without flaws. And we've already talked so much about this one defect, found only in certain women, that there's no need to say any more). Women in this situation love men even though they know them to be unworthy of their love. For at the beginning of their acquaintance, the men concerned probably pretended to be kind and loving (we've already noted this tendency of theirs), and even when the women discovered over time that the contrary was true, their love had already become so much a part of their life that they could not tear themselves away from it. For you all know the proverb:

Piaga per allentar d'arco non sana.

An arrow wound does not heal when the bow is
slackened.[1]

"But even in the case of family affection or friendship, where sexual attraction is not involved, women may be fully aware of the evil nature of the men they love, without ceasing to cherish and care for them. And the cause in this case is women's overwhelming natural charity and goodness, which can be compared to that divine mercy which lavishes love and concern on all creatures, however much they may offend it and however little they return its love.

"Finally, apart from these natural causes, many women's love, whether sensual or affectionate, proceeds from the influence of the stars. Many women are quite conscious of men's unworthiness and ingratitude, and aware that they are throwing away their time and energies foolishly on them, so that they would be all too happy to give up their perverse habit of love, and yet they still find themselves disposed to love, through the force of astral influence, which contributes more than any other factor toward both the inception and

1. The "proverb" is in fact the last line of a famous sonnet of Petrarch's (*RS*, 90), lamenting that his painful love for Laura shows no sign of easing as she ages.

the continuance of amorous passion. And even though it is said, quite correctly, that the heavens can influence but not compel us, it is not so certain that we should place an absolute and unquestioning faith in this axiom, where the case of love is concerned. Because, to tell the truth, we can't be sure about how things happen in this world; there's no certainty about it. Though, as I have said, as rational beings, we can avoid many evils and direct ourselves to the good by the exercise of prudence and virtue, whatever our natural inclination."[2]

"But couldn't these celestial aspects and positions influence men to love us, just as you claim they incline us women to love them?" asked Virginia.

"They could indeed," replied Corinna, "if they found the raw material in men suitable to receive their imprint (for, as you are well aware, it is impossible to impose a form on anything unless the matter is correctly disposed to receive it).[3] Women—or women's hearts—because of the innate goodness of their nature, are perfectly disposed to receive the imprint of true love. But men are both by nature and by will little inclined to love, and so, where love is concerned, they can be influenced only to a limited extent by the stars. In fact, all the stars in the sky would not be able to make them love us. They might *incline* them to love us, as I've said, but since men are by nature so remote from true love, that influence would not be enough to change their stubborn souls. And that's why the constellations cannot work on men in the way you suggest, Virginia, even though they do work their magic on women and on the lesser ranks of creation. Not that I'm saying that women can actually be compelled to act in a certain

2. Belief that the stars influenced human behavior was widespread in Fonte's day, among scientists as well as lay people, even though such astrological beliefs were difficult to reconcile with the Catholic doctrine of free will. An acceptable compromise position was that stated here and below by Corinna, that "the heavens can influence but not compel us" and that our reason is powerful enough to master astrally induced inclinations: see Tester 1987, 176–77, 201. For the specific point discussed here and below in the text, that astral influences play a large role in determining our attraction to (or repulsion toward) other individuals, see for example Leone Ebreo 1937, 73.

3. The terminology here derives from Aristotelian physics, the foundation of the scientific orthodoxy of the day. All natural objects were seen as a composite of *matter* (the physical substance of which they were composed) and *form* (the principle that determined their nature).

way by the stars, since we too are possessed of free will. But we are more easily inclined to love than men, because women are subjects more naturally disposed to compassion and love. And the truth of this can be observed in friendships, as well as love, because women make friends with other women more easily than is the case with men, and their friendships are more lasting."[4]

"It's certainly true what you're saying," said Lucretia, "that these celestial aspects exert a great, though not unlimited, power over us, especially where friendships are concerned. I can think of countless occasions, in church or at a dance or a banquet, when I have caught sight of people (of either sex, it doesn't matter), who, even though they are completely unknown to me, and may not be particularly attractive or have any obvious charms, nonetheless exert such an attraction over me that I immediately want to strike up a friendship with them (I'm talking about an innocent friendship, of course). And then, by contrast, there are people who have never done me any harm and who may be full of sterling qualities, but whom I take so strongly against at first sight that I can scarcely bear to look them in the face. So these wildly differing effects must be produced by supernatural causes rather than by the qualities of the people involved. I'd never realized the cause before."

"Yes, that's the reason," said Corinna. "You are attracted to people who were born under astrological influences compatible with your own. But friendship can also arise between two people because of the compatibility of their complexions and humors,[5] or because of a similarity of manners—you know the saying that like attracts like."

"That's true," said Cornelia. "But it is very uncommon to find this kind of rare, inseparable friendship arising between two men or between a man and a woman, because men's innate malignity stands in the way, even where these points of compatibility exist. For, as we've

4. This position is extremely distinctive within the copious literature on friendship produced in the Renaissance, which tends to treat friendship as an exclusively male phenomenon, whether it excludes women implicitly by simply ignoring them, or, as was the case in many Platonically inspired works, explicitly contrasts the spiritual friendship possible between males with the baser, because more sensual, attachments between men and women (for a famous example, see Michelangelo, 260 ["Non è sempre di colpa aspra e mortale"], lines 9–10 [Buonarotti 1991, 440]).

5. In medieval and Renaissance psychology, character was determined by an individual's "complexion," the balance of "humors" in their body.

already noted, men are by nature little inclined to love. They also have a natural tendency toward pride and vanity. The upshot is that they are so ridiculously obsessed with their reputations, and with gaining the respect of those around them, that they behave very stiffly and formally in the pretense that courtesy demands it, whereas in fact their behavior is dictated by artifice. Indeed, instead of honoring their friends by behaving in this way, they are dishonoring friendship and breaching its sacred laws, which banish all affectation. And they are revealing themselves as not only cold and lacking in affection, but also as ignorant, since they are apparently incapable of distinguishing between the behavior that is appropriate with someone you want to have consider you a real friend, and the kind of behavior we reserve for mere acquaintances."

"What they don't realize," Leonora added, "is that this sacred virtue of friendship is utterly pure and unaffected; it rejects all falsity, cares nothing for honor, scorns all boasting, pretense, and simulation, and is never idle, but always eager to show itself concretely in demonstrations of affection."

"There are many," said Corinna, "who do not make these distinctions, because they are incapable of real affection. They do not know how to treat their friends, because they are not real friends themselves. For a man who is a true friend to another must behave toward him in an absolutely frank and open manner: there must be no artifice in his behavior, no polite scruples, no hidden object or secret agenda. He should treat his friend just as he would a brother, a father, a son: that is, he should be as free and easy in all his dealings with him as he might be with a blood relative, even feeling at liberty to command favors when he needs them, and he should give his friend license to behave just as freely in return, never denying him anything he asks. And, believe me, anyone who doesn't take—and give—these liberties has no right to call himself a friend, but rather an acquaintance or a fair-weather friend.

"But there can be nothing better than friendship when it is genuine. Thus Scipio Aemilianus never left the court in the morning without having gained a new friend.[6] Alexander the Great used the treasures he acquired to buy himself friends, since he valued friends

6. The Roman general Publius Cornelius Scipio Aemilianus Africanus (185–129 BC) is a speaker in Cicero's dialogue *On Friendship*. This anecdote derives from Plutarch's *Sayings of Romans* (*Moralia*, 199E), where Scipio is said to have been following the advice of the Greek philosopher Polybius (Plutarch 1927–69, 3: 185–87).

higher than all the riches in the world.[7] Diogenes the Cynic—
thinking about friends' obligations to one another—used to say that
when he needed to, he would ask his friends for money not as though
it was theirs, but as though he was asking for the return of something
he had lent them in the first place.[8] Androcleidas, asked how one
could give men pleasure, replied that one should converse with them
as pleasantly as possible and provide them with the most vital and
necessary things.[9] Aristotle wrote that we should act toward our
friends just as we expect them to act toward us."[10]

Then Cornelia spoke. "I believe that you can tell your real friends
in adversity better than at any other time. As Ovid says,

> *Quando sarai felice numerarai molti amici*
> *Ma ne' tempi travagliosi ti ritroverai solo.*

When you are at the peak of your fortunes, you will have
many friends, but in the hard times, you will be alone.

And Ariosto wrote:

> *Alcun non può saper da chi sia amato*
> *Quando felice in su la ruota siede.*

No one knows who their true friends are, as they sit
blithely at the top of Fortune's wheel.[11]

"It was a saying of Seneca's," added Corinna, "that good fortune
dispenses friends, but ill fortune proves them.[12] And Demetrius adds

7. Alexander the Great was famed for his munificence, especially to men of learning:
Plutarch tells of his asking the philosopher Xenocrates, who had returned a lavish gift
from Alexander saying he had no need of money, whether this meant that he had no
friends, "for, in my case, the wealth of [the defeated Persian king] Darius was hardly
enough for my friends" (ibid., 3, 67).

8. This saying is recorded in Diogenes Laertius (*LP*, 6, 46).

9. This *sententia* derives from Plutarch's *Sayings of Spartans* (*Moralia*, 217D [4]), though
it is attributed there to the fourth-century Spartan general Antalcidas. The cause of
this misattribution, which may derive from some intermediate source, appears to be that
a single saying by a certain Androcleidas (not otherwise known) is recorded slightly
earlier in the same text (Plutarch 1927–69, 3: 301–2).

10. Aristotle wrote extensively on friendship in his ethical works, but this dictum
appears to derive from a secondary source (*LP*, 5, 21).

11. These lines are from *OF*, 19, 1, 1–2; the preceding quotation from Ovid's *Tristia*, 1,
9, 5–6.

12. The reference here may be to a passage in one of Seneca's *Moral Letters* (Seneca
1917, 1: 48–49).

that in good times, we should be able to call on our friends, but in bad times, they should call on us,[13] meaning that friends should help us in our times of need quite spontaneously and without waiting to be asked. There were many true pairs of friends in antiquity who voluntarily laid down their lives for one another, like Pylades and Orestes, Damon and Pythias, Phocion and Nicocles, Achilles and Patrocles.[14] Servius Terentius pretended to be Decimus Brutus in order to die in his place, but he didn't succeed.[15] And then there were many other pairs of friends like Scipio and Laelius, Nisus and Euryalus, Hercules and Philoctetes, and the philosophers Polystratus and Hippocleide, who were born on the same day, studied with the same master, and died at precisely the same time."[16]

13. The original's pun cannot be translated directly: in good times, friends are one's advocates (*avvocati*: literally "those summoned"), but in the bad, they should be one's *non vocati* ("those not summoned"). The saying is attributed to the fourth-century BC Greek statesman and philosopher Demetrius of Phalerum by Diogenes Laertius (*LP, 5, 83*). (Note that the Loeb translation interprets this somewhat obscure phrase in a different sense from that given here; Fonte's version, however, was the standard one in sixteenth-century Latin translations, and is preserved by some modern translators).

14. Pylades was the son of Strophius, king of Phocis, in central Greece, and of Agamemnon's sister, Anaxibia. He grew up with his cousin Orestes, and remained a faithful companion to him through the tribulations of his matricide and exile; Orestes later rewarded him by giving him his sister Electra's hand in marriage. The story of the fourth-century BC Pythagoreans Damon and Pythias (properly Phintias) is told by Valerius Maximus (*MSD*, 4, 7, Foreign Example, 1) and by Cicero in *On Duties*, 45. When Phintias was condemned to death by Dionysius II of Syracuse, his friend Damon offered to stand bail for him while he went to settle his affairs. When Phintias justified his friend's generosity and trust by returning at the time appointed for his execution, the tyrant was moved by the touching spectacle of their friendship to spare the condemned man's life. Phocion (d. 318 BC) was a famous Athenian statesman and general, who sponsored the limitation of the franchise in Athens and was condemned to death on the restoration of democracy. According to Plutarch's biography, Phocion's friend Nicocles, who was to be executed with him, begged as a last favor that he be allowed to die first: a favor reluctantly granted by his friend. The friendship of the Greek heroes Achilles and Patrocles is famously celebrated in Homer's *Iliad*. It is Patrocles' death, extravagantly mourned by his friend, that compels Achilles to renounce his resentment against Agamemnon and re-enter the war against Troy.

15. Decimus Junius Brutus (d. 43 BC) was a protégé of Julius Caesar and one of the conspirators in his murder; he was executed in Gaul during the Civil War on the orders of Antony, having been abandoned by his troops. Valerius Maximus (*MSD*, 4, 7, 6) tells the story of Servius Terentius's unsuccessful attempt to save his friend's life by impersonating him.

16. The friendship between the Roman statesman and orator Gaius Laelius and the great general Scipio Aemilianus was immortalized in Cicero's dialogue *De amicitia* (*On Friendship*), to which Corinna refers in her next speech. The touching tale of Nisus's grief at the death of his friend Euryalus is recounted in book 9 of Virgil's *Aeneid*. The Greek hero Philoctetes was a close friend of Hercules and was present at the latter's

"To be sure," said the Queen. "When a friendship is genuine, the two friends should be united in their desires and their dislikes, and should share everything."

"Yes," said Corinna. "But the first law of friendship, according to Cicero, is that we should ask of a friend only what is right, and do for a friend only what is right.[17] Friendship does not oblige us to go further than this. But there are certain unscrupulous wretches who claim (though they are unworthy of the name) to be the friend of some man, so that their 'friend' feels obliged to satisfy their every request, right or wrong. They don't care if what they are asking goes against all decency, or causes harm to others or endangers their friend's soul, as long as it serves their interests. And if their unjust requests are justly denied, they complain that they aren't being treated as friends—though I'm not so sure that they would do for others what they expect others to do for them. Then there are others who never acknowledge the favors they receive, and others who never return things they have borrowed, and then, when they are reminded of the loan, take offense and end up hating someone who has behaved lovingly toward them. And in this manner, through their own stupidity, they come to lose a good friend, whereas, if they had any sense, they would consider that, since having a dear and loyal friend is one of the greatest gifts one can have in life, one should be careful not to jeopardize such friendships through one's own foolishness. For in times of trouble, a good friend can often be more help than the closest relative.

"To move on, when one is choosing a friend, it is best to approach someone upright, decent, and virtuous, or at least someone who seems good and has a good reputation. For, by conversing with good people, we learn good habits and become better people through their example; and there's also the consideration that, in this way, we are able to share in their good reputation. For often when one is seeking information on someone, one asks what kind of company they keep and what kind of friends they have. And if someone is thought to be a person of sound principles and blameless life, then the same is thought of his or her companions; if the contrary, then the con-

death on Mount Oeta, where Hercules bequeathed him the poisoned arrows whose powers give him a key role in post-Homeric accounts of the Trojan War. Polystratus and Hippocleide were Epicurean philosophers of the third century BC. The "memorable fact" of their shared destiny is recounted by Valerius Maximus (*MSD*, 1, 8, Foreign Examples, 17).

17. The reference is to Cicero's *De amicitia*, 13, 44.

trary is thought. That's apart from the fact that, because of our natural inclination to vice, good people who keep company with bad friends risk losing their goodness and taking on their companions' vices."

"You're quite right," said the Queen, "And that's why fathers and mothers should keep their eyes open and not be too trusting and allow their children to take up with just anyone. Children very often turn to the bad as a result of bad examples and unsound advice."

"That's certainly true," said Corinna. "But, on the contrary, if, by some happy chance the friendships turn out to be good ones, what a joy! What a great blessing!"

Then Lucretia said, "A sensible person should test out a prospective close friend before confiding the least part of their secrets in him; then he should try to win his friendship by showing himself as much of a friend to him as he wishes him to be in return; and, finally, he should do all he can to keep his friendship. For a true friend represents a fortune in times of hardship, a helping hand in times of misfortune, health in illness, and life in death."

"In a word," said Corinna, "true friendship, true affinity, is the cause of all good. For it is friendship that keeps the world alive: friendship seals the marriages that preserve the individual in the species, while the friendship and bonding of the elements maintains health in our bodies, and brings fine weather to the air, calm to the sea, and peace to the earth, so that cities can be built, kingdoms grow to greatness, and all creatures live in comfort. When a man is at peace with his neighbor, he can walk in safety, eat in safety, sleep in safety; and all that he does is done in a spirit of tranquillity and repose. And, for this reason, man should devote all his energies to living in peace, in order not to add new miseries of his own making to the existing miseries of life. He shouldn't take offense at every nothing, every trifling incident; rather, he should be prepared to put up with a few little inconveniences, overlooking others' imprudence, pitying their benighted lives and trying his utmost to avoid conflict and scenes, and to live as harmoniously and as peaceably as possible. For whoever lives in peace is living in God, in a certain sense, since in paradise there is nothing but peace and charity; and God himself is peace and charity and paradise itself. But some people claim to have discovered certain natural agents that have the power to bring about peace and concord, and others that cause discord . . ."

"Ah, discord!" exclaimed Cornelia. "The destroyer of everything! It is when men fall out of harmony with each other that wars begin."

"And then, alas!" said Corinna, "provinces and families are exterminated, states overthrown, and whole peoples consumed. Meanwhile, in the air, disharmonies of the elements produce thunder and lightning; at sea, they provoke storms; and, on earth, earthquakes."

"Oh!" Helena said. "Talking of earthquakes, you reminded me of the one last year. Did you others feel it?"

"Didn't we just!" said the others. "And what a fright it gave us!"

As they talked on about the subject, Helena asked, "Corinna, my dear, what is it, do you think, that causes earthquakes?"

"The wind," said Corinna, "when, instead of wandering through its natural element, the air, it gets trapped underground for some reason, and cannot find a way out. And since, by its nature, it cannot stay enclosed, it puts all its energy into trying to escape, and it is this force that shakes and agitates the earth so violently."[18]

"It's fascinating to learn these secrets of nature," said Helena. "And the disturbances of the air and the sea: how do they come about? Perhaps you could tell us something about that?"

"Those are caused," replied Corinna, "by the different movements of the planets, especially of the sun and the moon."[19]

"Carry on a little with what you were saying earlier about these planets and the regions of the air," said Lucretia. "You started telling us about them, but never finished."[20]

"The sun, indeed, has a vast effect on this terrestrial globe of ours," said Leonora.

"There's no need for me to tell you anything more about the other planets," said Corinna. "As for the sun, it is an extraordinarily rapid-moving planet: speedier than its constitution would seem to permit, if we are to believe the astrologers. Passing, month by month, through all the various signs of the Zodiac, it brings us now heat, now cold, now long days, now short, as it approaches our hemisphere or recedes from it, and, with its equinoxes, it measures out our

18. This theory evidently held a certain imaginative appeal for Fonte, who includes a vivid description in her romance *Floridoro* of the jilted enchantress Circe constructing herself a mountain by imprisoning the winds within the earth and using their explosive force (Fonte 1995, 126 [8, 21]). Her source (whether direct or indirect) is probably Aristotle's *Meteorology* 366a, though Pliny also briefly alludes to this theory (*NH*, 2, 81, 192).

19. This notion is developed in Pliny (*NH*, 2, 39, 105–12; 2, 41, 108); see also Grant 1994, 576–77.

20. Lucretia is perhaps referring here to the mention of cosmic influences during the discussion of friendship, at pp. 121–23.

weather and our hours of daylight. This planet reforms the year, tempers the weather, and renews the world; it clothes the world in green, infuses the life force into plants and stones, and stirs animals' natural instinct to the act of generation, which is necessary for their survival. The sun concludes its daily course in twenty-four hours and its annual one in twelve months."[21]

"The moon," said Cornelia, "as I have heard, is a body that receives light from the sun. Does that mean that all its effects can ultimately be attributed to the sun?"

"No indeed," Corinna replied. "For even though the moon receives its light from the sun, its extreme humidity makes it very different in its properties and effects. The moon is closer to us than any other planet and as it follows its natural course, of waxing and waning, fullness, renewal, and eclipse, it causes an infinite number of different effects, sometimes alone and sometimes through the mediation of, or with the contribution of, other, accidental causes. In the air, the moon causes sometimes lightning, thunder, cloud mists, winds, rain, and storms, sometimes serenity and mildness. At the same time, it also alters the sea as it waxes and wanes, now swelling the waters in the middle of the ocean, now those around the shores; and it causes violent storms and dangerous squalls, as its movement stirs and churns up the ebb and flow of the waters. Nor has it lesser powers over the earth, over fields, crops, and trees, than those of the sun, which I've already described. And, what's more, with its great humidity, the moon is extremely harmful to our physical health and, as it passes through its phases, it exerts a great influence for better or worse over the course of illnesses. This is why doctors observe the phases of the moon very closely, because one could almost say that the moon disturbs and churns up the human body in the same way that it does the sea."[22]

"But how are clouds, and the rain that comes from them, generated?" asked Helena.

"Clouds (and hence rain) are generated," Corinna said, "from the vapors of the earth when they are swept up into the air by the

21. Corinna's speech, resting on the assumption that the sun moves around the earth, reflects the Ptolemaic and Aristotelian teachings that still constituted academic orthodoxy half a century after the publication of Copernicus's heliocentric theory (1543). On medieval and Renaissance cosmology, see Grant 1994, esp. 451–54 on the properties of the sun, and 393–402 and 459–66 on those of the moon.

22. On this belief, see Tester 1987, 223–24; and Grant 1994, 577.

southerly winds as a result of the movements of that same moon we've just been talking about. As I've said, the moon by nature loves humidity, and receiving excessive heat from the sun, as it does [. . .].[23] Similarly, fine weather is either caused by northerly winds, or else, very often, by the moon again, because when the moon finds that there are clouds in the air, since it needs humidity on account of its proximity to the sun, it turns to the sources of humidity closest at hand and absorbs the clouds into itself, with the result that the sky becomes clear and fine again. And the moon completes its orbit in nineteen days and twelve hours."

"Truly," said the Queen, "it's a remarkable testimony to man's wisdom that we can know even about these things that are so far away."

"If there are animals who know about these things," said Lucretia, "then why should we be amazed that man, with his divine intellect, has come to learn them as well?"

"I've heard that business about animals too," Adriana replied. "Especially birds, of which there are many that appear to know about these changes and indicate them to us by various signs."[24]

"We can see this every day," Corinna continued, "from our own experience of the domestic fowl we keep—cocks, geese, and so on—which, when they sense a change in the air, beat their wings, fly around, and screech far more than usual. But it is crows and ravens, above all, that act as harbingers of future events, good or bad. As the poet said:

Qual destro corvo, o qual manca cornice,
Canti il mio fato, o qual Parca l'inaspe.

What crow on the right or what raven on the left may sing
of my fate, or which Fate enspool it?[25]

23. The text appears to be corrupt here: the original reads, literally translated, "receiving excessive heat from the sun, as of humidity of the earth and the sea."

24. See *NH*, 18, 87, 362–63.

25. The lines are from Petrarch (*RS*, 210, 5–6). The references are to the classical myth of the Fates or Parcae, the three goddesses who were said to spin out human destinies on their looms, and to the Roman superstition (mentioned by Cicero in *De divinatione*, I, 39) that a crow flying to the right or a raven to the left were auguries of good luck. More generally, on the widespread belief in classical antiquity that birds' behavior could be read as an augury not just of changes in the weather but of future events, see Pollard 1977, 110–15.

"Oh come along now!" Leonora interjected. "Forgive me, Lucretia [*sic*], but you are breaking all the rules here. We're supposed to be discussing what's wrong with men (an extremely relevant subject and one that offers endless scope for discussion), and all you want to talk about is moons and clouds and birds and all that nonsense. Now, if you want an example of something unstable, why not talk about men? If you're interested in natural disharmonies—well, again, men will do fine. And if you're keen on talking about something that flies through the air, what need is there to look further than men's brains, which flit around exactly like birds, talking about this and that, with no direction at all. What's the point of all this astrology?[26] This kind of talk and this kind of study have nothing to do with us."

"I have not studied any discipline," said Corinna, "and this least of any, though it is an extremely important and fascinating one. But it is not for everyone, and I know little of it and care less about learning it. What little I have told you today has just been what happened to come up in the conversation: I wasn't trying to show off what I know, and, in any case, I've said nothing you didn't know already; indeed, that every schoolboy doesn't know. But astrology is in truth a very distinguished discipline, worthy of the loftiest intellects, and there were many ancients who wrote on the subject. In our own times, as well, there are numerous experts who have written a great deal on the subject."

"Could you perhaps name a few of these present-day writers, if you remember any?" Lucretia asked.

"There are quite a few of them," Corinna replied. "One whom I know personally is Signor Giovanni Niccolò Doglioni, a man of great refinement and one who, in addition to his other remarkable talents, has been gifted with incredible kindness and loyalty (things rarely found in men). This gentleman is an expert on many subjects outside his principal profession, and has written many books. And since one of his interests is astrology, he has written an extremely fine monograph on this same subject of seasons, the weather, and other related subjects. The title of this admirable little work is *L'Anno*, and a gentleman who is a great friend of his has composed a sonnet in his praise, which was published in the work.[27] But maybe you have all

26. What is meant here is, of course, astrology in the broad, Renaissance sense, encompassing cosmology and meteorology.
27. The sonnet, reproduced below, is by Moderata Fonte herself, and is reproduced under her name in the volume in question (published in Venice in 1587). This self-citation might fuel suspicions that the figure of Corinna is intended to be identified

seen it yourselves and don't need me to say any more."

The women all replied that no, this was all new to them, and they were very keen to see the book, or at least to hear the sonnet. And so Corinna, graciously recalling it to her memory, recited it to them as they sat listening attentively,

> Qual ricamo di perle in or cosparte
> O di fior copia in verde campo ameno
> Tal figura il tuo stil, felice a pieno
> Alta materia in gloriose carte.
> Gran saper, ch'uom mortal spiega e comparte
> Ogni poter celeste, ogni terreno,
> Termine, stato, moto, sito e seno,
> Tempo, elementi, ciel, natura ed arte.
> Sì con un cenno sol l'alto Architetto
> A sì gran mole diè spirito e forma,
> Qual tu rassumi in variato aspetto.
> Or per tant'opra, ei mentre al tuo crin forma
> Fregio di stelle, e inspira il tuo intelletto,
> Te picciol mondo in se stesso trasforma.

Like a scattering of pearls embroidered on gold, or a rich crop of flowers on a lovely green meadow, are the lofty thoughts scattered on each glorious page by your happy pen. What wisdom! That a mortal can decipher and distinguish each power of the heavens, each power below: limit, state, motion, site, and source; time, elements, heavens, nature, and art. In a similar way, with a single gesture the great Architect gave life and form to this vast mass whose various aspects you describe. And now, as you write this great work of yours, he fashions a wreath of stars to adorn your locks, and inspires your intellect, transforming you, microcosm that you are, into himself.[28]

---

with Fonte herself, since we have already heard (p. 67) that Corinna has the habit of modestly attributing her own work to others.

28. The last lines of Fonte's distinctly obscure sonnet carry to particularly ambitious extremes two Neoplatonic notions that had gained wide currency in Renaissance culture: the notion that man was a "microcosm," containing within him in miniature the same miraculous ordering of physical and spiritual forces that made up the greater universe, and the notion that man could become godlike through the act of contemplation, which utilized the divine part of his nature, his intellect. The text of this sonnet in the 1600 edition of *The Worth of Women* has *al suo crin* ("his [God's] locks")

The women were pleased to have heard this charming sonnet, which was new to them, even though it had already been published. And the Queen, who knew the gentleman who was the subject of the poem well, praised it highly, but added that Doglioni's merits were such as to deserve more than a mere sonnet: indeed, that it would take whole volumes of praise from the most learned pens to do justice to the virtues and rare qualities of that honored gentleman.

"Someone else who is famous in this field," said Corinna, "is Signor Giovanni Antonio Magini, who wrote that much-praised astronomical almanac.[29] And then, also worthy of note, there's Signor Lucio Scarano, who lectured on this subject (and still does, in fact), winning great reputation and universal acclaim."[30]

"I have also heard Signor Claudio Cornelio Frangipani mentioned as a great authority on the subject," said Lucretia.[31]

"Yes indeed, madam," said Corinna. "And there are also two Veronese gentlemen, Annibale Raimondo and Giovanni Padovani,[32]

and il suo intelletto ("his [God's] intellect") at lines 12–13. I have restored the version of the sonnet given in its original publication in Doglioni 1587, as this seems the more probable reading.

29. It is unlikely that Giovanni Antonio Magini (1555–1617) would have greatly appreciated being given second place to Doglioni in Fonte's list of authorities. A native of Padua, and from 1588 professor of mathematics at Bologna University, Magini was one of the most eminent Italian astronomers of his day, a correspondent of Kepler's and a rival of Galileo's (Drake 1978, 455).

30. Lucio Scarano, originally from Brindisi, held the chair of Latin in the university-level school of San Marco in Venice from 1586–1614 (Palmer 1983, 49n). He was one of the founder members of the second Accademia Veneziana in 1593, to which Doglioni also belonged, and is the dedicatee of Marinella's Nobility and Excellence of Women. No astronomical interests are apparent from the list of his works given in Stringa 1604, 424v.

31. Claudio Cornelio Frangipani (1553–c.1640), was a native of Friuli and the nephew of a famous lawyer. After studying at Padua and Bologna, he settled in Venice and began a career as a legal consultant to the Venetian state (Liruti 1760–1830, 2: 181–97). It may have been Frangipani's Friulian background (which he shared with Doglioni), or his prestige in the law (the profession of Fonte's husband, Filippo Zorzi), rather than his distinction as a scientist that led to his inclusion on this list, though it is true that his first published work (1573) was a contribution to the great astronomical debate excited by the appearance of a new star the previous year.

32. Giovanni Padovani (b. 1516) was a Veronese mathematician with an interest in astronomy (Maffei 1825–26, 1: 367–68; Thorndike 1923–58, 6: 124). Annibale Raimondo (c. 1505–post 1589), wrote on a range of astronomical and meteorological topics, and made significant contributions to two prominent controversies of the 1570s: that on the new star sighted in the constellation of Cassiopeia in 1572 (where his views attracted a virulent reply from the great Czech astronomer Tycho Brache), and that on the causes of the great plague of 1575–76 (Ulvioni 1982, 2–6; Preto 1984, 382; Maffei 1825–26, 1: 368–69; Thorndike 1923–58, 6: 473–75).

both highly expert in the field, and many others whose names I can't remember."

"Oh, that's splendid!" said Leonora. "That's all we need! After telling us all about astrology, now you're going to list all the astrologers you know, one by one. And then what? You'll get back on to the subject of birds and start listing each individual feather on their backs. Go on, I can't wait!"

"That's not such a bad idea," said Lucretia. "Go on, Corinna, carry on telling us about those birds you mentioned earlier: the ones that predict the weather and other things that are going to happen."

"Oh, yes, please!" said Leonora. "But I suspect you're asking her in all seriousness."

"Oh, go on, let her talk," said Lucretia.

"The ancients," said Corinna, "used to read auguries of future events in the behavior of many kinds of bird, but as good Catholics, we should pay no attention to these kinds of superstition. How many fantastic things the poets have written about birds like the eagle, the peacock, the magpie, and the swallow!"[33]

"Men like to compare us to magpies," said Helena, "because we are always chattering."

"And to which birds might we compare them?" asked Cornelia.

"To the crows we mentioned earlier," said Leonora. "Because when we see them, we know it means ill fortune for us."[34]

"One really lovely bird," Lucretia said, "is the peacock. Or, at least, it would be lovely if it weren't for that shrieking noise it makes."

"The peacock is generally thought to be both the most beautiful of flying creatures and the vainest," said Corinna. "It loves displaying the glory of its many-eyed feathers, but then, looking down and seeing its ugly little feet, it folds up its great wheel of feathers in

---

33. In the discussion that follows, on the characteristics of birds, Fonte draws on the extremely rich tradition of zoological anecdote and fable that Renaissance writers inherited from classical antiquity and the Middle Ages. Setting aside "the poets," mentioned here, the main classical scientific treatments of ornithology are Aristotle's *History of Animals*, Claudius Aelianus's *Characteristics of Animals*, and book 10 of Pliny's *Natural History*; to which we should add the so-called *Physiologus* (second century AD) and the medieval bestiary tradition that developed from it, enriched by the contributions of writers like Isidore of Seville. Fantastic things concerning eagles, peacocks, and swallows are recounted below in the text. Pliny describes talking magpies (*NH*, 10, 59, 118).

34. Crows and especially ravens were regarded as birds of ill omen in antiquity (Pollard 1977, 127).

shame and starts shrieking in that strident way, because it realizes that the rest of its body is not as perfect as it would wish it to be. And that should serve us as a useful lesson, to encourage us to keep striving toward perfection and not to rest on our laurels, just because we have one good feature.[35] The peacock is melancholy by nature and its flesh is not easy to digest, but it is a delicacy nonetheless, and highly prized. And there is no trouble involved in bringing up its chicks, as there is with other domestic fowls, which are kept inside, because peacocks make their nests in the open, in the fields, among the crops, or in some secluded hedge, and hatch out their eggs there and bring their chicks up in the open countryside, sleeping in the open and sheltering them under their wings. As for the other domestic fowls—ducks, geese, turkeys, and so on—I don't need to tell you about them, as you know better than me how they are kept on your country estates. These are all delicious to eat but not particularly nutritious."

"I'm extremely fond of pigeon," said Cornelia. "It not only tastes good, but it's very nutritious."

"One bird I find amazing is the swan, which is so similar to the goose," said Lucretia, "and which they say sings as it dies."[36]

"It sings," said Corinna, "because it predicts and foresees its death, which is caused by those three feathers that move into its brain as it ages. Certainly, it's a rare and lovely feature of this bird's behavior, and one we should imitate, since we have the intellectual capacity to foresee our deaths in a more rational way."

"And the phoenix?" said Helena. "Can it be true what we read about it, that there is only one of them, and that it renews its life in that way?"

"It may indeed be true," said Corinna, "even though it strikes us as so extraordinary. But, then, don't you think there may be many

35. The detail of the peacock's shame at the ugliness of its feet appears to be a late addition to ornithological lore: it is found in the early sixteenth-century Waldensian Bestiary (though with a more pious moral, equating the peacock's feet with the "baseness of the flesh"), but not in earlier Latin or vernacular bestiaries or in classical sources (McCulloch 1960, 153, n. 120).

36. The myth that swans sing before they die is found in Aristotle, Pliny, and the medieval bestiary tradition and it had become a commonplace of poetry and moralistic literature by the time Fonte was writing. The notion, mentioned below in the text, that swans' deaths were signaled by feathers moving into their brain, appears to be medieval in origin (see for example, Latini 1948, 147 [1, 161]), though Latini talks of a single feather rather than three, as here.

things in our own part of the world that seem quite normal to us because we see them all the time, but which must seem impossible and prodigious to people from elsewhere?"

"That's certainly true," said Cornelia. "But what does the phoenix feed on? It isn't a bird of prey, like the eagle; and it can't live on grain, because otherwise it would be seen around in the fields."

"I believe," said Corinna, "that it sups on celestial manna and the aromatic exhalations of those happy plants found in the sweet-smelling, shining Orient."[37]

"How about eagles?" said Cornelia. "I have heard that there are two kinds, one gray-brown and one white, but I think that's probably just a story."

"No, I think you're right," said Corinna. "The eagle is queen of all the other birds, and has a noble nature; it is known as the bird of Jove and that gives it a regal and sacred quality. It has remarkably acute and powerful vision, because alone of all birds it can look straight into the sun; and it's this that enables eagles to recognize their offspring. For as soon as the chicks are hatched, the parent exposes them to the sight of the sun and, if they are capable of looking into it, it recognizes them as legitimate—that is, as coming from its own eggs—but if the chicks are blinded by the light, it throws them out of the nest as impostors hatched from the eggs of other birds.[38] And what's more, although eagles are so huge, there is no bird that can fly higher, for they can soar above the clouds. They are extremely nimble on their wings and so powerful that they can lift up a sheep in their talons and carry it off through the air to eat it wherever they choose."

"Are eagles any good to eat?" said Helena.

"I've never read of anyone eating one," said Corinna. "They could be, but I suspect their flesh would be very tough, like the flesh of birds like kites and crows."

"You can't say that of falcons, though," said Lucretia, "because,

37. Classical sources differed on the topic of the phoenix's diet: some sources were inclined to think it ate nothing, while others had it eating incense (Ovid) or imbibing the sun's rays (Claudian) (Mermier 1989, 71).

38. The story of the eagle testing its offspring's eyesight is found in Aristotle (*HA*, 620a1–5) and Pliny (*NH*, 10, 3, 10), as well as in the medieval bestiary tradition. On the eagle as the sacred bird of Zeus or Jupiter, king of the gods, see Pollard 1977, 141–42. The detail, mentioned below in the text, of eagles flying above the clouds may reflect a legend recounted in medieval bestiaries, telling of elderly eagles' habit of flying up to the sphere of the sun to singe their wings before plunging into a fountain to restore themselves to youth.

apart from anything, Boccaccio tells us about a falcon being eaten and tasting delicious.[39] Yet falcons are birds of prey too."

"That's true," said Corinna. "But rather than the predators I'd still prefer to eat the prey—birds like doves, turtle-doves, thrushes, quails, and the different kinds of partridges,[40] which are delicious to eat, light to digest, and very good for you."

"Do you think it's true what some writers say about those partridges in Paphlagonia that have two hearts each?" Virginia asked.[41]

"If there are men," said Leonora, "who have twenty-five hearts each, then why shouldn't there be partridges in some far-off land that have two?"

"What do you mean?" asked Virginia. "Men with twenty-five hearts? I can't believe that."

"Fifty, even," Leonora replied, laughing.

"Have you ever met such a man?" Virginia asked.

"Only five hundred or so," Leonora replied. At that point all the other women burst out laughing at Virginia's naïveté, and Corinna said to her, "Leonora is speaking the truth: you had better believe her. I know men like that as well."

But Virginia replied, "If you'd told me they lived in some far-off country, like those monsters you hear about—men whose heads grow out of their chests or who have dogs' heads or a single enormous foot or something—well, then I could believe you.[42] But if you're claiming to know them, it's obvious that you're pulling my leg."

"You poor innocent creature!" Leonora replied. "Wouldn't you

39. The reference is to the ninth story of day 5 of Boccaccio's *Decameron*, where the impoverished Federigo degli Alberighi, stricken with shame at the inadequacy of his household when the woman he loves invites herself to dinner, proves his love for her by killing and serving up his much-loved falcon.

40. The original distinguishes between two species of partridge, the *starna* (*Perdix perdix*) and the *pernice* (*Alectoris rufa*).

41. The existence of two-hearted partridges in Paphlagonia (in northern Asia Minor) is reported in Theophrastus's *On Weather Signs* (Pollard 1977, 21).

42. The reference is to three of the mythical "monstrous races" described by Pliny, following Greek sources. The Cynocephali ("dog-heads") supposedly lived in India, as did the Sciopods, whose single, enormous foot served them as a sunshade. The Blemmyae (Shakespeare's "men whose heads/do grow beneath their shoulders") came from the Libyan desert (Friedman 1981). Belief in these exotic races, lively throughout the Middle Ages, suffered a blow in the sixteenth century when the New World (the "Indies") failed to yield the expected sightings, and Virginia's statement is probably better taken as further proof of her naïveté than as evidence of the continued currency of these notions.

conclude that a man must have twenty-five or more hearts if, when he's speaking to one woman and pretending to be in love with her, he tells her that he is pledging his heart to her, and then he goes straight on to another woman and swears in just the same way that his heart belongs to her, and then goes on to do just the same with the next twenty-five women he meets? Either that man must have at least twenty-five hearts to give away, or else, if he has only one, he must be lying to them all and not giving that one heart of his away to any of them. But let's get back to the subject in hand."

"Indeed," said Cornelia. "Trust men to lead us astray!"

"So," Corinna said to Virginia, "I'd say that the birds you were talking about do exist, among all the other prodigies of nature—for we have to allow for apparently incredible things."

"What I like," said Virginia, "are those little songbirds we keep in cages—goldfinches, chaffinches, linnets, and so on. But best of all are nightingales, which sing so sweetly, and those amazing talking blackbirds."

"One thing I really enjoy, when I'm in the country," said Leonora, "is hunting these little birds you're talking about. I'm just not so keen on getting out of bed at dawn to do it."

"Oh, Virginia, do you remember that time when we went sparrow-hunting with your uncle?" asked Helena. "We sat there in that reed hut in the middle of the meadow, not making a sound, waiting for the flocks of passing birds, which were tempted down by the decoys, singing their hearts out in their concealed cages or fluttering around on their strings, and by the tempting vista of the green bower, hung with nets. And then down they all swooped, crowding onto the branches, and the servant who had been sitting by on the alert jumped up and tugged hard at the rope attached to the nets, pulling them together and closing the nets and the bower and the little birds all in together, and then we all leapt out together and raced to see who could kill them all first; and we didn't uncover the bower or release the nets until they were all either captive or dead. What fun we had!"

"How could I forget it?" said Virginia. "In fact, I can't wait for this autumn, to go and enjoy those country pursuits again, though it won't be the same without you there."

"And how about thrush-hunting, how do you like that?" said Cornelia.

"I've sometimes seen my uncle doing it," said Virginia. "The same

uncle that Helena was talking about, who is still young and enjoys
that kind of entertainment. What he does is to lay out branches covered with birdlime in the thickets near the house and then put an
owl in the middle of the meadow. And the other birds—thrushes and
various other kinds—find it so monstrous that they all crowd around
to look at it and gradually, hopping around from branch to branch,
they get caught on the limed branches, their feet and wings get
stuck and then we come out of hiding and they are ours.[43] But it's
not as much fun as the other way of hunting."

"What I'd really like to do, if I were a man," said Leonora, "is to
ride out on a good horse with a falcon and bag some nice partridges
and quails. That's something I think I'd really enjoy."

"Oh come on!" said Helena. "We can't do any one of these
things without men to help us; in fact, we wouldn't enjoy them without men."

"Oh yes!" said Cornelia. "If there's one thing they *are* good at, it's
trapping, deceiving, ensnaring: that's their speciality, in fact. But it's
not something we would know how to do, left to ourselves, so when
we want to turn our hand to these pursuits, we need to learn from
men and draw on their help, since they are so expert and skilled at
them."

"To continue," said Corinna. "There's the swallow, the herald of
spring, which the poets make believe was once a woman, since it
makes its nest under the eaves of houses.[44] Then the diver, the

---

43. This mode of hunting was known in antiquity (Pollard 1977, 104), and is mentioned
in Aristotle (*HA*, 609a15). Fonte's speakers' enthusiasm for hunting doubtless reflects
contemporary social practice, but there may also be a feminist subtext here, given that
men's love of hunting was occasionally adduced by male writers as proof of their
superiority over women (see, for example, Bramoso 1589, 13: "Man, in a manner
consonant with his original, natural greatness, devotes himself to attempting to master
the birds of the air, the fishes of the sea and the wild beasts of the earth through the
wondrous power of his intellect: an enterprise quite alien to woman, who remains
timidly and fearfully cloistered within her own chambers, occupied with those domestic
tasks that are so well suited to the female species").

44. The allusion here is to the bloody and haunting myth of the sisters Procne and
Philomela, daughters of Pandion, King of Athens. Procne's husband, Tereus, fell in
love with his sister-in-law, raped her, and then hid his wife in the country, pretending
she was dead. He then married Philomela and cut out her tongue to hide his shame, but
she informed her sister by embroidering letters on a robe. Procne returned secretly,
killed her son, Itys, boiled him up, and fed him to his father. The sisters fled, but were
pursued by Tereus, escaping only when the gods granted their wish to be transformed
into birds. Procne became a nightingale, in the Greek myth; the tongueless Philomela,
a swallow (the Romans, less logically, made Philomela the nightingale, Procne the
swallow). It should be noted that the allusion to the Procne myth serves to evoke the

halcyon, the owl, the amorous dove, and the chaste turtledove—there's no need for me to tell you their stories and their characteristics, as you all know them anyway.[45] And then there are those birds they hunt with carbines in these lagoons of ours in winter, which are known by various names; they are very common and their diet is mainly small fish: I mean coots and so on."

"And then, would you believe it, they even taste of fish!" said Lucretia. "That is, if you don't get rid of the taste by boiling them and using a lot of spices to stuff them with, as is the custom."

"It would be nice," said Helena, "if you could eat them at Lent as well, since they feed on fish and spend most of their time in the water—you could call them duck-fish, just like you hear of dog-fish and cat-fish."[46]

The women laughed and Corinna said, "Isn't it enough at Lent to have so many different kinds of fish, which you might even say taste better than fowl, though they may not be so nutritious? Our fishing-grounds provide good bass and sturgeon, eels, flounders, various types of mullet, tuna, *morone,*[47] and all kinds of other fine fish. And that's

---

main theme of the dialogue, the disharmony between the sexes and, more specifically, men's violence against women.

45. As is the case with the swallow, the mythological associations of the birds in this list are amenable to a feminist reading, evoking as they do the themes of women's fidelity and compassion, men's cruelty, and women's capacity for learning. The halcyon, or kingfisher, was associated with the myth of Alcyone, daughter of Aeolus, king of the winds, whose happy marriage with Ceyx (the name means "tern") ended in tragedy when the gods caused Ceyx to be drowned in the course of a sea voyage, whereupon his grieving widow, attempting to drown herself, was changed into a halcyon. The story is told in book 11 of Ovid's *Metamorphoses* (710–48), where it is immediately followed by the tale of the Trojan prince Aesacus, who, after the nymph Hesperia was killed by a snakebite while fleeing his advances, attempted suicide by hurling himself off a cliff, but was transformed into a diving bird as he fell. Doves and turtledoves were famed for their fidelity to their mates, and, in Greek myth, were the birds that brought ambrosia to feed the infant Zeus in the cave on Crete where his mother Rhea had hidden him to protect him from his cannibalistic father Cronos (Pollard 1977, 58, 147). The owl was sacred to Minerva, goddess of wisdom (ibid., 143–44).

46. The last fish mentioned here is in fact *pesce colombo* (Pteromyleus bovina; lit. "dove-fish"); "cat-fish" has been substituted in translation to preserve Helena's joke.

47. *Morone* is an old Venetian dialect term for the Beluga sturgeon (*Huso huso*), known in Italian as the *storione ladato*. The discussion of fish initiated here is rich in dialect terms: this initial list includes, besides *morone, cièvolo* ("gray mullet"; cf. It. *cefalo*) and *varolo* (literally "pox-fish": "spotted sea bass" [Dicentrarchus punctatus]; cf. It. *spigola*); while the subsequent discussion mentions *gaiandra* ("turtle"; cf. Italian *testuggine*); *scarpenna* ("scorpion fish"; cf. It., *scorfano*); *folpo* ("octopus"; cf. It., *polipo*); *cuògola* (a type of large fishing net; cf. It. *cogolaria*); and *tratta, togna* (types of fishing net and line). The air of closeness to experience given by this use of dialect is, however, probably deceptive: the influence of classical and medieval literary sources is obvious (especially book 9 of

not counting all the smaller fish and the numerous different shell-fish, and the freshwater fish, like carp, trout, grayling, lampreys, shrimps, and countless others—it would take a good month to name them all."

"It certainly is a great convenience for us to have so many different kinds of fish," said the Queen. "Because whenever you can't find meat at the butcher's, you can get by with fish, which is always there, even if sometimes it's dearer than at other times. It's a blessing especially for the poor."

"I know I tend to eat fish most of the time," said Cornelia. "It tastes better to me than meat, and it agrees with me, as well."

"You must have a complexion that tends toward the hot and the dry," said Corinna, "because fish is bad for those whose complexion is dominated by phlegm.[48] And even though it tastes good, it isn't very nutritious because it's such a watery food: when you eat it, it reduces back down into its element, which is water, in which it is born and raised."

"Do fish hunt each other in the sea," said the Queen, "just as animals and birds do on earth and in the air?"

"Indeed they do, madam," said Corinna.

"Which do you think there are more of," asked Helena, "animals on land, birds in the air, or fish in the sea?"

"The experts all agree," said Corinna, "that there is a far greater quantity of fish than of other creatures."[49]

"And why do they say this is?" asked the Queen.

"I can't remember ever reading the reason," replied Corinna. "But one might suppose, since it is said that the oceans are bigger than the land, that the extent of the contents can be surmised from the extent of the containers.[50] And besides, since man doesn't intrude

---

Pliny's *Natural History* and Oppian's *Halieutica*).

48. Medieval and Renaissance dietary prescriptions, like medical thought in general, centered on the theory of the "humors." Foodstuffs, like human bodies, were thought to be characterized by differing combinations of the four basic "qualities" or "contraries" (cold, hot, dry, and moist). Imbalances could lead to ill health: thus people of "phlegmatic" complexion (cold and moist) were advised to avoid cold and moist foods like fish.

49. This was Aristotle's position, and remained the orthodox one, though it had recently been the subject of debate (see following note).

50. This sentence is obscure in the original; my translation reconstructs what seems the most likely sense of the passage. The proportions of the globe occupied by the land and the seas had been the subject of controversy in the decades preceding Fonte's composition of *The Worth of Women* (see Piccolomini 1568, Michele 1583, Berga

into the depths of the sea, where fishes build their nests, they can multiply more comfortably, with no one to prevent them or disturb their environment. For they are the sole inhabitants of the water."

"That last reason I'm happy to concede," said Leonora, "but not the first. Because if the number of inhabitants is supposed to be greater when their environment is greater in size, then birds would outnumber all other kinds of animal. For what part of the world is vaster than the air?"

"It's certainly true," said Corinna, "that the air is vaster than the other parts of the world, but I'm not prepared to concede on those grounds that there must be more birds than other animals. Because birds may fly through the air, but they don't build their nests there; they build them on land—on the ground or in the trees. And since the land is the most restricted part of the world and already occupied by men and by quadrupeds, there isn't much space for birds to breed in comfort, unlike fish. Some fish do get caught, obviously, around the coasts, but an infinite number remains out of reach in the seas and great rivers where ships pass infrequently. And there's further proof of the numbers of fish in the vast quantities of roe we find in their bodies at certain times of year."

"Do you think tiny fish breed in the sea?" asked Leonora.

"Yes, I think so," said Corinna. "But they don't last long because of the big fish—you know the proverb about the bigger fish eating the smaller."

"One thing I find amazing are those whales they talk about," said Helena, "that are so huge they look like reefs, so that sailors have often climbed onto them and then risked drowning."[51]

"Even more amazing, though," said Corinna, "is a certain fish they call a shark sucker, which is small but incredibly strong. They say it attaches itself to the bottoms of ships and stops them in their tracks and can threaten to drag them down; in fact, it does very often drag ships down, and there's absolutely nothing that can be done to save them."[52]

1589, all of whom also briefly discuss the question of the relative numbers of land and sea animals [at, respectively, 20v–21r; 3v–4r, 33]).

51. Anecdotes concerning sailors mistaking whales for islands are found in the bestiary tradition, but Fonte may be thinking here as well of the incident in canto 6 of Ariosto's *Orlando Furioso*, in which the enchantress Alcina lures the handsome paladin Astolfo onto a whale in order to carry him off (*OF*, 6, 37–41).

52. The shark sucker (*Remora remora*) has a large suctorial disc on its head, by which it can attach itself to other fish and to boats, a characteristic that gave rise to the

"The sea turtle," added Cornelia, "which is as big as an island, drags ships down as well. And the same fish opens its mouth and attracts other fish by the sweet smell of its breath, and then gobbles them up."[53]

"What's that fish," said Leonora, "that's small but deadly poisonous, but that is eaten nonetheless?"

"You must mean the scorpion fish," replied Corinna. "And then, how about the great weever fish, which has a venomous bite for which the only antidote is the flesh of the same fish?[54] The spider fish, as well, with its single spine can gore fishermen and wound them horribly."

"Let's not talk about that," said Helena. "Another thing I hate, though, is eels, because I've heard that they mate with snakes."[55]

"That happens in the summer," replied Cornelia, "so what does it matter? We don't eat them in that season. And they are really delicious to eat, especially the freshwater ones. One thing I've read about eels is that their skin is sometimes baked so hard by the sun that they can't swim; also that they are born without a father or mother and bring themselves up alone. But another remarkable thing is the swordfish, and how violently it tears apart ships when it collides with them, with that sword that nature has placed on its brow and that gives it its name, which sends tuna and other fish flying in terror, just like lambs fleeing from a wolf. And the fish known as the sea-ram does the same with its horn; it lurks under ships, waiting its chance to seize any man or animal that happens to fall or dive into

---

legend, reported by Aelian and Pliny, that it was capable of dragging ships to a halt (Davidson 1981, 166).

53. The beast referred to here is the *aspidochelone*, described in the bestiary tradition: a turtle of such prodigious size as to be frequently mistaken for an island by hapless sailors, who, if they were unlucky enough to anchor on the beast and attempt to light a fire on its back, would often find themselves dragged down to the deep by it along with their ships. (McCulloch 1960, 91–92).

54. The great weever fish (*Trachinus draco*) in fact poisons through its dorsal fins rather than its bite. Pliny notes the curative properties of the great weever's brain in his discussion of medicinal uses of fish (*NH*, 32, 17, 47). The other fish mentioned here is another weever (*Trachinus araneus*), known as the "spider fish" (*pesce ragno*) in Italian (Davidson 1981, 115). Pliny mentions its venomous sharp dorsal fin in his chapter on poisonous fish (*NH*, 9, 72, 155)

55. Pliny mentions as a rumor the suggestion that moray eels crawl out onto dry land and mate with snakes (*NH*, 9, 39, 76) (though he does not restrict their mating season to the summer, as Corinna does here). The story is also found in Aelian and in Oppian, who gives a particularly steamy description of this coupling.

the water.[56] The octopus, though, is man's friend, like the dolphin, and it takes on the color of anything that comes near it, just like a chameleon."[57]

"They say dolphins know when bad weather is on the way," said Cornelia.[58] "They are the heralds of storms and, as I said, a friend to man and especially a friend to young boys: you often see them playing with boys along the seashores. In fact, I remember once, when a boy was playing around, sitting on a dolphin's back, he accidentally speared himself in the rib with one of its fins, and he died of the wound. And the dolphin was so stricken by this that it refused to go back in the water but stayed out on the shore, out of its element, and shortly afterward died as well."[59]

"These are all great marvels of nature," said Lucretia, "but I've heard of a fish called a parrot-wrasse, which ruminates in the sea just like some land animals do."[60]

"It's true," said Lucretia, "if we can believe what we read. And that same fish, when it is caught in a trap, always contrives to get out by its tail, helped out by its fellow wrasses outside the trap.[61] The sturgeon, a most noble fish, is even more charitable[62] toward its species; it never abandons them and it is prepared to risk its own life to defend them."

"In that case," said Leonora, "what should men not be prepared to

56. The fish described here appears to be the (mythical) "sea-ram" described by Pliny (*NH*, 9, 67, 145), which sinks fishing boats and lurks "like a brigand" in the shadow of ships waiting for incautious swimmers.

57. Aristotle (*HA*, 622a8) and Pliny (*NH*, 9, 46, 87) talk of octopuses changing color to camouflage themselves. Both writers also mention that the octopus will approach a man's hand in the water, though they attribute this to the beast's stupidity rather than any love for humanity.

58. There may be an interjection from one of the other speakers missing at this point; as the text stands, Cornelia appears to speak twice in succession.

59. Dolphins' affection for humans, and especially young boys, is mentioned by Aristotle (*HA*, 631a7–13) and dwelt on at length by Pliny (*NH*, 9, 8, 24–28). Pliny's account contains various similar anecdotes, though none identical to this.

60. The parrot-wrasse (*Scarus cretensis*), highly prized by Roman gourmets, is described by Pliny (*NH*, 9, 29, 62), who includes the detail that it is said to be "the only fish that chews the cud and feeds on grasses and not on other fish."

61. The story of parrot-wrasses collaborating to save trapped companions is told by Aelian (*On Animals*, I, 4), and Oppian (*Halieutica*, IV, 40ff), the latter with much pathetic detail.

62. The original here has "far more charitable" (*molto più caritativo*), which reads oddly in the context; the original may be corrupt here.

do for women? For are we not of the same species as them? And instead they oppress us and treat us just as the hedgehog treated the viper: he was all spiky and she was rather delicate and they were crammed together in a small space, and when she complained he was hurting her with his spikes, he said, 'if you don't want to stay, you're welcome to leave.'"

"Men love us just as long as they think they are going to get something out of us," said Cornelia, "and, for the rest, they wouldn't risk a single hair on their head to help us. But, thinking of hedge-hogs, there's the marine equivalent, the sea urchin,[63] which moves through the sea using its spines instead of feet, and it can predict storms at sea and hides itself in the sand to protect itself. The cut-tlefish, by contrast, doesn't need to hide, as it fixes itself so firmly on the seabed that it isn't shaken, however fierce the sea."

"I can tell you a thing or two about those crazy little creatures," said Leonora. "Once when I was out staying in the country with some relatives (before I was widowed), and we went out fishing, there were some cuttlefish in our catch. And since I happened to be dressed in white, let me tell you, they really did a fine job on me; it looked as though someone had thrown an inkwell over my face and all down my dress."

"That's true," said Cornelia. "As soon as they're caught, they spurt out their ink in the fishermen's faces, as a form of self-defense. But fishing is at least as much fun as hunting birds: in fact, more so, in my opinion," she continued. "Especially when you get a good catch, either with nets cast from the boats, or with lines, or with fixed nets or octopus traps, or by whatever other means."

"And what do you think of that technique of inebriating fish, as people do in streams, just to amuse themselves?" said Leonora.

"Oh, that's great fun!" said Cornelia. "You see the fish floating up to the surface, as though they were asleep, and you can catch them with your hands."

"If you want to catch fish, though, whether saltwater or freshwa-ter, it's better to avoid times of drought," said Corinna, "because fish escape the heat by moving up-river or deeper into the sea. It's best to go fishing when it's raining or when there's the sirocco and the water

---

63. The sea urchin, in Italian, is known as the *riccio di mare* (lit. "sea hedgehog"). The detail mentioned below in the text about sea urchins predicting storms and anchoring themselves on the seabed is found in Pliny (*NH,* 9, 51, 100), who also mentions cuttlefish steadying themselves in rough weather (*NH,* 9, 44, 83).

is rising high and all churned up; it's then, in all that turbulence, that it's best to look for prey, and you can catch fish in great quantities. But this talk of fishing has made me think of the cleverness of the anglerfish, which you might almost say really does fish, lying on its back: it lurks under the sand and deftly casts out a series of natural fishing lines, with bait attached to them, designed to attract the incautious little fish, which race to feed on it and fall prey to the cunning of the predator."[64]

"Well, that's certainly a great secret of nature," said Cornelia. "But you haven't got on to shellfish yet, and yet there are very many kinds."

"What do you want me to say about them?" Corinna replied. "If I were to talk about them all, it would take quite a while. But there's one species of shellfish called the fan mussel, or pinna, that deserves a mention. It's blind by nature and incapable of foraging for food, but, in compensation, it's developed a marvelous trick. It makes friends with a shrimp, which comes to live in its shell with it and helps it out like this: the pinna lures little fish into its house, with its tongue, which hangs outside, and, as soon as they're in the shell, the shrimp, which is hiding in there, signals to its accomplice, which instantly closes the doors to its lodging and traps the prey in there; and then the two carry off their spoils and feast on them like merry dining companions."[65]

"What a fine trick!" said the Queen. "And it's proof of how useful it is to have good friends; for, as we were saying, when you can't do something yourself, you know you can rely on their help."

"Indeed," said Leonora. "But we would never get any help like that from men: in the same circumstances, they'd devour all the prey themselves and round the meal off with us, if they could."

"That's true," said Cornelia. "But, talking of shellfish, there's another kind in the sea known as the nautilus, which uses its shell as a boat and a wide, fine flap of skin as a sail, and sails along moving its limbs like oars and using its tail as a tiller."[66]

---

64. The ingenious fishing method of the anglerfish, or monkfish, is described by Aristotle (*HA*, 620b13–18) and Pliny (*NH*, 9, 67, 143).

65. The mollusk under discussion here is the *pinna nobilis*, once prized in the Mediterranean for its silky thread, which was harvested for cloth. Pliny (*NH*, 9, 66, 142) describes at some length the shell's relationship with its sentinel shrimp (or "pinna guard"), as do Oppian (*Halieutica*, 2, 186–98) and Aelian (*On Animals*, 3, 29).

66. The paper nautilus, or "mariner" (*Argonauta argo*) is described by Pliny (*NH*, 9, 47, 88); and Aristotle (*HA*, 622b5–20). Oppian (*Halieutica*, 1, 338–59) is the source for the

"That must be quite an amazing sight," said the Queen.

"Men must have learned to sail by observing that example," suggested Lucretia.

"Oh, but surely a greater master was needed to teach such an important science?" said Leonora.

"It's certainly true, when you think about it," said Cornelia, "that it must have taken extraordinary daring for the first man to set out to cross from shore to shore, venturing out to plow through the treacherous waves without any knowledge of seamanship and with no real idea what awaited him. And, similarly, just think what extraordinary ingenuity it took for the first man to start manufacturing ships, galleys, and all kinds of little craft."

"But intellects have become more refined through history," said Corinna, "and techniques of design have constantly improved through the ages. It's not as though all the marvelous technical achievements of the world were perfected at a single moment and by one sole inventor."[67]

"When it's good weather and there's a calm sea," said Cornelia, "it must be enjoyable sailing around our coasts. But on long sea voyages, especially when a great storm blows up, what a terror it must be! and what anguish for the poor sailors!"

"Yes, indeed," said Leonora. "But, then, think how many people there are who drown without ever going near the sea. Every time I go out, I hear someone say, 'Oh, poor girl, she's in deep water with that awful man.' Believe me, if women thought about it, they'd see that it's more dangerous to put yourself in the hands of a man than for a sailor to place himself at the mercy of the sea and the winds."

"It's certainly true," said Cornelia, "that many more ships reach a safe harbor than women do."

"Would that it weren't so!" said Corinna.

"Just think, though, what an enterprise sailing really is," said Cornelia. "Even if the ship is soundly built, of solid oak, lined with pine, well oiled, sealed, and smeared with pitch; even if it is well pro-

---

notion, mentioned below in the text, of its having been the inspiration for the invention of sailing.

67. There is a certain historical interest in this rejection of the widespread convention of attributing human inventions to legendary individuals (see, for example, Leonora's remarks on Penthesilea and Carmenta at pp. 100–101). See, however, *NH,* 7, 56, 206–9, for an account of the development of sailing through a gradual series of technological innovations.

vided with sails, tillers, anchors, rigging, and all the other appropriate equipment; even if it is manned by sailors who are highly skilled in managing the tiller, the sails, and the compass and all the rest; even if it is just the right size and weight for the cargo it is carrying— even if all this is in place, it's often of no avail, I can tell you. And so we see that of the various types of galley and little merchant ships and so on that set off for strange and distant lands, a good number come to grief, even though their navigators are guided by maps and the Pole Star, and know which passages to avoid and which to take; and even though their crews are highly experienced, and know the sea, the winds, and the rocks. They still often find themselves hurled to shore or driven onto hidden rocks by the raging of the winds and the long battering of storms; and many go down."

"Apart from all the other hardships they suffer," said the Queen, "what I can't understand is how sailors who do manage to arrive safely in some distant port at the end of all their journeyings can get used to living in such a strange climate, when they are used to the air of home."

"But you have to take into account," said Corinna, "that men who become sailors usually have a naturally strong constitution and can put up with a great deal. But, in any case, the change of air is not such a serious business, because they get used to the change little by little as they sail: it would be different if they could fly from one place to another like birds, as that kind of sudden change would be much harder to withstand. And, besides, there are places that may have a better climate than the port they were sailing from. It's true, though, that many sailors do get ill."

"If there weren't so many dangers in these sea voyages," said Leonora, "it would be a marvelous thing to go off and see the wonders of the world—those distant seas where they say pearls grow, and the Red Sea, famous for submerging those Egyptians long ago, and the North Sea, which in winter becomes so frozen that you can walk on it and pick fish up with your hands, as they lie frozen on the surface in their hundreds."[68]

"I believe," said Cornelia, "that the vastness of the seas derives from the fact that so many rivers flow into them."

---

68. The reference to the Red Sea is to the famous account in the Old Testament of its waters engulfing the pursuing Egyptian army after parting to allow safe passage to Moses and the Israelites (Exodus, 14, 26–28). I have not been able to trace a source for the story about the North Sea freezing over.

"That can't be true," said Corinna, "because if (as is the case), all rivers come from the sea and keep the same water in them, and if the sea is always more or less full, depending on the waxing and waning of the moon (as we've already mentioned), then it cannot be that the sea derives from the rivers; on the contrary, the rivers derive from the sea and eventually flow back into it. But that doesn't make the sea grow, because it yields up to the springs the same amount of water as it receives from the rivers."

"So river waters come from the sea, then, even though rivers have fresh water and the sea is salt?" asked Lucretia.

"They do indeed," said Cornelia, "for, as the waters pass through the inner reaches of the earth, they are purified and freshened and take on another taste, as though they had been distilled. And that's why there are so many different qualities of springwater."[69]

"The properties of springs: that's something I've heard about as well," said the Queen. "There's one, for example, the Lyncestis, whose waters make people drunk, like wine."[70]

"That's what the natural historians say," said Corinna. "And there's another in Cyprus that according to some sources has the power to rekindle a lamp that has gone out, and another that hardens and petrifies wood that is placed in it."

"And then there are those others that the poet talks about," said Virginia, "one of which makes those who drink from it die of laughter, while the cure is to drink from the other.[71] And then there's

69. This theory of the circulation of waters is found in Pliny (*NH*, 66, 166), who described water being filtered from the sea through a vast network of veins in the earth until it is forced out through springs. The notion that seawater undergoes a kind of distillation in the course of this process is found, for example, in Seneca 1972, 1: 216–17 (3, 5, 1); see also 1: 246–47 (3, 20, 1).

70. This fountain is described by Pliny (*NH*, 2, 106, 230), whose two discussions of the miraculous powers of springwaters, in books 2 and 31 of the *Natural History*, are the source of most of the examples cited subsequently in the text: see *NH*, 2, 106, 228, for a mention of a fountain with the power to rekindle extinguished torches (though Pliny locates it in mainland Greece rather than Cyprus, at the shrine of Zeus at Dodona); also 31, 20, 29–30, on petrifying springs; 2, 106, 229, on the "Fountain of the Sun"; and 31, 16, 19, on "Cupid's fountain" and its power to dispel love ("Cirico" may be a distortion of Cyzicus, the town on the Propontis (the modern Sea of Marmara, in Turkey), where Pliny locates this last spring).

71. The poet in question is Petrarch (*RS*, 135, 76–79), who locates these springs, following Pomponius Mela, in the "Isles of Fortune" (the Canaries). The same canzone also contains mentions of two of the "Plinian" springs mentioned here: the Fountain of the Sun and the spring that relights extinguished lamps.

that other one that's known as the Fountain of the Sun, because it boils at night and cools down by day. And then there's the one they call the Cirico spring or Cupid's spring, which has the power to chase love from our hearts, as some people claim."

"Then there are other springs known as spas," said Cornelia, "whose waters are so beneficial to men's ailments."

"Oh, if only there were some spring," said Leonora, "that could cure men of their various hidden ailments, which they pay no heed to curing, yet which are the most pernicious and incurable of all!"

"What are these hidden ailments?" asked Helena.

"Infidelity," said Leonora. "Deception, ingratitude—that kind of thing."

"The worst thing is," said Cornelia, "that it's they who have these ailments, but we who feel the pain."

"Oh," said Corinna [sic], "when I talked about spa water being good for men's ailments, I was talking about both sexes. And I was speaking of physical infirmities, for the kind of mental indispositions you're speaking of in men could not be cured by all the waters of the ocean."

"I was beginning to wonder how long you were going to be able to continue without someone intervening to make mischief," said Helena. "Now do please go on with what you were saying."

"Calm down!" said Corinna, with a laugh. "You'll just have to put up with what we've been saying—and with what we are going to say later. Now, the spa waters I was talking to you about are of various kinds and found in various different places. There are extremely cold ones, tepid ones, hot ones, and even boiling ones—I remember seeing some of those in the mountains around Padua, and they say that the reason why they come out so hot is because there's so much sulfur around in that area.[72] There are other hot springs in other areas and they have excellent curative properties, as we can see every day from experience. But springs of that kind don't appear to flow into rivers. For, although all rivers have their sources in springs (though this has been called into doubt in the case of the Nile),[73] that

72. The reference is perhaps to the famous springs at Abano Terme, near Padua, celebrated in the sixteenth century for their efficacy against gout (Chambers 1992). More generally, on spas, see book 31 of Pliny's *Natural History*, esp. 2, 4–8, 12 and 32, 59–61.

73. The source of the Nile was a subject of much speculation in antiquity and the Renaissance (see, for example, *NH*, 5, 10, 51).

doesn't mean that all springs flow into rivers: in fact, the waters of some flow back to the sea by subterranean paths."

"Is it true," asked Leonora, "what they say about the Nile, that the rushing of its waters is so loud that no one can live within miles of it without going deaf?"[74]

"Indeed it is," said Cornelia [sic]. "Or at least that's what we read."

"And that river called the Pactolus," said Lucretia. "Do you believe what they say, that the sand of its shores is made of gold?"[75]

"It could be true," replied Corinna. "I haven't seen it with my own eyes."

"Oh, you're one of those people who never want to believe anything," said Helena.

"The best plan is just never to believe in men," said Leonora.

"Oh, you can believe some of what they say," replied Corinna. "Just not what they say to women. Now, for goodness' sake, let's leave men alone for a moment. There's another river as well, known as the Ebro in Thrace, the Tagus in Spain, the Ganges in India, and the Po in Italy that is also reputed to have golden sands."[76]

Then Lucretia spoke up, "Why is the river Tigris known by that name? Is it because tigers come from it?"

"No," said Corinna. "It's known as that because it's so fast.[77] It's said that both the Tigris and the Euphrates come from the Earthly Paradise."

"Which do you think is the vastest of all rivers?" said Cornelia.

"There's the Ganges," replied Corinna. "That most immense of rivers, which is said to be twenty miles wide and bottomless in depth and which runs through India and Arabia Felix. Then there's the Don, that icy-cold river, and the Danube and Rhine, that flow through Germany and other northern parts; all rivers much celebrated by writers."

74. See *NH*, 6, 35, 181; Seneca 1972, 2: 25 (4a, 2, 5–6).

75. The Pactolus was a river in Lydia (Asia Minor), the mud from whose banks was rumored in antiquity to contain particles of gold. It is mentioned in Ariosto's *Orlando Furioso* (*OF*, 17, 78, 5), which may well be Fonte's source.

76. This statement seems extraordinary enough to prompt the suspicion that the text may be corrupt. The Ebro is, of course, like the Tagus, in Spain, rather than Thrace.

77. Fonte's source is probably, ultimately, Pliny (*NH*, 6, 31, 127), who notes that the name Tigris means "arrow" in Persian. The legend mentioned immediately below in the text, that the Tigris and Euphrates had their source in the Earthly Paradise, derives ultimately from a passage in Genesis, 2, 10–14, and is mentioned in Dante's description of the Earthly Paradise in *Purgatory*, 33, 112–14.

"Petrarch," said the Queen, "gathered up almost all the most famous rivers in a few lines, in that poem which starts,

Non Tesin, Po, Varo, Arno, Adige e Tebro

Neither Ticino, Po, Varo, Arno, Adige, nor Tiber[78]

"But, leaving aside those far-distant rivers," [continued Corinna], "there's the Piave, that vast and extremely fast-flowing river, which passes through great tracts of land and finally pours its fresh waters into the Adriatic. And then there's that most noble of rivers the Po, known as the king of rivers, which flows along its seven branches, irrigating and fertilizing our lands on all sides; it flows through the most noble city of Ferrara and, passing through many different places, finally comes out into our lagoon.[79] A lady made a very honorable mention of this river in a sonnet she wrote in praise of a Ferrarese lady called Laura Peverara (she was from Mantua, actually, but lived at the court of the Duke of Ferrara)."[80]

"Corinna, darling," said Leonora, "can you remember how the sonnet goes? Go on, tell us, please."

"Oh, I don't know," she replied. But Virginia and the others begged her for it, and she recalled it to mind and recited it as the others listened.

Splendea nel regal Po chiarezza tanta,
Ch'ogn'altro fiume a le sue egregie sponde
Cedea di ricche palme e di feconde,
E grate olive, onde si pregia e vanta.
Ma poi ch'or presta ombra più lieta, e santa
Anco il bel lauro a le sue lucid'onde,

---

78. The first quatrain of the poem referred to (*RS*, 148), a famous Petrarchan tour de force, consists of a list of twenty-three rivers and a sea in Europe and Asia, all of which combined, according to the poet, could do less to dampen the burning in his heart than the little Sorgue, which ran through his beloved valley of Vaucluse, near Avignon.

79. The Po in fact flows close to, but not actually through, Ferrara, before reaching its delta at the bottom of the gulf of Venice, below Chioggia.

80. Laura Peverara, or Peperara (c. 1545–1601), the daughter of a wealthy Mantuan merchant, entered the court of Ferrara in the early 1580s as lady-in-waiting to the new duchess, Margherita Gonzaga, and in 1583, married a Ferrarese nobleman, Count Annibale Turchi. She was famed for the beauty and virtue mentioned below, but also for her remarkable musical talent, which she displayed in the celebrated female vocal consort of the Ferrarese court.

> *Può sì 'l valor de l'onorata fronde,*
> *Che insino il mar l'alte sue lodi canta.*
> *Se fu virtù, se fu bellezza rara*
> *Ne l'arbor già, che al gran Toscano piacque,*
> *Tutto in quest'è via più famosa e chiara.*
> *Poiché, se quella in picciol borgo nacque,*
> *Questa Mantoa creò, nutre or Ferrara,*
> *Degno ornamento a le sue nobil'acque.*

Already in the past the regal Po shone with such glorious
fame that all other rivers bowed before its noble shores,
and all had to cede to its rich palms and fruitful and
pleasant olive groves. But now a still happier and more
sacred shade is cast over its gleaming waters by the lovely
laurel tree, whose glorious leaves compel the sea itself to
sing this great river's praises. If virtue, if singular beauty
once resided in that tree that so pleased the great
Tuscan, this present laurel is more famed and glorious yet.
For if that laurel of old was born in a small town, this
modern one was created by Mantua and is now nourished by
Ferrara: a worthy ornament to the noble waters that flow
through that city.[81]

The women were delighted with the sonnet Corinna recited for
them; even if it did not strike them as particularly elegant, they still
enjoyed it a great deal for its novelty and aptness to the conversation.

"Now, that same river," continued Corinna, "also passes through
other Italian cities, like Cremona, Piacenza, Casale, and many others."

"You may sing the praises of any river you like," said Helena, "but
I'll always love my dear Brenta the best: it's our nearest river, for one
thing, and it passes through the most noble and ancient city of
Padua, which is such an honorable and glorious place, the birthplace
of studies and the beneficiary of so many great intellects, a city rich

---

81. In this sonnet, Laura Peverara is compared to her namesake, the beloved of Petrarch
(the "gran Toscano" of l. 10) and a native of Avignon, whom the modern Laura
outshines, not least because of the greater dignity of her birthplace. The mention of
palm trees at l. 3 of this sonnet is unexpected in a description of the banks of the Po;
it may be that Fonte's botanical observation here is swayed by the metaphorical sense of
the word ("honors," "victories"). The punning use of a laurel tree to symbolize Laura is
Petrarchan in origin.

in fine gardens and distinguished families, and full of so many lovely and virtuous ladies that it is like paradise living there."

"That's true," said Cornelia, "and you have every reason to praise this Brenta of yours, as your estates lie on the river and you enjoy its waters half the year."

"Apart from anything," said Lucretia, "how on earth would we manage in the summer, during periods of drought, when there's no rain and the wells are dry, if it weren't for the waters of the Brenta?"

"You are teasing me, I know," said Helena. "But in fact that *is* important."

"And I," said Leonora, "am very fond of the Adige, because when I was in Verona in the governor's entourage I had a marvelous time on the river with a party of ladies who were my companions there."

"To be sure," said the Queen, "Verona too is a fine and much-respected city, as is Vicenza, which lies on the charming river Bacchiglione, and, though small in size, is well populated and rich, full of fine buildings and charming gardens. But Verona is a most ancient city and existed in Roman times; it was a Roman colony and there are still Roman remains there, like the arena they called the amphitheater, and many other buildings. It's a city that has often been sacked by barbarian invaders, but it is now more flourishing than ever. And somewhere nearby that deserves a mention is Lake Garda, famous for its *carpioni* that people say feed on gold."[82]

"Well, you're all welcome to your own opinions," said Cornelia, "but to my mind Brescia is the most flourishing and comfortable of the cities of Italy, and the surrounding area is extremely fertile. I stayed there with my grandfather when he was in the administration there;[83] it's a very civilized area, even though there are mountains on one side of it and many important castles and fortresses in the vicinity. Four well-known rivers, the Navilio, Mola, Oglio, and Sperchio pass through Brescian territory, and they also carry their waters to

---

82. The *carpione* (*Salmo carpio*), found exclusively in Lake Garda, was a celebrated delicacy in this period, and sufficiently rare and valued to have been the subject of protective legislation by the Venetian government in the fifteenth century. Legends surrounding the fish included that mentioned here concerning its unusual diet; see Lenotti 1977, 21; and Bertoluzza 1972, 84 (I am grateful to Corinna da Fonseca-Wollheim for these references).

83. Brescia, though in Lombardy, was under Venetian rule in this period and remained so until the fall of the Venetian republic in 1797.

many other places in the area, especially the Oglio, which passes through the border area and provides water for, among others, the towns of Pontevico, Orzinovi, and Soncino, that splendid town, with its noble fortress, home to many refined souls.[84] And then there's the river Mincio, which forms a kind of lake around the noble city of Mantua, famous for many things and especially for being the birthplace of Virgil. Then there's the Ticino, which passes through the lovely city of Pavia, another seat of learning, which has that highly respected university which has always been well stocked with distinguished scholars. Pavia is ancient, but not so ancient as Milan, which is traversed by the river. . . .[85] It was first raised in the middle of Lombardy by Breno during the Roman period, and then it was destroyed by the Frank Belovese, and then it was enlarged and rebuilt like so many other Italian cities."[86]

"But surely the river Arno has a greater claim to distinction than any other river?" said Cornelia.

"Indeed it does," said Corinna. "For the Arno is that much-celebrated river that flows through the lovely city that bred so many remarkable intellects: Dante, Boccaccio, and Petrarch (whom we've just mentioned) and others from the past and the present, whom it would take too long to mention. Besides which Florence is now so rich in fine buildings, beautiful gardens, and illustrious citizens that one might say it is the greatest city in the world. The river Ombrone passes through the charming city of Siena, also a center of learning,

---

84. Orzinovi and Soncino, with its fifteenth-century fortress, lie on the river Oglio between Brescia and Crema, to the southwest of the former. Pontevico is a little to the east, on the road between Brescia and Cremona. The whole area was under Venetian rule in the sixteenth century. The unexpected amount of detail in Fonte's description of this area, and her praises of Soncino in particular, may perhaps be accounted for by the fact that the physician Orazio Guarguanti, praised below at two points in the text and evidently a part of her circle, was a native of the town. Of the four rivers named here, only the Oglio is straightforwardly identifiable, though the "Mola" is probably the Mella, the "Sperchio," the Serio, and the "Navilio," the Naviglio Grande Bresciano, a canal of ancient construction.

85. There is a lacuna in the text here (unsurprisingly, as no well-known river flows through Milan).

86. Fonte's interest in this distinctly obscure reach of history is perhaps explained by her friendship with Giovanni Niccolò Doglioni, who, as a historian and a native of Belluno, had a particular interest in the legendary Frankish prince Belovese (sixth century BC), conjectured to be the founder (not the destroyer, as Fonte states here) of both Milan and Belluno (see Doglioni 1588, 4–6; and 1606, 1: 53 and 2: 287; also Doglioni 1594, 69, on "Breno," another legendary founder of the city).

famous for the academies that flourish there and for many other excellent qualities, which make it the equal of many other cities, however famous. But the imperial Tiber advances all other rivers in dignity: the river that has seen, over so many centuries, so many remarkable things in the ancient city of Rome that lies on its banks (I don't need to go into detail, since you already know all about them). So there are infinite rivers, rising from the sea, as we have seen, and flowing back into the sea, as we have seen."

"To get back to what we were talking about," said Lucretia, "it seems very odd to me that water, which is heavy by nature, can, as you claim, rise so high as to give rise to rivers from mountain springs."

"If you think that's so amazing," said Leonora, "then just think of the way in which men, who are inferior to us and so should by rights stay below us, in a lowly and humble position, manage to rise above us and dominate us, against all reason and against all justice. So you shouldn't be surprised if water too, though such a base element, is presumptuous enough to ascend to the summit of mountains. At least water then flows back to its natural level again, whereas men remain obstinately fixed in their stern position of eminence."

"It certainly seems strange," said Corinna, "that water, which is a heavy element (though also a mobile one) can go upward. But in fact this movement reflects a natural instinct. Nature occasionally breaks its own laws—dramatically at times: if you think about it, it's more amazing that humidity should rise from the earth and the sky and turn into air, as it does when clouds are formed, than that the sea should be able to rise up mountains. Also, what element is lighter than fire and more resistant by nature to a low position? And yet, following another law and natural tendency, it does consent to remain on earth, which is the lowest element of all. In fact, one element converts into another over time, so we find the earth gradually turning into water, water into air, and air into fire. And we also find the opposite: fire becomes air; air, water; and water turns back into earth."

"If the earth is round and surrounded by air, how does it hold together?" asked Leonora.

"That's the way it was made to be," replied Corinna. "That's how the Prime Mover designed it. The earth is anchored at its center by its own weight and solidity, and is content with its status as the humblest of the elements. And, cold and dry as it is, in its solidity it is the ancient mother of all created things."

"Since the earth is contained in a narrower space than all the other elements," said Cornelia, "it is remarkable that it has generated so many animals, and produced so many plants, and that it contains so many different materials."

"It is indeed," said Corinna. "If you consider all the different species of animals that live and breed on the earth, it seems miraculous that there can be so many, and it would be impossible to describe even a tiny fraction of them."

"I can believe it," said Cornelia. "And the number of animals in the wild must be far greater than the number of domestic ones."

"Without a doubt," said Corinna.

"Don't be so sure," said Leonora. "There are more animals in the home than you think, they just aren't recognized as such."

"Oh, do be quiet, for heaven's sake!" said the Queen.

"Ah, madam!" said Leonora. "How many lions are there, how many tigers, how many bears that we forget to include in the total? How many even more savage and terrifying creatures? Don't try to tell me about them!"

"Let it go!" said the Queen. "I know very well what you're talking about. I pity men, when you're around!"

"On the contrary," said Leonora. "You should pity us, when they're around. Do you know, I've heard that the lion, that noble beast, always shows sympathy for the most humble creatures and does not harm them: in fact, when a lion comes across a man and a woman together, it tends to leave the woman alone and attack the man, as though it sensed our humility and innocence through some natural instinct and took pity on us—ferocious, savage beast though it is.[87] So that the beast behaves toward us as men should, while men, who so often injure us without reason, behave toward us in a manner befitting the most savage of beasts."

But Helena broke in to stop her at this point, "I think I've heard that the lion, for all its fierceness, fears the voice of the cockerel. Is that true?"

"Well, that's what the natural historians say," said Corinna. "It's also afraid of the sight of fire.[88] But even so, the lion is known as the king of beasts, because of its strength and courage, even though

87. Fonte's source here may well be Pliny, who notes lions' reluctance to attack women in his *Natural History* (*NH*, 8, 19, 48) (though Pliny represents lions' tendency to direct their attacks against men in preference to women or children as evidence of their gallantry toward the weak, rather than of their intuition of men's lesser deserts).

88. The source is, again here, Pliny (*NH*, 8, 19, 52), who adds turning wheels to his list of lions' fears.

there are larger beasts, like the elephant; crueler ones, like the tiger; and more ferocious ones, like the wild boar and so on."

"Are tigers and leopards the same thing?" asked Lucretia.

"No, madam," said Corinna. "But there are great similarities between them, both in their skin and in their cruelty and fleetness of foot. For tigers are faster than any other animal, and, in this connection, I remember reading that huntsmen find great difficulties in taking these animals' cubs from the nest. For even when they see that the mother is far off and they carry the cubs off on swift horses and set off with an enormous advantage, the sources say that as soon as the mother realizes, she runs behind them so fast that she immediately catches them up. So that, in order to get away, the huntsmen are forced to throw her one of the cubs; and she's so fast that she can pick it up, go back to the nest and leave it there, and then catch up with the huntsmen to get the others back; and they have to throw her another cub, and so on until they can reach a port and sail out to sea to escape her fury.[89] Another notorious animal trait is the stolid and irascible nature of the bear (an animal whose flesh is good to eat). Bears are born as a mass of formless animate matter and only gradually take on their natural shape, through time and the efforts of their mothers."[90]

"But isn't the deer just as swift as the tiger?" said Lucretia. "After all, the poet says,

I dì miei legger, che nessun cervo

My days [flee] swifter than any deer . . .[91]

"The deer," said Corinna, "besides being fleet of foot, is an animal of immense longevity, and lives on for many centuries, renewing its horns and its skin, which changes from fawn to white. Deer contain no bile, except in their innards, and there is a bone in their hearts. The snake is another creature that lives to a great age, and, besides that, it is an extremely vigilant animal and has been endowed by nature with the highest degree of prudence possible in an animal.

89. A similar account is found in Pliny (*NH,* 8, 25, 66).

90. Fonte's most likely source of information is, again, book 8 of Pliny's *Natural History:* see especially *NH* 8, 54, 126, for the bizarre detail of bears' supposed formlessness at birth ("The cubs are born a white, shapeless lump of flesh, hardly bigger than a mouse, eyeless, hairless and with only the claws protruding. This is then gradually licked into shape by the mother.")

91. The line (slightly misquoted) is from Petrarch (*RS,* 319).

Many useful medications are derived from snakes (only from certain species, though); and there are also snakes that are good to eat."[92]

"You must be joking!" said Helena. "I wouldn't touch them myself. Give me a nice plump heifer instead, any day—what do you say, Virginia?"

"I'll join you!" said Virginia.

"Do you know, though," said the Queen, "I'm just as happy eating a nice piece of young beef, as I am veal."

"Yes indeed," said Lucretia. "I must say I quite agree. But apart from that, what else can you tell us about cows and oxen, Corinna?"

"What can I say?" said Corinna. "In my opinion, they are the most useful animal nature has provided us. For, while they are alive, they are extremely useful in farmwork, and also (I'm talking about cows here, of course) they provide us with all kinds of milk products, necessary to human life. And, once they are dead, what part of these animals is not of some use to us? Everyone knows how useful their skin is for various purposes: we eat their flesh, and we even use their horns and hooves for various things. They are docile, slow creatures, rather melancholy by nature; and their meat is healthy and pleasant-tasting, but difficult to digest for those of delicate stomach; and that's why veal is more expensive, as it's more easily digested and nutritious."

"I've heard," said Cornelia, "that if you boil down a calf's foot for forty days, the liquid can get rid of wrinkles and make your skin as smooth as that of a girl of fifteen."

"The flesh of kids is healthy to eat," said Lucretia. "But lamb is not; it's too humid. And what about wild animals, like the deer you were just talking about: are fallow deer and roe deer more or less digestible than domestic cattle?"

"They are lighter to digest and more nutritious," said Corinna.

"I'm so enjoying this conversation," said Lucretia, "that I'd be

---

92. The longevity of stags is mentioned by Pliny (*NH*, 8, 50, 119) and by the medieval bestiary tradition (which occasionally has them living 900 years), though Aristotle dismisses this as a "fabulous story" (*HA*, 578b25; see also *HA*, 506a32 for an allusion to deer's lack of a gallbladder and the bitter taste of their gut). The notion that the deer had a bone in its heart was perpetuated in medical literature (where this bone was recommended as a cure for poison and plague) despite the skepticism of doctors like Antonio Maria Brasavola and of the pioneering anatomist Andrea Vesalio (Mattioli 1573, 275; Thorndike 1923–58, 5: 454). The juxtaposition of stags and snakes in this passage probably betrays the influence of the medieval bestiary tradition, where the two beasts (linked by the deadly enmity they supposedly bore one another) were generally portrayed together (McCulloch 1960, 174).

quite happy to forget about detailing men's deficiencies, if you others
were in agreement. I'd rather listen to Corinna and learn something
new than talk about men's flaws, which are something of which we
are all only too aware."

"I'm not sure about that," said Corinna. "Women aren't as aware of
men's failings as they should be, or else they'd know how to protect
themselves from men better than they do. In fact, it's easier for us to
understand the properties of irrational animals (even though they
should be more mysterious to us, since their nature is so alien from
ours and they can't speak) than to understand those false creatures
who are close to us in nature, but quite different in their character
and desires, and who never speak the truth."

"I despair of you," Leonora said to Lucretia. "You're always going
off the subject. I'm surprised at our Queen, allowing you to break the
rules like that."

"Oh, I'm not too worried about their going off the subject," said
the Queen, "since *you* never forget it for a moment. Besides, you say
quite enough to make up for any deficiencies on their part."

"If I speak ill of men," said Leonora, "it's in order to speak the
truth and to say what I genuinely feel. Not like men, who speak honeyed words, but underneath are pure poison."

"Absolutely," said Corinna. "All the antidotes the pharmacists
make up, and all the powers of the unicorn's horn, wouldn't be
enough to protect us from men's malice."

"It really is a marvelous property of the unicorn," said Helena,
"that its horn is so effective against poison."[93]

"It's also useful against many diseases of the heart," said Corinna.
"And the natural historians say that unicorns so love virgins that they
happily fall asleep with their heads in their laps, and that's how
hunters catch them. But I wonder whether you ever read the fable of
the unicorn?"

"No, I haven't," said Helena; and all the others said the same,
and begged her to tell them the story, if she could remember it. And
she began the fable, with these words:

"The poets write that at the time when the thunderstruck

93. The myth of the unicorn was not widely doubted by naturalists until well into the
seventeenth century (Thomas 1984, 79–80; though see Shepard 1930, 158–61 for one
sixteenth-century skeptic). Venetians had particular cause for belief, as no fewer than
three unicorn horns were preserved in the treasury of St. Mark's (ibid. 1930, 106–8).

Phaeton, the son of Apollo and Clymene, had fallen to earth, and his sisters were transformed into poplars and his wretched mother was left wandering the earth in her grief, there ruled in the regions of the Orient, in a noble city of India called Felicia, a king called Alciteo, the younger son of that same father, Apollo, by another of his mistresses.[94] This Alciteo was showered with so many blessings and maintained such a splendid and noble court, that he was visited and honored by all the leading men of Asia, and his virtue and noble demeanor drew the most respected princes and the finest knights of the age to his court to pay homage to him. And among the others who came there to honor him, attracted by the legend of his fame, was Prince Lioncorno of Phrygia, who was welcomed most honorably by Alciteo and soon contracted a close friendship with him, for the two men were alike in their virtue and courtesy; and such was the love they came to bear one another that they were rarely seen apart.

"Alciteo had a very beautiful sister of marriageable age, called Biancarisa, who only very rarely exposed herself to human gaze. Now, it happened one day that, when Alciteo was throwing the discus with Lioncorno, the discus flew in through the sister's window, as she sat within, with her ladies-in-waiting, involved with their feminine labors. She picked it up from the floor without knowing whose it was and, on a whim, went over to the window; at the same time Lioncorno came running up to find his lost discus, and, when he saw the lovely girl and she him, cruel Love worked its usual trick in both their hearts, wounding both with the same dart and leaving them cold, pale, dumb, and senseless. In this manner the love sprang up between these two most noble lovers, and as happens, before long, Lioncorno found a way to communicate his feelings to the girl, who, quite unable to withstand the raging love for him that tormented her day and night, welcomed his love and responded to it; and the end of it was that they secretly agreed to become husband and wife. Alciteo knew nothing of what was going on and continued in the love he bore his great friend Lioncorno; and he continued, as well, to hold court, welcoming and courteously playing host to all strangers who turned up in

94. Phaeton, died after his father, the sun god Apollo, reluctantly acceded to his son's desire to be allowed to drive the chariot of the sun; the chariot veered out of control and Jove killed the boy with a thunderbolt to prevent him from setting the world alight. His grieving sisters were subsequently turned into poplars (Ovid, *Metamorphoses*, 2, 340–66) This famous classical myth is used by Fonte to lend dignity to the ensuing fiction of Lioncorno (or "Unicorn"), which is seemingly her own creation.

his land. And so happy was his lot that his father Apollo, delighted to have such a son, gradually forgot the pain that the death of Phaeton had left in his heart.

"But then one day the inconsolable Clymene, Phaeton's mother, arrived and was warmly welcomed by Alciteo. And seeing and envying his happiness, and comparing her continuing misery over her thunderstruck son with Apollo's present happiness (now that Alciteo's good fortune had driven his other son's accident from his mind), how Clymene suffered! How she resented Alciteo! And her grief was such, along with her envy and jealousy of Alciteo, that she secretly resolved to do all she could to destroy and exterminate Alciteo, to spite Apollo, as soon as the opportunity offered itself. And since she was a great expert on poisons, having stored in her memory much that she had heard from her once beloved Apollo concerning the properties of plants, she made an arrangement with a corrupt servant, who agreed, out of greed for the reward she was offering, to betray his lord and poison the innocent young man. And so, having undertaken the task of preparing the potion herself, and having agreed the manner and date of her return, she took her leave and left the court.

"Meanwhile the amorous Lioncorno had managed to win over his lady, to the point that, overpowered by her great love, she had agreed (strictly on the understanding that she was now his wife, however) to introduce him into her chamber; and having agreed on a plan and fixed a time, Lioncorno hid himself in a little dressing room that lay close to Biancarisa's room. And at that very moment, the perfidious Clymene arrived with her deadly potion and started to speak to the treacherous servant, not noticing the young man hiding there, so that Lioncorno was able to overhear everything as she gave the man the flask of poison he was to offer to Alciteo in some devious way, and spurred him and encouraged him with lavish promises of reward to commit the dastardly act. When they had gone, young Lioncorno was so stunned and dismayed that he felt as though he had been dreaming; and although, on the one hand, he was enflamed by a burning desire to be with the young woman he loved so much, on the other hand, considering the gravity of the situation, and the dangers of delay, his reason overcame his appetite, and, more concerned for his dear friend's life than his own pleasure, he ran at once to Alciteo's chamber, who at that very moment, deceived by his faithless servant, whom he trusted, was lifting to his lips the little flask in which his death was lurking. Lioncorno cried out to him not to drink, and swiftly snatched the flask out of his friend's hand himself and threw it to the ground, where it smashed, spilling the poison. And, after revealing the whole story to Alciteo, and disclosing the plot that had been hatched against him, he had his friend instantly seize the death-dealing servant, who was too bemused by what was happening to escape his fate, and instead confessed under torture to everything and was condemned to death by due process of justice.

"The hapless Clymene, seeing that the plot had not only been discovered but forestalled, that the servant had been punished, and that she herself risked experiencing the eminently justified wrath of Alciteo, took to her heels and fled weeping through the nearby forests, and crying out with burning tears, she addressed these wicked prayers to the listening Venus:

"'Hear me, lovely goddess! You know how faithfully I have always worshiped you and how devoutly I have venerated your holy flames. But see now how that ingrate Apollo, whom I love so faithfully, has betrayed and deceived me, taking a new mistress and fathering that proud youth Alciteo, who has made him forget me and my own poor son Phaeton. Generous goddess, even if my interests are not enough to move you to avenge this injury, pray be moved by your own interest and your own honor! You well know how much our common enemy Apollo has injured you in the past, and there could be no better way to punish him than by the death of his son Alciteo. This was to have been our revenge and our glory, and I had laid my plans well, and ordered everything and done exactly what was needed, but that cruel Lioncorno foiled our plans so thoroughly that there is now no remedy. So, at the very least, kind Cytherean goddess,[95] visit instant punishment on this meddler, as a revenge for our ruined revenge, and as an example to others, to make them think twice before interfering in other people's affairs.'

"Venus, though she loved Lioncorno as one of her most faithful subjects, also hated Apollo, who had injured her so intolerably, and extended her hatred to all his race. She was thus thrown into some confusion by Clymene's prayers, but, in the end, her long-nurtured spite against Apollo prevailed, and, resolving finally to grant the wishes of her evil supplicant, she waited until the young man,

---

95. Cythera, in Greece, was the site of a famous shrine to Aphrodite, the Greek prototype of Venus.

delighted at having foiled such wickedness, returned to his waiting lover, who was there on tenterhooks, her heart racing as she hoped for the arrival of her dearest love, worrying and fearing and trembling and not knowing what to think. And at that moment, just as he was eagerly anticipating enjoying his dear wife, the angry goddess, in an unstoppable fury, rooted him to the spot and threw a certain magic powder over him and made some utterance, whereupon Lioncorno felt himself suddenly changing in his outer form, though not in his spirit. His arms, the arms that were aching to enfold that dear neck, were changed into legs (alas! cruel impediment) and the hands into feet; his white garment was converted into a white coat of hair, and his handsome face into a strange animal head, armed with a daunting horn; all this so quickly that there was not even a moment for his eager mouth to take leave of his hapless, stunned wife, nor to give her a last kiss. I leave you, ladies, compassionate as you are, to imagine the state the poor girl was left in, seeing all her hopes vanish so cruelly before her very eyes, and being left with the heartrending spectacle of her dear husband gazing on her with his pitiful eyes, with a gaze that still looked human, and seemingly more stricken by having lost her than by his own cruel misfortune. So keenly did he lament, so many tears did he shed, that the sound of his wretched sighs drew the whole household to the room, and with them Alciteo, to whom his sister pitifully recounted the whole story of her love, finishing with the tragic incident of the young man's transformation, to the horror and misery of all who were listening, especially Alciteo, who wept long and bitterly over the story, considering that his friend had saved his life. And Biancarisa after this would never remarry, for the sake of her own honor and that of her dear lover, who seemed to her neither living nor dead. He, after some time, retreated into the nearby woods to forage for food, and in his new form, he retained his old manners, which are still preserved in his descendants. His sweet, loving nature still has a particular instinct for and power against poison; for, as I have said, his horn is remarkably effective as an antidote to poison, and there have been noteworthy cases of this. At the same time, he also preserves a memory of the sweetness of his love, so that he is affectionate when he sees any young virgin, and happily comes up and sleeps in her lap, since she reminds him of his Biancarisa, from whose sweet company he was so cruelly severed."

The tragic sufferings of the unfortunate youth drew tears to the listeners' eyes many times as Corinna was telling the story. Leonora commented on the story, "Well, that's a very fine tale, but it seems to put men in a rather better light than women."

"Ah, but you have to remember," said Corinna, "that what you've just heard was a fairy tale."[96]

"Oh, I know," said Leonora. "Go on, tell us about some other animals. And don't worry if it means speaking ill of women: we all know that it's only in fairy tales that it's possible to speak ill of women or good of men."

"But what shall I say?" replied Corinna. "Should I launch into an account of the agility of the horse, the greed of the wolf, the meekness of the sheep, the fox's cunning, the cat's patience, the hare's timidity, the dog's loyalty? But all that kind of thing is better suited to a written treatment—and besides, Pliny and the other authorities on the subject have already discussed these and other animals at length, and one can also find many noteworthy facts in other reliable authors."

"Something I've been wanting to know for a long time," said Helena, "is the nature of the hidden enmity that exists between the wolf and the lamb, the lion and the sheep, the fox and the chickens, the cat and the mouse, and between other animals of the air and the water. What is the cause of this great discord between the animals, so that one is always chasing, the other fleeing from it?"

"The cause is not any enmity on the part of the stronger beast," said Corinna. 'It's just prompted by the natural instinct it has to feed on the other animal; and it doesn't pursue its prey or devour it out of any hatred it feels for it, or any disagreement that exists between the two species, but simply because one is the food that Nature has provided for the other.[97] And, on the other side, the weaker beast—for example the sheep—doesn't flee from the lion be-

96. Fonte's speakers' alertness to the gender implications of fictional stories is an interesting feature of the dialogue; see also p. 194, where Leonora herself is accused of having told a joke that could be interpreted as misogynistic.

97. Corinna's denial that any enmity exists in nature is interesting in that it contrasts quite sharply with the position of Fonte's main classical source, Pliny, who adduces as evidence for the claim that animals are sentient the fact that natural enmities exist between species (*NH*, 10, 95, 203–6). Corinna's position is closer to that of Aristotle (*HA*, 608b25–610a30), who does not deny that such enmities exist, but identifies their source in animals' feeding habits. Fonte's insistence on the harmony between animals may be seen as part of her strategy in Day 2 of the dialogue of emphasizing the unnatural character of men's ill-treatment of women.

cause it hates it, but rather because it fears it, since it too knows, by a natural instinct, that the other animal is pursuing it with the aim of devouring it and using it for food. And that's why it flees it as a mortal enemy, in order to escape death."

"If only women too had this intuition and instinct to flee from their pursuers and from death," said Leonora, "we wouldn't see so many of them perishing or suffering as we do. But instead, poor trusting creatures, they deliver themselves into their predators' hands; and then, when they are caught, it's too late to have regrets."

"You're still at daggers drawn with men," said Virginia, who couldn't help laughing in spite of herself. Then she went on. "But couldn't we come up with some kind of remedy to improve them a little? If you have wine in the house that has gone off, if you mix in some good wine it very often improves it; if you have a ragged old dress, you can mend it so it passes as new; and unappetizing dishes can be improved by adding butter and spices."

"Dearest sister," said Leonora. "I wouldn't know where to start, to try to disguise the taste of these rotten men. They are like mature trees, that have laid down roots: they are incapable of change."

"But even with trees," said Corinna, "it's possible to change their nature by grafting them. But I'm not so sure about men: they never really change their ways—except from bad to worse."

"It would be more of a miracle if men improved," said Cornelia, "and started producing good effects from their bad nature, than the strangest freak of nature one could think of, like birds being born out of trees."

"That's truer than you think," said Corinna. "For, though the former is impossible, the latter does actually happen: we read, in fact, that there's a land beyond Holland where there's a miraculous kind of plant that instead of fruit, grows birds rather like ducks."[98]

"I can't believe my ears," said the Queen. "That really is an incredible natural phenomenon. Perhaps it's true then what they say about the trees of the Hesperides, which grew golden apples."[99]

98. The "land beyond Holland" is Scotland; the ducklike birds, barnacle (or brent) geese, which were widely believed in the Middle Ages and Renaissance to grow like fruit on trees, dropping off like ripe pears on maturity (or, alternatively, to be born from fungus growing on floating timber) (McCulloch 1960, 198–99).

99. The Hesperides were nymphs appointed to guard (with the aid of a dragon) the golden apples that had been given by Juno to Jupiter as a wedding present and which Eurystheus ordered Hercules to steal as one of his twelve labors.

"No, madam," said Corinna. "That really is just a legend."

"And how about those bushes that produce balsam," said Lucretia. "That's not made up, is it?"

"No, that's the sober truth," said Corinna. "They are found in Arabia Felix, where they also gather manna, which is a heavenly dew; and all kinds of aromatic plants grow in the same land, like cinnamon, aloes, spikenard, ginger, nutmeg, and all kinds of other spices, more or less hot according to their different properties, which are used all over the world and have countless different uses.[100] And then there are endless different kinds of tree and shrub, growing all over the world, whose roots, seeds, leaves, flowers, and fruit have various different properties. For different parts of plants are used for different purposes—it's possible to find species, for example, where the roots are cold and the fruit warm."

The Queen interjected at this point, "In how many different ways Divine Providence works to provide for our needs! God has even thought to place these powers in plants to aid us in our infirmities. How grateful we should be!"

"Another thing this proves," said Leonora, "is how little gratitude we owe to men, and what a disservice they do us. For all things were created for their benefit and ours, and in fact men themselves were created specifically to help us in life. And yet they do their job far worse than trees and other irrational creatures, which never fail in their duties. Here's all the help they are to us: they don't look after us, as they should, but rather set out to injure us and deprive us of all those good things we could be enjoying if it weren't for them— wealth, freedom, reputation, and the favor and respect of all the creatures of the world."

"Oh, stop interrupting Corinna," said Lucretia. "In any case, if I remember right, you're contradicting what you yourself said earlier, about woman being born after man, as his helpmate. So we should be looking after them, rather than their looking after us."

"If that's the case," said Leonora, "if they need our help, when we are just the same as them in every quality and substance, then that must mean that they are inferior to us and should cede power to us. But I'm not denying that we should look after them out of love, since they are the same flesh as us; I'm just lamenting the fact that they

---

100. It should be remembered here that Venice had traditionally been the center of the vastly lucrative spice trade with the East, and remained an important importer of spices in this period, despite competition from the Portuguese.

aren't prepared, in the same spirit of love, to help, support, and look after us, and that they don't accord us the respect we deserve. And yet, as I've said, all the other creatures recognize us as the rulers of the world, just as much as men, if not more."

"You just said that there was no water in the world that could cure men of their defects," said Lucretia. "Why don't you try to see now whether you can think of any plant that might help, since you've talked about the virtues residing in plants."[101]

"They say balsam cures all infirmities," said Cornelia.

"True balsam," said Corinna, "which is gathered from certain bushes in Arabia, using little ivory knives, is a divine liquor (as long as it isn't doctored in any way) and extremely good for our whole body, for a taste of it revives flagging spirits, restores strength to the body, and generally puts new life in you.[102] Balsamic ointment applied to the living keeps the face looking fresh and young, while, applied to dead bodies, it acts as a preservative against putrefaction and decay. So all in all, it's the ideal remedy for everything—except the disease you're talking about."

"I thought manna was the best thing in the world," said Lucretia. "Surely there's nothing sweeter than manna?"

"Even if it was the sweetest thing to taste," said Corinna, "that wouldn't make it the most powerful cure. Manna falls on certain aperient herbs, and you can gather it just like honey.[103] It's warm and humid, in a temperate way, and the whiter it is, the better. It's

101. The long list of remedies that follows draws on the rich tradition of classical, medieval, and Renaissance writings on herbal medicine (see Arber 1986, Rohde 1971; also Palmer 1985; Findlen 1994, 240–87). By the time Fonte was writing, this doctrine was widely diffused in the vernacular as well as Latin, in manuals like Pierandrea Mattioli's much-published *Commentary on the Six Books of Dioscorides* (first published in Venice, 1544) and Castor Durante's *New Herbal* (Rome, 1585). Pliny's *Natural History*, Fonte's most likely source in her discussions of animals, birds, and fish, also contains a long discussion of the medicinal properties of plants (*NH*, books 20–27). These written authorities must of course have been supplemented by oral sources, including the recommendations of commercial pharmacists, who sold genuine or fake specimens of all the substances listed here. It should not be forgotten, either, that Padua was a center for research into medicinal plants, and contained Europe's first botanical garden (est. 1545).

102. The resin balsam (or balm of Gilead) and its properties are discussed in Mattioli 1573, 55–57; and *NH*, 12, 54, 115. Mattioli stresses that true balsam is unavailable in Italy and warns against the incompetent fakes sold by pharmacists (though see Findlen 1994, 270–71).

103. On manna, see Mattioli 1573, 90–92. The manna sold by Renaissance Italian pharmacists was probably a juice obtained from the bark of the manna ash (*Fraxinus ornus*) in Southern Italy.

extremely sweet to the taste, has great powers to purify the blood, and is effective against acute fevers, together with cassia (which is another plant that's useful against high blood temperature, as well as purging the stomach)."

"I've heard that rhubarb is very good against fevers, once the temperature has dropped," said Cornelia.

"Yes, it's good in cases of tertian fever, single and double," Corinna replied, "because it acts against choler. For it to work, you have to choose a full, heavy specimen (it's a root, and comes from India). When you break it open, there are separate veins inside, some red, others white; then, as you chew it, it loses its color and has a bitter taste. It's hot and dry to the second degree, like senna, and is very similar to the kind of rhubarb we use in cooking."[104]

"Isn't senna good for melancholics?" asked Lucretia.

"It's good against melancholy, yes," replied Corinna, "and against disfunctions of the liver. It's also effective against quartan fever, when mixed with colocynth. And colocynth is also good against hardening of the spleen (the marrow of the plant, that is, mixed with a solution of hart's tongue fern) or you can make it up into a decoction with vinegar as a cure for toothache or a poultice to use against worms. It's not to be used alone, though, as it's poisonous."

"In that case, it must resemble man," said Leonora, "who is noxious when alone, and needs women's company as his antidote."

"I don't know of any better remedy against worms than aloe," said Lucretia. "And I should know, having used it so many times."

"Aloe is hot and dry in the second degree," said Corinna. "It's the sap of a plant of the same name, which can be of three types. The best is known as *cicotrino*, and can be distinguished by its coloring, as it's the color of saffron. Aloe purges choler and phlegm and melancholy, calms the nerves, and alleviates dropsy and constipation; and mixed with rosewater, it's good for clearing the vision. Aloe is very bitter and has an extremely strong smell, but it's never as bitter as agaric."

"Agaric!" said Lucretia. "I've heard great things about that."

"It's used in cases of severe illness," said Corinna. "But its principal property is purging phlegm, and, after that, melancholy; it's also

---

104. The distinction being made here is between two types of rhubarb: the medicinal root (*Rheum officinalis*, or *reubarbaro* in Fonte's Italian), which had been known since antiquity, and culinary rhubarb (*Rheum ponticum*, or *reupontico*), a variant introduced to Italy only in the sixteenth century.

very effective in healing suppurating wounds and intestinal ailments. Though something else that's very good against that kind of thing is saffron, which is hot and dry to the first degree, and is also good for digestion, and is cordial and sweet-smelling."

"If you're talking about aids to digestion," said Lucretia, "I know a lady who uses nutmeg and mace, which is the very fine outer membrane of the nut; and she swears by them."

"Nutmeg," added Corinna, "is very good in pregnancy, and effective as an aid to digestion for delicate stomachs, as are pepper, ginger, cinnamon, cardamom, and carnation seeds and other such spices, all of which are well suited to those of a cold complexion, but which those of a choleric or sanguine complexion should take only in moderation. Tamarind purges choler and purifies the blood. Scammony too helps draw choler from the veins, and is cordial, when mixed with red sandalwood."

"Oh Lord!" said Leonora. "You're no nearer to finding the medicine I was asking about. You can find all the remedies you like against bad blood and choler, but men's stomachs and blood can never be purged, as their hearts and minds are terminally sick. But if only it were at least possible for us to find some cure for our naïveté, and the compassion and love we bear for these sick companions of ours!"

"That's a remedy you won't find in Galen," said Corinna. "And none of the other authorities on the subject seems to have discovered it either—or, if they did, they certainly didn't record it. After all, it would hardly have been in their interests, for wolf doesn't eat wolf, and men know very well which side of their bread is buttered: if we stopped loving them, they'd be in a fine state!"

"You do find, though, in some books, all kinds of remedies against love," said Lucretia, "like the skin of a freshly killed sheep, or the dust where a mule has rolled (not to mention, of course, the miraculous spring we mentioned earlier). And they also talk about making the lover drink the blood of the person he loves and endless other things. But I think that's all nonsense: when love has really found its way into someone's heart, I don't believe that anything except death can really cauterize and cure it. But we're not just talking about grand passions, but about affection in general, since, as we've already established, we women have such a tendency to be affectionate by nature."

"While we're on the subject," said Corinna, "I've read that if a man carries a hyena's intestines around, on the left-hand side of his body, any woman he looks at will be mysteriously enflamed with love for him.[105] Now let's forget about such nonsense! Goat's rue and sweet flag are both good cordial medicines, while licorice is incredibly effective against chest ailments, as are linen seeds. You can either apply them externally, rubbing them on with butter, or you can add them to food."

"I'm getting so sick of these cures of yours," said Leonora, "that, for my part, I'd be keen on putting an end to the feast. It's as though you're all just waiting for me to get ill so I can try them all! Come now, please, if we can't find what we're looking for, let's put an end to this long rigmarole."

"If you'd just let Corinna talk," said Lucretia, "then she might be able to come up with some cure. You're such a pest, interrupting all the time."

"All right, then, on that condition, you may carry on," said Cornelia. "Though I suspect your promises are like the promises one makes to one's children to persuade them to go to school, with no intention of keeping them."

"Myrrh," said Corinna, "is another plant that is good for chest complaints and aids digestion, when mixed with fine quality styrax resin."[106]

"Yes, but when it comes down to it," said the Queen, "I'm not sure I know of any better medicine for the chest and stomach than a nice sweet wine or a malmsey or muscat[107]—what do you say to that, ladies?"

"Quite right," said the other women, laughing. "A drop of malmsey, taken without food, is very good for weak stomachs, especially in those of cold complexion."

"Normal wine is excellent too," said Corinna, "though only when taken in moderation and by people in good health. The whites and lighter reds, especially, are good (though whites can cause wind); heavier reds are harder to digest. But wines of whatever type, if drunk

---

105. The target of Corinna's sarcasm here may well be Pliny, who includes a long list of the miraculous properties of the hyena's body parts in *NH,* 28, 27, culminating with the observation that a hyena's anus, carried in an amulet on the left side, will make a man irresistible to women.

106. The original has *storace calamita;* for an explanation of the term, see Mattioli 1573, 84–85.

107. The original has *una malvasia moscatella:* "a malmsey made of muscat grapes" (rather than the *malvasia* variety that gives malmsey its name). This seems unlikely, but it may be that the word *malvasia* is being used generically in this phrase, to indicate any kind of sweet wine. Malmsey was imported into Venice from Crete in vast quantities in this period, for home consumption and export throughout Northern Europe.

in too great quantities, cause headaches and nerve disorders, swell the belly, prevent digestion, and inflame the liver."

"There are those who say that herbs boiled in wine are very good for one," said Cornelia.

"Rosemary, in particular, is often boiled with wine," said Corinna. "It's the best of the lot, and it really is amazingly effective against all kinds of ailments."

"How about wine made from pomegranates?" said Lucretia. "Do you think that's any good?"

"Yes, it's good when you have the fever," said Corinna. "And, on the subject of acidic fruits, they are also good as an astringent— quinces, for example."

"I like quinces only when they're cooked with grapes," said Cornelia.

"Don't let's get sidetracked," said Corinna. "Quinces are useful for all kinds of things: they help in healing wounds, and quince oil is good as a cure for spitting blood and vomiting. It's also amazingly good for quenching thirst. Then there are domestic apples, of which there are various kinds (though they are all humid and tend to cause wind): when they're cooked with sugar, they are good for relieving constrictions of the chest, and the syrup is effective against quartan fever."

"I'm very fond of pears," said the Queen. "More so than apples. They are very digestible when cooked, but, if you eat them raw, you need to follow them with wine."

"How about plums?" said Helena. "What are their properties? I've eaten such a lot of them this last year, and I don't know whether they've been good for me or bad."

"Plums are cold and damp fruits," said Corinna. "Some are black, others red. The black ones are good for people with fever, as they have cooling and soothing properties, as do cherry plums."

"Oh, cherry plums!" said Lucretia. "They're extraordinary. I've heard, among other things, that if you mix their powder with powder of aloes, it can help prevent hair loss."

"They also serve to purge phlegm and melancholy, when you cook them with the roots of senna or spurge," said Corinna.

"My favorite kinds of fruit," said Virginia, "are date plums and peaches."

"They *are* good to eat," said Corinna, "but date plums quickly start decaying in the stomach. Peaches, though, are cordial, and their skin and pulp counteract any harmful effects they might have. It's said that peaches were poisonous in their original habitat, but that they lost that malign quality as they were transported over here, and became as good as we now know them to be."[108]

"Of all fruit," said Cornelia, "those I love best are grapes, figs, and melons."

"Grapes," said Corinna, "come in many different species, and are delicious to eat. When they are fully ripe, they are not particularly harmful to eat, even though they are a little humid and tend to cause wind. Grapes have laxative properties, though their pips are astringent. Figs have laxative properties as well and are good for the chest and the lungs. And the same goes for raisins and pine nuts."

"I've never eaten pine nuts fresh, as one eats almonds and walnuts," said Lucretia. "But I'm sure they're very good like that—pistachios, too."

"That might be true," said Corinna, "but since they come from so far away, you can only eat them dried."

"I like fresh walnuts," said Cornelia, "but I always seem to get a headache when I eat them."

"Walnuts and hazelnuts do cause headaches," said Corinna, "and they're very hard to digest. But walnuts are a good antidote to toxins, and they're almost like chestnuts, though they're colder in nature. Sweet almonds are hard and indigestible; the bitter ones, though, can be used in medicine."

"The Lord be praised!" said Leonora. "We're on to chestnuts now! And how about going on to beans after that, and cherries? This is like counting sheep: we're never going to get to the end. I'm sure you're just doing it to make fun of me and provoke me into interrupting."

Helena and Virginia were laughing helplessly at Leonora's desperation, and the Queen said, with a grin, "Now do let Corinna carry on for just a little while, and tell us whether, by eating too many melons this summer, I'm storing myself up a nice quartan fever for the winter, for they do say that fever is brought about by humid and cold things."

"Well yes, I suppose they are cold and humid," said Corinna. 'But

---

108. Peaches in fact originated in China, but the "original habitat" referred to here is Persia, from which land they were first imported into Europe in antiquity, reputedly by Alexander the Great (hence their Latin name, *Persicum malum*, or Persian apple). The legend referred to here, that they were poisonous in their original environment and became edible only when transplanted, had much currency in the Renaissance (see, for example, Alciatus 1985, no. 143). The origin of the story appears to be a confusion of the peach with another fruit tree of similar provenance: see Mattioli 1573, 195 and 223; and Columella 1960–68, 3: 42n (*On Agriculture*, 10, 405–10).

if you eat good ones, and in moderation, they aren't particularly harmful. And pumpkins, lemons, watermelons,[109] and other such fruit are
also cold; in fact, doctors call them 'cold-seed fruits.' They are all
effective against burning fevers, especially lemons, which have very
strong medicinal powers. The flowers, fruit, and pips of the lemon—
even its smell—are cordial. Its peel is hot, and the pith and marrow of
the fruit are temperate, while the pips have a cooling effect and are
an excellent remedy against worms. Its leaves are always green, like
those of the laurel, sacred to Apollo and the Muses. Orange trees are
much the same."

"Ah, the laurel tree!" said Cornelia. "We must show due respect,
for it is:

> *L'arbor vittoriosa e trionfale*
> *Onor d'imperadori e de poeti.*

> That glorious, triumphant tree, the crown of emperors and
> poets.[110]

"The laurel, too, has curative properties," said Corinna. "They
make an oil out of its berries that has a warming effect, since the
plant is hot and dry by nature, and it's very good against head ailments
caused by cold. Other evergreens are the box tree, the myrtle,
Venus's tree, and the pungent juniper."

"These shrubs you're talking about may remain green all year," said
Lucretia, "but (apart from citrons), they don't produce flowers or
fruit."

"Indeed," said Corinna. "But, then again, you find some plants
that bear fruit without producing flowers, like fig trees, and others
that produce flowers but not fruit, like the rose."

"You should rather say," said Leonora, "like men, who look lovely
when they're in flower, but then turn out to produce no fruit, and
whose fine appearance lasts no longer than that of the rose."

"The rose," said the Queen, "is truly remarkable and singular in
its beauty and its smell, and leaves all other flowers far behind."

"Indeed," said Corinna. "And it's noteworthy, as well, from a
medicinal point of view, as it's included in many remedies for its

---

109. The list in the original contains two words that normally signify "watermelon"
(the Northern Italian *anguria* and the Tuscan *cocomero*). This may be an oversight, or
anguria is perhaps being used in a second, rarer, sense, to indicate a kind of cucumber.
110. The lines (slightly misquoted) are from Petrarch (*RS*, 263).

refreshing properties and as a dissolving agent. The rose is Venus's flower, and comes in many species. You can cook roses into a syrup with honey, or make them into a sugar, an oil, a vinegar, an ointment, a balm, or into rose water. Dried rose petals can be made up into a bath that is extremely good for the nerves (though the petals are humid when fresh). And, all in all, there is no sweeter or more delicate smell than that of the rose."

"Violets may not be as sweet as roses," said Cornelia. "But they are rightly prized as the first flowers to open, at the beginning of the season."

"You're right," said Corinna, "and, besides their beauty, they have many medicinal uses, as they have soothing and hydrating properties; they are good against headaches, help send you to sleep, and, mixed with sugar, make good cough medicine."

"Aren't you going to mention the narcissus and the hyacinth, which have such famous legends attached to them?"[111] said Helena.

"The narcissus, hyacinth, jasmine, and carnation," replied Corinna, "are among the stronger-smelling flowers. The first two have a short life, while the second two last rather longer. And each of them has particular properties, which I shan't go into in detail for the sake of brevity, in case Leonora gets annoyed with me. And the same can be said of white lilies and irises, which have aperient and warming properties. But then there's another flower that lurks underground, dried and shriveled, while the others are flowering, and then, as the others begin to dry up, it emerges and starts putting out its leaves. That, too, is a flower of extraordinary curative powers; and it's known as the cyclamen or sow bread."

"Well, that's amazing," said the Queen. "But leaving aside these sweet-smelling flowers, I think I remember you saying, a little while ago, that rosemary was good for one, boiled in wine."

"Yes it is, to get back to that," said Corinna. "It's extremely effective, especially for weak stomachs and limbs, and they say that if you take a dose every day, it cures all kinds of ailments. And another good cure is the flowers of mallow and other herbs, which can be made up into fine preserves with sugar. But, then, all plants have

111. In Greek myth, both flowers were said to have sprung from the blood of handsome youths struck down by untimely deaths (Narcissus killed himself in desperation after falling in love with his reflection in a fountain, while Hyacinth was accidentally killed by Apollo as they played at quoits).

their uses—their roots, their flowers, their leaves, even though plants vary greatly in their properties. For dill and southernwood are hot and dry, and the first is good for chest complaints, while the second is good for the spleen, while sage is hot and humid, and is good for. treating boils and preventing hair loss. Then, tansy is good for the lungs; lovage for urinary complaints; capers for the spleen; chamomile for headaches, the liver, and pains in the side; maidenhair for the chest and spleen, and against fevers; and they say cinquefoil, when it is found by chance, improves people's appearance and makes them more attractive."

"I've also heard it said of the *cento capi*, whose root comes in two forms, male and female, that if a man carries the male root around, it makes him more attractive, while if a woman does the same with the female root, it has the same effect,"[112] said Cornelia. "They also say that the Egyptian herb that they call *nepenthe* relieves all melancholy.[113] Fennel is very good for the eyes, and can be made up into a fine preserve with vinegar, salt, and pepper; marjoram, celery, thistles, artichokes, parsley (all those hot and dry plants), and asparagus all have purgative properties; while aniseed and coriander are good against wind. Borage, bugloss, sorrel, radicchio, endives, and lettuce—all these cooling herbs, as everyone knows, are administered in a decoction in cases of fever. But it would be take all night to tell the properties of every kind of plant."

"Well, I prefer the white cabbage or the thistles we eat in the winter with fowl to all these decoctions and medicines of yours," said Cornelia.

"Cabbage isn't very good for you, though," said Corinna. "It generates black choler and makes the stomach humid and bloated. Beets are a better staple food, if you like them."

"I like all kinds of staple food," said Lucretia, "but my favorite is rice."

112. The *centum capita* (literally "hundred heads") is described by Pliny (*NH*, 22, 9, 20–22), who mentions the male root's capacity to make the bearer attractive to women, but does not mention the corresponding powers Cornelia attributes here to the female root. Durante identifies the plant as a species of asphodel; other herbalists as a kind of eryngo.

113. This is the herb served to Telemachus by Helen in book 4 of Homer's *Odyssey* (221ff.), which has the power to banish the most dreadful sorrows. Pliny mentions it twice (*NH*, 21, 91, 159; and *NH*, 25, 5, 12, where he mentions its Egyptian origins). For speculation on what it may have been, see Heubeck, West, and Hainsworth 1988, 206–7.

"I prefer beans and barley," said Lucretia.

"Rice," said Corinna, "is healthy and nutritious, and has astringent properties. Various kinds of bean are good to eat, but they are hard to digest and cause wind. But barley is very healthy and refreshing indeed: in fact, as well as an excellent foodstuff, it's a medicine for those with ailments caused by too much heat."

"I don't like that cereal they call panic grass," said Lucretia. "Nor wheat, except when it's used to make bread. Though bread made with millet is just as tasty when it's fresh, with its Damascene raisins inside."[114]

"Well, you can eat it if you like," said Cornelia. "I'm happy enough sticking with wheat bread."

"Millet," said Corinna, "is not particularly nutritious, but it's good as a stomachic and against urinary disorders. And sorghum[115] has astringent qualities."

"Oh, Lord!" said the Queen. "I always ask myself how the poor manage, especially out in the countryside, where they have to live on crops like these—when they can get them, that is, which hasn't always been the case, especially in these years of famine. It's seems a miracle that they survive at all—but the Good Lord helps them."

"Poor creatures!" said Lucretia. "They should at least be shown some compassion when they can't come up with the whole rent for the land, because their harvests really are now only amounting to half of what they used to get before these lean years. Though this year's harvest has been better than the last few, Lord be praised."

"Corinna, dear," said Cornelia, "what do you think causes these poor harvests that we sometimes see?"

"Sterility and poor yield can result from a whole series of causes," she replied. "One is when the fields are badly prepared or ill tended, or when the seeds are sown at the wrong time. It can also result from the inclemency of the air, which sometimes sends down mists and

114. These are raisins made from the Damascene, or zibibbo grape (a kind of muscat): see Mattioli 1573, 817; see also 316 for the comment that millet bread is palatable only when fresh. This discussion of alternatives to wheat bread was topical at a time when, owing to a series of bad harvests in 1590–91 (mentioned below in the text), the price of wheat had risen catastrophically (Pullan 1968, 155–56; see also 164 on the Venetian populace's reluctance to accept alternatives to wheat flour.)

115. Sorghum or Indian millet was grown in Europe from antiquity until the early modern period. It is still a staple food crop in Africa and China. With sorghum, millet, and panic (another variety of millet), the conversation is moving toward the poorest peasant food: hence Adriana's next comment.

burning vapors, which can dry out and destroy the crops just as they are ripening. At other times, it is caused by droughts, or by excessive rain, when it comes out of season and causes the wheat to go to seed or rot. Another frequent cause is when the sirocco blows too much in the winter, when the grain is germinating: little worms grow and gnaw away at it before it starts growing. And then finally, of course, there's the danger of storms when the grain is already ripe—but that only affects the few farmers whose fields are touched by them. Many of these defects can be remedied, but many can't be, so we have to resort to and submit to God's will, where crops, trees, and plants are concerned, as in all things."

"We may feel the effect of poor harvests," said Lucretia, "but the people who really feel it are the poor country folk, who suffer for the whole year, if the harvest is worse than expected."

"This year, though, I'm hoping the harvest will be good, to judge from how things look now," said Helena. "I've just been to our estate in the country, to make rose water."

"I don't like going to the country at this time of year," said Cornelia. "I prefer going in August or September, which are the really enjoyable months there."

"I'm going next month," said the Queen, "and staying until the end of September, for the sake of the harvest. I have to: if I don't keep an eye on the workers there, the poor things will try to make up for the thin years they've been having and I'll be left with nothing."

"These are the months of business in the country," said Lucretia, "and the autumn is the time of pleasure."

"Oh, but there are pleasures to be had there even now," said Virginia. "In this hot weather, on feast days, to see the little shepherdesses in their Sunday best, going off to join in the dancing—there can be nothing more charming. We always go along to the feasts in the carriage with ladies from the other estates nearby—and that's the most enjoyable part, because it can be tedious to be in the country unless one has some contact with one's equals."

"I love being in the country at this time of year, as Helena has just been, to enjoy the beauty of the flowers and plants and the lovely birds and all the other charms of the springtime," said Corinna.

"You should add," said Helena, "that it's a great delight to watch the goats and sheep being driven out to pasture at this time of year, some pregnant and some already with their sweet little kids and bleating lambs, skipping through the meadows. And that's not to mention the practical benefits we get from these creatures: milk and dairy products and wool."

"Dairy products are certainly good to eat," said Corinna, "but milk and ricotta are cold and cause wind. Butter is good for easing constriction of the chest, but cheese is hard to digest and, eaten in quantity, it harms the stomach and the brain."

"All in all," said Lucretia, "the country in the summer is a paradise, with all these pleasures we've been talking about and the good things it produces. But in the winter, it's a kind of hell, stripped bare of all its treasures: barren of crops and barren of pleasures."

"If only it were possible to preserve fruit all year, as you can preserve other things," said Virginia.

"Fruit, in the modern world," said Corinna, "is more of a delicacy than a staple part of our diet. So it makes sense that the Lord has willed that the most important things can be preserved: grain, wine, and herbs of all kinds, so that we can both nourish ourselves and dose and cure ourselves in all the various infirmities to which we are subject."

"That's not quite right," said Lucretia. "For everything can be preserved in some manner, for a certain period, at least."

"Yes," said Cornelia, "except for the love and loyalty of men."

"Heavens above!" said Leonora. "I can't believe what I'm hearing! You're being so ridiculous, and we're being so ridiculously patient. I keep waiting for your good sense to reaffirm itself, but looking at the great leaps you've made today in the conversation, I can only laugh. Do you know, you're just like another Phaeton, plummeting down from the skies into the water—except that, fortunately, instead of drowning, as he did, you've somehow managed to get back to shore and drag yourself out onto the earth.[116] You were meant to be keeping to the subject, but instead you've launched into this great rigmarole about animals, trees, plants, and medicines. Don't you realize that it's already past three o'clock and we still haven't really started? What have the kind of things we've been talking about got to do with us, may I ask? Are we doctors, by any chance? Leave it up to them to talk about syrups and poultices and all that kind of thing. It's absurd for us to be talking about them."

---

116. For the myth of Phaeton, see above, note 94. Leonora is referring to the "leaps" in the subject matter of Corinna's disquisitions on nature, from the air to the waters to the earth and its inhabitants.

"You're quite wrong," said Lucretia. "On the contrary, it's good for us to learn about these things, so we can look after ourselves, without needing help from men. In fact, it would be a good thing if there were women who knew about medicine as well as men, so men couldn't boast about their superiority in this field and we didn't have to be dependent on them."[117]

"Well, heaven preserve us from the need to rely on doctors, in any case," said Helena, "for there are times when we really need them."

"For my part," said Virginia, "whenever I've been ill, I've got better without doctors or medicine, and I hope I'll be able to do the same in future."

"I couldn't say that myself," said the Queen. "For, if it were not for the goodness of the Lord, in the first place, and the skill and diligence of our family doctor, in the second, I can tell you, I'd have died a thousand times over."

"The same goes for me," said Cornelia. "I must say, I'm extremely grateful to our family doctor, as well. You don't know what you're talking about if you've never been seriously ill."

"Ours has done wonders for us, as well," said Lucretia.

"Who's your doctor?" asked Cornelia.

"We used to have that most distinguished man, Massaria," she replied, "before he went to Padua.[118] He's really extremely impressive and worthy of being summoned anywhere. But our present doctor, also excellent, is Zarotti."

"Oh, what an admirable man!" said the Queen. "He really is a fine doctor, and one of the kindest and most conscientious I've come

117. In making this point, Fonte may have been conscious that herbal medicine was a field in which women had been thought to excel in the ancient world: see *NH*, 25, 5, 10; and Mattioli 1573, dedication p. 3v, where the figures of the enchantresses Medea and Circe are interpreted as the mythologized record of great female herbalists of the distant past.

118. Alessandro Massaria (c. 1510–98), originally from Vicenza, was one of the most distinguished Italian physicians of his day. A plague specialist, he had a lucrative medical practice in Venice, before being appointed to a chair at the University of Padua in 1587. Of the doctors mentioned subsequently in the conversation, a number featured in the lists of prominent Venetian doctors given in the popular and much-published guidebook to the city, originally by Francesco Sansovino (d. 1583), entitled *Delle cose notevoli della città di Venezia* (*On the Remarkable Features of the City of Venice*): see, for example, the edition of 1587, 200, where Leandro Zarotti is mentioned, or the 1624 edition, revised by Giovanni Niccolò Doglioni, which includes Ottavio Amalteo and Benedetto Flangini in its list (Goldioni 1624, 192).

across. Not that he's our doctor, but he does serve some of our friends and relatives."

"I don't care for doctors," said Leonora. "You can summon your doctors all you like, but I'm with Virginia on this. What do you say, Cornelia?"[119]

"I'm certainly someone who, when I feel ill, always likes to consult a doctor," she replied. "I don't know how people manage without."

"And who's your doctor?" said Lucretia.

"We have that extremely distinguished gentleman Orazio Guarguanti, who really is a remarkable man,"[120] she said. "I can tell you, he has worked wonders in cases that other fine doctors had given up as desperate, both in our household and those of many of our friends and acquaintances."

"Oh, Guarguanti!" said the Queen. "I don't know him personally, but I've heard him being praised as a man of the soundest judgment, and possessed of all those qualities that characterize a person of refinement."

"Oh, I can assure you that he is a paragon of erudition and experience, as well as being extremely kind to his patients," said Corinna.

"When I need a doctor, I always call on Stabile,[121] who is extremely learned in both sciences, physic and surgery," said the Queen.

"Yes, I've often heard him praised as a very skilled and experienced doctor," said Lucretia.

"Do you know Amalteo, our doctor?"[122] said Helena.

"How could I not know him?" replied the Queen. "He is a justly

119. This passage bears the mark of hasty composition; Cornelia's opinion has already been expressed.

120. Orazio Guarguanti (1554–1611), a prominent physician and the author of several medical works, is praised later in the text for his literary talents. He appears to have been an acquaintance of Fonte's uncle and biographer, Giovanni Niccolò Doglioni, who later dedicated to him a guide to the sights of Venice (Goldioni 1603). On his life and works, see Ceruti 1982, 200–206.

121. Francesco Stabile was one of the Venetian state's medical advisors during the severe plague of 1575–77. In 1592, Stabile was again called on, along with others of the doctors mentioned here (Ottavio Amalteo, Parisan Parisani, and Leandro Zarotti), to advise on a plague in the Venetian dependency of Crete (ASV, *Provveditori alla Sanità*, reg. 736, f. 75v; I am grateful to Richard Palmer for this reference).

122. Ottavio Amalteo (1543–1626) was a member of a well-known family of physicians and humanists from the town of Oderzo, northeast of Venice. After studying philosophy at Padua, he spent most of his life as a physician in Venice.

famous man, and has a distinguished and much-respected practice, and he enjoys a great and admirable reputation: indeed, his remarkable abilities are such as to deserve lasting fame."

"And how about that distinguished gentleman Benedetto Flangini?" asked Lucretia.

"Oh, Flangini!" said Corinna. "He too is a highly skilled doctor, and, besides that, he is a man of great refinement, pleasant, and extremely conscientious. He deserves the highest praise."

"I know the man you mean," said Cornelia, "and, indeed, he can't be praised too highly. But then we should also mention the famous Parisan, the much-respected Saffronia, and the learned Scarn. They too, as everyone knows, are among the leading doctors of the city and no less skilled and conscientious than those we have been talking about."

"And I've heard of many others, just as famous as these, but I can't recall them at present," said Corinna. "This art of medicine is a truly miraculous one; in fact, there's something almost divine about it. For all other arts are directed toward obtaining the goods, comforts, and pleasures annexed to life, while medicine addresses itself to the conservation of life itself—that is, to maintaining our souls in our bodies, in that composite only God can create. For men are quite capable of generating bodies by purely human means, but only God can infuse these bodies with a soul: this is something he jealously guards for himself, without permitting human intervention. But medical science has now reached such a point that the souls that God has introduced into our bodies can be maintained there for many years, in spite of the infirmities that assail us, depleting our strength and reducing our bodies to a state in which they are on the point of bidding our souls farewell. This science of maintaining our souls in our bodies, imitating and shadowing as it does that first divine act of infusion of the soul, has rightly come to be called (in a way that intends no blasphemy, though) a kind of second creation, an everyday miracle, a superhuman act of grace—or rather, a heavenly power humanized within our hearts and brains."

"You're certainly very eloquent, Corinna," said the Queen, "and, certainly, one couldn't find a more worthy or useful or necessary activity. Of course, there are endless people who go around carping about medicine and the medical profession, but they can't have much need of doctors themselves (and heaven help them if they do). For even if some individual doctors don't practice their profession as judiciously as they might, there's no need to extend the blame to those who do, and still less to the art of medicine itself, which is a heaven-sent blessing. Because God would hardly have placed so many curative powers within plants and stones as he has, if we didn't need them and if we weren't intended to use them."

"The fact is," said Lucretia, "that those gentlemen who practice medicine, if they wish to help their patients and not harm their profession, need to have both a keen intelligence and a tenacious memory, and they must never cease to study and learn, and never just fall back on age and experience, for there is such a multitude of factors they must take into account, to be able to treat different individuals at different moments."

"You're quite right," said Corinna, "for they must know not only the different effects of medicines, but also all about diseases and their causes. And they need a fine judgment to select the right treatment for each different ailment, taking into account not just the nature of the ailment, but the age and constitution of the patient. For we are all made up of four elements, which combine to form the four principal substances or dispositions of the human body: that is, phlegm, which is generated from air; blood, from water; choler, from fire; and melancholy, from earth. If one of these humors predominates in the patient's body, the doctor must be able to recognize this and choose the appropriate remedy for correcting the balance and tempering the dominant element. A remedy that works for one person isn't always good for another: patients differ in constitution and age, and doctors must vary, alter, and adjust their cures accordingly. This is no easy matter, so it is best to ignore the foolish suggestions of many people who are not doctors by profession and are completely ignorant of natural philosophy, but who have heard that a certain remedy cured a certain patient of a certain ailment, and deduce from this that the same remedy must work for everyone, without taking all the relevant circumstances into account. And when one finds a good doctor, who is not only intelligent, but looks after the patient lovingly and conscientiously, he certainly deserves to be handsomely rewarded for it; for what greater thing can one man do for another than to restore life and health to him? It's not a good idea, either, to consult various different doctors when one is ill, for the conflicting opinions of different doctors can often be the death of some poor wretch."

"That's enough about doctors," said Cornelia. "What you're saying is very sensible, but we must get back to the subject at hand. We've now talked all about the stars, the air, birds, rivers, fish, and all kinds of animals, plants, and herbs, and we still haven't found anything with the power to work a change in men's minds and make them respect us and love us as we deserve."

"Well, they do say," said Lucretia, "that great powers reside in stones and in words, as well as in plants."

"It's true that stones do have special properties and can work miraculous effects,"[123] said Corinna. "But as for the problem in hand, I'm not sure a stone exists that could perform that particular magic."

"I've heard that the stone they call a heliotrope has the power to make people invisible,"[124] said Lucretia. "Is it true, do you think?"

"Let's not get sidetracked by those old yarns," said Corinna. "There are many kinds of stones that have curative powers. Coral, both the red and the white kind, has a mysterious power to counter-act epilepsy, and powdered coral mixed with tragacanth gum and barley water can stem nosebleeds. Powdered coral, drunk in a potion, stanches blood flow in general, and, taken in pill form, it is good for those who are spitting blood. Lapis lazuli is extremely good against melancholia and complaints of the heart and spleen. Diamonds are extremely cold—so cold as to be poisonous, and they are so hard that nothing can break them, except ram's blood."[125]

"And jasper?" asked the Queen. "Doesn't that help blood clot?"

"Yes indeed," said Corinna. "Hematite, too, is an excellent rem-edy against bleeding from the nose, and internal bleeding, as well."[126]

Helena interjected, "I think I heard somewhere that oritis could bring peace where there was discord."[127]

---

123. The discussion that follows, on the medicinal properties of stones, gemstones, and metals, draws on sources similar to those mentioned in n. 101 above: see especially *NH*, books 33–34 and 37; and Mattioli 1573, books 5–6.

124. The heliotrope was a mythical precious stone, resembling a red-veined sapphire, which was said to confer invisibility on its bearers (though Pliny is skeptical of this: *NH*, 27, 60, 165–66). A famous story in Boccaccio's *Decameron* (8, 3) tells of the mishaps endured by the gullible Calandrino after being convinced by two malicious friends that some stones he has found in a valley near Florence are heliotropes.

125. This detail is from *NH*, 37, 15, 55–61.

126. Hematite or bloodstone is red oxide of iron, recommended as a styptic by Pliny (*NH*, 36, 37–38, 144–48; and 37, 60, 169).

127. This stone is variously referred to by Pliny as oritis or sideritis ("ironstone"). If Pliny is her source here, Fonte's memory may be faulty, as he in fact attributes to this stone the opposite property, that of stoking discord (*NH*, 37, 67, 182).

"Well, that's what one reads," said Corinna. "Now, what can I say of the eaglestone, which has so many amazing powers? Its main use is as an antidote to poison; and it's because of this that the eagle, from which it takes its name, carries it to its nest, as protection against snakebites. It's also good for pregnant women: if a woman, when she's pregnant, wears it on her left arm, it protects her from miscarriages, and if she takes it off when the moment comes and hangs it by her left thigh, it eases the pains of delivery amazingly.[128] And it's also effective in cases of worms, vertigo, and other ailments. And then there's turquoise, which is very good for drying and cicatrizing wounds, and which is especially good for the eyes, mixed with rose water."[129]

"Sapphires, as well," said Cornelia, "as I know from experience, can do wonders for your sight, if you gaze on them."

"Aren't pearls supposed to have all kinds of powers, as well?" asked the Queen.

"Yes," said Corinna. "Apart from their beauty, pearls are a very good form of nourishment for the weak and the sick, if they are dissolved in foods—as is gold, which is the most noteworthy of all the metals and the noblest.[130] Gold is a life-giving substance, but also often a death-dealing one, for men have such a greed for gold that they often do things for its sake that are unworthy of a rational creature who is heir to all the riches of Heaven."

"As for the other metals," said Lucretia, "I'd think they were to be prized more for their beauty and usefulness when worked than because of their medicinal properties."

"Oh, don't say that!" said Corinna. "They all have their proper-

128. The mythical eaglestone or aetites (in fact probably "a hollow geode or concretion containing loose crystals, pebbles or earth" [Albertus Magnus 1967, 87]), is described by Pliny (*NH*, 10, 12; 36, 149–51). Its use in pregnancy was prescribed by Dioscorides (Mattioli 1573, 891–92).

129. The original here has *pietra di tucia.* Turquoise, which is variously referred to in sixteenth-century Italian as *turchese, turchina,* and *turcica,* seems the most likely translation, especially since medieval and Renaissance lapidaries attribute the property of preserving sight to it (Albertus Magnus 1967, 123; Dolce 1617, 64–65). Another possibility, however, is that it may indicate the metal antimony (sometimes referred to as *tuzia*), also used in this period to treat eye ailments (see Ramusio 1978–88, 1: 806, n. 5).

130. The medicinal use of gold was widely practiced in the period, though its use was not uncontroversial (Ulvioni 1982, 51; Thorndike 1923–58, 5: 664–65; 6: 457, 459).

ties, especially mercury, which has the power to dissolve substances and to incise metals. Then litharge, which is the froth from gold and silver, is good for cleaning, closing, and healing wounds, and you can make up an eye bath with it, mixed with rose water, or a cosmetic bath for the face.[131] And the others, too, have properties that it would take too long to describe in detail."

"Talking of silver and gold," said Cornelia, "what do you think of that modern-day Midas, who wanted to turn us all to gold?"[132]

"It was a trick that certainly gave us all something to talk about," said the Queen, "and a harmless bit of fun."

"What can I say?" Corinna added. "I've never believed in that kind of miracle, and I don't believe in alchemy, either. I think it's just a whim, a kind of obsession, that finishes up reducing men from something to nothing, rather than, as they claim, creating something from nothing. For myself, I don't know any better alchemy for making gold and silver than for a man to study hard and develop skills and then to work hard to make money through the sweat of his brow. That, for me, is an alchemy that never fails."

"You're right," said the Queen. "How many men have driven themselves to distraction with this foolish obsession with changing the nature of metals? But, then, people are never happy with things the way they are."

"The problem is more that many people want to get on in the world without lifting a finger," said Cornelia, "so they turn to all these quackeries and frauds, and call themselves alchemists or astrologers or herbalists or lapidaries in order to conjure coins out of the purses of those who don't know any better. Which is why it's better to keep a safe distance from these charlatans and not to believe a word they say."

"But, to get back to stones," said Lucretia, "they say that black

---

131. Copious recipes for such preparations are found in contemporary cosmetic manuals like Marinelli 1562 and Cortese 1588. Cortese is particularly fond of litharge as an ingredient: see for example 144–45, 155, 196–97, 200, 203.

132. The reference is probably to the flamboyant Cypriot impostor Marco Bragadin, or Mamugna, who thrilled audiences throughout Europe with his apparent ability to change mercury into gold before coming to an ignominious end in Munich in 1591, where he was beheaded on the orders of the Duke of Baveria. Bragadin stayed in Venice for a few months in 1589–90 on the invitation of the Venetian government, where he aroused great curiosity and (after his imposture was revealed) scorn (Kallfelz 1971).

magnets have the power to draw iron toward themselves, and that the white variety has the power to draw hearts into love.[133] So that sounds like just what we need."

"Alas, madam!" said Cornelia. "How well a stone works depends on the nature of the heart it is working on. It doesn't take much to bend a woman's heart and incline it toward a loyal and virtuous love, but all the powers of calamite are not enough to affect the heart of a man. Nor can the magnet of a woman's love draw a man into taking pity on her. For not only will he refuse to comfort her in her suffering or to help her in her needs, but he will also, into the bargain, refuse to believe what she is going through (or pretend not to believe it). In fact, he will positively revel in her torments, and find them a source of amusement, lapping up her tears as young shoots of grass drink in a soft April shower, and glorying in her pain."

"I don't know what makes you hope that any of these stones can have any effect on a man," added Corinna. "Men's hearts are made of stone, anyway, and a metal harder than any we find on this earth. The only way to get through to men using stones would be to use them in the manner of that gardener we heard about, when he was chasing off the thief from the fruit trees."

"If only men could be moved by force of words!" said Leonora. "If they could be, I'd try my hand at a public oration in the demonstrative genre:[134] I'd shower them with praise and lavish every term of affection I knew on them, if only I thought it would work."

"Oh, that would really be something to hear!" said Corinna. "Would you really dare stand up in front of all those censors, those know-alls, who do nothing but carp and jeer and mock? You could try all your best logical arguments, dialectical syllogisms, rhetorical colors, but it would all be to no avail. You could form fine concepts, clothe them in fine words, alter your voice, vary your style, draw on all the right figures of speech to construct arguments, prove laws, or

133. Pliny (*NH,* 36, 25, 128) talks of magnets as being divided into black and white varieties (the white being in fact possibly a kind of talc), which could also be male or female. White magnets (as well as "female" black magnets!) did not possess magnetic force.

134. The demonstrative, or epideictic, was one of the three genres of oratory identified by the classical authorities on rhetoric. It comprised speeches of praise and criticism delivered on ceremonial occasions. Another was the deliberative genre, mentioned below, which comprised speeches of (generally political) advice. The third genre, the forensic, is not mentioned in connection with Leonora's oration, even though her speech clearly seems to fall within that genre.

recall examples, but you'd still have lost your case even before you
started it, and even as you began your proem, you'd find your narration
and epilogue already mapped out for you."

"Oh, I'm no coward," said Leonora. "If I thought it would be any
use, I'd have no problem in putting my case."

"I have no doubt of that," said Cornelia. "But you're too fiery; you
wouldn't try hard enough to win them over."

"What a lovely orator you'd make!" said Helena. "Go on, pretend
we're the men you want to address and give us a taste of your speech:
what would you say?"

"It would be better for you to speak in the deliberative genre,
addressing men on behalf of all women, and persuading them to love
and respect us," said Corinna.

"You're right," said Helena. "Now go on, do start."

"What do you expect me to say?" asked Leonora. "I haven't had a
chance to study or prepare anything. Are you trying to catch me out?"

"Don't you know what the poet says?" Cornelia interjected.

Molti consigli delle donne sono
Meglio improviso che a pensarvi usciti.

Women's counsel is often more reliable when spontaneous
than when carefully thought out.[135]

"All right, then, listen," said Leonora. "I'm going to begin."

"Go on, give them something to remember!" said Cornelia; and
the other women crowded around, trying hard to hold back their
laughter, and she began,[136] "Dearest and most cherished menfolk, so
prudent are you and so warm in your affections, that I am confident
that you will lend your ears to one who speaks on behalf of all women
(for only one speaker may be heard at any one time, and the others
have graciously accorded me this privilege, even though I am the least

135. The lines are from *OF*, 27, 1, 1–2.

136. It was not completely unknown in the period for a woman to compose or deliver an
oration for an official occasion: on the public performances of the well-known
Venetian humanist Cassandra Fedele, see King 1991, 199–201; on Ipsicratea Monte's
public orations in Venice and its environs in the 1570s and 80s, see Contarini 1597,
71r; and Sansovino 1584, 277–85. These instances are exceptional, however:
Renaissance moralists never tired of repeating St. Paul's injunction against women
engaging in public speaking, and in general oratory (and the study of rhetoric in
general) were exclusively masculine fields.

of their number), on a subject that touches profoundly on the interests of all of us. And inasmuch as the cause I bring before you is the most just you will ever hear, and my arguments the most unimpeachable, I can have no doubt but that listening, as you surely will, not as interested parties but as the most impartial of judges, you will finally give sentence in our favor. The case is this: that you men, as you well know, have until now been so much our enemies as to have devoted yourselves to oppressing and abusing us with all the words and actions that lie in your power. And since we are entirely innocent and have done nothing to justify this enmity on your part, we now wish to move you to take pity on us, swayed by the force of our innocence and our merits (of which you are fully cognizant, however much you seek to dissimulate it), by the force of your obligation to us, and of the prayers and oblations we are about to offer to you, and of all our other arguments; and to treat us henceforth with a respect that corresponds to the great respect and love we bear you.

"For, to begin, you know full well that we were born with the same substance and qualities as you, and that we were given to you as companions in this life, not as slaves; and you are also quite aware that because of our humble and unselfish nature and because of the love we bear you, we serve you and follow you, and are respectful, obedient, patient, and utterly faithful, and devoted to you, accompanying you throughout life and even to the tomb (for how many of us have died alongside you and on your behalf?) So, dearest, dearest men, what reason can you have for not loving us? Loving fathers, what possible cause can there be for your favoring your male over your female offspring? (I shall not mention the actual physical cruelty that has often been shown by fathers to their daughters). Are we not your flesh and blood, as much as your male children are? Why do our claims go unrecognized, both during your life and at your death? And you, cherished brothers, why are you so cruel to your sisters? Why do you fail to care for them, if they find themselves penniless, through the fault of their fathers or of Fortune? Why do you not trouble yourselves to settle them, and prevent the poor creatures from turning to the bad? Why, pray, when you happily pay for and nourish brute animals in your household—dogs, cats, and birds—why are you so unwilling to do the same for us, when we were born from the same womb as you and are of the same flesh and blood?

"And you, beloved sons, why do you show such little regard to your mothers, who have suffered so much for you? You came from our wombs and drank our milk, your first nutriment, at our breasts, and we have spent so much effort in raising you, suffering endless labors and travails. Come, in the name of our blood, which is in you, and of the labors we so willingly endured in order to nurture you, teach you manners, guard you from every danger—in short, to make you the men you are today—can you not show us some compassion, some respect? Do not despise us, do not abandon us; consider that if you are now men, it is because we are women.

"And you, darling, darling husbands, pray do not hold your poor wives in contempt: you know full well that you are one flesh with us and that only death can sever you from our companionship. Why then do you abandon us? Why do you so often strip us of all our worldly goods? Why do you fail to cherish us as it is your duty to do? Alas! Is not all our devoted service, all the love we bear you, all the deference we show you—is not all this enough to bend you to make yourselves one flesh and one spirit with us, as you should be by rights? And do not attempt to justify yourselves by the fact that now and then a woman may dishonor her husband, for the many should not suffer for the offenses of the few, the universal for the particular; and, in any case, you have only yourselves to blame for these few women's errors, since you are always laying siege to each other's wives, until the poor creatures are led by all your pestering and by their own ill fortune to fall into the trap. And, indeed, it is often husbands themselves who are the causes of their wives' downfall, for, by giving them such a miserable life, they bring them to a state of such desperation that they hardly care what they do any more. So hear our plea, dearest friends and inseparable companions, for you belong to us by all laws, both divine and human, just as we belong to you. Come, be good and loving companions, and show us an example: for if you love us, then we will love you; if you pay us the regard due to a wife, we will pay you that due to a husband—we will even regard you as our masters, not through obligation, but through love.

"And now you lovers, you crafty and importunate schemers after our freedom and honor, I beg you, in the name of all women, think well about what you are doing, and resolve to mend your ways and stop attempting to lead us to our ruin. Come now, please, if you really love us, don't set out to endanger our honor, our life, and our immortal souls: for those are the acts of an enemy, not a friend. Or if you don't really love us, if you are simply out to trick us, what is it that makes you want to destroy someone who never did you any harm? That is a cruelty too excessive. Please let us be, and put an end to your attempts to dishonor us, molest us, and deceive us. For we want no part of it: we completely and utterly refuse to bend to your desires. In other respects, we are prepared to remain your friends and well-wishers, but at a distance.

"And so, O supremely wise and supremely just men, since, as was stated earlier (and as you well know in any case), we are like you in substance, in form, and in our natural qualities, and since all things love their like, then, pray, why do you not love us? And since divine law, human edicts, the ties of nature, and the laws of grace all conspire to oblige you to love us, then why do you fail to love us? And if we love you, and if love permits no love to go unreturned,[137] then why do you not love us? Especially when all the persuasive force of our humility, our patience, and our kindness is added in, along with all our other merits, which should be sufficient to win your love by any rational calculation. And we might add to this the extra inducement of an armistice: we hereby promise, if you come round, to be reconciled to you, forgetting all your past offenses, and we pledge in future to be even more loving and submissive to you than ever—submissive, that is, as a free choice, out of love for you, not under compulsion. For Love reigns over his empire without need for a sword. We have made you judges of the case even though you are one of the parties; we have submitted ourselves entirely to your decision; now we beg and beseech you to listen to justice and be convinced by the strength of our case and pass sentence against yourselves. Though, in fact, this sentence will rather be in your favor—pass it, O men! and you will find yourselves happier with every new day. Grant our requests (and I know your goodness and wisdom will not allow you to do otherwise) and you will remove any cause for further resentment on our part, so that we can live out that short space of life that the Lord has given us, loving one another and living together in peace, charity, and love. And in this way the effects will validate the justness of your sentence."

Leonora's listeners enjoyed this speech of hers immensely and it was a long while before their laughter died down afterward. Then the

---

137. This phrase echoes a famous line from Dante's *Inferno* (5, 103) in which Francesca da Rimini, condemned to hell for lust, attempts to justify her affair with her brother-in-law. A phrase below, "Love reigns over his empire without a sword," is another embedded quotation, this time from Petrarch (*RS*, 105, 11).

Queen said, "Well, Leonora, you certainly go down very well presenting your case among us women, since we are all on your side anyway.
But I'm not sure how much success you'd have persuading the men!"

"Are you suggesting that I'd suffer the same fate as the ironmonger's son?" replied Leonora.

"What happened to him?" the Queen asked. "Go on, tell us."

"There was once an ironmonger," said Leonora, "who sent his son
off to study, in the hope that he would turn out to be intelligent and
achieve his doctorate in time. Now when, after a few years, the time
arrived that the father had longed for for so long, he summoned his
son back home and started quizzing him about the degree examina-
tion, asking him, among other things, whether he thought he would
be able to stand up to the interrogation and give the right answers to
all the questions and criticisms with which he would be confronted.
The young man replied that he thought he would; at which, 'Come,
lad,' said the father, 'I'd like to put you to the test beforehand, to see
whether you're up to it. Let's have a go: it will all be good practice.'
And he took him into a room stacked with the pots and pans he made
for a living, and he picked up a selection of them and lined them up
on a tabletop, and then said to the son, 'Now you stand here opposite
and pretend that these are your audience, and these others are your
examiners. Now, let's hear what you have to say.' And the young man
pulled all his knowledge together in his head in the best way he
could, and started arguing his case and stringing together such a mass
of tangled arguments that the father, who understood about as much
about logic and learning in general as an ass does about playing the
lyre, had the impression that his son was arguing brilliantly and resolving all kinds of problems that *he* didn't understand a word of, and that
the young man's head was as well stocked with philosophy as his shop
was stocked with saucepans. So, when the performance was finished,
he cried happily, 'Away with you, lad! You really are quite an expert;
you know more than a hundred examiners put together. Now let's go
and get things organized: I don't want to hang around any longer.'

"And so off they went, and arranged things with the examiners.
And shortly afterward, the examiners assembled in front of a large
audience to interrogate the young man, with the father present; but
the boy, from the very first question, was completely bemused and got
so abashed that he couldn't say a single thing to anything he was
asked. The father was profoundly shocked and dismayed, and asked,
'But when we were at home, in front of those saucepans and crocks,

you were arguing away and disputing away like Tully himself.[138] Why on earth are you so confused and tongue-tied now?' 'Oh, respected father,' the young man replied. 'Men aren't at all the same thing as saucepans, you know.' So that young man really came a cropper—but I don't quite think the same would happen to me."

Her listeners laughed a great deal at Leonora's joke; then Cornelia said, "So, Leonora, you're comparing us women to an audience of old crocks?"

"Oh, don't get the wrong end of the stick," laughed Leonora. "My comparison wasn't supposed to reflect at all on women's dignity or learning: what I was thinking of was how intimate and easy we all are with each other, and if you take the analogy that way it's quite proper and fitting. Anyway, as I was saying, despite this warning, I'm not afraid that my courage would fail me in front of a different audience; in fact, I think I'd be able to speak up even better than I did just now, if I thought there were any chance of making some headway with these men of ours."

"There was one man," said Lucretia, "(and this is a true story), who was supposed to be talking to a gathering of gentlemen about a matter of some importance, but whose memory went completely, so he couldn't even make a start on what he was supposed to be saying. And he was so embarrassed that all he could think of to say was, 'Respected sirs, I had rather a tasty little morsel for you, but for the moment I've quite forgotten it'; and with that he took his leave."

"I heard about another man," Corinna added, "who had written all the main points of his speech inside his cap. He appeared before his honored audience and politely took off his cap, glancing surreptitiously into it to see where to begin, but, as luck would have it, he couldn't find the beginning of his notes. So he stood there turning the cap around and around in his hands without ever finding the first lines of his speech, until finally, at a loss for what to do, he decided to cut his losses, made a deep bow, put his cap back on his head, and took himself off."

"It's certainly true enough that this art of oratory is no light matter, when you think about it," said the Queen, "and advocates have to be brave indeed to stand up in public and lay themselves open to the censure of all those many people who are less interested in listening

138. Marcus Tullius Cicero, the great Roman orator, whose name was a byword for eloquence.

to their arguments than in picking their speeches to pieces."

"You're quite right," said Corinna. "That's why they say that that most celebrated orator Demosthenes broke down when he had to speak before Philip of Macedon.[139] And, what's more, just think of what a memory lawyers need to have! They have to remember all the laws, the whole of courtroom procedure, the entire defense case, and all the relevant precedents, so that they don't go off the track, or do the wrong thing at the wrong time, or fail to exploit the strong points of the defense, and so that they aren't lost for an example when they need one. They need to be able to study the depositions carefully, understand all the arguments and construct new ones of their own, spot the traps their opponent is setting them, devise strategies and counter those of their adversary, and consult other lawyers about the case (and that often brings new difficulties, because very often opinions differ: one person thinks one thing, another, something quite different, and trying to reconcile them means going back and thinking the whole thing through again, and racking one's brains over it). And then, when the case is prepared, the advocate has to be ready to speak in front of the tribunal, which takes great courage, a powerful voice, a prompt memory, and strong arguments. He has to be able to win over the judge and also to uphold justice in all its rigor, convince his listeners of the piteousness of his client's position or the necessity that forced him to act in the way he did, and maintain the justness of the prosecution or defense."

"And even so, they lose so many cases," said Lucretia.

"Well, what do you expect?" Corinna replied. "There's always a loser as well as a winner. But do you know where clients often go wrong? They often meddle too much, and aren't prepared to entrust their cases to a single lawyer, even when they have no reason to doubt his reliability, thoroughness, and loyalty. Because just as conflicting advice from different doctors can be the end of a patient (as we've said), so the conflicting opinions of different lawyers can kill off a case."

"But you hear people say that the only way to get on in the world is to watch out for your own interests," said Helena.

139. The story of Demosthenes' nervous confusion and inability to speak during an embassy to Philip of Macedon (346 BC) is told by an ill-disposed fellow orator, Aeschines, in a defense speech composed for the latter's trial for treachery (*On The Embassy*, 34–35, in Aeschines 1919, 187).

"That may be true," replied Corinna, "but you have to know where to stop."

"I must say," said Lucretia, "that among all the miseries this miserable life of ours has in store for us, I do think the sufferings of all those poor souls engaged in litigation are not among the least. They never get a moment's peace! And I should know, for when I was involved in a lawsuit myself, I was in continual agonies. It wasn't the endless expense that got me down as much as the endless worries this kind of tedious business inevitably brings with it."

"Did you win?" asked Helena.

"I did indeed," she replied, "through the grace of God and the merits of our superb lawyer."

"And who was that?" the Queen asked.

"He was (and still is)," Lucretia replied, 'that excellent man Usper. You must all know his name: he's one of the foremost lawyers of the city and everyone knows how learned he is and how eloquent—there can be few lawyers anywhere in the world who can match him.[140] I really am very much obliged to him."

"When we need a lawyer," said the Queen, "we always use that other much-respected man Balbi.[141] Again, he's someone else of rare ability and quite remarkable learning, and he doesn't only excel in the legal profession: he's someone of very wide-ranging talents."

"When my father was involved in a lawsuit," said Cornelia, "I heard him showering praise on Trento and Vicenzi,[142] who were our lawyers and, according to him, two of the finest in the whole palazzo."

"He was quite right," said Corinna. "And what's more, besides

---

140. Lucretia's praises of Lodovico Usper's learning appear well grounded, from the evidence of his library inventory, which reveals him as a man of broad and somewhat heterodox cultural interests (Ambrosini 1982, 18–19). Usper, along with several others of the figures mentioned in the ensuing discussion (Luigi Balbi, Camillo Trento, Giovanni Vincenti, Michiel Marini, Filippo Pincio), is mentioned in a list of prominent Venetian lawyers in late sixteenth-century editions of the famous Venetian guidebook, *On the Remarkable Features of the City of Venice*; see, for example, Sansovino 1587, 200.

141. On Luigi Balbi, a prominent lawyer and orator, and noted for his fine library, see Cicogna 1824–61, 3: 17–18.

142. Giovanni Vincenzi (or Vincenti) is among the lawyers thanked by Fonte in her romance *Il Floridoro* (1581) for assisting her in a lawsuit of her own (Fonte 1995, 46 [3, 5]). A figure of the same name is later mentioned by Doglioni as occupying the highly prestigious post of Secretary to the Council of Ten (Goldioni [Doglioni] 1624, 192).

their eloquence, they are very loyal men, and well-mannered and most conscientious. Then there are Marini, Bardelini, Pincio, Squadron[143]—all celebrated and leading figures in their profession, and there are countless more highly distinguished men, whom it would take far too long to list."

"And who is your own lawyer? One of those just named?" asked the Queen.

"No, indeed," she replied. "I use Signor Filippo Giorgi, who is also advocate fiscal for that most honored institution, the Officio dell'Acque, and whose diligence, loyalty, and efficiency are much appreciated by our much-respected Senate.[144] And it's certainly true that, even if he is not as famous as some other lawyers, because of his age (for he's very young), he is on a par with the most celebrated men where talent, decency, and integrity are concerned; and he is extremely conscientious and throws himself into his cases with great energy. So he is highly regarded for all these reasons; and, what's more, where preparing cases is concerned, he really is in the first rank."

"I've heard that too," said Leonora, "and, if I were ever in the position of having to call on some man's services, in a lawsuit, I should most certainly choose him."

"Lawyers," said the Queen, "should try to be as brief and concise in their speeches as possible, for long perorations (besides the fact that they allow more scope for error) tend to bore the judge."

"Oh, that's something I can't bear either," said Lucretia, "those types who draw their speech out far beyond what's necessary, and dissect everything that's said word by word like some pedantic old grammarian."

"It's best for lawyers, as well, to avoid using Latin tags," said

143. Filippo Pincio, whom a document of 1600 indicates to have served, like Fonte's husband, Filippo Zorzi, as a tax lawyer in the Venetian civil service (ASV, Senato Terra, reg. 70, 110), is praised for his oratorical excellence in the dedicatory letter of a well-known anthology of vernacular orations (Sansovino 1584). Pietro Squadron (d. 1615), too, was famed for his "learning and eloquence" (Cicogna 1824–61, 1: 283).

144. Filippo Giorgi (or Zorzi, in the Venetian spelling) was, of course, Moderata Fonte's husband. Her tribute to him here has an important function within the dialogue's debate on marriage (at least for those readers aware of her identity), serving both to distance the author from some of her speakers' more drastic generalizations about the iniquity of husbands, and at the same time to lend weight to the dialogue's condemnation of the ills endured by many married women by pre-empting any attempt to dismiss it as the expression of a personal grievance.

Corinna. "It's got an old-fashioned ring about it, and it's not really done any more."

"It's a strange thing," said Cornelia, "that Latin teachers are not particularly highly regarded these days; and yet it can't be denied that the first thing children need to be taught is this most useful of disciplines, which opens up the way to all the others."

"If men were a bit more as they used to be," said Leonora, "that is, if they were less bad (as their forefathers were), I might try to address a good, old-fashioned proem to them; and, if the vernacular didn't seem to be working, I'd use Latin. But I'm not sure it would be worth the effort: they'd just try to avoid listening to me, knowing I'd be speaking the truth,

> *Com'aspide suole*
> *Che per star empio il canto udir non vuole.*

> Like an asp, which, as it is evil, does not wish to hear the singing.[145]

"And besides," said Corinna, "your Latin grammar wouldn't coincide with theirs, for in men's Latin, the agreements are always wrong. With them, a relative never agrees with its antecedent, for, if yesterday, they smiled on you and had a good word for you, you can be sure that today they will be inconsistent with the past and will show themselves your enemy. They have the passive of the first verb, but not the active, which belongs to women alone, because we love and they are loved; their conduct is punctuated with the black marks of their misdeeds, but their appetites know no parentheses. Of the genders, they have the masculine and the indefinite; of the cases—well, the accusative is theirs, because they are always accusing us of something or other; the dative, because they sometimes give us a good hiding; and the ablative, because another of their habits is taking things away from us (like themselves, and everything we possess). Whereas we have the nominative, for always speaking their names with reverence; the genitive, for being all theirs, and the vocative, since we are always lovingly calling out to them."

---

145. These lines, from *OF*, 32, 19, 7–8, refer to the legend, alluded to in the Psalms and recounted in medieval bestiaries, that the asp resists attempts to charm it to sleep by pressing one ear against the ground and blocking the other with its tail (McCulloch 1960, 88–90).

"Now men aren't going to understand you if you carry on like that," said the Queen. "And, anyway, how do you expect them to love us if we're always speaking so badly of them?"

"Do you know the reason why our speaking ill of them makes them dislike us?" said Leonora. "It's because,

L'ossequio gli amici, e la verità partorisce odio

Flattery makes us friends, the truth, enemies.[146]

And besides, they offended us before we started complaining about them; and they were already speaking ill of us, before we started speaking ill of them."

"Well, maybe we should just try keeping quiet for a while," said Helena, "and perhaps they'll change their tune."

"We've already done too much keeping quiet in the past," Leonora replied, "and the more we keep quiet, the worse they get. On the contrary, in order to move a judge to pass a just sentence, one needs to speak out freely, not suppressing any argument that might support the truth. If a man needs to reclaim some money from a person who has refused to pay him and he keeps quiet about it, the unscrupulous debtor will never give him satisfaction, but if he speaks up, if he brings the case, if he complains in front of the judge, then sooner or later he will get back what is his by right."

"But if it were the judge himself who was the debtor," said Cornelia, "then I'm not as sure as you seem to be that he would give the sentence in the plaintiff's favor."

"Well in that case he would be an unjust and cruel judge," said Corinna, "because a true judge should be dispassionate and shouldn't let himself be swayed by his own interests; he should judge soundly even when it means passing sentence against himself."

"It's certainly true," said the Queen, "that judges must have extremely good judgment and that they need to be men of the highest integrity to be able to pass judgment on the conflicting parties correctly and sincerely. And when a judge is known to be of this character, no one has any cause for complaint, even when the sentence goes against him."

"I'm sure all kingdoms and republics draw up laws and appoint judges to ensure that the people are well governed," said Lucretia.

146. I have not been able to identify the source of this quotation.

"But nowhere does the justice system work better than in this glorious city of ours, whose venerable laws are worthy of being embraced and adopted by any realm on earth, just as the laws of that wisest of cities, Athens, were adopted by others in antiquity. And as for our senators, who sit in judgment, words cannot express their wisdom, justice, and compassion."

"Oh, quite so!" said the Queen. "But then, what can one say about the extraordinary goodness and civility of the Venetian nobility in general? The city can justly be proud of its ruling class, as also of its loyal and devoted *cittadinanza* and its populace."[147]

"But, then, while we're on the subject," said Corinna, "what can one say about the divine and quite extraordinary merits of our most serene Prince, the Doge?"

"Oh!" exclaimed the Queen. "It would be impossible even to know where to begin."

And Lucretia added, "Whenever I see and admire that venerable presence that moves the souls of his subjects (indeed, of everyone, without exception) to love and revere him, I am reminded of that famous victory in which he played a part so glorious that before long he exchanged his honored sword for the glorious ducal *corno* he now wears."[148]

"What a happy event!" cried the Queen, "A victory worthy of perpetual remembrance! And our Doge's name, too, deserves to be echoed throughout the whole world and down through the ages. For, even were it not for his other merits, his share in that great victory alone would be enough to guarantee the great honor and joy that the famous name of PASQUAL CICOGNA, Doge of Venice, evokes in the republic."

"And what a lovely sight it is," Virginia added, "when our Doge

147. The notion that the Venetian patriciate constituted a uniquely talented, con-scientious, and disinterested ruling class was a central commonplace of the political "myth of Venice," on which see Finlay 1980, 27–37; Queller 1986, 3–16. (On the degree to which this vision corresponded to reality, see Queller.) The *cittadini* were the second elite class of Venice, excluded from political power, but prominent in the civil service and the professions. The *popolo* was the third estate, ranging down from wealthy merchants to poor laborers.

148. The victory referred to here is probably the great sea battle at Lepanto in 1571, where the combined Western forces succeeded in winning a rare victory against the Turks. Pasquale Cicogna (1509–95), doge of Venice from 1585, was governor of Crete at the time of the battle, and played an important administrative role in the Christian victory, though not the heroic military role implied here. The *corno* (lit. "horn") was the horn-shaped beretta worn by the doge and symbolic of his office.

passes by on his way to some ceremony or other, accompanied by all the pomp and splendor of the foreign ambassadors and our wonderfully dignified senators and most noble secretaries."[149]

"Indeed," said Corinna, "one feels one is seeing a collection of precious jewels, the greatest treasures of our country passing before one's eyes. For these are the men who govern Venice and sustain her; these are the men who, after God, are responsible for providing her with all her needs. These men embody all the virtues that ensure the survival and well-being of this great republic of ours: courage, shrewdness, wisdom, learning, intelligence, piety, and true fear of God. These men, though they are lords of the city, nonetheless, like loving fathers, work unceasingly, unstintingly, and unwearyingly for the benefit of all, without any thought of the cost to themselves, in money and energy, of their labors for the common good. These men administer justice, aid the poor, reward the deserving, and punish criminals (though this last duty they perform with compassion, imitating God's own mercy); and, besides this, they diligently oversee public works, keeping a careful eye on the state of the Lagoon and the outlying regions, as well as the fortresses and the public buildings so necessary to the life of the city. And besides that, they are kind, loving, and respectful to every one of their subjects, and while the others sleep, they keep an anxious vigil, so that under their wings, like children nestling in the care of their mothers and fathers, their subjects can rest securely and without a care in the world. O venerable vigilance! O venerable institutions! O venerable laws! O venerable fathers! Anyone intolerant of such venerable and happy protection is wretched and foolish indeed."

"I couldn't agree more," said Cornelia. "But when you mentioned public building works earlier, you reminded me of the reconstruction they're engaged in at the moment of the Procuratorie, and the new Rialto bridge.[150] What do you think of all this new building, at such

---

149. Such ducal processions were a central part of Venetian civic ritual (Muir 1981, 188–211), and served as a frequent visual reminder to the populace of Venice's elaborate social and political hierarchies. An interesting detail here, considering Fonte's *cittadino* background, is the prominence given in her account to the representatives of this estate (the "most noble secretaries"), though these high-ranking civil servants were indeed allotted an honorable place in Venetian political ritual.

150. The first stone bridge over the Grand Canal, at the Rialto, was built between 1588 and 1591, to a design by Antonio da Ponte. The Procuratorie Nuove (Offices of the Procurators of St. Mark) on the south side of Piazza San Marco, were under construction between 1582 and 1586, under the direction of Vincenzo Scamozzi.

sumptuous expense? What do you think of these new marvels, following on so many others?"

"It's certainly a most admirable and remarkable project," said the Queen. "But then, as that lines goes,

> *Sempre Venezia ha maraviglie nove.*

Venice always has some wondrous new thing.[151]

"When they were just starting work on this marvelous construction," Corinna said, "I saw a sonnet written by a gentleman, a relative of mine, in praise of this building and the city as a whole. If I could only remember it, I'd love you to hear it, but I can't recall how it went."

"Well, you'd better try," said the Queen, "or else you shouldn't have mentioned it in the first place." Corinna, who had a written copy with her, unfolded it with a smile and read it out as her eager audience listened.

> *Inclite maraviglie apportar suole*
> *Varia età, vario luogo e vario ingegno*
> *In oro, in carta, in bronzo, in marmo, in legno*
> *Fabriche, imprese e forme elette e sole.*
> *Ma questa tua quanto 'l mar gira e 'l sole*
> *Venezia, avanza ogni mortal disegno.*
> *Opra è degna di te, lavor condegno*
> *A l'eterno esser tuo, l'eterna mole.*
> *Le piramide, i tempii, i mausolei,*
> *Nulla son; questo è nuovo onor del mondo,*
> *Degno di penna d'oro e d'aurea cetra.*
> *Non più fral legno or ti congiunge; or sei*
> *Fondata in pietra, in CHRISTO, o caro pondo*
> *Ch'in eterno ei sostien, felice pietra.*

Lofty and remarkable monuments have been created by diverse ages, places, and talents: choice and rare constructions, enterprises and artifacts, in gold, paper, bronze, marble, and wood. But this new marvel of yours, O Venice, far outstrips all other mortal designs on the face of the

---

151. I have not been able to identify the source of this line, which is probably modeled on the Greek proverb quoted by Pliny and much cited in the Renaissance, "Out of Africa, always some new marvel" (*NH,* 8, 17, 42).

earth. It is a creation worthy of you, a work well fitted to
your immortal destiny and vast immortal fabric. The pyramids, temples, and mausoleums of the past are nothing:
this is the new wonder of the world, worthy of being celebrated with pens and lyres of gold. No longer, fair city, are
you joined with fragile wood; now you are founded in
stone, on the rock of CHRIST. O happy rock! O dear
burden, that he will bear to all eternity![152]

The women praised to the skies this novel sonnet, read to them
by the charming Corinna. And the Queen then continued, "But we
shouldn't just talk about these architectural splendors. When you
think about it, what is done by those destined by their rank to be the
fathers of our city that is not rare and remarkable and carried out with
great prudence? For before doing anything, they discuss it at length
with those fine judges of theirs, especially those of the Pregadi and
the Council of Ten, who are charged with the highest affairs of the
state (for the only business transacted in the Great Council is the
election of magistrates and other minor business)."[153]

"This city has always had the good fortune to be governed most
wisely," said Lucretia, "and it has always found leaders of good sense
and great integrity to regulate and guide its affairs. Now, for example,
apart from having such a great man as doge, we also have men of talent as ducal councilors, procurators, *savi*, *avogadori*, and censors,[154]

152. The last lines of this sonnet depend on a pun untranslatable in English, on *pietra*
(the "stone" of which the new bridge is built, but also the "rock" of faith on which
the city is founded). An allusion may be intended to Venice's rival, Rome, the "eternal
city" and the burial place of St. Peter, the rock—*petrus*—on which Christ founded his
church (it should not be forgotten that Venice boasted a competing apostolic
connection, with St. Mark).

153. The institutions referred to here were the principal political organs of the
Venetian state. The Pregadi ("the elect"), also known as the Senate, was an elite
council of Venetian patricians, chosen by the members of the Great Council, an
assembly of male patricians over the age of twenty-five. The Council of Ten was a
smaller council (though larger than its name implies), elected from the Senate.
Originally established to supervise domestic security after a conspiracy in the
fourteenth century, by the sixteenth, it had accrued vast, wide-ranging, and rather
sinister powers, though these were curtailed in a sweeping reform of 1582–83.

154. Lucretia's list encompasses some of the most important of what a seventeenth-
century English ambassador described as the Venetian state's "infinitie of officers"
(*VDH*, 26). The ducal councilors were six in number, and, together with the sixteen
savi [lit. "sages" or "experts"], who were organized into three committees, and the
heads of the Courts of the Forty (see following note), made up the so-called Collegio,
the steering committee of the Senate, memorably described by another English

besides a formidable crop of excellent magistrates, who look after those in their charge with remarkable and unwearying scrupulousness, and who maintain justice and watch over individuals' interests with the greatest imaginable impartiality. And then, besides these grave elders of the city, there are also those remarkably prudent younger men, who seem to be born already wise, as though exercising justice came naturally to them (as it does, indeed): I mean the judges of the Courts of the Forty, the *savi di ordini*, the magistrates of the lower courts and so on."[155]

"Good Lord!" said Leonora. "I can't believe what I'm hearing! I despair of you! How can you let me down like this? Are you really quite determined to spend the entire day talking about anything rather than the subject at hand? What on earth do magistrates, law courts, and all this other nonsense have to do with us women? Are not all these official functions exercised by men, against our interests? Do they not make claims on us, whether we are obliged to them or not? Do they not act in their own interests and against ours? Do they not treat us as though we were aliens? Do they not usurp our property?"

"That's all too true, sadly," said Cornelia. "Now let's really get down to discussing these men of ours."

"I'm happy to defer to Leonora, since she has such a trick of hitting on the essential points," said Corinna.

"I don't have much to say," said Leonora, "nor much faith in the power of my words. What I've said in the past has never had any effect, and I don't hold out much hope that what I'm going to say in future will carry much weight with men."

"People do say, though, that, just as beasts are bound with ropes, so men are bound by the power of words," said Corinna.

"That's all very well," said Cornelia. "But not all those who have the outer form of men are really men underneath: don't you know the

---

ambassador as "that member of the state where (as in the stomach) all things are first digested." The procurators of San Marco, elected from the Senate for life, were charged with administering the vast revenues of the basilica. The *avogadori del comun* were state attorneys. The censors had the thankless task of policing electoral corruption in the Great Council.

155. There were three Courts of the Forty (*Quaranta*) charged with administering justice in, respectively, criminal cases, civil cases in Venice, and civil cases on the mainland (*VDH*, 53–54). Their members sat on the Collegio, as did the *savi agli Ordini*: a committee charged with maritime affairs. Both posts, though prestigious, were relatively junior and regarded as the beginning of the Venetian *cursus honorum* (Davis 1962, 30, 89–90).

story about the sage who searched high and low for a man, torch in hand, and didn't find a single one?[156] So that saying about words having the power to bind men works only in a minority of cases, since there are few men who can truly be called men."

"It's certainly true," said the Queen, "that fine speech, infused with emotion and ordered by the natural eloquence of the intellect, even without those formal refinements that are the hallmark of a trained orator, still possesses a remarkable, almost miraculous, capacity for moving and swaying the souls of its listeners, be they men (when I say 'men' I'm not applying Cornelia's exacting standards) or the very stones themselves. And besides, a finely tuned harmony of ideas, expressed in a copious flow of well-chosen words, apposite to the subject under discussion, can be a source of great pleasure, whether it is spoken aloud or gathered on the page."

"I must say," said Lucretia, "that writers of fine prose are to be much commended, but those who succeed in writing poetry well deserve both our commendation and our reverence."

"Writing in verse," said Corinna, "is a thing of such high worth that the sages affirmed the true poet to be moved by divine fury, seeing poetry as a divine gift, a supernatural form of insight, innate in poets. That's why there's that proverb about poets being born, prose writers made."[157]

"The kind of poetry I love best," said Cornelia, "is poetry that has substance, and combines gracefulness and dignity: an unforced style of poetry whose simplicity gives it an appropriate measured grandeur."

"It's certainly true that there are different styles of poetry," said Corinna, "for the style must vary along with the subject matter. So, when writing about grave matters, or on sad occasions, or when writing in praise of princes, one should compose weighty, resonant lines, full of gravity; while pleasant subjects and happy occasions require lighter and more charming concepts and words. But regardless of the subject, the meter should always be firm and not lax, and the words should be choice and the epithets apt, and all harsh and jarring language should be excluded, for it can make poetry sound forced— worse, clumsy and unrefined."

"But, in conclusion," said Leonora, "it has to be said that even if

---

156. The story is told by Diogenes Laertius of the Greek Cynic philosopher Diogenes (fourth century BC) (*LP*, 6, 41).

157. The proverb was a Roman one: *Poeta nascitur, orator fit.*

a gifted poet is capable of writing successfully on any theme, to write something of real excellence, it's necessary to have the right subject."

"That's quite right," said Corinna, "and, thinking about it straight, what more worthy and what lovelier subject can one find (limiting ourselves to secular themes) than the beauty, grace, and virtues of women? Because even though, when a poet writes in praise of a prince or some other illustrious person of rare and marvelous talents, the resulting piece may be very fine and a delight to the ears, it's nonetheless true that the gravity of the subject seems more suited to an elegant prose treatment than to the sweetness of verse, for the subject does not in itself possess that vivacity, that power to steal away our senses, to separate our souls from our bodies and lift our spirits into ecstasy, that we find in a fit and polished description of the outer or inner beauties of some noble and worthy woman: a subject that offers the diligent poet the charmingly varied prospect of a thousand delightful conceits."

"While we're on this subject," said Lucretia, "which would you say was preferable: the inner form of the soul, with all the fine proportions of its different faculties, or the outer form of the body, in all its fine disposition of line, feature, and color?"

"I'd say," said Corinna, "that a perfectly composed outer corporeal form is something most worthy of our esteem, for it is this visible outer form that is the first to present itself to our eye and our understanding: we see it and instantly love and desire it, prompted by an instinct embedded in us by nature. But the beauty of the mind and spirit are nobler and more estimable by far, not only because it resides in a nobler part of us, but because this beauty itself is of a nobler quality. For, like a fragile flower that opens up in the morning in all its tenderness and freshness, but by nightfall (or earlier, if it is smitten by rain or wind) falls wilted and dry to the earth, so corporeal beauty, whether through illness or fatigue or gradual aging, fades away utterly and loses all its worth. By contrast, the beauty that truly and inalienably belongs to us (that is, virtue in its various forms) is not only infinite, but also ineffable and immortal, and of such a kind that its divine glories can barely be expressed in prose or verse. It is because of this discrepancy that it is an unworthy sight to see some refined soul (as often happens) blinded by a lovely surface, losing itself in pursuit of the fragile appearances of outer beauty and lavishing too much love on that part of us that is less worthy in itself and that soon fades, and ignoring what is more important in us and more worthy of being loved."

"Oh, don't try to argue that!" said the Queen. "For a lovely face has a great power to attract men's souls and inflame their bodies, and it sometimes seems to me that two fine eyes have the capacity to move a mountain, let alone the heart of an eager young man, predisposed to such accidents and passions of love. Oh, how much what can be seen matters! How much more than what can't!"

"Well, now," said Corinna. "You're quite right when you say that in the short term what we see and what pleases the eye has far more power over us than what we cannot see or grasp in an instant. But, over time, if a man is given the opportunity to spend time in the company of a woman who is physically beautiful and another possessed of beauty of mind, there can be no doubt that even if he initially prefers the first, when he discovers her to be silly and ignorant or haughty and impudent, then for all her beauty, he will find himself unable (or he *should* find himself unable) to love her with a genuinely deep and passionate love. But, by contrast, as he converses with her less beautiful companion (as long as she isn't actually hideous); as he gradually discovers her to be a woman of refinement, intelligent, virtuous, quick-witted and well-mannered—I ask you, madam, what will you say of such a creature? You must admit that, if she is not beautiful, she is nonetheless all charm, and this charm of hers will work its magic, so that her eyes, though not beautiful, will seem quite ravishing, and her mouth, as it utters fine words with a lovely smile, will come to seem equally lovely. And, in the same way, the vivacity of her keen and lively mind will make her a faultless and charming companion, and, if she does not impress at first sight, her rich store of inner beauties will gradually reveal themselves over time, in the form of words and gestures and virtuous actions. And these are the kind of beauties that do not fade or wither, but last our whole lives and even live on after our deaths, in our fame."

"Well, I must say that Corinna has put her case very well and very reasonably," said Lucretia, "and I'm sure it's true that any person of sound judgment would be compelled to feel more warmly toward such a woman than a woman whose beauty resided solely in her outer appearance, and moreover that the love he conceived for her would be more firmly grounded and less liable to fade over time. For the kind of love that is aroused by physical beauty fades as rapidly as it is generated— or at most, lasts only as long as the woman's beauty lasts."

"When we're talking about love," said the Queen, "it's all very well to give advice, but it's very hard to overcome people's natural inclinations. For there are some who will choose a woman for her physical beauty, others who will prefer another for her beauty of mind, and still others who will choose a woman who has neither of these beauties to recommend her and yet who will, for some reason, quite fascinate him. And, in the same way, you'll find a woman falling in love with a man who has nothing whatsoever to recommend him, and yet, whether because of a natural inclination on her part or an act of will, she will find him more attractive than any other man, however handsome or charming. Haven't you heard of how the noble maiden Hipparchia fell passionately in love with that philosopher, even though he was so gaunt and twisted that he looked like a monster?"[158]

"That's nothing: at least he was a man of talent," said Cornelia. "If you want to hear something really bad, I was told a supposedly true story about a very pretty and well-mannered young woman who fell in love with the ugliest, most insalubrious scarecrow you could imagine, and eloped with him and lived with him, as happy as can be. And someone, I don't know who, took it into their head to write a humorous little madrigal, inspired by these lovers; and since I doubt you've heard it, I'll recite it for you, to follow Corinna's example."

And she started:

> *Gionta a spino pungente*
> *Fresca rosa ridente;*
> *Et or lucido e terso*
> *Giacer nel fango immerso*
> *Vidi e stupii, veggendo in gran piacere*
> *Del fango e spin la rosa e l'or godere.*
> *Allor diss'io, qual più sprezzato core*
> *Piagnerà per Amore?*
> *S'ei fa in virtù di sua potente face,*
> *Che spesso il bello annoia, e 'l brutto piace.*

158. The philosopher in question is the Cynic Crates (c. 365–285 BC). Diogenes Laertius (*LP*, 6, 96–98) relates how Hipparchia fell in love with him after hearing him lecture and, undeterred by his physical hideousness and his unsavory habit of dressing in pieces of sheepskin (6, 91–92), finally persuaded him to marry her.

A fresh, laughing rose joined to a sharp thorn; a piece of
bright, polished gold lying enveloped in mud: I saw these
things and stood amazed, seeing the rose embracing its
thorn with relish, the gold wallowing in its mud. And I
said to myself: what rejected lover will ever again weep at
Love's cruelty, when we see that the power of his brand
can make beauty indifferent to us, and ugliness attractive?

This novel little madrigal, recited by the witty Cornelia, found
great favor with the ladies, and the Queen said, "All these things are
extravagances and miracles wrought by this cruel passion of love,
which has such great power over our hearts that it blinds our intellect
and deprives us of our reason; and that's why people say that love
knows no laws, and that love is stronger than death. But to get back
to what we were talking about, I have to recognize that Corinna
knows better than I do, so I'm quite prepared to concede, rationally
speaking, that inner beauty is far more worthy of love than the beauty
that appears on the surface."

"It's certainly true, though," said Corinna, "that when you find
these two kinds of perfection united in a single person, the one
adorns the other in such a way that the individual who contains two
such signal graces seems more like a god than a human being. But
since it's a rare thing to find such a sublime conjunction in a single
person and it's more usual to find oneself having to choose someone
with just one of these perfections, it seems to me that, in both
sexes, a person who is not beautiful but who is sensible, intelligent,
and virtuous is to be preferred over someone handsome but foolish and
shameless. But to get back to what we were saying, both these kinds
of beauty are noble subjects for poetry and ideally suited to stimulate
poets' intellects and dispose their minds to search out novel conceits, pleasing words, and resonant lines, full of power and spirit, for
it seems that this is the subject, by nature, that pleases us more than
any other."

"You're quite wrong," said Cornelia, "in what you were saying earlier, about there not being many women around who are beautiful in
both body and mind, for in this city alone there are very many women
who meet that description and would make worthy subjects for the
most polished verse."

"I know many such women as well," said the Queen, "and I'd name them for you one by one, but I can't recall all their names, only those of the few I have had most to do with personally. There's the most excellent Signora Marina Pisani, for example, the worthy consort of the most excellent Signor Tommaso Contarini, a most noble couple and deserving of the highest praise for their rare qualities and virtues, of which everyone is aware. She is a lady whose outer beauty matches and is matched by her beauty of mind; and both are so sublime that words cannot express them."[159]

"I know the lady," said Corinna, "and her two most noble sisters as well, who rival her in their surpassing beauty, grace, and virtue. There's Signora Cecilia, the worthy consort of the most excellent Signor Niccolò Sanuto, a gentleman endowed with a rare intelligence and the highest degree of refinement and virtue. She is remarkable for her beauty and for her rare virtue and courtesy; and, on the happy occasion of her marriage, among the many rhymes written about her, there was a sonnet written by a gentleman of my acquaintance, who was kind enough to show it to me."[160]

The women then all begged Corinna to recite the poem to them if she could remember it, and she, after thinking for a moment, courteously obliged:

> *Insolita beltà, ch'ascosa ogn'ora*
> *Si stette, qual tesor guardato e caro,*
> *Folgorò d'improviso e'l sol men chiaro*
> *Parve dinanzi a sì lucent'aurora.*
> *Al suo vago apparir, quando uscì fuora,*
> *S'allegrò il mondo e del miracol raro,*
> *Leggiadro sposo e di lei degno a paro*
> *Amante e possessor divenne allora.*

159. Marina di Vincenzo Pisani was married to Tommaso di Gaspare Contarini in 1584, in the church of San Salvatore (ASV, Avogaria del Comun, Matrimoni, reg. 2, 60). This couple, like the other figures praised over the following pages, were members of the highest strata of the Venetian nobility. The original indicates their rank by preceding their name with the word *clarissimo* or *clarissima*, which is somewhere between an adjective ("most excellent"; lit. "most glorious" or "most famed") and a title ("His/Her Excellency"). Figures of a lesser rank mentioned elsewhere in the dialogue, like the doctors and lawyers mentioned above, mostly *cittadini*, are designated by the adjective or title *eccellente* or *eccellentissimo*, which I have translated "most distinguished."

160. Cecilia Pisani married Niccolò di Federico Sanuto (or Sanudo) between March 1588 and February 1589 (ASV, Cronaca Matrimoni). The sonnet referred to, like those that follow, is likely to have been written by Moderata Fonte herself, and together they provide interesting evidence of her real or aspirational social connections among the patriciate in the late 1580s and early 1590s.

A tal atto del mar le rive e l'onde
S'empier di gioia e 'l grido alto e sonoro
Mosse Adria e i dolci cigni al canto arguto.
Proteo ogni ben promise e dalle sponde
E da gli antri di gemme e conche d'oro,
Eco PISANA rimbombò, e SANUTO.

A rare beauty, which had been lying hidden, like a coveted and jealously guarded treasure, suddenly flashed forth like lightning; and the sun itself seemed dimmer before such a radiant dawning. When she appeared in all her loveliness, the world rejoiced, and a charming bridegroom, well-deserving of her, stepped forward to declare his love and claim the possession of this rare marvel of nature. At this happy event, the shores and waves of the sea were filled with rejoicing, and their thundering cry of joy roused Adria and her fair swans to piercing song. Proteus was eager to shower them with gifts, and from the far shores and the jeweled caves and the golden shells, Echo chorused back the names of PISANA and SANUTO.[161]

The ladies listened to the sonnet with great pleasure and praised it highly; then Corinna went on, "But what can I say about that most noble and refined lady Isabetta, the third of the sisters, and consort of the most excellent Signor Daniele Dolfin, a man fully deserving of his extraordinary good fortune in possessing such a glorious creature as his wife? What praise, what honor, what newly coined tribute to her miraculous beauty and other rare gifts might one offer this sublime creature that would not fall far short of her lofty and incomparable deserts? To be sure, no human tongue, no mortal thought could express or even imagine a thousandth part of the celestial qualities of this most excellent lady. For my part, I am so devoted to her and so enraptured by her that I can never tire of serving her in any way I can, and I could wish to have a thousand tongues with which to praise her loveliness of feature and graciousness of manner."

The Queen and the other ladies, who were all well acquainted

---

161. This sonnet, like the others that follow, transcribes into poetic language the habit of the Venetian patriciate of keeping their daughters in close confinement until their marriage, which was a "coming out." Of the deities mentioned here, Adria (a humanistic invention) was a sea nymph and tutelary deity of the Adriatic; Proteus, a sea god; and Echo the river nymph who pined away and died for love of Narcissus, leaving only her plaintive voice, which echoed other sounds.

with this lady, approved Corinna's words and added many of their own in her praise. And Corinna recited another sonnet for them, composed for the lady's wedding,[162] which went like this:

> *Questa leggiadra giovenetta accorta*
> *Ch'or esce in luce e appar sposa novella*
> *Co 'l suo bel viso e sua dolce favella*
> *A 'l mondo gaudio, e meraviglia apporta.*
> *Ogni cor mesto in lei si riconforta,*
> *Ogni virtù per lei si rinovella,*
> *Ogni donna, ogni ninfa e ogni stella*
> *Le cede e riverenza e onor le porta.*
> *Degna è tanta beltà di alteri onori*
> *Ch'onestà tenne in sé chiusa, qual suole*
> *Gemma in or, sol in nube e fiore in cespo.*
> *Benché a' begli occhi suoi cede oggi il sole*
> *E alle guanze i più leggiadri fiori,*
> *E l'oro agguaglia il crin lucido e crespo.*

This charming and well-mannered young girl, now coming out into the light as a new bride, rejoices and astounds the world with the loveliness of her face and the sweetness of her utterances. Each sad heart is cheered by her presence, each slumbering virtue awakened; every woman, every nymph, and every star cede to her, honor and revere her. This beauty, deserving of the highest praises, was formerly kept shrouded by modesty, as jewels are shrouded by gold, the sun by clouds, or a flower by its leaves. But now she has emerged, her lovely eyes can outshine any sun and her cheeks out-glow any flower, while her bright, rippling locks rival gold itself.

The eager ladies praised the sonnet as it deserved, and then Lucretia said, "In their charm and refinement, those three sisters show themselves worthy daughters of that most respected of mothers, the most excellent Signora Bene[de]tta Pisani, a paragon of worth, wisdom, piety, and every other fine and remarkable quality a person can possess, and a worthy consort to a senator as illustrious as the most excellent Signor Andrea Dolfin, a man fully deserving of his

162. Elisabetta Pisani married Daniele di Lorenzo Dolfin in San Salvatore on 22 January 1590 (ASV, Avogaria del Comun, Matrimoni, reg. 3, 102).

office as procurator of San Marco and a shining exemplar of nobility and grandeur, of lordly high-mindedness, liberality, wisdom, and infinite courtesy.[163] May the Lord God grant them a long and happy life together!"

All the other ladies warmly seconded her good wishes, and Corinna continued, "Do you know Signor Dolfin's two nieces, the most excellent Signora Chiara Dolfin, who is married to Signor Giovanni Corner, and Signora Gracimana, consort of the most excellent Antonio Nani?[164] Those two ladies, as well, are most deserving of being placed in the ranks of women lovely in body and mind; in fact, so captivating are they and so remarkable their gifts that the world is left wondering whether they are mortal women after all or goddesses. On the occasion of Signora Gracimana's marriage, a dear friend of mine wrote a sonnet, which, if I remember rightly, went like this:

> *La più bella stagion di fior ridente*
> *Con la fervida state luminosa*
> *Del verno si ridea, che secca e ombrosa*
> *Avea la spoglia, e 'l crin di never algente.*
> *Quand'ei nel maggior freddo il più lucente*
> *Sol fé apparer, e così fresca rosa*
> *v'aggiunse, e seco una qual cara sposa*
> *Ch'a se diè gloria ed allegrò ogni mente.*
> *Coppia gentil, del divin merto vostro*
> *Quando pompa spiegar con maggior vanto*
> *Fior più leggiadri, o più giocondi spera?*
> *Se tal miracol dura, il secol nostro*
> *Bramerà 'l verno: or che ei vince di tanto*
> *Il sol di state, e i fior di primavera.*

The loveliest of the seasons, with its laughing flowers,
and the fervid and brilliant Summer used to laugh together

---

163. The three sisters praised above in the text were born to Benedetta di Andrea Pisani (d. 1595) in her first marriage, to Vincenzo di Marcantonio Pisani. She remarried in 1575, following Vincenzo's death (ASV, Avogaria del Comun, Matrimoni, reg. 2, 98); on her second husband, Andrea di Giovanni Dolfin (1540–1602), a wealthy patrician banker, see Grendler 1979, 334.

164. Chiara di Lorenzo Dolfin married Giovanni di Marcantonio Corner (1551–1629), a future doge (1625–29), in the Church of San Salvatore, on 10 February 1578 (ASV, Avogaria del Comun, Matrimoni, reg. 2, 64v). Her sister Gracimana married Antonio di Giorgio Nani on 10 February 1587 (ibid., 202).

at Winter, with his dry, gloomy old frame and hoary locks.
And then he suddenly brought out, in the bitterest cold,
the brightest sun imaginable and the freshest rose, and
the loveliest bride, bringing honor to himself and pleasure
to all. Noble couple, when could the pomp of Spring ever
hope to bring forth a flower gayer or more lovely than your
divine merits? If this miracle lasts, we shall come to long
for Winter, now that Winter can so far outdo the sun of
Summer and the flowers of Spring.

The ladies took great delight in hearing Corinna recite one
lovely sonnet after another on such deserving and charming subjects.
And when they had praised her, Lucretia said, "There's one gentlewoman I know in this city who can truly be called an ideal, a miracle,
and a marvelous freak of nature for her near-angelic beauty, her superhuman grace, and her utterly miraculous virtues. You must all know
her, surely: she's so remarkable and so much talked-of."

"And who is that?" said the Queen.

"The very lovely Signora Chiara Loredana,"[165] Lucretia replied,
"wife of the most excellent Giovanni Querini, a gentleman of remarkable gifts, regal bearing, and great refinement of manners."

"Of course we know her!" cried the Queen. "It's like asking
whether we've ever noticed the sun! She is graced to such a degree
with every supreme glory of mind and body, and the heavens have
showered their gifts on her so lavishly and splendidly, that even
before you named the person you were talking about I was almost prepared to wager I knew whom you meant."

"I can believe that," said Corinna. "Now there was a sonnet written about that lady by someone very close to her and utterly devoted
to her, who loves and greatly admires her extreme beauty and her gracious and noble manners. I don't know whether any of you have heard
it?"

The other ladies replied that they had not, and the Queen said,
"You'd better let us hear it, then, as you have all the others—all the

<hr/>

165. Chiara Loredana, the daughter of Girolamo Loredan, married Giovanni di Girolamo
Querini in 1580 (ASV, Avogaria del Comun, Matrimoni, reg. 2, 221v). Her sister Laura,
mentioned below in the text, married Francesco di Ermolao Morosini in San Vitale in
1573 (ibid., reg. 1, 253). Their sister-in-law, Laura di Girolamo Querini, also mentioned,
married their brother Leonardo at the Gesuati in 1574 (ibid., reg. 1, 224v).

more so since I'm quite convinced that you yourself are the 'gentleman' who has written all these poems."

Corinna laughed and agreed to recite the poem, in order not to appear ill-mannered.

Quanto è di bel, di caro e di gentile
Fra noi, quanto può 'l cielo e gli elementi
Tutto è in voi, nobil donna, e in Dio possenti
Vi fer le stelle a voi sola simile.
Ridonvi nel bel viso i fior d'aprile,
Sembran dui soli i begli occhi lucenti,
Oro è 'l crine e tra perle e rose ardenti
Movete il dir, ch'avanza ogn'altro stile.
Ne i regali costumi avete inserto
Un non so che, che gli animi incatena
E l'aria di più luce orna e rischiara.
Non giunge umana gloria al vostro merto,
Idolo di beltà, del ciel Sirena,
Per sangue, per virtù, per nome Chiara.

Noble lady, you are the epitome of all that is loveliest, dearest and most precious in this world; the finest efforts of the heavens and the elements are all concentrated in you; of all God's creation, only the stars can rival you. For in your face can be seen the laughing flowers of April; your shining eyes seem like two suns; your locks are like gold and your speech (which is of surpassing eloquence) flows out between pearls and glowing roses. In your queenly deportment there lurks a certain ineffable something that binds the souls of those that behold you and infuses the air around you with a new and brighter light. No human glory can match your high deserts, O idol of beauty, Siren of the skies, Chiara [i.e., "Glorious"] in name, in breeding, in virtue.

The ladies found this sonnet, which was new to them, quite delightful and very charming, and they showered Corinna with praise until she blushingly broke in to interrupt them, "Equally worthy of praise for every fine quality that can be desired of a beautiful and noble matron is that lady's sister, the most excellent Signora Laura,

consort of the most excellent Signor Francesco Morosini, a gentleman of exemplary goodness, good sense, and valor. And there's also
the most noble Signora Laura Querini, who is their sister-in-law by
her marriage to the most excellent Lunardo Loredan, their brother (a
noble spirit, and a man admirably endowed with every most excellent
virtue): she too is stupendously beautiful both in body and in mind."

"Oh yes, indeed," added Lucretia, who knew the lady in question.

"But the grace, beauty, and goodness," Cornelia broke in, "of that
most illustrious young lady, Signora Elena da Mula, who is married to
the son of the most illustrious Signor Iacopo Foscarini, the renowned
procurator of St. Mark's, are also most worthy of note.[166] In fact, I
can't imagine how they could be improved. I am extremely devoted to
her, for when I first came to know her, apart from her thousand other
lovely and winning qualities, I had the feeling of speaking to an
angel, to a being of almost superhuman gifts. So, both for her outer
and her inner beauties, every fine spirit and eloquent tongue is bound
by solemn duty to celebrate her splendidly and shower her with immortal tributes."

"If one wished to list all the beautiful and virtuous ladies of this
city," said Corinna, "one would need to know them all by name, and it
would be an impossible task, as there are so many that they would provide material for all the poets who have ever lived and will ever live to
write noble volumes in their honor (just as it would be a task that
would wear out all the pens in the world to speak as much ill of men
as they deserve)."

"It's quite true," said the Queen, "that whatever people say, there
is no better subject for poetry that the praise of feminine beauty. It's
a subject (as Corinna has pointed out) that offers poets much fine
inspiration. What would the divine Petrarch have done if the physical
and spiritual beauties of the woman he loved, which he describes so
sublimely, had not provided him with such ample material for him to
forge his way to immortality? It can't be denied that even though he
wrote various other extremely fine works, it is his love poetry alone

166. Elena da Mula, daughter of Andrea, married Giambattista Foscarini on 6 February
1589 (ASV, Avogaria del Comun, Matrimoni, reg. 2, 118v). The young man's father,
Iacopo Foscarini (1523–1602), a former naval commander, was one of the most powerful
political figures in the republic in this period (Grendler 1979, 331–32n). A further
connection between Foscarini and Fonte's circle is that Doglioni chose him as the
dedicatee of his *History of Venice* (1598) (Cicogna 1824–61, 2, 24).

that has lifted him to the summit of poetic glory, as he himself confirms a thousand times in those miraculous works of his.[167] And the same can be said of many other remarkable intellects who have devoted themselves to this noble pursuit and succeeded brilliantly at it."

"Such rare and miraculous intellects certainly flourished in the old days," said Lucretia. "But one doesn't seem to find them in our own day, whether the world is getting older or men are getting worse."

"How can you say that?" cried Corinna. "I'm sorry, but you're quite wrong. There are poets now who can rival any in the past, and maybe even surpass them."

"You must know some poets, of course," said Lucretia, "since you're so fond of poetry and write yourself."

"I have heard of many, but I know few poets personally," said Corinna, "though I did know one who was the leader and mainstay of them all and the pride and joy of this city of ours and who would be still if cruel death had not snatched him away from us so soon." She sighed, and went on, "I'm talking about the most excellent Signor Domenico Venier, whose glorious memory will continue to live for all eternity and will always remained fixed in my heart for as long as I live.[168] But, thinking of those alive now, one remarkable poet is that noble spirit, the most excellent Signor Orsato Giustiniano.[169] Then

167. The fact that much great poetry has been inspired by women's beauty was often used by sixteenth-century defenders of women as an argument for women's dignity and contribution to civilization (for a famous example, see Castiglione 1994, 264 [3: 52]).

168. Domenico Venier (1517–82) was a highly influential figure in Venetian literary life in the mid-sixteenth century, revered both for his talents and for his stoicism in supporting the long illness that forced his retirement from public life in the 1540s (Erspamer 1983, 191–96). It might be noted that Corinna's description of Venier as "allegrezza e gloria di casa nostra," which I have interpreted as referring to Venice ("this city of ours"), could also mean "the pride and joy of our family." This would open up the intriguing possibility that some of Fonte's speakers, at least, might be historically identifiable figures; in the absence of other indications to this effect, however, this suggestion should be treated with caution.

169. Orsatto Giustinian (1538–?1603) was one of the best-known Venetian petrarchists of the generation following Domenico Venier's (Erspamer 1983, 218–19). His name was often linked with that of Celio Magno, as the two men were close friends and published a joint collection of their poetry in 1590. Giustinian was also the author of the translation of Sophocles's *Oedipus Rex* performed at the opening of the Teatro Olimpico in Vicenza in 1585.

there is the most excellent Signor Giorgio Gradenico, a man of exceptionally elegant intellect and a singular master of the Muses; and that most refined spirit Signor Celio Magno, who finds time amid the grave concerns of his post as a most praiseworthy and deserving secretary of this state, besides all his other noble qualities, to reveal the riches of his extraordinarily keen mind in the glorious exercise of poetry.[170] And there's the most illustrious Signor Erasmo di Valvassone, who has opened a new Hippocrene through the lovely meadows of the noble land of Friuli.[171] And there's Signor Giuliano Goselini, famous for his mastery of Apollo's lyre, and celebrated in every other virtue besides.[172] And then there's that learned gentleman Valerio Marcellino, who, besides all his other famous and glorious intellectual endeavors, sweetens the salty waters of our city with a fresh spring of choice and pleasing rhymes.[173] And then there's the most excellent Signor Orazio Guarguanti, whom we've already mentioned today, who, in addition to his principal activity (which, as we've said, is that of a most accomplished philosopher and physician), is also a respected and elegant poet;[174] and among other things, his divine intellect has

170. Celio Magno (1536–1602) is generally regarded as the outstanding poet of his generation in Venice (Erspamer 1983, 219–21). That Fonte names him after Giustinian and the lesser figure of Giorgio Gradenico (1522–1600) may reflect his lower social standing, as a *cittadino* rather than a patrician.

171. The collected lyric poetry of the Friulian nobleman Erasmo da Valvassone (1523–93) was published in 1592, the year of the composition of *The Merits of Women*. His other works include a poem on the hunt, a translation of Statius, and, most significant in the present context, several works in genres that interested Fonte: an unfinished chivalric romance, *Il Lancillotto*, and religious poetry in *ottava rima*. Hippocrene was the name of a fountain near Mt. Helicon, sacred to the Muses.

172. The presence in this list of the Piedmontese, Milan-based historian and poet Giuliano Goselini, or Gosellini (1517–87) is something of a surprise, as the other writers mentioned are all from Venice or (in the case of Erasmo da Valvassone) its territories. However, Goselini was a correspondent and admirer of Domenico Venier (Venier 1751, xxxi–ii, 80, and 108), and this may account for his inclusion here, as in the similarly Venetian-dominated list of poets in Fonte's early *Floridoro* (Fonte 1995, 160).

173. Valerio Marcellino was a Venetian lawyer and a member of the circle of Domenico Venier, whose wit, learning, and piety he commemorated in a dialogue, *Il Diamerone* (1565). Marcellino was hardly well known as a poet, and his presence in this list can probably be explained by personal motives, in that he appears to have been acquainted with Fonte's father (ASV, Avogaria di Comun, Suppliche e scritture inespedite, b. 433, no. 4, 6: third testimonial, dated 2 January 1590) and may well also have been a professional acquaintance of her husband.

174. Orazio Guarguanti (1554-1611) has already been mentioned earlier in the day's discussion, in connection with his eminence as a physician. As in the case of Valerio Marcellino (see preceding note), Fonte's inclusion of Guarguanti in the present list is

produced a remarkable work in which he describes the various perfections, physical and spiritual, of the Virgin MARY, our Lady, in *ottava rima:* a poem almost too deep and profound in its insights for mortal minds to penetrate."

"From what I hear," said Helena, "he is also an excellent musician. Now there's an art I'm extremely fond of: in fact, what really brings poetry to life is when it's sung sweetly and fitted to the harmonies and consonances of music. It's then that it has the power, as the poet said, to

> *Romper le pietre, e pianger di dolcezza.*

> To break stones open and make them weep with sweetness.[175]

"For all that," said Leonora, "all the poetry and music in Parnassus wouldn't be enough to break the malice of men, or to draw a tear from their eyes, unless it was a feigned one."

"That's true," Corinna replied. "Now there was a sonnet written in praise of the most honored Guarguanti, for the work on Our Lady that I mentioned just now. It went like this:

> *Di sì pronto, vivace, alto intelletto,*
> *Che novella virtù spiega ed esprime;*
> *Di spirto sì profondo, e sì sublime,*
> *Certo era indegno uman senso e soggetto.*
> *MARIA, bellezza eterna, onor perfetto*
> *Della prima cagion, delizie prime,*
> *Sol degno scopo è a sue celesti rime*
> *Poiché d'angelo ha stil, voce e concetto.*
> *Non mai chiaro pittor d'ombre e colori,*
> *Finse un volto sì ben, com'ei cantando,*
> *L'alma figura, in cui Dio si compiacque.*
> *Degno è perciò d'alti immortali onori,*

---

more likely to be motivated by personal friendship and esteem than an objective assessment of his literary standing. At the time Fonte was writing, Guarguanti's only published literary work was the poem celebrated below in the text, the *Excellences of the Virgin Mary in Ottava Rima*, published first in 1588 and again in 1592, in a volume edited by Giovanni Vincenti, another acquaintance of Fonte (Tansillo 1592). The sonnet quoted below in praise of Guarguanti's work, presumably by Fonte, is not found in either edition.

175. The line quoted is the concluding line of a Petrarch sonnet (*RS*, 304).

Che 'l suo ingegno altamente al ciel sacrando
Molto ardì, molto seppe e molto piacque.

No mere human subject could possibly have sufficed for an intellect so keen, fertile, and elevated, and possessed of such unwonted talents, or for a spirit so penetrating and sublime. The only fit subject for his celestial rhymes (for indeed, in style, tone, insight, he shows himself an angel) is MARY, eternal beauty, paragon of honor, prime delight of the First Cause. No celebrated painter has ever conjured a face from shadows and colors so well as he has portrayed in his song that lovely form which so delighted God. This achievement merits the loftiest and most immortal honors, for his genius, as it soared up in consecration to Heaven, showed itself rich in ardor, rich in insight, and rich in inspiration.

I can hardly express how delighted the ladies were with this elegant sonnet, with its resonant conclusion; indeed, they preferred it to any of the previous ones they had heard. And Lucretia said, "Where music is concerned, I have heard that someone of great talent is the most excellent Signor Mario Belloni, who is also a very successful lawyer."[176]

"Music," said Corinna, "which is, strictly speaking, a consonance of voices or instruments or persons, is something that requires variety of style, voice, tempo, harmonies, and rhythms (this is true of both instrumental and vocal music). It's an art truly worthy of being embraced by every person of refinement, since music imitates on a human level the melodies of Paradise, and it's something that delights both the performer and the audience, and, even when played by a single performer, can delight a multitude of listeners. Moreover, it refreshes the spirit wonderfully."

176. Although Fonte is described in Doglioni's biography as an accomplished musician herself, her coverage of the art in the dialogue is curiously perfunctory, more so even than the treatment of painting that follows. The choice, as a representative of Venetian musical culture, of the obscure Mario Belloni (presumably a professional acquaintance of Fonte's husband), rather than, say, the great Giovanni Gabrieli (1553–1612), principal composer at St. Mark's at the time of her writing, seems extraordinary. On the contacts between musical and literary culture in this period in Venice, see Feldman 1994).

"Oh, but I'd heard that even if music enhances the pleasure of those who are already happy, in the case of melancholics, it deepens their melancholy," said Lucretia.

"Well, that's true," said Corinna, "but it's also true that music is a great consolation to us at times of misfortune or illness."

"There is nothing in the world I love more," said Helena, "than to listen to the singing of four or six people, whose voices are of the necessary standard and who have mastered the art to perfection (for there's no use in having one of these qualities without the other)."

"Which do you prefer?" asked Lucretia. "Vocal or instrumental music?"

"Vocal," said Cornelia. "For it contains two elements, the sense of the words and the sweetness of the voices, whereas instrumental music has only one element, which is the sweetness of the harmonies (which, in any case, cannot be compared with the sweetness of singing at its best)."

"Indeed," said the Queen, "I have sometimes heard madrigals sung in four or six-part harmony by some young relatives of mine who are experts in this art, and I really did feel as though I was in Paradise among the angels: I could easily have forgotten to eat or drink in the pleasure of listening to them. In short, as Corinna has said, music is a most enjoyable thing."

"I once heard a madrigal sung in praise of a young woman's singing," said Cornelia. "I'd like to tell you how it went, if I could only remember."

"Oh yes, please!" said Corinna. "It's about time you others came up with something: it's a shameful thing that I've been left all day so far to act the poet and keep you all amused."

"Well then, listen," Cornelia replied, "and I'll recite it as best I can."

Leggiadra fanciulletta,
Il tuo cantar d'amore
Ci ha già trafitto il core:
Ma se quel detto è vero,
Che l'un contrario cura
L'altro per sua natura,
Deh ritorna a cantare,
Ma non d'amor, che dà ferite amare,
Canta d'odio e di fiero

Sdegno, talché la dura
Piaga ne i petti umani,
Che fé 'l primo cantar, l'altro risana.

O charming maid, your songs of love have pierced our
hearts to the quick. But if it is true, as they say, that
everything can be cured by its contrary, then sing again,
I pray you. Not of love, though, this time, which inflicts
such unlovely pain; sing rather of hatred and of cruel
wrath, so that the gaping wound the first song has opened
up in our breasts may be cured by this second!

When the charming Cornelia had finished reciting the madrigal,
her listeners showered it with praise, and Corinna said, "I told you
that the best was just beginning! And I imagine you know many
others?"

"Oh, hardly," replied Cornelia. "But why don't you let us hear
that madrigal you recited for me that time when we were on the river
once, on the way to our estates in the country."

"Do you mean that poem on an amorous theme," said Corinna,
"that was given to me (honestly!) by a gentleman, a relative of mine?"

"Yes, that's the one," replied Cornelia. "Go on, recite it for us."

And Corinna then, racking her memory, recited the following
madrigal for them.

Voi mi affligete a torto,
E volete ch'io taccia,
Ed io che di piacervi ho sol desio
Sofro il gran dolor mio,
E morrò volontier, quando vi piaccia;
Anzi morendo avrò gioia e conforto,
Pur che sappiate poi,
Crudel, che al fin sarò morto per voi.

You torture me unjustly and bid me be silent; and I, whose
only desire is to please you, suffer this great anguish
happily and am willing to submit to death, if that is your
pleasure. Indeed, death will be a joy and a comfort to me,
as long as you one day learn, my torturer, that I have died
for you.

"In my opinion, all forms of poetic composition require a resonant concluding line," said Cornelia. "But madrigals, in particular, should have, one might almost say, more conceits than they have words, and should end resonantly."

"You're quite right," said Corinna. "But, while we're on the subject, listen to another."

> *Deh, come cieco io sono*
> *Della mente, foss'io de gli occhi ancora*
> *Per non veder oimè quel, che mi accora:*
> *O pur, sì come io veggio*
> *Pur troppo, oimè, con gli occhi de la fronte*
> *Le luci avess'io ancor de l'alma pronte,*
> *Che così amore o sdegno*
> *Di me compita avrebbe intera palma*
> *Sendo Argo, o talpa tutta e d'occhi e d'alma.*

Alas! would that I were as blind of eye as I am blind of mind, so that I did not have to see what so torments me— or else, would that the eyes of my mind were as keen as the eyes on my face, which see all too much. For, that way, either love or anger would have complete sway over me [rather than my being caught between these warring emotions], since I would be either an Argus[177] or a mole in both eyes and spirit.

"These reprises or symmetries are a very fine thing in poetry,"[178] said Leonora, "but I'd much prefer to see them in men's behavior toward us. That would really be the sweetest and the loveliest music you could ever hear in the world, if men and women could make peace with each other and live together in harmony."

"Oh, wouldn't it just?" said Corinna.

But Helena remarked, "I have no problem in living in harmony with my husband; and if you others haven't been fated to experience the same happiness, the fault lies with your ill fortune, not with men."

"Oh, do be quiet, for goodness' sake, before you make me say something I'll regret!" said Leonora. "Didn't you yourself admit just now that your husband is a jealous man and that there was disharmony

---

177. In classical mythology, a many-eyed monster.

178. Such elaborate and sustained parallelisms were a stylistic hallmark of the poetry of Domenico Venier, reaching their most extreme development in his famously virtuosic exercises in correlative verse (Taddeo 1974, 57–60).

between you because of that?[179] And anyway, just think of what the poet says,

> *Che raro a bel principio il fin risponde.*

Promising beginnings rarely lead to good ends.[180]

"It's quite true, as Leonora says," said Cornelia, "that men should devote themselves to practicing no other kind of music than that of living in harmony with us women. For their current state of disharmony with women produces such an awful sound: all one hears all day is carping, scorn, abuse, and a thousand other ills, as we are forced to curse, insult, and dishonor them, quite against our natural inclination, habits, and will (because, by nature, we would be inclined to put up with anything and suffer our mishaps in silence, but men are so pestilential and importunate that eventually they wear down even *our* patience)."

"As you know," said Leonora, "a single slack string or a single discordant voice can ruin a whole performance, so it's scarcely any wonder if all those false and discordant minds we find in men are out of harmony with us women. In fact, the difference between the sexes is so immense that even if they wanted to, I'm not sure they could find any accord between their great malice and our great goodness."

"That's only too true," said Cornelia. "But, thinking of those poetic symmetries we were talking about, I wanted you to hear a stanza in *ottava rima* that was given to me by a person of great refinement.[181] I'm sure you'll enjoy it; it goes like this:

> *Arsa dal crudo Amor, che la tormenta*
> *Orenia, che nel mar supero nacque,*

179. See pp. 46–47 and 69 above.

180. The line may perhaps be a misremembering of the eighth line of Vittoria Colonna's sonnet "Oh che tranquillo mar, che placide onde": "mentre al principio il fin non corrisponde" (Colonna 1982, 7).

181. *Ottava rima* (eight hendecasyllabic lines, rhymed ABABABCC) was generally a narrative meter and was much used as such by Fonte in her poetic works (see Fonte 1582b, 1592, and 1995). Occasionally, however, as here, a single stanza in *ottava rima* was composed as a self-standing poem. "Orenia," the protagonist of the stanza that follows, is an invented figure, a Venetian sea nymph (the "upper sea" of line 2 is the Adriatric).

Mentre è tutta al suo ben volta ed intenta
Con le fiamme, c'ha in sen, consuma l'acque;
Teme e duolsene il mar, che si ramenta
Fetonte e 'l foco, ond'arso in fondo giacque,
Ed ella: alcun timor già non vi tocchi,
Quanto vi toglie il cor, vi rendon gli occhi.

Burnt by cruel Love, which torments her, Orenia, child of
the upper sea, as she sits brooding on the object of her
desire, dries the waters with the flames in her breast. The
sea is struck with fear and complains to her, mindful of
Phaeton and his fires, which once seared it to its core.
She replies, "Sea, fear not. Whatever waters of yours my
heart dries up are amply recompensed by my eyes."

The ladies were charmed by this stanza; in fact, they liked it so
much that they insisted on Cornelia's reciting it again. Then the
Queen said, "Poetry, it seems to me, enjoys a special pre-eminence
over all other human endeavors, because, besides what we've already
said about its being an innate and God-given talent, there's also the
fact that poetry, as it were, embraces all other disciplines, for a poet
is equipped to write on anything whatsoever, and can do so well and
pleasingly."

"It seems to me," said Lucretia, "that the poet has much in common with the painter, for just as painters, with their brushes, paint
all manner of forms and colors, using fullness and hollows, shadows,
lines, indentation, and relief, so skilled poets, with their pens, flesh
out with all variety of words the beautiful designs that they have
imagined and conceived in their minds."[182]

"You're exactly right," said Corinna. "In fact, the comparison is
so apt that it would be impossible to deny it."

"Oh, I'm not so sure," said Cornelia. "Think of a fine portrait,
painted from life by some excellent painter, in which the form, the
air, the lineaments, and the features of the sitter are vividly rendered,

---

182. This comparison between poetry and painting, which originated in an offhand
comment in Horace's *Ars Poetica*, was one of the most frequently repeated commonplaces
of Renaissance aesthetic theory. The discussion that follows in the text reflects
contemporary debate on the relative merits of the two arts (see, for example, Barocchi
1971–77, 1: 263–69).

so that the image seems to breathe, to speak, to have feeling and motion. To see such a portrait, in my eyes, is far preferable and far more satisfying than to read ten lines of verse, however perfect."

"You're quite wrong there," replied Corinna. "You have to realize that the painting is like a body the soul has left, while the verse is like a soul without a body; and so, just as the soul is far nobler than the body, so a composition in words is far nobler than one in colors."

"In that case," said Cornelia, "painting would be the embodiment of poetry and poetry the soul of painting."

"That's right," said Corinna. "But let's not pursue the issue. It's still certainly a remarkable thing, this art of painting, which allows us to preserve people's living images for posterity after their death."

"Indeed," said the Queen. "But the painter has to be of the first quality if he is to do justice to the art."

"Who is there alive today who is worthy to be called a remarkable and celebrated painter?" asked Cornelia.

"I've heard people mention Signor Giacomo Tintoretto, and a daughter of his, apparently supremely talented," said Lucretia.

"Signor Paolo Veronese is someone else who has achieved great things in his profession, as I have seen with my own eyes," said the Queen.[183]

"Well, I'm happy to admit that painting is a miraculous art," said Helena, "but I think sculpture, as well, has much to recommend it. In fact, in some ways, it is a nobler art than painting, since it has the vitally important quality of relief, which allows it to represent the true nature and form of an image better than painting.[184] For, even if, in painting, it's possible to create an impression of relief using

---

183. Iacopo Robusti, known as Tintoretto (1519–94), and Paolo Caliari, known as Veronese (1528–88), are still of course regarded as the greatest Venetian painters of their day. Tintoretto's daughter Marietta (?1560–90) was trained in her father's workshop along with her brothers and, according to the seventeenth-century art historian Carlo Ridolfi, produced portraits of such quality as to arouse the interest of international patrons such as Philip II of Spain. Her devoted father, however, preferred that she marry a local goldsmith and remain with him in Venice, where she died at the age of thirty (Ridolfi 1984, 97–99).

184. The question of the relative merits of painting and sculpture, known as the *paragone* (lit. "comparison"), was the subject of heated debate in the Italian Renaissance, drawing comment from many of the greatest artists and art theorists of the age (Barocchi 1971–77, 1: 465–74). Fonte's abbreviated treatment of the issue, in these two exchanges, is entirely conventional, though a Venetian influence may perhaps be identified in her giving the last word to painting, on the grounds that it employs color (see Rosand 1982, 15–26; Barocchi 1971–77, 1: 548–53).

shadows, it is never going to be as dramatic and immediate as what can be achieved in sculpture."

"You've got it all wrong," said Corinna. "Painting is a far nobler art than sculpture in all respects, and it is numbered among the liberal arts. Above all, it is a more vivid means of representation than sculpture, because, even though it's true that sculpture has relief, as you say, painting does not lack this quality, as you yourself confess (I'm not talking about what is revealed to our sense of touch here, but simply about how things appear to the eye). And, moreover, painters deploy color, in all its vivacity, to refine their means of expression and bring their works to perfection."

"In ancient times," said Helena, "the Romans, in their wisdom, chose for the most part to immortalize their image and memory by means of sculpture rather than painting, as you can tell from all those ruined statues strewn about in Rome."

"The reason was perhaps that they judged images in stone to be more durable than those on canvas or wood," said Corinna. "But, for all that, they didn't neglect the art of painting."

"Oh!" exclaimed Leonora. "If only it were possible to find a painter or sculptor skilled enough to paint or sculpt the form of men's inner selves from life, so that women could see the secret regions of their hearts on open display and men could no longer deceive the poor guileless souls with the false appearances they present to the world. Because even if it's true (as Lucretia pointed out) that some women are fully aware of men's malice but still cannot help falling in love with them and allowing themselves to be duped, there are nevertheless many others who, if they realized what men were like, would no longer fall victim to all the vile tricks men play on them, with their deceptions and their plausible lies."

"That is something devoutly to be wished!" said Virginia.

"Nowadays," said Corinna, "it seems as though painting is generally much preferred to sculpture. Few sculptures are commissioned now, except to commemorate some important person, like a prince or a lord or a famous captain. Such men frequently receive the honor of having statues, columns, and other similar constructions erected in their honor, to reward their merits and preserve their fame for posterity. And our own rulers here in Venice have done just that on various occasions in the past, to the glory of deserving soldiers and citizens of the republic."

"It's certainly very fitting," said Lucretia, "that such people should be given honors of this kind, whether statues or paintings or immortal verses. For those who give their life for their country or their prince deserve to have it restored to them in some way. One such individual, in our own day, is that most glorious gentleman, Signor Tommaso Costanzo, a knight of marvelous skill and courage, whose life was much admired, whose death much mourned, and whose name much celebrated.[185] His bones, brought back from Flanders to Padua and honored with unceasing tributes of marble and praise, now lie at rest, enjoying their glorious reward for the tireless labors he performed in his lifetime, while his rare military talents, celebrated by his many eminent admirers, remain as an example to posterity of good and virtuous action."

"I've heard his name mentioned with great reverence," said the Queen, "and I seem to remember that one of his tributes was a remarkable work entitled *The Mausoleum*."[186]

"I've seen some other poems as well on the same subject," said Corinna. "One of them I learnt by heart—a sonnet, which, if I remember rightly, went like this:

> *Leggiadro spirto in prezioso velo*
> *Che arricchì Dio di grazie e di favori*
> *Scese da l'alto Empireo, e frutti e fiori*
> *Di valor, di beltà portò dal cielo;*
> *Sue divine virtù l'armar di zelo;*
> *Religioso, e i giovenili ardori,*
> *Onde ei Marte d'invidia arse e i furori*
> *Di Marte vinse, e di Fortuna il telo.*
> *Fur l'opre in somma angeliche e la forma,*
> *E pendea 'l mondo, in sì mirabil manto*

185. Giovanni Tommaso Costanzo (b. 1554), of Castelfranco Veneto, near Treviso, died at the age of twenty-six, fighting in the siege of Valenciennes in 1581. The tragic case attracted much attention, especially since the young man's father, the *condottiere* Scipione Costanzo, had some years earlier orchestrated a long campaign for his son's release after he had been taken hostage by the Turks at the age of seventeen (Sansovino 1609, 295r–296v; Stefani 1868).

186. The habit of commemorating the deaths of prominent figures by collections of verse was a common one in this period, but I have found no record of the *Mausoleum* to Costanzo mentioned here. Doglioni, in his life of Fonte, records her writing a canzone for inclusion in this volume on the request of Costanzo's father. The sonnet that follows in the text may also be assumed to be her work.

S'egli era eletto spirto, od uom mortale,
Ma troppo, ahimé, d'onor seguend'ei l'orma
More, e morto per lui, che 'l fé immortale
Trasse il mondo di dubbio, e 'l pose in pianto.

A lovely spirit, wrapped in a precious veil and adorned by
God with all graces and gifts, descended to us from the
high Empyrean, bringing with him the fruits and flowers
of beauty and high worth. His divine virtues and youthful
ardor so fired him with religious zeal that Mars himself was
consumed with envy [at his martial prowess], as he made a
mockery both of Mars's furor and of Fortune's grip on men's
fate. In short, his deeds were those of an angel, as was his
form: and the world was left doubting whether this creature, encased in such a miraculous shell, was an elect
spirit or a mortal man. But running too keenly, alas! at the
heels of honor, he met his death. And dying, as he did,
for him who had made him immortal, he relieved the world
from fear, at the same time thrusting it into mourning.

"It's quite right," said the Queen, "that people should honor the
life and preserve the fame of their heroes in this way, for by doing so
they encourage others to give up their lives for their country, inspired
by a noble hope to be so honored themselves. But leaving the dead
aside, a remarkable living soldier is that most illustrious and excellent
lord, Giovanni Battista Borbone, Marquis of Monte Santa Maria, who
has few peers anywhere in the world, either as a leader of armies in
the field or a defender of cities left under his guard.[187] But artillery
and guns have been the ruin of the brave knights of our time, for
they prevent them from displaying their valor and courage to the full,
and no army, however strong, is capable of resisting them."[188]

"At least in the past they could fight without having to worry
about things like that," said Cornelia. "How splendid they must have

187. For an account of the career of this rather obscure Tuscan *condottiere* (whose
presence here is something of a mystery), see Sansovino 1609, 261v–262v.

188. Artillery had been in use for well over a century at the time Fonte was writing, and
there are grounds for suspecting that she may be echoing a complaint of early
sixteenth-century writers like Ariosto rather than reflecting a sentiment still current
in the culture of her day (see *OF*, 11, 26–27).

looked, those knights one reads about, who carried off their victories through the courage of their heart and the might of their arm."

"If only those times were still with us!" said Leonora. "I'd like to see us women arming ourselves like those Amazons of old and going into battle against these men. At any rate, it's generally believed that there are more women than men in the world, so our greater numbers would compensate for the disadvantage of our physical weakness, which results from our lack of military training."

"Well, I must say that *I* wouldn't be accompanying you on your campaign," said the Queen, "for I'm a peace-loving soul."

"[If we don't do such a thing],"[189] said Corinna, "it is because it would be beneath our dignity to do battle against our natural inferiors. Because, for the rest, even if we are physically weaker, the victory would certainly be ours, as right is on our side."

"Indeed it is," said Lucretia. "But tell me, Leonora darling, what emblem would you carry into battle?"

"I'd wear an image of a phoenix on my helmet,"[190] she replied; at which Helena spoke up, "So you'd be emulating that great Marfisa, who had the phoenix as her emblem, and of whom that elegant poet said,

> *O sia per sua superbia, dinotando*
> *Se stessa unica al mondo in esser forte,*
> *O pur sua casta intenzion lodando*
> *Di viver sempremai senza consorte.*

[She bore a phoenix as her emblem], either out of arrogance, to declare herself unique in her strength and courage, or else to boast of her chaste resolve to live forever without a mate.[191]

189. The phrase in parentheses, not in the original, has been supplied as the sense seems to require it.

190. It will be remembered that the phoenix figures among the emblems chosen by Leonora's aunt to symbolize her commitment to a life without marriage, listed and glossed in the description of the allegorical fountain at the beginning of Day 1 of the dialogue.

191. The warrior Marfisa, a character in Ariosto's *Orlando Furioso,* is an appropriate point of reference for Leonora, as one of the very few examples in the literature of the period of a female character consistently resistant to marriage for other than religious reasons (though an interesting point of comparison is the eponymous heroine of Campiglia 1588). The lines quoted below in the text are from *OF,* 36, 18, 1–4.

"And what colors would you wear?" asked Virginia. "What livery would you adopt?"

"I'd wear the white armor and white surcoat of the novice knight, and bear on my shield a golden yoke broken through the middle, signifying freedom."

"That shining whiteness," said Cornelia, "would be just the thing to symbolize our simplicity and purity,[192] but it strikes me that green would be much better, to bring us hope of victory. So I think the emblem of a laurel tree would be better suited to our purpose, if you think of that line

Arbor vittoriosa e trionfale

O, tree of victory and triumph . . .

or that other one:

A la vittoriosa insegna verde.

Beneath the victorious green ensign.[193]

"Fine," said Leonora. "If only we really were in that position! I'd be perfectly happy then to allow whatever colors you preferred."

"I think green mixed with yellow would be a more exact and appropriate expression of our state," said Corinna, "as it would convey how thin our chances are ever to win our way into the good graces of men.[194] For they are so obstinate and so perverse in their feelings toward us that even if we were to succeed in conquering their persons by force, we could never win over their will by love."

"Rather, we'd be better off dressing in vermilion to signify our aim of vengeance," said Lucretia, "with an emblem showing the sun

192. White armor was traditional wear for female knights in chivalric romance: Ariosto's Bradamante wears it (*OF*, I, 60, 3–4), as does Risamante, in Fonte's own *Floridoro*. The next phase of the conversation assumes some knowledge of the conventional color symbolism outlined in works such as Lodovico Dolce's *Dialogue on Colors*. Of the colors mentioned in this first speech, see Dolce 1565, 29r, on white as a symbol of purity of heart, and 22r-v on green as symbolic of hope.

193. The lines are from Petrarch (*RS*, 263 [slightly misquoted] and 325, 32). Laurels were associated with victory in ancient Rome, where their leaves were used to crown conquering generals, as well as poets.

194. Dolce 1565, 34v–35r, identifies greenish yellow (the color of wilting grass) as symbolic of fading hope; see also 24v, on vermilion (mentioned in the following speech) as symbolic of "lordship, and the desire for revenge."

behind some clouds, but on the point of breaking out, with the motto: *In nube spero* ['Even amid the clouds I have hope']."

"No, no," said Helena. "Since the desire for revenge has no place in a magnanimous heart, such as we claim ours to be, we would do well to wear dark red, signifying our happiness not at the prospect of our hoped-for victory, but at the thought of winning men over entirely to our side.[195] Because, after overcoming them in combat, I'd want us to overcome them in courtesy as well and to redouble our glory by showing clemency toward them."

"In my opinion," said Virginia, "it wouldn't be inappropriate for us to wear black arms decorated all over with white doves, to allude to the steadfastness with which we love these men of ours and the purity and sincerity of the love we bear them."

"I love inventing emblems like this," said Lucretia, "but, as well as the charm of the images, you also need a nicely pointed motto, for, without that, the emblem is mute and dead."

"There are various books on the subject, which you must have seen," said Corinna. "So let's not bother talking about it."

"All these various emblems and colors," said the Queen, "are like a language that doesn't use words, and that allows people to reveal the innermost reaches of their hearts in a delightful manner. It's as the poet says, describing knights preparing for the joust,

> *Chi sopra l'elmo, o nel dipinto scudo*
> *Disegna Amor, se l'ha benigno, o crudo.*

> Some on their helmets or on their painted shields, bear an
> image of Love, benign or harsh as appropriate.[196]

"There are many languages that communicate without using words," said Leonora, "but the language of sighs is, I think, the most eloquent of all. As one elevated spirit said in a canzone, touching on this theme:

> *Certo non così puote*
> *Diserta lingua in note*
> *Di profonda eloquenza in prosa, o in rima*

---

195. Red had traditional associations with Christian charity, and it may be these that underlie Helena's choice of the color to symbolize her magnanimous proposal.

196. The lines (slightly misquoted) are from *OF*, 17, 72, 7–8.

Mover un cor, quant'alma, che ben ami,
E mercé muta sospirando chiami.

Certainly, the most practiced tongue speaking in prose or
verse, however supreme its eloquence, cannot move a heart
like a soul that truly loves and mutely sighing pleads for
mercy.[197]

"Say what you like," said Cornelia, "but in my opinion, the most
persuasive of these languages is the language of the eyes, which can
in all truth be said to speak and to reveal in their outward gaze the
inner secrets of the heart. Oh, what eloquent orators the eyes are
when they are seeking to defend their cause! What valiant soldiers
when they seek to wound their enemies! What sweet flatterers they
prove when they woo a heart that is already well disposed to them!
And hatred, love, hope, fear, pain, happiness, anger, shame, and all
the movements and passions of our souls are reflected in the eyes."

"Yes, when they're telling the truth," said Corinna. "But the
eyes very often deceive, as well, showing one emotion in place of another. Sighs, on the other hand, never lie, for it has to be admitted
that although one can pretend to sigh without meaning it, it's very
easy to detect the lie."

"Fie!" said Leonora. "In men, everything is feigned: looks, sighs,
colors, words, and deeds. You can never discover the truth of their
souls or tell whether they are acting sincerely—except when they are
perpetrating some particularly grave offense against women."

"What you say is quite true," said Corinna. "But I really can't see
you ever allowing yourself to be deceived by a man again."

"Certainly not," she replied. "But I cannot rest easy, for I'd like
to see all of you safe from men's wiles as well. But to keep to the subject of colors, how many men dress in pink or green to play the lover,
when dull gray or black would be more appropriate, to express the fraud
and practiced deceit lurking in their hearts!"[198]

"In this city of ours," said the Queen, "men, after a certain age,

197. I have been unable to identify the source of this quotation.
198. In conventional color symbolism, green signified hope, while pink signified
"amorous pleasure" and was thus suited either to successful or aspiring lovers (Dolce
1565, 33r). Black, on the other hand, often symbolized madness or malignity (24v–27v),
though it could also signal gravity, as a speaker in Dolce's dialogue notes, and as
Lucretia remarks below. For Dolce (33r), however, gray means humility, rather than
deceitfulness, as here.

tend not to wear colors as they do elsewhere, but always to dress in black.[199] And you don't often see women, either, wearing colors outside the house, except before they are married."

"Yes," said Lucretia. "It's as though black conferred a certain air of reputation and dignity on the wearer, more than any other color."

"One thing that's certain," said Cornelia, "is that Venetian women dress in a more attractive manner than women elsewhere. Just consider whether it doesn't seem to you that there's something truly feminine about our dress: it has a grace and a delicacy that are peculiarly suited to women, and proper to them. Women from outside Venice, on the other hand, often look mannish rather than feminine."

"More than anything," said Helena, "the Venetian fashion for women to wear their hair blond seems to confer an air of femininity and refinement, even nobility.[200] In fact, for a woman to have a fine head of blond hair is usually enough for her to be thought a fine-looking woman."

"Oh!" cried Cornelia, "If men could hear us talking about these things, how they'd mock us! As it is, they're always saying that it's the only thing we're interested in, preening ourselves and making ourselves beautiful."

"Oh, let them say what they want!" said Corinna. "It's not such an insult, anyway, for the refinement and neatness of our appearance is a sign of the nobility of our soul. Just think, by contrast, of those base yokels (I'm not talking about baseness of birth now, but of manners), who go around coarsely and untidily dressed: who knows what kind of thoughts are breeding in all that sloppiness of dress and body? You all know about the impression Lucius Sulla formed of Julius Caesar, which made him warn the Roman senators that they should beware of that ill-girt youth."[201]

---

199. Venetian men of rank, both patricians (after the age of twenty-five, when they entered political life) and *cittadini*, wore a distinctive "uniform" of a long wide-sleeved black robe (except for some high officials of the state, who wore red) (see Newton 1988, 9; and, on *cittadini*, Zannini 1993, 71).

200. Sixteenth-century portraits amply testify to Venetian noblewomen's penchant for tinting their hair blond; one popular contemporary cosmetic manual, *On Women's Adornment* by Giovanni Marinelli, gives twenty-six recipes for hair dye (Marinelli 1562, 64r–69r).

201. The Roman dictator Lucius Cornelius Sulla (c. 138–78 BC) was mistrustful of Caesar, who opposed him, and predicted that the young man would prove in future a danger to the Republic. Specifically, his comment on Caesar's suspiciously effeminate habit of girding his toga loosely is reported by Suetonius, *Divus Julius*, 45, 3; and by

"That's all very well," said the Queen, "but how about those curls, those horns, that men are always carping about: what do you say to them? I can't say I'm particularly keen on that fashion."[202]

"I'd say," said Corinna, "that that style too is something that should be not merely tolerated, but accepted and praised, just as much as any other feminine adornment. Because this is nothing more than a fashion, a custom, and a pastime of ours; and when it is done judiciously and with moderation, it sets the face off very charmingly. But, anyway, what on earth has it got to do with men, whether we dress our hair on one side rather than another? And what has it got to do with them if we do what we can to look beautiful, and do what we like with our hair? After all, women were created to adorn and bring gaiety to the world."[203]

"There are certain women who don't look good with their hair dressed that way," said Lucretia. "But I don't think the style can be blamed for that: it's more a matter of those individuals' lack of judgment and the fact that they don't dress their hair in a manner that suits their faces. It's just the same with women who don't take any care to ensure that their clothes fit well and that everything's in place, so you'll see them with their dresses slipping off their backs and armlets that come down to their elbows and other such oversights, which make them look terribly untidy and slatternly. Because in all things we should try as hard as we can to avoid extremes. It's like those women who wear colors that don't suit their complexions: that's one area in which you sometimes see women slipping up very badly, and becoming a laughingstock for those idle youths who have nothing better to do than to mock us and laugh at us."

"That's true," said Cornelia. "But not every woman can be perfect at everything, and women who make these mistakes must have their minds on other and higher things, so that even though they want to follow the fashions of other women and look good, they don't put

---

Dio, *Roman Histories*, 43, 43, 4; see also Suetonius 1982, 107, on the connotations of this style of dress. The story would have had a particular significance in a Republican culture like Venice.

202. These were horn-shaped mounds of hair at either side of the head. Moderata Fonte herself wears a relatively discreet version of this style in a portrait, dated to the final year of her life, reproduced above on p. 42.

203. This speech of Corinna's, and the discussion on dress in general, lend support to the recent suggestion that the extravagant dress of patrician women in Venice in this period may be seen as a means of self-assertion in a society that accorded them considerable personal wealth but no political power (Chojnacki 1980, 68; see also Cox, 1995, 551–54).

enough work into it or give the matter enough thought. Besides which, often some blame should also fall on the men to whom these women are subject, who either don't care about whether their women look after themselves and dress smartly, or who actively discourage it. So the poor things have to dress in a hurry or on the sly, when they can find a moment, and as they don't really know how to go about it, they lose interest altogether and finish up just throwing things together anyhow."

"But then there are all those other women who throw away enormous amounts of time in preening themselves," said the Queen. "In fact, I remember, when I was young it was a consuming interest of mine, trying to look beautiful (and I succeeded very well, to go by what people said about me at the time). Though I have the impression that nowadays women dress up more extravagantly than ever and there are all these striking new fashions."

"It's not unfitting for us women to express our natural inner refinement outwardly, in feminine dress and adornments," said Corinna. "Of course, men say that all this finery we wear betrays a corrupt heart underneath, and often endangers our virtue. But they're quite wrong: as I said earlier, women's dress could hardly endanger their virtue if men would only stop pestering them. And to prove it, just think how frequent it is to see women of low estate importuned by men and coming to grief, in spite of the fact that they dress plainly and, one might say, without any form of adornment. It is far rarer to see gentlewomen suffering the same fate, in spite of all their finery, for they aren't dressing up for any vicious reason, but simply, as I've said, out of a spirit of gaiety and to follow the custom of the city."

"While we're on the subject," added Leonora, 'many men also refuse to allow their women to learn to read and write, on the pretext that learning is the downfall of many women.[204] As though the pursuit of virtue (which is where learning leads) led straight to its contrary, vice! What they don't see is that what you just said about women dressing up can be said with even more justice about their acquiring an education. For it's obvious that an ignorant person is far more liable to fall into error than someone intelligent and well read; and we see from experience that far more unlettered women slide into vice than educated women who have exercised their minds. How many

204. For examples of this view, still widespread in the late sixteenth century despite many humanists' advocation of education for women, see King 1991, 185–87.

illiterate maidservants, how many peasant girls and plebeian women give in to their lovers without putting up much of a fight! And the reason is that they are more gullible than women like us, who have read our cautionary tales and learnt our moral lessons and developed a love for virtue: we may still feel some pricking of the senses, but we know how to discipline our desires, and it's only very rarely that an educated woman allows herself to be carried away by her appetites. And those few who do would do just the same if they didn't know how to read as if they did, for the means to do evil have never been lacking to those who are truly determined to satisfy their desires."

"It really is something," said Cornelia at this point, "that men disapprove even of our doing things that are patently good. Wouldn't it be possible for us just to banish these men from our lives, and escape their carping and jeering once and for all? Couldn't we live without them? Couldn't we earn our own living and manage our affairs without help from them? Come on, let's wake up, and claim back our freedom, and the honor and dignity they have usurped from us for so long. Do you think that if we really put our minds to it, we would be lacking the courage to defend ourselves, the strength to fend for ourselves, or the talents to earn our own living? Let's take our courage into our hands and do it, and then we can leave it up to them to mend their ways as much as they can: we shan't really care what the outcome is, just as long as we are no longer subjugated to them. And then, having achieved equality, we'll be in a sufficiently strong position to mock them as they now mock us; and we'll have a thing or two to say about how they spend a thousand years combing and setting the few paltry hairs they have on their heads and their chins; and how they wear their cravats so long and drooping one minute that they can easily be taken for napkins or kerchiefs, and so tight around their necks the next that they make them look like so many puppets; or how they sometimes wear their breeches so tight with their long doublets that they look like frogs, and sometimes wear them so loose that they could easily jump around inside them. And what's more, many of them have now taken to wearing platform shoes almost as high as the ones they are always criticizing women for wearing.[205]

205. The items of footwear referred to here (*pianelle* or *zoccoli*) were wooden overshoes, originally adopted for the practical reason of protecting footwear in the wet Venetian streets. By the late sixteenth century, however, the fashion was for *pianelle* so high that their wearers were scarcely capable of walking in them without support from their servants (see Rodocanachi 1907, 149–50 and 174; Labalme 1980, 136).

And there are endless more silly fashions and crazes of theirs—far too many to go into."

"You make me laugh," said Helena, "with all this talk about how men jeer at us for our concern with dress. That's not my impression. What they *would* find ridiculous, I'd think, is hearing us talk about some of the things we've been discussing today, which they think only men should talk about. As for clothes and beauty, they don't mind us being interested in them, because they see them as women's proper concern."

"Well, they shouldn't find anything to laugh at in our having discussed various different subjects either," Corinna said. "For one thing, we've talked about them (or rather, touched on them) just casually and in passing, not because we consider ourselves experts. And, for another, we have just as much right to speak about these subjects as they have, and if we were educated properly as girls (as I've already pointed out), we'd outstrip men's performance in any science or art you care to name."

"Well, that's it!" said Virginia. "I heard so many fine things about men yesterday, and I've heard so many more today, that I'm beginning to feel almost converted to the position of Leonora and her companions. They've made me inclined to think I'd prefer not to submit myself to any man, when I could be living in peace and liberty alone."

"Don't say that, daughter dear!" said the Queen. "Because I have no choice but to find a husband for you.[206] But I do promise that when the time comes, I'll keep searching until I find a companion with whom you'll be able to live happily, for I shall strive to find someone noble, sensible, and virtuous, rather than someone rich, spoilt, and unreliable."

"Oh, but please, mother dearest!" said Virginia. "I'll be much happier staying with you. What if he turned out to be a proud and arrogant man: what would I do then?"

"You'd be as humble as you could in return," said the Queen. "Because, since we must needs be subject to them, the only thing to do is to flatter them and spoil them."

"Well, yes," said Leonora. "Most of them are so stubborn and determined to have their own way, there isn't much choice."

"But there are some men who are less proud than others," said the Queen, "and if women play their cards right, they can be brought

206. See above, p. 48, where Adriana explains the reasons why her daughter must marry.

around. And besides, if this husband we're talking about is noble, as I've said (I mean noble in his soul and his bearing, if not by birth), then there's nothing to worry about, because humility is the mark of true nobility."

"But what if he were stern and terrifying, what should I do then?" asked Virginia.

"You'd be patient and silent and long-suffering," said the Queen.

"It wouldn't be any use," said Leonora, "because men often attack us even when we haven't said a thing."

"But we've said that he's a sensible man," said the Queen, "so he will soon calm down and see reason—all the sooner if you don't stoke up the fires of his anger by answering him back."

"And what if he were jealous, how should I behave then?" her daughter asked.

"You wouldn't give him any occasion for jealousy," said the Queen. "And, since it wouldn't be your business to be attractive to anyone apart from him, if he didn't want you to dress up and adorn yourself, then you'd stop doing so; and if he didn't want you to leave the house, you'd stay in to please him. And by doing this, you'd win him over and gain his trust to such an extent that after a while he'd let you do just as you liked."

"A jealous man," said Leonora, "is never going to change."

"He will if you follow this method," replied the mother. "In any case, if he is a noble and a sensible man, as we've said he is, he is bound to change, for the sake of his honor, and because good sense dictates it."

"But if he didn't," said Virginia, "then what a miserable life I'd have!"

"If the thought of that life doesn't appeal to you," the Queen replied, "just imagine what will happen if I don't marry you off. You'll still have to stay within four walls all day and dress soberly, without any of the finery and fripperies you're allowed now, because that's what happens to young girls who don't want to get married. And, what's more, you'll be deprived of that companionship that could be the joy of your life."

"But what if my husband turns out to be given to vice, then what could I do about it?" asked Virginia.

"If that were the case," the Queen replied, "you'd have to try, as cautiously and tactfully as possible, to wean him away from his vicious habits, by reminding him of God's wrath and the world's judgment, offering up the example of other men who behave decently, and reproaching his defects obliquely by criticizing them in other people."

"That's wouldn't work at all," said Leonora. "She'd only succeed in making him hate her, and then he'd go from bad to worse."

"If he's essentially a decent man," replied the Queen, "then his vices will not be able to hold out against his basic decency, and since we've stipulated that he's also a noble and a sensible man, he will succeed in shaking off any vicious tendencies he may have in his nature. And if that's the case, and you end up a happy woman, then you can thank the Lord; if not, you have the consolation that a husband like yours may still be better than some others you could have had, and that you're better off than many wives."

"Well, I say it's better to be happy alone than unhappy with your companion," said Corinna.

"And I say," said Lucretia, "that even admitting that men are as flawed as we've been saying, with things the way they are in the world, it's still preferable to have their protection and company than to be without it. For we poor women are constantly being assailed and abused, and cheated of our money, our honor, our lives; so it seems better to have one man at least as a friend, to defend us from the others, than to live alone with every man against us. But if, by some chance, as sometimes happens, one's husband is a good man (whether because he is innately good-natured, having taken after his mother, or whether his upbringing has been such as to make him a paragon of virtue and kindness, and an example to the others), then it's impossible to imagine how happy a woman's life can be, living with such a man in an inseparable companionship that lasts until death. And so, dearest girl, you shouldn't lose heart, for you have no way of knowing yet what kind of future God has prepared for you."

"If she could be sure to find a husband like the one you've just described," said Leonora, "I'd certainly advise her to take him. But there are so few good ones around that to be on the safe side (remembering that once you've chosen, there's no going back) I would urge her in the strongest possible terms to shun marriage like the plague. And I remember once hearing a very beautiful poem of Corinna's, which taught me the reason why the men who pretend to love us today don't feel the kind of genuine passion they used to in the old days, when they would even die for the sake of their beloved. And perhaps she could be persuaded to recite the poem for us now: she would be doing me a great favor and giving me great pleasure, and I am quite sure all you others would love to hear it as well."

"Oh, I don't think I should start on that now," said Corinna. "It's a longish poem, and it would be evening by the time I finished."

"Oh, go on," said the Queen, "let's hear it. In fact (let me pull rank on you), I command you to let us hear it."

"Well, since I can see you're all so determined to hear it, I certainly wouldn't wish to deny you any pleasure that's within my power," replied Corinna. "And so, without any further preamble (for the subject of the poem will be obvious enough as you hear it) here it is:[207]

I

Dal ben composto e splendido suo tempio
Di dorici archi e di gemmati fregi
Mosso era Amor, superbo in vista ed empio,
Onusto e altier d'almi trionfi egregi;
Poiché nel ciel più non trovava essempio,
Che cedea Giove a' suoi più rari pregi,
Con maggior facilità prese speranza,
Ch'alla sua qui cedesse ogni possanza.

II

Sparse e spiegò le ventilanti penne,
E scese e venne a innamorar la terra;
E com'era il desio l'effetto ottenne
Con dolce, interna e faticosa guerra.
Ogni cosa creata amar convenne,
Gli uomini, gli animai, l'acqua e la terra:
E mentre vince Amor queste e quell'alme
Orna il bel tempio suo d'illustri palme.

207. Doglioni, in his life of Fonte, cites this short narrative poem in *ottava rima* as an example of her remarkable speed of composition; according to his account, it was conceived of one evening and dashed off the following morning. The piece revisits, in a mythological idiom, some of the main themes of the first day's dialogue, including men's perfidy in love (stanzas 34-36), and the injustices of the dowry system (stanza 15). In her use of the fiction of a primitive Golden Age to sketch out an ideal view of the relations of the sexes, Fonte may have be influenced by the famous choruses in Torquato Tasso's *Aminta*, 1, 2, and, more particularly, Giambattista Guarini's *Pastor fido*, 4, 9 (note the references to the pastoral tradition in stanza 10). More certain is the influence of Ariosto, Fonte's main source in the *Floridoro*; compare especially the allegorical sequence at *OF*, 14, 74-97.

III

Non era cuor di qualità sì dura,
Ch'al suo possente stral non desse loco;
Né petto di sì rigida natura,
Che non ardesse il suo cocente foco;
Però accadea, ch'una gentil figura
(Quantunque fusse il suo merito poco)
Avea tal forza in mente alta e proterva,
Che 'l Re sposava, e 'l Prencipe la serva.

IV

Inganno, falsità, villan pensiero
Nell'animo de' giovani non era;
Il lor'affetto ardente era e sincero,
E la lor servitù costante e vera.
Beata, chi patia sotto il suo impero,
Si riputava ogni pena aspra e fiera.
Né l'uom restava mai d'esser fedele,
Benché la donna fusse empia e crudele.

V

Questo perché l'aurato, acuto dardo
Lor trafigea profondamente il core.
E 'l dolor della piaga era gagliardo,
Né mai scemava, anzi crescea l'ardore,
Era poi mercè degna un dolce sguardo
D'un lungo, ardente e ben provato amore;
O mio fiero destin, malvagio e rio,
Perché non nacqui a sì bel tempo anch'io?

VI

Quei ch'avevano 'l desio corrispondente
Al desiato fin giungeano tosto:
Ma ad alcuno accadea d'amar sovente
Tal ch'avea in altri il suo disegno posto
E perch'era l'amor vero e fervente,
E 'l dolor rendea l'animo indisposto,
I rivali venian con dura sorte
Spesso ad arme, a ferite, a sangue, a morte.

VII

Quivi occorrea ch'Amor, sì come il sole
Penetrando co' rai dentro il terreno,

Gli dà virtù, che concepir vi suole
Fior delicati e fresche erbette a pieno:
Tal egli con sue fiamme interne e sole
Penetrando de gli uomini nel seno
Lor porgea tal valor, che d'onor degni
Fea germogliar mille felici ingegni.

VIII

Questi s'udian con chiari e dolci stili
Del cor gli affetti esprimere diversi,
Fiorian da questi l'opere gentili,
Le dolci rime e i leggiadretti versi.
Lontani da pensieri ingrati e vili
Gli intelletti purgati eran e tersi;
Che ciascun per gradire a chi più amava
A gara onori e meriti acquistava.

IX

Per le floride spiaggie e nell'erbose
Rive de i chiari e liquidi cristalli,
Al cantar delle Naiade amorose
Guidavan le Napee vezzosi balli;
Queste di gigli e d'odorate rose,
Quelle ornate di perle e di coralli,
Ciprigna bella in mezo [sic] lor si serra,
che co' begli occhi fa fiorir la terra.

X

Sempre in lor compagnia star si vedea
De' pastorelli una ridente schiera,
Chi canta, chi contempla la sua dea,
Chi fior le dona e chi la chiama altera.
V'era Aci e la fugace Galatea,
Che del crudel Ciclope si dispera.
V'era Mopso e Tirennia e Tirse [sic] e Filli,
E Titiro e la sua dolce Amarilli.

XI

Se le forze amorose in piani e monti
Eran possenti e sviscerate a pieno:
E così nelle selve e nelle fonti
Fra satirelli e ninfe albergo avieno:
Per le città volar veloci, e pronti

I dardi suoi vedevansi non meno,
E trappassar de' molli giovenetti,
E delle donne i delicati petti.

XII

Da cagion sì gagliarda e sì possente
Spinta la gioventù degna e reale,
Non guardava né a dote, né a parente,
Ch'a sua condizion non fusse eguale:
Ma per dar loco alla sua fiamma ardente
Celebrava Imeneo santo e leale;
Tanto ch'in breve Amor scacciò dal mondo
L'Ambizion e l'Avarizia al fondo.

XIII

Quell'altier, ch'i suoi dì tutti avea spesi
In mercar dignità, gradi ed onori;
E per gara de' ciò molti avea offesi,
Né pur mirar degnava i suoi maggiori;
Trafitto a mezo il cuor da strali accesi
Di questo Re, per mitigar gli ardori
Una vil donna, ancor che bella, prende
Per consorte legitima e si rende.

XIV

Quell'altro avaro, ingordo di tesoro
Tutta la vita sua strazia e patisce,
Non veste mai, non si dà alcun ristoro,
A pena che scacciar la fame ardisce;
Poi tocco dallo stral di costui d'oro
Le sue ricchezze in pochi dì finisce,
O contradote, o spesa altra, ch'importa,
Per goder la sua dea di far comporta.

XV

Felici voi che con sì caldi amanti
Donne vi ritrovaste a quell'etade,
Dove per non aver doti bastanti
Non invecchiava mai vostra beltade,
Né con false lusinghe e finti pianti
Vi cercavan por macchia all'onestade
Ma con debito mezo [sic]*, onesto e grato*
Godeano il fin da lor tanto bramato.

XVI

Già dall'orto all'occaso Amor lasciava
Del suo invitto valor chiari trofei,
Su l'are il foco pio morto restava,
E la religion de gli altri dei:
La vitima [sic] a lui sol si consacrava,
E l'odorato incenso de' Sabei,
Ed era ancor per dilatar più il regno,
S'alla gelosa dea non venia a sdegno.

XVII

Giunon d'invidia e di superbia piena,
Di rabbia, di furor, di gelosia,
Veggendo Amor condotto alla terrena
E prima alla celeste monarchia,
Tal cordoglio ne sente e sì gran pena,
Ch'ad implacabil sdegno apre la via,
E perché vendicarsi al fin conchiude,
Nella secreta camera si chiude.

XVIII

Iri seco ha la sua fedele amica,
Con cui si sfoga e seco parla e dice:
Dunque preposta è Venere impudica
A me, che son del cielo imperatrice?
Dunque la stella a me crudel nimica,
Mi vuol far sempre viver infelice?
Dunque per sempre Amor pres'ha partito
Di far, ch'altra si goda il mio marito?

XIX

Non per una cagion, per mille deggio
Vendicarmi di lui, che sì m'offende,
La terra e 'l ciel soggetto essergli veggio
Obedienza ogni mortal gli rende,
Il nostro culto va di mal in peggio,
La fiamma al nostro altar non più risplende,
Che più voglio aspettar? Ch'un dì s'opponga,
E me di questo mio seggio deponga?

XX

Poi ch'ebbe dato loco al gran lamento
Con lunga e acerbissima querela,

Per isfogar il suo fiero tormento
In fosca nebbia il chiaro aspetto cela.
Sempre ad alta vendetta ha 'l cor intento,
Né pur ad Iri il suo pensier rivela,
In terra scende sconsolata e mesta,
Ed Iri in ciel locotenente resta.

XXI

Per aspra, incolta e disusata via
Con gran dolor la dea va caminando,
E la Superbia incontra, che fuggia
A cui del mondo avea dato Amor bando,
E l'Avarizia era in sua compagnia,
La dea se le venne approssimando,
E dove elle di gir s'avean proposto
Lor fé dimanda, onde le fu risposto.

XXII

Dannate siam disse, in perpetuo essiglio,
L'empia Superbia, all'adirata dea,
Dal maledetto e scelerato figlio
Della malvaggia [sic] e brutta Citerea,
Il qual con certo suo soave artiglio
Gli animi tira alla sua voglia rea,
E se 'l mondo terrà troppo il suo stile
In breve diverrà povero e vile.

XXIII

Come che gravi sian nostri dolori
Che tenevam in terra il primo loco
E stavam nelle corti de' signori,
Anzi nel cuor più che in ogni altro loco,
Via più c'increscé de' nostri maggiori,
Ch'ad Amor come veggio a poco, a poco,
Giove obedisce e le sante alme, vinte
Da certe sue dolcezze amare e finte.

XXIV

A questo dir Giunon di rabbia accesa
Ne gli occhi, e più nel cor sfavilla ed arde
E le risponde: Son d'ogni mia offesa
Le vendette maggior, più che son tarde.
Gran tempo ho comportato esser offesa,

Non che le forze mie non sian gagliarde;
Ma mi parea viltà d'usarle seco,
Essendo vil fanciullo, ignudo e cieco.

XXV

Ma poi ch'è divenuto sì arrogante
Che voi discaccia ed osa offender noi
Per noi tre insieme, ancor che sia bastante
Io sola a far quel che farete voi
Vada all'ingiuria la vendetta inante,
Sieno tutti spuntati i strali suoi.
Il parer della dea fu a tutte caro,
E subito nel mondo ritornaro.

XXVI

L'assunto all'Avarizia fu dato
Di condur ad effetto il lor pensiero:
Ella, c'ha 'l tempo commodo appostato,
Ritrova Amor di sue vittorie altero:
Co 'l sembiante di Venere a lui grato
Se gli appresenta e copre il volto fiero,
E l'invita a posar, com'ella suole,
Nel suo perfido sen con tai parole.

XXVII

Dolce mia speme, in così fervid'ora,
Che 'l sol ci offende e sei sudato e stanco,
Cessa di saettar, vieni a quest'ora,
E nel mio sen riposa il tuo bel fianco.
Le consente l'incauto e in grembo a Flora
Getta il bel corpo suo tenero e bianco,
E nel sen di chi offenderlo propone
La bionda testa e innanellata pone.

XXVIII

Il sonno entrò ne' begli occhi amorosi,
Che la fatica fa 'l riposo grato.
La brutta arpia, che i strali luminosi
Nella faretra ha visti al manco lato;
Perché 'l dolce Cupido a i suoi famosi
Nomi dia fine più non sia pregiato,
Con l'empia, ingorda man, ch'egli non sente,
Gli la dislaccia e leva pianamente.

XXIX

La gelosa Giunon tutta contenta
Con la Superbia allor si fece inante;
E perché sia d'Amor la gloria spenta,
Fé nascer ivi un monte di diamante,
In cui l'empia Superbia s'argomenta
Di spuntar le saette invitte e sante.
E poi che ben l'effetto lor successe
Furo al loco, ove tolte, ancor rimesse.

XXX

Sparir poi tutte e solo il bel Cupido
Lasciar fra fiori a canto alle fresch'onde.
Che poi svegliossi e con vezzoso grido
Chiama la madre sua, che non risponde,
Stimando, che sia gita in Pafo o in Gnido
O in altro loco, più non si diffonde,
Ma spiega l'ali al ciel di più colori,
E torna ad impiagar mill'altri cori.

XXXI

Il suo gran danno il misero non vede,
Che chiusi gli occhi tien d'un velo schietto.
E perché acuti i suoi strali esser crede,
Spera, che debbian far l'usato effetto.
Incurva l'arco e com'io ho detto riede
A ferir, come suol, questo e quel petto,
Ma non che penetrar possan nell'osse
A pena i panni segnan le percosse.

XXXII

Da questo avvien, ch'al mondo or non si puote
Né vera fé, né ver'amor trovarsi.
Né un vero par di fide alme divote,
Che d'interno fervor possa vantarsi,
Poi che Cupido in van fere e percuote
E sono i colpi suoi deboli e scarsi;
Egli, che la cagion non può sapere,
In van si duol, che manca il suo potere.

XXXIII

Per questo cade ogni gentil costume,
Ogni pregiato e generoso gesto.

Un leggiadro pensier più non pressume
Di far suo nido in petto, che sia onesto.
Le preclare virtù co 'l lor bel lume
Escon del mondo e 'l lascian cieco e mesto.
Quelle al ciel si ritornano e in lor vece
Moltiplicano i vizi a diece a diece.

XXXIV

Però voi donne a questi, che sapete,
Che vi chiamano ingrate, empie e crudeli
Gli occhi, gli orecchi e 'l cor sempre chiudete
Poi che non son più gli uomini fedeli.
Cercan di farvi cader nella rete
E di voi si lamentano e dei cieli.
E quando pur gli usate alcun favore
per tutta la città s'ode 'l romore.

XXXV

E poi che né virtù, né gentilezza
Può del misero Amor scontare i danni,
Né vostra grazia e natural bellezza
Può crear ne' lor petti altro, che inganni;
Cingete il vostro cor d'aspra durezza
Sì, che lor falsità mai non v'inganni,
Che son del vero Amor le forze dome,
E sol riman d'Amor nel mondo il nome.

XXXVI

Per non far dunque error, sì ch'a pentire
Non ve ne abbiate poi con danno e scorno
Sdegnate il loro instabile servire,
Né la pietà con voi faccia soggiorno.
E rivolgendo il vostro alto desire
A miglior opre ed a più bei studi intorno,
Ornatevi d'un nome eterno e chiaro
A onta d'ogni cuor superbo e avaro.

I

From his splendid, well-proportioned temple, with its
Doric arches and jeweled friezes, Love came forth,
haughty and malicious, proudly decked out in the fine and
noble spoils of his past victories. For the heavens now

held no one who could rival him: Jove himself yielded
before his matchless skills. All the more certain, then,
was he that no earthly power could stand against him.

II

So Love fanned out his wings on the air and swooped
down to make the whole world fall in love; and it came
about just as he wished, through a sweet, wearisome, inner
struggle. All created things were compelled to love—men
and women, animals, the waters, and earth—and as Love
vanquished each successive soul, he adorned his lovely
shrine with ever more glorious triumphal palms.

III

No heart, however hard, could resist his powerful darts; no
breast, however rigid, was not melted by his burning fires.
A winsome form (however lowly the person's status) came
to exert such power over the proudest and most arrogant of
hearts, that kings and princes married their servant girls.

IV

Deception, falsity, and base thoughts found no place in
the minds of young men: their affections were ardent and
sincere, their wooing constant and true. Those who suffered under Love's reign considered the harshest pains a
blessing, and men did not cease to be faithful even when
women showed themselves cruel and malign.

V

The reason for this was that their hearts were pierced
through with Love's sharp golden dart. The pain of their
wound was keen and its burning never diminished, rather
increasing over time. Moreover, a sweet glance from the
beloved was considered ample reward for even the longest
and most ardent and enduring of devotions. What a bitter,
cruel, malign destiny is mine, that I too was not born in
this happy age!

VI

Those whose chosen objects returned their love were not
long in reaching their desired end. But it often happened
that a young man would fall in love with a girl whose
sights were set on someone else, and since love in that
age was genuine and ardent, and the pain affected men's

minds, the two rivals would often be led by their harsh
fate to the clash of arms, and wounds, blood, and death
would ensue.

VII

Another effect of Love was that just as the sun, when it
penetrates the earthly sphere with its rays, infuses it with
vital spirit so that it blossoms forth with delicate flowers
and fresh green shoots, so too, as Love penetrated men's
breasts with his unique hidden flames, he filled them with
such prowess that a thousand gifted minds began to flourish, each worthy of great esteem.

VIII

And these could be heard expressing the various passions
of their hearts in clear, sweet tones; refined compositions, sweet rhymes, and charming verses poured from
them. Remote from any base or ungrateful thought, men's
minds then were pure and polished, and each of them, to
please the woman that he loved, vied with the others to
win honors and prove his worth.

IX

Along the blooming seashores and the grassy banks of the
clear and liquid crystal [streams], to the singing of the
amorous Naiads, the Napaeae performed charming dances;
the latter adorned with lilies and sweet-scented roses, the
former with pearls and corals. And lovely Venus sat encircled by them: Venus who with her fair eyes makes the
earth bloom.[208]

X

And always in their company there was a laughing band of
young shepherds, some singing, some gazing on their
"goddesses," giving them flowers or bewailing their haugh-
tiness. Acis was there, and the fleeing Galatea, driven to
despair by the cruel Cyclops;[209] and Mopso was there, and

208. The Naiads were freshwater nymphs (though Fonte appears, from the attributes
she gives them, to think of them as sea nymphs); the Napaeae, nymphs of forests and
groves. Venus, the goddess of beauty and love, was the mother of Love or Cupid, the
protagonist of this poem. She is referred to in the original as "Ciprigna" ("Cypriot"), as
it was off the coast of Cyprus that Aphrodite, her Greek equivalent, was supposed to
have been born from the waves.

209. Galatea, a sea nymph in Greek myth, was wooed by Polyphemus, a one-eyed giant,

Tyrrenia and Thyrsis and Phyllis, and Tityrus and his sweet Amaryllis.[210]

XI

If the forces of love were so powerful and heart-wrenching in the plains and mountains, and if they were equally powerful when they haunted the woodlands and streams where nymphs and frisky little satyrs dwelt, Love's darts flew no less swiftly and directly in the cities, piercing the delicate breasts of languishing youths and ladies.

XII

The noblest and most elevated youths of the cities, spurred on by such a powerful and irresistible motive, gave no thought to dowries, or to the shame of kinship with those below their status; instead, hoping for some respite from the flames of their love, they hastened on to contract holy and faithful marriage. So, before long, Love had driven Ambition and Avarice from the world and banished them to the depths.

XIII

The haughtiest of men, who had spent their lives trading in dignities, ranks, and honors, and trampling others underfoot in their ambition, once almost too proud to deign to glance even at their betters, now found themselves pierced through the heart with the flaming arrows of this Monarch of the World, and to ease their fierce ardors they would take a woman of low birth (though great beauty) as their legitimate spouse, yielding to Love's power.

XIV

Others, miserly and greedy for treasure, had spent their whole lives scrimping and suffering, never dressing properly, never allowing themselves a moment of recreation, hardly willing to consume enough even to drive off

---

or Cyclops. When he discovered her with Acis, the youth she loved, the jealous Cyclops threw a great boulder at him, whereupon Galatea (who had meanwhile flown back to her native element, the sea), turned Acis into a river to save him.

210. These last names, with the exception of Tyrennia, all derive from classical and Renaissance pastoral literature, which describes in idealized terms the life of shepherds in Arcadia during a mythical golden age.

hunger, until suddenly, struck by Love's golden shafts,
they burned up their savings in a few days, lavishly dower-
ing the brides they worshiped or spending freely on anything that might give them pleasure.

XV

O happy you women of that age, who enjoyed such ardent
lovers and whose beauty was never suffered to wilt in solitude for the lack of a sufficient dowry! Nor did men at
that time lay siege to your honor with their false flattery
and feigned sufferings; rather, they pursued the objective
they desired so passionately by correct, decent, and
acceptable means.

XVI

By now, the glorious monuments of Love's unconquerable
prowess were strewn across the broad reaches of the earth.
On the altars the holy fire was reduced to ashes and the
worship of the other gods had fallen into disuse; to Love
alone were the sacrificial victims destined and all the aromatic Sabaean incense.[211] And he would have extended
his realm still further, had he not awakened the anger of
the jealous goddess.[212]

XVII

Juno was brimming with envy and pride, with rage, fury, and
jealousy, seeing Love elevated to the monarchy of the
earth (as he had been previously to that of the heavens);
and the pain and misery she felt on account of this gradually gave way to a fierce and implacable anger. Finally
deciding to take revenge, she locked herself away in her
private chamber.

XVIII

She had with her her faithful companion, Iris, to whom
she poured out her feelings thus: "So, I see that that trol-

211. Saba, the biblical Sheba and the present-day Yemen, was famed in antiquity as a
producer of incense.
212. The "jealous goddess" is, as we learn in the following stanza, Juno, sister and wife
of the habitually unfaithful Jove, or Jupiter, king of the gods. Iris, mentioned below,
was the goddess of the rainbow, who acted as messenger to the gods and was often
portrayed, as here, as a particular confidante and servant to Juno.

lop Venus has been elevated above me, the rightful empress of the skies. Can it be that the cruel stars, my enemies, have fated me to live perpetually in misery? Can it be that Love has permanently decreed that other women should enjoy my husband?

XIX

And not just this one reason, but a thousand others press me to avenge myself on this great enemy. I see that both earth and sky are now subject to him, and that all mortals obey him, while the cult of us other gods goes to rack and ruin and the flames no longer burn on our altars. What am I waiting for? For him to rise up against me and depose me from my rightful throne?"

XX

Having given vent to her great sense of wrong with bitter and long drawn-out lamenting, she set out to assuage her fierce torment, shrouding her glorious aspect in a dark mantle of cloud. Her heart was firmly set on revenge, and she did not reveal her plans even to Iris. Dismayed and miserable, she descended to earth, leaving Iris her lieutenant in the heavens.

XXI

Along a rough, overgrown, and disused path, the goddess trekked, accompanied by her misery. In the other direction came Pride, in flight from Love, who had banished her from the world, with Avarice alongside her. As the goddess approached, she asked the two where they were heading, and they replied.

XXII

"We have been damned to perpetual exile," malign Pride said to the angry goddess, "by the vicious, cursed offspring of that wicked hag Venus, who seizes souls in those sweet talons of his and bends them to his twisted will. If the world remains under his sway for long, it will soon sink into poverty and baseness.

XXIII

"But although our own sorrows are acute (for we used to enjoy the highest rank on earth, and dwelt in the courts

of princes—or rather, deep within their hearts), what
hurts us more keenly is to see what has happened to our
superiors. For we see Jupiter himself gradually bending to
the dominion of Love, along with the other divine spirits
who dwell with him, vanquished by those sweetnesses
Love proffers (sweetnesses bitter and false)!"

XXIV

Hearing this, Juno's eyes flashed with fury, while her heart
burnt more fiercely still. She replied, "My revenge, when I
have been offended, is always the more terrible the more it
is delayed. If I have tolerated Love's offenses against me
for a long while, it is not because I lacked the strength to
avenge myself; it's simply that I felt it would be beneath
my dignity to use my powers against a helpless, naked,
blind child.[213]

XXV

"But since he has now become so arrogant as to banish you
two and to dare to offend me, let the three of us combine
our efforts to avenge the injuries he has done us (though,
of course, I should be quite equal to the task alone). Let
us blunt those arrows of his!" The goddess's proposal was
applauded, and the three at once set off back toward the
earth.

XXVI

The execution of the task was allotted to Avarice, who,
after calculating the most apposite moment, searched out
Love, as he basked in the glory of his victories. She
appeared before him in the semblance of his beloved
Venus, disguising her unlovely face, and invited him, as
was Venus's wont, to rest in her perfidious lap. These were
her words:

XXVII

"Sweetest treasure, in this fervid hour of the day, when
the sun is assaulting us and you are hot and tired, you
should cease your labors with the bow and come rest your

---

213. Cupid was generally represented in art as a naked and blind (or blindfolded) child,
a figuration obviously intended to symbolize the arbitrariness of love.

lovely flank in my lap." The incautious boy consented and flung his lovely body, tender and white, among the spoils of Flora, and in the lap of she who planned to offend him, he laid his blond, curly head.

XXVIII

Sleep crept into his lovely, amorous eyes, for bodily fatigue makes us crave rest. The ugly harpy, who had glimpsed his gleaming arrows lying at his left side in their quiver, to ensure the end of Cupid's fame and glory, untied the quiver with her fell, voracious hand and eased it off his body, as the sleeping youth lay impervious.

XXIX

The jealous Juno then delightedly rushed up, with Pride beside her. And in order to extinguish Love's glory altogether, the goddess raised up a mountain made of solid diamond, and Pride then busied herself blunting that youth's glorious sacred arrows against the rock.[214] And once this had been done, they restored the arrows to their customary place.

XXX

Then the three vanished, leaving handsome Cupid alone among the flowers, beside the flowing waters. He awoke and, in his charming tones, called out for his mother, who did not reply. Imagining her to have left for Paphos or Cnidos,[215] or some other place, he did not trouble himself further, but unfurled his many-colored wings and took flight to wound another vast consignment of hearts.

XXXI

The wretch could not see the great harm he had suffered, for his eyes were bound by a tight veil. And believing his shafts to be as sharp as ever, he imagined that they would have the usual effect. He drew his bow and, as I said, devoted himself to the task of shooting this breast or that. But his arrows, far from penetrating to the bone, as

---

214. Diamond was famed for its exceptional hardness.
215. Both places were the sites of famous shrines to Venus in antiquity.

was their wont, would now scarcely even mark the garments
of their victims.

XXXII

And that is the reason why, in the world today, true faith,
true love are never found, nor a true pair of devoted, faithful souls, who can boast a genuine inner fire. For Cupid
wounds and strikes in vain and his blows are weak and in-
effectual; and he, incapable of discovering the cause,
vainly bemoans his lost powers.

XXXIII

And because of this, the refined behavior of olden times
has lapsed, elegant and noble deeds are no longer seen,
and charming thoughts of love no longer make their home
in virtuous breasts. Virtue and genius, in their splendor,
have abandoned the world, leaving it blind and dreary; they
have returned to heaven, leaving the vices to multiply in
their place.

XXXIV

And so, ladies, you should keep your eyes, ears, and hearts
firmly closed against these suitors (though you know they
will call you ungrateful, fell, and cruel). For men are no
longer faithful: they merely seek to trap you in their nets,
complaining the while of your harshness and the harshness of their fate. And then, if one of you does grant
them some favor, the news of it spreads immediately
throughout the city.

XXXV

And since neither virtue nor gentility can ever reverse the
wrongs poor Love has suffered, and women's grace and natural beauty are not enough alone to inspire anything but
cunning and trickery in men's breasts, you must gird your
hearts with stony hardness, so that their trickery can
never take you in. For the forces of true Love have been
blunted, and all that remains of love in the world is the
mere name.

XXXVI

And, in order not to fall into an error that will cost you

long and painful repentance, you must scorn their faithless wooing and steel yourself against pity. Instead, turn
your lofty desires to higher objects and finer studies, and
adorn yourselves with immortal fame, spurning all those
whose hearts are prey to avarice and pride.

Words could not have expressed how thrilled Corinna's listeners
were by the beauty of this poem and its striking inventiveness, and
each begged for a copy. But then Helena, to continue the interrupted conversation, turned to Leonora and said, "But in spite of all
this, and in spite of everything we've been hearing, I'm sure you must
still be prepared to allow that there is some goodness to be found in
men."

"Oh, I'm happy to allow it," Leonora replied. "But I'll leave it up
to you to find out exactly where."

"That's enough!" said the Queen. "I'm not going to settle on a
husband for Virginia until I've managed to seek one out who is as
good as I promised. It shouldn't be hard to tell who is suitable by looking at their behavior (for I'm going to research this very thoroughly)."

"That's a very sensible plan," said Lucretia. "The thing is not to
lay too much stress on wealth and beauty in a marriage partner (and
that goes for both men and women), for it's that kind of vain concern, which many people are far too swayed by, that is the downfall of
many husbands and wives."

"It's certainly true," said Leonora, "that since men are rotten for
the most part, women should do what our Queen says and put their
energies into seeking out that quality in husbands which is hardest
to find and yet ultimately the most important: goodness."

"Oh, stick to your ground if you must!" said Helena. "Go on,
don't give an inch! If men knew what you were thinking when they
saw you walking past in the street—if they had the least suspicion of
how much ill will you harbor against them—I'd have to start fearing
for your safety."

"On the contrary," replied Leonora, "men have good cause to
honor me and take my part, for, when it comes down to it, nothing of
what I've said has been intended to offend good men; rather, it's all
been directed toward converting bad men—if only they'd listen. So
they should be grateful to me, really, since I haven't been speaking
out of any hatred for men, but rather in a spirit of charity, and moved

by the compassion I feel for the many suffering women I see around me, one made unhappy by her father, another by her brother, another by her husband, still another by her son, and so on across every relationship one person can have with another. For many men see the world in a blinkered way, and are so firmly convinced by the unwarrantable fallacy that they are created women's superiors, and so incapable of seeing past this lie, that they believe themselves fully justified in treating women as tyrannically and brutally as they like. But if they could be persuaded of their error, they might just change their ways—for it must be acknowledged that man is under the same obligation to help his neighbor as himself, since we were all created to help one another, as we have already said. So I don't feel that men would have any cause to be offended by what I've said, even if I had spoken publicly in their presence."

"Oh, if only you had!" cried Cornelia. "Countless women would have had cause to be grateful to you, both for the useful warnings you'd have given them, which would save them from all kinds of errors, and for having done such a good job of persuading those men who fail to behave as they should toward women to mend their ways and become better."

"Talking away like this," said the Queen, "we have amused ourselves so delightfully that the time we had for speaking about these men of ours has run out before what we had to say on the subject was exhausted. Indeed, I'm quite sure that it would take not just days but months and years to get to the end of what might be said on the subject and for you all to be satisfied. So, in order not to stretch things out to infinity, since the day is drawing to a close, it seems appropriate for me to renounce my sovereignty to your good graces, thanking you for the obedience and loyalty you have shown me. And, to conclude, I'd just like to beg Leonora to change her mind about marriage, since she's still such a slip of a girl, and to try to seek out a worthy and charming companion for herself, with whom she can lead a long and happy life—if only to avoid the risk of giving occasion for malicious gossip and slander."

"Well, let's see Virginia married first," said Leonora, "since it's her first time. And, in the meantime, I'll think it over, and, who knows? Perhaps eventually I'll come round to accepting your counsel, along with all the sound and sensible advice you have given me."

With that, the women arose from their seats, for the sun was on the point of setting, and, as they walked through the garden in the cool of the evening, Corinna and Virginia started singing a madrigal:

S'ornano il ciel le stelle
Ornan le donne il mondo,
Con quanto è in lui di bello e di giocondo.
E come alcun mortale
Viver senz'alma e senza cor non vale,
Tal non pon senza d'elle
Gli uomini aver per sé medesimi aita,
Che è la donna de l'uom cor, alma e vita.

If the stars adorn the heavens, women adorn the world, with all that is lovely and pleasant in it. And just as no mortal can live without a soul and a heart, so men cannot get by without women, for woman is man's heart, his soul, and his life.

When they had finished, the women all took their leave of one another and went off to their respective homes.

APPENDIX
THE THEME OF WOMEN'S EQUALITY
WITH MEN IN FONTE'S *FLORIDORO*

The passage that follows is from Moderata Fonte's first work, *Tredici canti del Floridoro* (Venice, 1581), canto 4, 1–5. It is cited from the recent edition of the text by Valeria Finucci (Bologna: Mucchi, 1995), 61–62, with one minor departure, where I have retained the punctuation of the 1581 edition.

> *Le donne in ogni età fur da natura*
> *Di gran giudizio e d'animo dotate,*
> *Né men atte a mostrar con studio e cura*
> *Senno e valor degli huomini son nate;*
> *E perché, se comune è la figura,*
> *Se non son le sostanze variate,*
> *S'hanno simile un cibo e un parlar, denno*
> *Differente aver poi l'ardire e 'l senno?*
>
> *Sempre s'è visto, e vede (pur ch'alcuna*
> *Donna v'abbia voluto il pensier porre)*
> *Nella milizia riuscir più d'una,*
> *E 'l pregio, e 'l grido a molti uomini torre,*
> *E così nelle lettere e in ciascuna*
> *Impresa che l'uom pratica e discorre,*
> *Le donne sì buon frutto han fatto, e fanno,*
> *Che gli uomini a invidiar punto non hanno.*
>
> *E benché di sì degno, e sì famoso*
> *Grado di lor non sia numero molto,*
> *Gli è perché ad atto eroico, e virtuoso,*

Non hanno il cor per più rispetti volto.
L'oro che sta ne le minere ascoso;
Non manca d'esser or, benché sepolto;
E quando è tratto e se ne fa lavoro
E' così ricco e bel come l'altro oro.

Se quando nasce una figliuola il padre,
La ponesse col figlio a un'opra eguale,
Non saria nelle imprese alte, e leggiadre
Al frate inferior né diseguale;
O la ponesse in fra l'armate squadre
Seco, o a imparar qualche arte liberale;
Ma perché in altri affari viene allevata,
Per l'educazion poco è stimata.

Throughout the ages, women have been endowed by
nature with excellent judgment and great courage, and
they are born no less well fitted than men to display wisdom and valor, if properly trained and nurtured. And,
indeed, if men and women share the same bodily form, if
they are composed of like substance, if they eat and speak
in the same way, why should they be thought to differ in
courage and intelligence?

Numerous women throughout history have attained success
in military life, outstripping the achievements of many of
their male comrades, and the same still occurs whenever a
woman turns her energies to this kind of activity. The
same may be said of the profession of letters, and all other
activities in which men engage: women's achievements
have been and are such that they have no cause to envy
men.

And even if there are not many women who have attained
this degree of excellence and fame, that is only because,
for various reasons, they have tended not to turn their
energies toward heroic and challenging deeds. The gold
that lies buried in the mines is still gold, even though it
is buried from sight, and when it is mined and worked, it is
as precious and exquisite as any other gold.

If, when a daughter was born to him, a father were to have
her engage in the same pursuits as a son, the girl would

not prove inferior to her brother in any lofty and glorious
enterprise, whether she were placed alongside him in the
ranks of an army, or set to learn some liberal art. But
because girls are given a different kind of upbringing,
their abilities are not rated highly.

WORKS CITED

PRIMARY WORKS

Aeschines (1919). *The Speeches of Aeschines*. Edited and translated by Charles Darwin Adams. Loeb Classical Library. Cambridge, MA: Harvard University Press.

Agrippa, Henricus Cornelius (1996). *Declamation on the Nobility and Preeminence of the Female Sex*. Edited by Albert Rabil, Jr. Chicago: University of Chicago Press.

Alberti, Leon Battista (1969). *The Family in Renaissance Florence*. Translated by Renée Neu Watkins. Columbia: University of South Carolina Press.

Albertus Magnus (1967). *Book of Minerals*. Edited and translated by Dorothy Wyckoff. Oxford: Clarendon Press.

Alciatus, Andreas (1985). *The Latin Emblems: Indexes and Lists*. Edited by Peter M. Daly, with Virginia W. Callahan, assisted by Simon Cuttler. Toronto: University of Toronto Press.

Andreini, Isabella (1607). *Lettere*. Venice: Marc'Antonio Zaltieri.

Ariosto, Ludovico (1975). *Orlando Furioso*. Translated by Barbara Reynolds. 2 vols. London: Penguin Books.

Aristotle (1986). *The Complete Works*. Edited by Jonathan Barnes. 2 vols. Princeton: Princeton University Press.

Astell, Mary (1986). *The First English Feminist: Reflections on Marriage and Other Writings*. Edited with an introduction by Bridget Hill. New York: St. Martin's Press.

Bacci, Andrea (1582). *Dell'alicorno*. Florence: G. Marescotti.

Bandello, Matteo (1974). *Novelle*. Edited by Giuseppe Guido Ferrero. Turin: UTET.

Barbaro, Francesco (1978). *On Wifely Duties*. Translated by Benjamin Kohl, in Kohl and R. G. Witt, eds., *The Earthly Republic*, 179–228. Philadelphia: University of Pennsylvania Press.

Barocchi, Paola, ed. (1971–77). *Scritti d'arte del Cinquecento*. 3 vols. Milan: Ricciardi.

Bembo, Pietro (1954). *Gli Asolani*. Translated by Rudolf B. Gottfried. Indiana University Publications in the Humanities, 31. Bloomington: University of Indiana Press.

Berga, Antonio (1589). *Discorso della grandezza dell'acqua e della terra, contra l'opinion del S. Alessandro Piccolomini*. Turin: Heirs of Bevilacqua.

Bergalli, Luisa (1726). *Componimenti poetici delle più illustri rimatrici d'ogni secolo*. Venice: A. Mora.

Bestiario valdese (1984). Edited by Anna Maria Raugei. Florence: Olschki.

Boccaccio, Giovanni (1963). *Concerning Famous Women*. Translated by Guido A. Guarino. New Brunswick, NJ: Rutgers University Press.

‒‒‒‒‒ (1987). *Decameron*. 6th ed. Edited by Vittorio Branca. Turin: Einaudi.

‒‒‒‒‒ (1993). *Corbaccio or The Labyrinth of Love*. Translated by Anthony K. Cassell. 2d rev. ed. Binghamton, NY: Medieval and Renaissance Texts and Studies.

Bramoso, L'Academico [Cipriano Giambelli] (1589). *Discorso intorno alla maggioranza dell'huomo e della donna, fatto nell'Accademia de' Solletici di Trevigi*. Treviso: Angelo Mazzolini.

Bronzini, Cristoforo (1622–24). *Della dignità e nobiltà delle donne: Settimana prima e giornata prima [-terza]*. Florence: Zanobi Pignoni.

‒‒‒‒‒ (1625). *Della dignità e nobiltà delle donne . . . Settimana prima e giornata quarta [-sesta]*. Florence: Zanobi Pignoni.

Bruni, Leonardo (1987). "On the Study of Literature (1405) to Lady Battista Malatesta of Montefeltro." In *The Humanism of Leonardo Bruni: Selected Texts*, trans. and introd. Gordon Griffiths, James Hankins, and David Thompson, 240–51. Binghamton, NY: Medieval and Renaissance Texts and Studies.

Buonarotti, Michelangelo (1991). *The Poetry of Michelangelo: An Annotated Translation*. Edited and translated by James M. Saslow. New Haven: Yale University Press.

Bursati da Crema, Luciano (1621). *La vittoria delle donne*. Venice: Evangelista Deuchino.

Campiglia, Maddalena (1588). *Flori, favola boschereccia*. Vicenza: Heirs of Perin Libraio and Tommaso Brunelli.

Capra, Galeazzo Flavio (1988). *Della eccellenza e dignità delle donne*. Edited by Maria Luisa Doglio. Rome: Bulzoni.

Castiglione, Baldassare (1994). *The Book of the Courtier*. Translated by Sir Thomas Hoby (1561), edited by Virginia Cox. London: Everyman.

Cicero, Marcus Tullius (1922). *De senectute, De amicitia, De divinatione*. Edited and translated by William Armistead Falconer. Loeb Classical Library. Cambridge, MA: Harvard University Press.

Colonna, Vittoria (1982). *Rime*. Edited by Alan Bullock. Bari: Laterza.

Columella, Lucius Junius Moderatus (1960–68). *On Agriculture, and On Trees*. Edited and translated by E. S. Forster and Edward H. Heffner. 3 vols. Loeb Classical Library. Cambridge, MA: Harvard University Press.

Contarini, Luigi (1589–97). *Il vago e dilettevole giardino ove si leggono i vari et mirabili esempi di virtù et vitii de gli huomini, l'origine e l'imprese delle Amazzone, i meravigliose essempi delle donne*. 2 parts. Vicenza: Heirs of Perin Libraio.

Cortese, Isabella (1588). *I segreti*. 4th ed. Venice: Heirs of G. Simbeni.

Dardano, Luigi (1554). *La bella e dotta difesa delle donne in verso e in prosa*. Venice: Bartolomeo detto l'Imperatore.

Doglioni, Giovanni Niccolò (1587). *L'Anno, dove si ha perfetto e pieno ragguaglio di quanto può ciascun desiderare, sì d'intorno alle cose del Mondo Celeste, et Elementare, come d'intorno à quelle de' tempi e del Calendario*. Venice: G. A. Rampazetto.

_____ (1588). *Della origine et antichità di Cividal di Belluno, et brevemente de' successi di quella città*. Venice: G. A. Rampazetto.

_____ (1594). *Compendio historico universale di tutte le cose notabili già successe nel Mondo, dal principio della sua creatione fino all'anno di Christo 1594*. Venice: D. Zenaro.

_____ (1606). *Del Theatro universale de' prencipi et di tutte l'Historie del Mondo*. 2 vols. Venice: N. Misserini.

See also Goldioni, Leonico.

Dolce, Lodovico (1565). *Dialogo nel quale si ragiona delle qualità, diversità e proprietà de i colori*. Venice: Giovanni Battista and Melchiorre Sessa.

_____ (1617). *Trattato delle gemme che produce la natura, nel quale si discorre della qualità, grandezza, bellezza e virtù loro*. 2d ed. Venice: Giovanni Battista and Giovanni Bernardo Sessa.

Elyot, Thomas (1980). *Defence of Good Women: The Feminist Controversy of the Renaissance*. Edited by Diane Bornstein. Facsimile Reproductions. New York: Delmar.

Erasmus, Desiderius (1965). "Courtship," "The Girl with No Interest in Marriage," "The Repentant Girl," "Marriage," "The Abbot and the Learned Lady," and "The New Mother." In *The Colloquies of Erasmus*, trans. Craig R. Thompson. Chicago: University of Chicago Press.

Fonte, Moderata [Modesta Pozzo] (1582a). *Le feste: Rappresentazione avanti al Serenissimo Prencipe di Venetia Nicolò Da Ponte il giorno di S. Stefano, 1581*. Venice: D. and G. B. Guerra.

_____ (1582b). *La Passione di Christo descritta in ottava rima da Moderata Fonte*. Venice: D. and G. B. Guerra.

_____ (1592). *La Resurrettione di Giesu Christo nostro Signore . . . descritta in ottava rima.* Venice: G. D. Imberti.

_____ (1988). *Il merito delle donne.* Edited by Adriana Chemello. Venice: Eidos.

_____ (1995). *Tredici canti del Floridoro.* Edited by Valeria Finucci. Bologna: Mucchi.

Franco, Veronica (1995). *Rime.* Edited by Stefano Bianchi. Milan: Mursia.

Giovio, Paolo (1978). *Dialogo dell'imprese militari e amorose.* Edited by Maria Luisa Doglio. Rome: Bulzoni.

Goldioni, Leonico [Giovanni Niccolò Doglioni] (1603). *Le cose maravigliose dell'inclita città di Venetia, riformate, accommodate e grandemente accresciute.* Venice.

_____ (1624). *Le cose maravigliose et notabili della città di Venezia, riformate, accommodate, et grandemente ampliate.* Venice: Ghiradro e Iseppo Imberti.

Guarguanti, Orazio (1588). *Eccellenze di Maria Vergine in ottava rima.* Venice: G. Dagano. *See also* Tansillo, Luigi.

Kempe, Margery (1986). *The Book of Margery Kempe.* Translated by Barry Windeatt. New York: Viking Penguin.

King, Margaret L. and Albert Rabil, Jr., eds. (1981). *Her Immaculate Hand: Selected Works by and about the Women Humanists of Quattrocento Italy.* 2d rev. ed. Binghamton: Medieval and Renaissance Texts and Studies, 1983.

Klein, Joan Larsen, ed. (1992). *Daughters, Wives, and Widows: Writings by Men about Women and Marriage in England, 1500–1640.* Urbana: University of Illinois Press.

Knox, John (1985). *The Political Writings of John Knox: The First Blast of the Trumpet against the Monstruous Regiment of Women and Other Selected Works.* Edited by Marvin A. Breslow. Washington: Folger Shakespeare Library.

Kors, Alan C., and Edward Peters, eds. (1972). *Witchcraft in Europe, 1100–1700: A Documentary History.* Philadelphia: University of Pennsylvania Press.

Krämer, Heinrich, and Jacob Sprenger (1971). *Malleus Maleficarum.* Translated by Montague Summers. London: Pushkin Press, 1928; reprint, New York: Dover.

Landi, Ortensio (1562). *Sette libri de' cataloghi a varie cose appartenenti non solo antiche, ma anche moderne: opera utile molto alla historia, et da cui prender si po materia di favellare d'ogni proposito che ci occorra.* Venice: Giolito.

Latini, Brunetto (1948). *Li livres dou trésor.* Edited by Francis J. Carmody. Berkeley: University of California Press.

Leone Ebreo [Jehudah Abarbanel] (1937). *The Philosophy of Love (Dialoghi d'amore).* Translated by F. Friedeberg-Seeley and Jean H. Barnes, with an introduction by Cecil Roth. London: Soncino Press.

Lorris, William de, and Jean de Meun (1983). *The Romance of the Rose.* Translated by Charles Dahlbert. Princeton: Princeton University Press, 1971; reprint, Hanover, NH: University Press of New England.

Maggio, Vincenzo (1545). *Un brieve trattato dell'eccellentia delle donne . . . di lingua latina in Italiana tradotto.* Brescia: Damiano de Turlini.

Marinella, Lucrezia (1601). *Della nobiltà et l'eccellenza delle donne.* 2d ed. Venice: G. B. Ciotti.

Marinelli, Giovanni (1562). *Gli ornamenti delle donne.* Venice: Francesco de' Franceschi.

Mattioli, Pierandrea (1573). *Discorsi nelli sei libri di Pedacio Dioscoride Anazarbeo della materia Medicinale.* 6th ed. Venice: Heirs of Valgrisi.

Mexia, Pedro (1564). *Selva di varia lettione, di Pietro Messia Spagnuolo, da lui divisa in tre parti, alle quali s'è aggiunta la quarta di Francesco Sansovino.* Venice: G. de' Cavalli.

Michele, Agostino (1583). *Trattato della grandezza dell'acqua e della terra, nella quale . . . dimostrasi l'acqua essere di maggior quantità della terra.* Venice: N. Moretti.

Navarre, Marguerite de (1984). *The Heptameron.* Translated by P. A. Chilton. New York: Viking Penguin.

Passi, Giuseppe (1599). *I donneschi difetti.* Venice: I. A. Somasco.

———— (1602). *Dello stato maritale.* Venice: I. A. Somasco.

Petrarca, Francesco (1991). *Remedies for Fortune Fair and Foul (De remediis utriusque Fortune).* Translated and edited by Conrad D. Rawski. 5 vols. Bloomington: University of Indiana Press.

Piccolomini, Alessandro (1568). *Della grandezza della terra et dell'acqua.* Venice: G. Ziletti.

Pizan, Christine de (1982). *The Book of the City of Ladies.* Translated by Earl Jeffrey Richards. Foreword by Marina Warner. New York: Persea Books.

———— (1985). *The Treasury of the City of Ladies.* Translated by Sarah Lawson. New York: Viking Penguin.

Plato (1961). *The Collected Dialogues, including the Letters.* Edited by Edith Hamilton and Huntingdon Cairns. Princeton: Princeton University Press.

Plutarch (1927–69). *Moralia.* Translated by Frank Cole Babbitt and others. 15 vols. Loeb Classical Library. Cambridge, MA: Harvard University Press.

Ramusio, Giovanni Battista (1978–88). *Navigazioni e viaggi.* Edited by Marica Milanesi. 6 vols. Turin: Einaudi.

Ridolfi, Carlo (1984). *The Life of Tintoretto and of His Children Domenico and Marietta.* Edited and translated by Catherine Enggass and Robert Enggass. University Park: Pennsylvania State University Press.

Ruscelli, Girolamo (1552). *Lettura sopra un sonetto dell'illustriss. marchese della Terza: Ove con nuove e chiare ragioni si pruova la somma perfettione delle donne.* Venice: G. Griffio.

———— (1563). *Del modo di comporre in versi nella lingua italiana.* Venice: Giovanni Battista and Melchiorre Sessa.

———— (1584). *Le imprese illustri.* 3d ed. Venice: Francesco de' Franceschi.

Sansovino, Francesco (1584). *Delle orationi volgarmente scritte da diversi huomini illustri de' tempi nostri*. 4th ed. Venice: Altobello Salicato.

_____ (1587). *Delle cose notabili della città di Venetia*. Venice: Altobello Salicato.

_____ (1609). *Della origine et de' fatti delle famiglie illustri d'Italia*. Venice: Altobello Salicato.

Seneca (1917). *Ad Lucilium epistulae morales*. Edited and translated by Richard M. Gummere. 3 vols. Loeb Classical Library. Cambridge, MA: Harvard University Press.

_____ (1972). *Naturales quaestiones*. Edited and translated by Thomas H. Corocan. 3 vols. Loeb Classical Library. Cambridge, MA: Harvard University Press.

Spenser, Edmund (1978). *The Faerie Queene*. Edited by Thomas P. Roche, Jr. with the assistance of C. Patrick O'Donnell, Jr. New Haven: Yale University Press.

Stringa, Giovanni (1604). *Venetia città nobilissima et singolare, descritta già in XIII libri da M. Francesco Sansovino, et hora con molta diligenza corretta, emendata, e più d'un terzo ampliata dal M. R. D. Giovanni Stringa*. Venice: Altobello Salicato.

Suetonius (1982). *Divus Julius*. Edited by H. E. Butler and M. Cary, with a new introduction, bibliography, and additional notes by G. B. Townend. Bristol: Bristol Classical Press.

Tansillo, Luigi (1592). *Le lagrime di San Pietro del Signor Luigi Tansillo, con le lagrime della Maddalena del Signor Erasmo da Valvassone, di nuovo ristampate, et aggiuntovi l'Eccellenze della Gloriosa Vergine Maria del Signor Horatio Guarguanti da Soncino*. Edited by Giovanni Vincenti. Venice: S. Cornetti.

Tarabotti, Arcangela (1654). *La semplicità ingannata*. Leiden: Sambix [Elzevir].

_____ (1994). *Che le donne siano della spezie degli uomini (Women Are No Less Rational Than Men)*. Edited by Letizia Panizza. London: Institute of Romance Studies.

Teresa of Avila, Saint (1957). *The Life of Saint Teresa of Avila by Herself*. Translated by J. M. Cohen. New York: Viking Penguin.

Venier, Domenico (1751). *Rime*. Edited by Pierantonio Serassi. Bergamo: Pietro Lancelotto.

Vives, Juan Luis (1524). *The Instruction of the Christian Woman*. Translated by Rycharde Hyrd. London: Thomas Berthelet.

Weyer, Johann (1991). *Witches, Devils, and Doctors in the Renaissance: Johann Weyer, De praestigiis daemonum*. Edited by George Mora with Benjamin G. Kohl, Erik Midelfort, and Helen Bacon. Translated by John Shea. Binghamton, NY: Medieval and Renaissance Texts and Studies.

Wilson, Katharina M., ed. (1984). *Medieval Women Writers*. Athens: University of Georgia Press.

_____ (1987). *Women Writers of the Renaissance and Reformation*. Athens: University of Georgia Press.

Wilson, Katharina M., and Frank J. Warnke, eds. (1989). *Women Writers of the Seventeenth Century*. Athens: University of Georgia Press.

SECONDARY WORKS

Ambrosini, Federica (1982). *Paesi e mari ignoti: America e colonialismo europeo nella cultura veneziana (secoli XVI–XVII)*. Venice: Deputazione.

Arber, Agnes (1986). *Herbals, Their Origin and Evolution: A Chapter in the History of Botany, 1470–1670*. Cambridge: Cambridge University Press.

Barzaghi, Antonio (1980). *Donne o cortigiane? La prostituzione a Venezia: Documenti di costume dal XVI al XVIII secolo*. Verona: Bertani.

Beilin, Elaine V. (1987). *Redeeming Eve: Women Writers of the English Renaissance*. Princeton: Princeton University Press.

Benson, Pamela J. (1992). *The Invention of the Renaissance Woman: The Challenge of Female Independence in the Literature and Thought of Italy and England*. University Park: Pennsylvania State University Press.

Bertoluzza, Aldo (1972). *Casa e cucina trentina in otto secoli di principato: Usi, costumi, folclore nella nota della spesa*. Trento: Dossi.

Bloch, R. Howard (1991). *Medieval Misogyny and the Invention of Western Romantic Love*. Chicago: University of Chicago Press.

Boerio, Giuseppe (1829). *Dizionario del dialetto veneziano*. Venice: Andrea Santini.

Bouwsma, William J. (1980). *Venice and the Defense of Republican Liberty: Renaissance Values in the Age of the Counter-Reformation*. 2d ed. Berkeley: University of California Press.

Burstein, Stanley M. (1982). "Arsinoe II Philadelphos: A Revisionist View." In *Philip II, Alexander the Great, and the Macedonian Heritage*, ed. W. L. Adams and E. N. Borza. Washington: University Press of America.

Butler, Christopher (1970). *Number Symbolism*. London: Routledge and Kegan Paul.

Casagrande di Villaviera, Rita (1968). *Le cortigiane veneziane nel Cinquecento*. Milan: Longanesi.

Caujolle-Zaslawsky, Françoise (1989). "Arète de Cyrène." In *Dictionnaire des Philosophes Antiques*, ed. Richard Goulet. Vol. 1. Paris: Éditions du CRNS.

Ceruti, Paolo (1982). *Biografia Soncinate*. Milan: Giulio Ferrario, 1834; reprinted Cremona: Turris.

Chambers, D. S. (1992). "Spas in the Italian Renaissance." In *Reconsidering the Renaissance: Papers from the Twenty-Sixth Annual Conference of the Center for Medieval and Early Renaissance Studies*, ed. Mario A. di Cesare, 3–28. Binghampton, NY:

Medieval and Renaissance Texts and Studies Chemello, Adriana (1983). "La donna, il modello, l'immaginario: Moderata Fonte e Lucrezia Marinella." In *Nel cerchio della luna: Figure di donna in alcuni testi del XVI secolo*, ed. Marina Zancan, 95–170. Venice: Marsilio.

———— (1988). "Gioco e dissimulazione in Moderata Fonte." In Moderata Fonte, *Il merito delle donne*, ed. Adriana Chemello. Venice: Eidos.

Chojnacki, Stanley (1975). "Dowries and Kinsmen in Early Renaissance Venice." *Journal of Interdisciplinary History* 5: 571–600.

———— (1980). "La posizione della donna a Venezia nel Cinquecento." In *Tiziano e Venezia: Convegno internazionale di studi, Venezia 1976*, 65–70. Vicenza: Neri Pozza.

———— (1988). "The Power of Love: Wives and Husbands in Late Medieval Venice." In *Women and Power in the Middle Ages*, ed. Mary Erler and Maryanne Kowaleski, 126–48. Athens: University of Georgia Press.

Cicogna, Emmanuele Antonio (1824–61). *Delle iscrizioni veneziane*. 6 vols. Venice: Giuseppe Orlandelli.

Cinelli Galvoli, Giovanni (1734–47). *Biblioteca volante, continuata dal Dottor Dionigi Andrea Sancassiani*. Venice: G. B. Albrizzi.

Clark, Elizabeth A. (1986). *Ascetic Piety and Women's Faith: Essays on Late Ancient Christianity*. Lewiston, NY: Edwin Mellen Press.

Collina, Beatrice (1989). "Moderata Fonte e *Il merito delle donne*." *Annali d'Italianistica* 7: 142–64.

Conti Odorisio, Ginevra (1979). *Donna e società nel Seicento*. Rome: Bulzoni.

Cowan, Alexander F. (1982). "Rich and Poor among the Patriciate in Early Modern Venice." *Studi veneziani*, n.s. 6: 147–60.

———— (1986). *The Urban Patriciate: Lübeck and Venice*. Cologne: Böhlau.

Cox, Virginia (1992). *The Renaissance Dialogue: Literary Dialogue in Its Social and Political Contexts, Castiglione to Galileo*. Cambridge: Cambridge University Press.

———— (1995). "The Single Self: Feminist Thought and the Marriage Market in Early Modern Venice." *Renaissance Quarterly* 48/3 (1995): 513–81.

Daenens, Francine (1987). "Eva, mulier, femina: Étymologies ou discours véritables sur la femme dans quelques traités italiens du XVIe siècle." *Les lettres romanes* 41: 5–28.

Davidson, Alan (1981). *Mediterranean Seafood*. Harmondsworth: Penguin.

Davis, James C. (1962). *The Decline of the Venetian Nobility as a Ruling Class*. Johns Hopkins University Studies in History and Political Science, 80ii. Baltimore: Johns Hopkins University Press.

———— (1975). *A Venetian Family and Its Fortune, 1500–1900: The Donà and the Conservation of Their Wealth*. Philadelphia: American Philosophical Society.

Davis, Natalie Zemon (1975). *Society and Culture in Early Modern France*. Stanford: Stanford University Press.

De Ceuelneer, Adolf (1919). "La Charité romaine dans la littérature et dans l'art." *Annales de l'Académie Royale d'Archéologie de Belgique* 67: 175–206.

De Jean, Joan (1991). *Tender Geographies: Women and the Origins of the Novel in France*. New York: Columbia University Press.

Dixon, Suzanne (1992). *The Roman Family*. Baltimore: Johns Hopkins University Press.

Drake, Stillman (1978). *Galileo at Work: His Scientific Biography*. Chicago: Chicago University Press.

Endrei, Walter, and László Zolnay (1986). *Fun and Games in Old Europe*. Budapest: Corvina.

Ercole, Francesco (1908/1910). "L'istituto dotale nella pratica e nella legislazione statuaria dell'Italia superiore." *Rivista italiana per le scienze giuridiche* 45: 191–302; and 46: 167–257.

Erspamer, Francesco (1983). "Petrarchismo e manierismo nella lirica del secondo Cinquecento." In *Storia della cultura veneta*, ed. Girolamo Arnaldi and Manlio Pastore Stocchi. 6 vols. Vol. 4/i, *Dalla controriforma alla fine della repubblica*, 189–222. Vicenza: Neri Pozza.

Feldman, Martha (1994). *City Culture and the Madrigal at Venice*. Berkeley: University of California Press.

Ferguson, Margaret W., Maureen Quilligan, and Nancy J. Vickers, eds. (1987). *Rewriting the Renaissance: The Discourses of Sexual Difference in Early Modern Europe*. Chicago: University of Chicago Press.

Ferraro, Joanne M. (1995). "The Power to Decide: Battered Wives in Early Modern Venice." *Renaissance Quarterly* 48/3 (1995): 492–512.

Findlen, Paula (1994). *Possessing Nature: Museums, Collecting, and Scientific Culture in Early Modern Italy*. Berkeley: University of California Press.

Finlay, Robert (1980). *Politics in Renaissance Venice*. London: Benn.

Finucci, Valeria (1992). *The Lady Vanishes: Subjectivity and Representation in Castiglione and Ariosto*. Stanford: Stanford University Press.

Friedman, John B. (1981). *The Monstrous Races in Medieval Art and Thought*. Cambridge: Harvard University Press.

Gardner, Jane F. (1986). *Women in Roman Law and Society*. London: Croom Helm.

Gilbert, Felix (1980). *The Pope, His Banker, and Venice*. Cambridge: Harvard University Press.

Giornale di medicina (1763). Vol. I, no. 49 (7 April): 387–88.

Grant, Edward (1994). *Planets, Stars, and Orbs. The Medieval Cosmos, 1200–1687*. Cambridge: Cambridge University Press.

Grendler, Paul F. (1979). "The Tre Savi Sopra Eresia, 1547–1605: A Prosopographical Study." *Studi veneziani*, n.s. 3 (1979): 283–340.

_____ (1989). *Schooling in Renaissance Italy: Literacy and Learning 1300–1600*. Baltimore: Johns Hopkins University Press.

Grimal, Pierre (1986). *Dictionary of Classical Mythology*. Translated by A. R. Maxwell-Hyslop. Oxford: Blackwell.

Günsberg, Maggie (1987). "'Donna Liberata'? The Portrayal of Women in the Italian Renaissance Epic." *Italianist* 7: 7–35.

Guthmüller, Bodo (1992). "'Non taceremo più a lungo.' Sul dialogo *Il merito delle donne* di Moderata Fonte." *Filologia e critica* 17: 258–79.

Hallett, Judith P. (1984). *Fathers and Daughters in Roman Society: Women and the Elite Family*. Princeton: Princeton University Press.

Herlihy, David (1985). "Did Women Have a Renaissance? A Reconsideration." *Medievalia et Humanistica*, n.s. 13: 1–22.

Heubeck, Alfred, Stephanie West, and J. B. Hainsworth (1988). *A Commentary on Homer's "Odyssey"*. Oxford: Clarendon.

A History of Women in the West (1992–93). Vol. 1, *From Ancient Goddesses to Christian Saints*, ed. Pauline Schmitt Pantel; vol. 2, *Silences of the Middle Ages*, ed. Christiane Klapisch-Zuber; vol. 3, *Renaissance and Enlightenment Paradoxes*, ed. Natalie Zemon Davis and Arlette Farge. Cambridge: Harvard University Press.

Horowitz, Maryanne Cline (1976). "Aristotle and Woman." *Journal of the History of Biology* 9: 183–213.

Hull, Suzanne W. (1982). *Chaste, Silent, and Obedient: English Books for Women, 1475–1640*. San Marino, CA: Huntington Library.

Jones, Ann Rosalind (1990). *The Currency of Eros: Women's Love Lyric, 1540–1620*. Bloomington: Indiana University Press.

Jones, Verina, and Letizia Panizza, eds. (forthcoming). *A History of Italian Women's Writing*. Cambridge: Cambridge University Press.

Jordan, Constance (1990). *Renaissance Feminism: Literary Texts and Political Models*. Ithaca: Cornell University Press.

Kallfelz, H. (1971). "Marco Bragadin." In *Dizionario biografico degli italiani*, 13: 691–94. Rome: Istituto dell'Enciclopedia Italiana, 1960–.

Kelly, Joan (1984). *Women, History, and Theory: The Essays of Joan Kelly*. Chicago: University of Chicago Press.

Kelso, Ruth (1978). *Doctrine for the Lady of the Renaissance*. Foreword by Katharine M. Rogers. Urbana: University of Illinois Press, 1956; reprinted.

King, Margaret L. (1991). *Women of the Renaissance*. Foreword by Catharine R. Stimpson. Chicago: University of Chicago Press.

Kirkham, Victoria (1978). "Numerology and Allegory in Boccaccio's *Caccia di Diana.*" *Traditio* 34: 303–29.

Kolsky, Stefan D. (1993). "Wells of Knowledge: Moderata Fonte's *Il merito delle donne.*" *Italianist*, 13: 57–96.

Labalme, Patricia H. (1980). "Women's Roles in Early Modern Venice: An Exceptional Case." In *Beyond Their Sex: Learned Women of the European Past*, ed. Patricia H. Labalme, 129–52. New York: New York University Press.

_____ (1981). "Venetian Women on Women: Three Early Modern Feminists." *Archivio veneto*, 5th ser., 117: 81–109.

Laqueur, Thomas (1990). *Making Sex: Body and Gender from the Greeks to Freud.* Cambridge: Harvard University Press.

Lazzaro, Claudia (1990). *The Italian Renaissance Garden.* New Haven: Yale University Press.

Lenotti, Benedetto (1977). *Leggende del Garda: Cenni storici, miti, tradizioni, usanze, folclore.* Calliano (Trento): Vallagarino.

Lerner, Gerda (1994). *The Creation of Feminist Consciousness, from the Middle Ages to 1870.* Women and History, 2. Oxford: Oxford University Press.

Liruti, G. G. (1760–1830). *Notizia delle vite ed opere scritte da' letterati del Friuli.* 4 vols. Venice: Modesto Fenzo; Udine: Fratelli Gallici; Venice: Alvisopoli.

Lochrie, Karma (1992). *Margery Kempe and Translations of the Flesh.* Philadelphia: University of Pennsylvania Press.

McCulloch, Florence (1960). *Medieval Latin and French Bestiaries.* University of North Carolina Studies in the Romance Languages and Literatures, 33. Chapel Hill: University of North Carolina Press.

Maclean, Ian (1977). *Woman Triumphant: Feminism in French Literature, 1610–1652.* Oxford: Clarendon.

_____ (1980). *The Renaissance Notion of Woman: A Study of the Fortunes of Scholasticism and Medical Science in European Intellectual Life.* Cambridge: Cambridge University Press.

Macurdy, Harriet Grace (1932). *Hellenistic Queens: A Study of Woman Power in Macedonia, Seleucid, Syria, and Ptolemaic Egypt.* Johns Hopkins University Studies in Archeology, 14. Baltimore: Johns Hopkins University Press.

Maffei, Scipione (1825–26). *Verona illustrata.* 3 vols. Milan: Società Tipografica de' Classici Italiani.

Malpezzi Price, Paola (1989). "A Woman's Discourse in the Italian Renaissance: Moderata Fonte's *Il merito delle donne.*" In *Annali d'Italianistica* 7: 165–81.

_____ (1994). 'Moderata Fonte.' In *Italian Women Writers: A Biobibliographical Sourcebook,* ed. Rinaldina Russell, 128-37. Westport, CT: Greenwood Press.

Martin, Ruth (1989). *Witchcraft and the Inquisition in Venice, 1550–1650.* Oxford: Blackwell.

Matter, E. Ann, and John Coakley, eds. (1994). *Creative Women in Medieval and Early Modern Italy*. Philadelphia: University of Pennsylvania Press.

Megna, Laura (1991). "Comportamenti abitativi del patriciato veneziano (1582–1640)." *Studi veneziani*, n.s. 23: 253–323.

Mermier, Guy R. (1989). "The Phoenix: Its Nature and Its Place in the Tradition of the *Physiologus*." In *Beasts and Birds of the Middle Ages: The Bestiary and Its Legacy*, ed. Willem B. Clark and Meredith T. McMunn. Philadelphia: University of Pennsylvania Press.

Molmenti, Pompeo (1905–8). *Storia di Venezia nella vita privata, dalle origini alla caduta della repubblica*. 3 vols. Bergamo: Istituto italiano di arti grafiche.

Monson, Craig A., ed. (1992). *The Crannied Wall: Women, Religion, and the Arts in Early Modern Europe*. Ann Arbor: University of Michigan Press.

Muir, Edward (1981). *Civic Ritual in Renaissance Venice*. Princeton: Princeton University Press.

Newton, Stella Mary (1988). *The Dress of the Venetians, 1495–1525*. Pasold Studies in Textile History, 7. Aldershot: Scolar [for] the Pasold Research Fund.

Okin, Susan Moller (1979). *Women in Western Political Thought*. Princeton: Princeton University Press.

Ossola, Carlo (1976). "Il 'queto travaglio' di Gabriele Fiamma." In vol. 3 of *Letteratura e critica: Studi in onore di Natalino Sapegno*, 239–86. 5 vols. Rome: Bulzoni, 1974–79.

Pagels, Elaine (1988). *Adam, Eve, and the Serpent*. New York: Harper Collins.

Palmer, Richard (1983). *The Studio of Venice and Its Graduates in the Sixteenth Century*. Sarmeola di Rubano (Padova): LINT.

——— (1985). "Pharmacy in the Republic of Venice in the Sixteenth Century." In *The Medical Renaissance of the Sixteenth Century*, ed. A. Wear, R. K. French, and I. M. Lonie, 100–117. Cambridge: Cambridge University Press.

Pollard, John (1977). *Birds in Greek Life and Myth*. London: Thames and Hudson.

Pomeroy, Sarah B. (1976). *Goddesses, Whores, Wives, and Slaves: Women in Classical Antiquity*. New York: Schocken Books.

Preto, Paolo (1984). "La società veneta e le grandi epidemie di peste." In *Storia della cultura veneta*, ed. Girolamo Arnaldi and Manlio Pastore Stocchi. Vol. 4/ii, *Dalla controriforma alla fine della repubblica*, 377–406. Vicenza: Neri Pozza.

Pullan, Brian (1968). "Wage Earners and the Venetian Economy, 1550–1630." In *Crisis and Change in the Venetian Economy in the Sixteenth and Seventeenth Centuries*, ed. Brian Pullan, 146–74. London: Methuen.

——— (1971). *Rich and Poor in Renaissance Venice: The Social Institutions of a Catholic State, to 1620*. Oxford: Blackwell.

Queller, Donald E. (1986). *The Venetian Patriciate: Reality versus Myth*. Urbana: University of Illinois Press.

Rodocanachi, Emmanuel Pierre (1907). *La femme italienne à l'époque de la Renaissance: Sa vie privée et mondaine et son influence sociale*. Paris: Hachette.

Rohde, Eleanour Sinclair (1971). *The Old English Herbals*. London, 1922; reprinted New York: Dover.

Romanello, M. (1991). "Doglioni, Giovanni Niccolò." In *Dizionario bibliografico degli italiani*, 40: 368–69. Rome: Istituto dell'Enciclopedia Italiana, 1960–.

Rosand, David (1982). *Painting in Cinquecento Venice: Titian, Veronese, Tintoretto*. New Haven: Yale University Press.

――― (1984). "Venezia e gli dei." In *"Renovatio urbis": Venezia nell'età di Andrea Gritti (1523–1538)*, ed. Manfredo Tafuri, 201–15. Rome: Officina.

Rose, Mary Beth, ed. (1986). *Women in the Middle Ages and the Renaissance: Literary and Historical Perspectives*. Syracuse: Syracuse University Press.

Rosenthal, Margaret F. (1992). *The Honest Courtesan: Veronica Franco, Citizen and Writer in Sixteenth-Century Venice*. Chicago: University of Chicago Press.

――― (1993). "Venetian Women and Their Discontents." In *Sexuality and Gender in Early Modern Europe*, ed. James Grantham Turner, 197–232. Cambridge: Cambridge University Press.

Santore, Cathy (1988). "Julia Lombardo, 'Somtuosa Meretrize': A Portrait by Property." *Renaissance Quarterly* 41: 44–83.

Shemek, Deanna (1989). "'Of Women, Knights, Arms, and Love.' The *querelle des femmes* in Ariosto's Poem." *MLN* 104: 68–97.

Shepard, Odell (1930). *The Lore of the Unicorn*. Boston: Houghton Mifflin.

Smarr, Janet Levarie (1995). "The Uses of Conversation: Moderata Fonte and Edmund Tilney," *Comparative Literature Studies* 32, no. 1: 1–25.

Soleiti, Angelo (1902). "Le rappresentazioni musicali di Venezia, dal 1571 al 1605, per la prima volta descritte." *Rivista musicale italiana* 9: 503–38.

Stefani, F. (1868). "Nota sui Costanzo di Castelfranco." In *Della necessità di conservare la cavalleria di grande armatura nello esercito veneziano: Ricordo di Scipione Costanzo alla Signoria di Venezia, 1577*, [ed. F. Stefani], 25–29. Venice.

Stuard, Susan M. (1987). "The Dominion of Gender: Women's Fortunes in the High Middle Ages." In *Becoming Visible: Women in European History*, ed. Renate Bridental, Claudia Koonz, and Susan M. Stuard, 153–72. 2d ed. Boston: Houghton Mifflin.

Taddeo, Edoardo (1974). *Il manierismo letterario e i lirici veneziani del tardo Cinquecento*. Biblioteca di cultura, 56. Rome: Bulzoni.

Tester, S. J. (1987). *A History of Western Astrology*. Woodbridge, Suffolk: Boydell Press.

Tetel, Marcel (1973). *Marguerite de Navarre's "Heptameron": Themes, Language, and Structure*. Durham, NC: Duke University Press.

Thomas, Keith (1984). *Man and the Natural World: Changing Attitudes in England, 1500–1800*. Harmondsworth: Penguin.

Thompson, D'Arcy Wentworth (1947). *A Glossary of Greek Fishes*. St. Andrews University Publications, 45. London: Oxford University Press.

Thorndike, Lynn (1923–58). *A History of Magic and Experimental Science*. 8 vols. New York: MacMillan.

Tomalin, Margaret (1982). *The Fortunes of the Warrior Heroine in Italian Literature: An Index of Emancipation*. Ravenna: Longo.

Treggiari, Susan (1991). *Roman Marriage: Iusti Coniuges from the Time of Cicero to the Time of Ulpian*. Oxford: Oxford University Press.

Ulvioni, Paolo (1982). "Astrologia, astronomia e medicina nella repubblica veneta tra cinque e seicento." *Studi trentini di scienze storiche* 61: 1–69.

Vergani, Raffaello (1989). "Miniere e metalli dell'alto vicentino." In *Storia di vicenza*, vol. III/1, *L'età della repubblica veneta (1404–1797)*, ed. Franco Barbieri and Paolo Preto. Vicenza: Neri Pozza.

Walsh, William T. (1987). *St. Teresa of Avila: A Biography*. Rockford, IL: TAN Books and Publications.

Warner, Marina (1976). *Alone of All Her Sex: The Myth and the Cult of the Virgin Mary*. New York: Knopf.

Weaver, Elissa (1986). "Spiritual Fun: A Study of Sixteenth-Century Tuscan Convent Drama." In *Women in the Middle Ages and the Renaissance: Literary and Historical Perspectives*, ed. Mary Beth Rose. Syracuse: Syracuse University Press.

Wiesner, Merry E. (1993). *Women and Gender in Early Modern Europe*. Cambridge: Cambridge University Press.

Willard, Charity Cannon (1984). *Christine de Pizan: Her Life and Works*. New York: Persea Books.

Wilson, Katharina, ed. (1991). *An Encyclopedia of Continental Women Writers*. New York: Garland.

Zancan, Marina, ed. (1983). *Nel cerchio della luna: Figure di donna in alcuni testi del XVI secolo*. Venice: Marsilio.

Zannini, Andrea (1993). *Burocrazia e burocrati a Venezia nell'età moderna: I cittadini originari (sec. XVI–XVIII)*. Memorie della classe di scienze morali, letteratura ed arti, 47. Venice: Istituto Veneto di Scienze, Lettere ed Arti.

Zeno, Apostolo (1753). *Biblioteca dell'eloquenza italiana di Monsignor Giusto Fontanini con le annotazioni del Signor Apostolo Zen*. 2 vols. Venice: G. Pasquali.

INDEX

Tullia, 105–6
Tullia d'Aragona. *See* d'Aragona, Tullia
Tyrrenia, 252

unicorns, 161–65
Usper, Lodovico, 196
uterus (*hystera*), in Greek psychology, ix

Valvassone, Erasmo da, 218
Varo River, 153
Venice: dress in, 234, 235n, 237n; legal profession in, 196–97; medical profession in, 181–83; painting in, 226; poetry in, 217–18; political culture of, 44n, 56n, 200–201; political institutions of, 203–4; position of women in, 2, 3, 17, 39, 47n, 62n, 235n; praises of, 43–44, 199–204; Procuratie Nuove, 201; publishing industry in, 3; Rialto bridge, 202; San Leonardo, 32; San Rocco, 39; San Samuele, 33; Santa Marta (convent of), 33–34; social hierarchy of, 31n, 200, 201n, 210n, 218n, 234n
Venier, Domenico, 5, 217, 218n, 223n
Venus, 30, 59n 175, 176; as character in Fonte's fable of Lioncorno, 164–65; mentioned in Fonte's fable of Love disarmed, 254, 255–56
Verginia (Roman heroine), 45n, 105
Verona, 155
Veronese (Paolo Caliari), 226
Veturia. *See* Volumnia
Vicenza, 155
Vincenti. *See* Vincenzi
Vincenzi, Giovanni, 196, 219n
Virgil, 100n, 112n, 126n, 156
Virginius, 105

Virgin Mary, xiii, 91n; praised, 94, 219–20
virgins, 91; favored by unicorns, 161, 165
Vives, Juan Luis, *On the Education of a Christian Woman*, xxii, xxv
Volumnia (Coriolanus's mother), 94n, 103

warfare, 229–30. *See also* women, and warfare
Weyer, Johann, xx
wine. *See* diet
witchcraft, xx *See also* magic
women: and chastity, xxii–xxiii, 54, 84–91, 101, 105, 112, 236–37 in Christian thought, xi–xii and the church, xv–xvi as daughters, 62–63, 66–67, 103–6, 112–13, 190 and dress, xxv, 234–36 in Greek thought, viii–x, 59n, 83n, 92n and learning, xxi, xxv, 101, 236–37, 238, 261–63 and medicine, 10, 181 in medieval literature, xii–xiv as mothers, 64–67, 107–9, 190–91 and power, xxiii–xxiv, 59, 204, 237 in Roman law, x–xi; as sisters, 63–64, 106–7, 190 and speech, xxiv, 18, 101n, 188–94 superior to men, 59–61, 83–84, 91–95, 99, 115, 157, 168 and vice, 72, 87–89, 105–6 and virtue, xxii, 84–86, 99, 100–103 and warfare, xxiv, 5–6, 100, 102–3, 230–32, 261–63 as wives, 68–72, 91–92, 99–100, 109–11, 113–16, 191, 238–40 and work, xiv–xv as writers, xx–xxi, 2–4, 16, 21–22, 49, 101. See also *querelle des femmes*; Venice, position of women in
Xenocrates, 88

Zarotti, Leandro, 181
Zenobia, 102, 112